CASEBOOK IN PUBLIC
ADMINISTRATION

CASEBOOK IN PUBLIC ADMINISTRATION

R. JOSEPH NOVOGROD   Long Island University

GLADYS O. DIMOCK

MARSHALL E. DIMOCK

HOLT, RINEHART AND WINSTON, INC.

NEW YORK   CHICAGO   SAN FRANCISCO   ATLANTA
DALLAS   MONTREAL   TORONTO   LONDON   SYDNEY

Copyright © 1969 by Holt, Rinehart and Winston, Inc.
All rights reserved
Library of Congress Catalog Card Number: 77–91334
SBN: 03-077255-9
Printed in the United States of America
1 2 3 4 5 6 7 8 9

PREFACE

In the teaching of public administration, cases provide the feel of actual situations. Ideally, a casebook should also cover the principal areas of public administration to provide related materials for teaching purposes. This casebook attempts to meet these objectives.

This book is distinctive in two respects: first, the cases are brief; and second, they include administrative profiles, consisting of a short biography of the official, his career development, and his insights into the administrative process. This treatment focuses on the events arising in specific situations as well as on the personality factors that affect leadership—since, in attempting to solve problems, administrators are influenced by the situations in which they find themselves.

Some of our cases, such as the Employment Service, are presented in an expository and chronological form. Most of them combine administrative history, personalities, interpersonal relations, and administrative techniques, relating these to such matters as civil liberties, the welfare of the Indian population, or the determination of accounting policies for the federal government. Ten cases are in dialogue form as transcribed from the actual taped interview or conference.*

---

* Cases numbered 1, 3, 6, 10, 11, 12, 13, 14, 15, and 17.

The pattern of collaboration that we have used may be of some interest. The three authors together planned the objectives and selection of cases; Marshall and Gladys Dimock contributed two of the cases; R. J. Novogrod developed and initially wrote the rest; then all three authors participated in the editing and polishing of the final manuscript.

Professor Novogrod's method of research relied primarily on capture-and-record, depth interviewing, and group dynamics. Much advance planning of agenda for interviews was necessary, and tentative key questions were submitted in advance. Nearly all the interviews were tape recorded, transcribed, and edited; participants were invited to review and sharpen any points they had made. In many instances, several sessions were devoted to defining the issues and providing a full account of the events of the case.

The authors have deliberately combined administrative history with the analysis of concrete situations having immediate relevance, for every administrative situation has a past history, a future history, a cast of characters, and congeries of tensions. One objective has been to capture these clashes of forces, personalities, and issues that are the heart of the political science approach. The authors do not distinguish sharply between "policy" and "administration," for to do so seems to set up an unworkable dichotomy; rather, the attempt throughout is to emphasize the cutting edge of policy, especially in areas of the greatest controversy, for it is here that administration faces its hardest tests.

The method used could be criticized as too journalistic, too close to those of political reporters and columnists. We believe, however, that since public administration is an earthy, politically significant field of study, its true character is not likely to be understood until the tensions and nuances of complex situations are described. These cases can be thought of as the raw data for more systematic analysis.

No attempt has been made to suggest what the solutions *should* have been. Each case reports what was done, what the experience was at a given point in the development of a problem, what the expected results of decisions would be in matters of policy and method, and what the continuing tensions are in matters of policy and technique. The purpose has been to encourage lively class discussion.

The subject headings under which the cases are listed are only guides to their content. Each case involves more than one theoretical problem— as would be expected in real-world situations—and teachers should find multiple uses for cases not evident even to the authors. A key to some of the many uses of the cases can be found at the end of this book. In addition, a listing of relevant cases from this and other casebooks can be found at the end of each chapter of Marshall and Gladys Dimocks' *Public Administration,* 4th ed. (New York: Holt, Rinehart and Winston, Inc.,

1969), although the cases in the present collection can be used with any textbook.

Because three authors have been involved and the number of their associations is sizeable, it is difficult to express adequately our indebtedness to all who have helped to develop this casebook. Particular thanks go to all participants in the interviews, for their time and for their continuing interest and cooperation. We would also acknowledge the assistance of Mrs. Cyd Smith, secretary of the Political Science Department at Long Island University; of Kevin Gregg Halpern, a former student in the Governmental Administration class at Long Island University, who willingly evaluated many sections of the manuscript; and of Mrs. Frances Cohen, who was continuously resourceful and patient in the final typing of it.

Members of the Holt, Rinehart and Winston staff were most helpful. Political Science editor Herbert J. Addison provided critical support and balanced suggestions. Karen Dubno made sound technical and literary comments, and William Ryan put the galley proofs in final shape. All were meticulous and cooperative partners, from rough draft through the concluding stages of the manuscript. Each brought a special quality to the entire effort, and the authors appreciate their sustained interest and concern.

R. J. N.
M. E. D.
G. O. D.

Brooklyn, N.Y.
Bethel, Vt.
June 1969

CONTENTS

CASEBOOK IN PUBLIC
ADMINISTRATION

I
OVERVIEW

1
COMPTROLLER GENERAL

The General Accounting Office (GAO) provides direct assistance to the Congress and its members and committees in carrying out their legislative and oversight responsibilities; prescribes standards and principles of accounting in the federal agencies and departments; provides advice and renders decisions on the legality of governmental expenditures, both retro-active and prospective; settles claims for and against the United States; and audits and reviews federal programs and the manner in which they are conducted.

At the head of this vast undertaking is the Comptroller General of the United States, Elmer Staats, who personifies the best in public service—Mr. Public Administrator to his fingertips. During his twenty-eight years in national affairs, Staats has been closely associated with many major deci-sions and individuals through the terms of several Presidents. As he sees his job, "The magnitude and complexity of the operations of the federal government today, involving an outlay estimated for fiscal 1969 of $189 billion, places a tremendously heavy responsibility upon my staff and offers a challenge unique in government annals."

Congress created GAO as an independent agency in 1921 when it passed the Budget and Accounting Act of that year. It was to be organizationally responsible only to the Congress and totally independent of the executive agencies whose work was reviewed. GAO's staff manual contains statements on "independence" that are lessons for all public administrators: "Independence is an impartial attitude . . . toward situations, organizational and individual relationships, emotional factors, and other environmental conditions. Independence is both a power and a privilege to which attaches the responsibility for utmost fairness and objectivity in its exercise. . . ." Objectivity is the avoidance of unsubstantiated impressions from fact-finding, analysis, interpretation, and reporting, and this factor also is strongly stressed at GAO.

Elmer Staats's office combines tidiness with informality. It contains much of his own furniture, including an old-fashioned grandfather's clock. On his desk are many piles of papers, precisely marked for action.

Staats arrived punctually from a meeting. He is a tall man, informal yet courtly, and commands attention by his mere presence. In our discussion he spoke modestly yet with undebatable authority. It was restful to listen as he described situations in which he had been involved, budgeting his words with rarely a wasted phrase.

Staats has a dry humor, a strong awareness of human goals and needs, and a calm and judicious attitude that makes one think of a school headmaster, a college dean, or a court judge. He is a close listener and answers each question carefully.

Staats was born in Kansas in 1914, graduated from McPherson College as a member of Phi Beta Kappa, and has an M.A. degree from the University of Kansas. He worked in the research department of the Kansas Legislative Council at Topeka in the summer of 1936, was a staff member of Public Administration Service at Chicago in 1937–1938, became a Brookings Institution Fellow, received a Ph.D. from the University of Minnesota in 1939, and in the same year joined the staff of the Bureau of the Budget in Washington. During the following years he served the bureau in such capacities as Assistant Director for Legislative Reference and Executive Assistant Director. In 1950 President Truman named him Deputy Director.

In 1953 Staats left the bureau, briefly, to become Research Director for Marshall Field and Company in Chicago, but a year later he returned to Washington when President Eisenhower appointed him Executive Officer of the newly established Operations Coordinating Board of the National Security Council. Staats occupied this position until rejoining the Bureau of the Budget in September 1958 as Assistant Director, and was reappointed Deputy Director a few months later. He was again reappointed by President Kennedy in 1961 and continued in this assignment under President Johnson until assuming the Comptroller Generalship on March 8, 1966.

Commenting on his long career in public administration, Staats once said: "If someone were to say to me: 'Well, if you had the opportunity to choose over again between a career in commerce or industry, academic profession, or government, would you choose differently?' My answer would be that if I had the choice to make again, my choice would be the same."

Staats's lifelong interest in public service is reflected in his associations as well as his career. As a charter member of the American Society for Public Administration, he was its national president in 1961–1962. He is a member of several boards and committees interested in public service, including the Advisory Council of the Brookings Institution's Conference on Public Affairs, the board of directors of the American Academy of Political and Social Science, the board of directors of Public Administration Service, and the Research Advisory Committee of the Council of State Governments. He has written articles for the *American Economic Review, Public Personnel Review, Public Administration Review,* and *American Political Science Review.* He received the Rockefeller Public Service Award in 1961 and an honorary Doctor of Laws degree at McPherson College in 1966. From time to time he lectures at universities.

Elmer Staats is married, has three children, and lives in Washington, D.C.

Could we perhaps start with a matter that has long intrigued me. Are there individuals in your long span of public experience—I believe it runs into 28 years—who have influenced you, rather heavily, in your response to administrative problems?

I assume that you refer here to individuals after I entered the public service or, at least, after I concluded my academic program.

Surely, although if you want to include certain teachers—I guess we never stop being a student—I'd be delighted to hear of any references to the academic period of your career, as well.

Well, I suppose one of the important things to keep in mind is that if you stop being a student, you stop thinking, you stop learning new ways of doing things and new approaches to problems. Certainly the government has changed a great deal since 1939 when I first joined it. It's a difficult question, always, to try to relate your attitudes or your own development, actually, to individuals as against situations. I suppose my thinking initially, in coming to the government, was influenced heavily by the Report of the President's Committee on Administrative Management which. . . .

Oh, the Brownlow. . . .

Yes, the Brownlow, Gulick, Merriam report, which was, of course, very new at the time. I had been a Fellow at the Brookings Institution to complete my doctoral dissertation, intending to return to Public Administration Service in Chicago—which, as you know, is a management consulting organization for state and local governments and, to some degree, for the federal government.

But I suppose that report plus the fact that I was at Brookings, where I was brought into contact with individuals in the government, gave me more of a "feel" of being a part of the governmental scene. These contacts were arranged initially through the Brookings Institution. Seminars and meetings were also sponsored by Brookings at that time. The Brookings fellowship, plus the fact that Harold Smith, who had been Director of the Budget in Michigan, and Donald Stone, who had been head of Public Administration Service, both joined the Bureau of the Budget, were responsible for my decision to accept an appointment there, too. This was in 1939, and the challenge then was the reorganization of the federal government. Individuals like Wayne Coy, who joined the bureau at that time and had worked easily and closely with President Roosevelt, and Harold Smith developed the bureau and gave it an influential role with the President.

The Executive Reorganization Act of 1939, and later the President's order, which established the Executive Office of the President, also played a part, I suppose, in my own thinking. These developments opened up a lot of doors and windows to my thinking—in other words, it was a very stimulating atmosphere with lots of challenges. I was relatively junior at the time, but still I was thrown into some of these problems and was challenged by them.

And then the government itself was going through a strenuous period, trying to deal with the economic problems of the time. Also, of course, beginning in 1940, we met a whole series of new problems with the emergence of the war in Europe. Being in the Bureau of the Budget, we were thrown directly into this by virtue of the needs of the wartime organization. Ironically, one provision in the establishment of the Executive Office of the President that had been a matter of foresight, but perhaps not fully understood even then by Harold Smith and Brownlow, was the authority for the President to establish new organizations, as in the case of the Office for Emergency Management, which was made an integral part of the Executive Office. It was under this authority that President Roosevelt created a number of organizations to deal with the wartime situation. As members of a unit of the Budget Bureau concerned with wartime problems, a number of us were given the job of helping to develop organizational concepts for this defense period. And then, later on, as the United States became involved in the war directly, we took on, I suppose, responsibilities all out of all proportion to our experience, by virtue of the fact that we'd had the background and were more familiar with the antecedents of some of these organizations than anyone else. All of this opened up tremendous problems, so that President Roosevelt, on the basis of Harold Smith's advice, issued orders that we were not to be brought into the military service, but were to stay on in the Budget Bureau working in this area. This background I cite partly to explain and answer your question as to how I happened to develop my own views and what kind of influences were important at that time.

I would add that the charter of the Budget Bureau itself tends to cause individuals to try to seek new approaches to problems. This is, in part, what the bureau is all about—why it was established: to give continuing consideration to ways of carrying on programs more efficiently, more economically, with better rationalization of organization, clearer lines of responsibility. Then as new legislation developed, after the war, all of these new programs created tremendous challenges; in many cases, we were frankly experimenting.

Innovation was involved in the organization, for example, of the Atomic Energy Commission. I was involved deeply in the drafting of legislation that led to the Atomic Energy Act, and in the Bureau of the Budget I handled the budget for the commission when it was first established. Similarly, the National Science Foundation presented another kind of a problem, which grew out of the views that were held by most scientists that the United States was not properly organized in this area and not carrying on an adequate research program. Vannevar Bush, Conant, Lloyd Berkner, and many others felt that unless we changed the concept of the federal government's role in this respect we might be in serious difficulty in the event of another emergency. The NSF grew in part out of the experience and impetus of the work of the Office of Scientific Research and Development. Eventually the National Science Foundation emerged, and James Webb, who was then Director of the Budget, Don Price, who is now at Harvard, and I were the three people from the Budget Bureau side paying most attention to how the federal government should organize in this area.

I mention these as only two examples of matters with which I was most directly involved in this immediate postwar period.

You've been in on the birth of many new programs and dealt with some individuals who have become almost legendary in the literature of public administration. As you look at the administrative process, are there certain concepts that you believe continue to be dependable in the solution of daily problems?

I would have to sort this out in terms of organizational concepts as contrasted with, you might say, management concepts. For one thing, in establishing a new organization, it's important to make sure that it receives proper focus and attention. It's easy for the theoretician to say that you should organize according to program lines or functional lines, but one of the things we learned during the war and subsequent to the war—I think we're still learning it in dealing with problems of urban areas—is that it is terribly important to organize flexibly, to be able to set up special-type agencies to deal with new special-type problems. Forget about neatness in these cases, and how the function fits in with old-line agencies. But at the same time, there has to be some recognition of the need to blend these functions back into the established agencies at some point in time, because obviously you can't have special organizations for every problem of government.

They might start bumping into one another.

That's right. We're facing this today in the anti-poverty program, in my opinion. The idea of a special agency to give focus to the anti-poverty program is fine. Question: How long should it continue as a separate organization? Because only about 10 percent of the federal government's effort in this area is being funded through this agency. The anti-poverty program is supposed to be related to all these other efforts through the Office of Economic Opportunity, the director of which wears two hats: one as director of an operating program and the other as coordinator of the total program. Question again: Can he operate a function and carry on his coordinating role at the same time? In carrying out his operating program he is a competitor for funds and political support with other programs that he is supposed to coordinate.

Are the motives in setting up a new function separately from the rest of the establishment, first, to give it the spotlight, and second, to protect it from encrusted methods of doing things? I'm thinking of creativity or innovation.

It's both, or all three if you want to add creativity to it, in my opinion. But don't overlook the importance of undivided time and effort on the part of top management. To some degree, in a big department like Agriculture, Commerce, or Housing and Urban Development all programs are competing for funds and for the time and leadership of top management.

I think Appalachia, in a somewhat different way, also illustrates what we're talking about. That program was developed for the single purpose of trying to interrelate and integrate all of our efforts in the Appalachia area. At some point in time the parts of this program have to be tied back into the economic development efforts of the commerce department and other agencies. The point I would make is that there has to be a flexible concept of organization, there has to be certainty, when embarking on a new program, that it will not get lost because it does not have the single, undivided time and attention of an organization.

There also seems to be a galloping spirit manifest in a new agency that the older agencies often lack. New agencies are making precedents, building new teams, pioneering as it were.

And they're on the spot—you ought to add that—to make good. But the tendency, in a program of this kind, is that you do draw in people from the outside who are—we won't use the word zealots, but enthusiasts—people who are motivated by a desire to participate in this new effort.

And it's quite a bit of fun, I've discovered.

It is *great* fun. I think during World War II we saw this in an organization like the Office of Price Administration, which was a whipping boy, certainly, all through this period. But it did, in hindsight terms, an excellent job—an almost unbelievable job—in restraining prices and preventing inflation at a time when it was vital to do so. The TVA, in a different field, was a similar effort because here was a new, unchartered kind of a program, also under attack, which brought to it people who wanted to enter the fray and try to bring this big program about.

All these factors do play a part in deciding how to organize the government. Any President—any party in power—is always going to be as much concerned about getting his program accomplished as he is about how neatly it is organized. And, in fact, you can't just say that a new and separate organization is more efficient in dollars-and-cents terms, because if you don't make the program work—assuming it's a good program in the first place—you've lost everything, or you've lost virtually everything, and it may be far more expensive than if you had tried to organize it in a more traditional way.

This is not to say that you don't have a basic problem of how you organize any governmental effort, or for that matter any private effort. There's no one best way to organize. Look at the natural-resources field, as a case in point. There are long overdue changes involved here. Look at—in my opinion, at least—the science education programs, where similar overdue changes also are called for.

Organizations tend to get entrenched—I should say organizational patterns tend to become entrenched—and there is great difficulty in changing them if you don't have some instrumentality for throwing the spotlight on them. It's a difficult problem.

Now, to turn to the management process. What concepts have proved reliable; which have, in my opinion, paid off? I think some of the old concepts that we talked about thirty years ago still hold, such as the importance of delegation. We think of this especially now, with the growth in the size of government and in the size of our grant-in-aid programs for state and local governments. The importance of delegation is to get timely and informed action at the level where it needs to be taken. This is a terribly important point that I think is just as relevant today as it was thirty years ago.

I think the importance of leadership is just as great now as it was then. Leadership from the top man in the organization cannot be separated from the effectiveness of the organization. How does he do this? I think he does it, in part, by communication, imparting to the organization an understanding of his objectives, showing an interest in his subordinates' ideas—what I would call the flow-up theory of idea generation. It is an aspect of the participative process which we hear a lot about now in private management.

It is terribly important. The more you can get people to participate in decisions, the more they're going to understand them and the more faithfully they will carry them out.

... because these decisions ultimately affect their daily operations as well as their careers.

That's right. And if they feel all decisions are coming down to them from on high, particularly if they happen to disagree and if they don't feel there's been an understanding of the "real problem," then you're not going to get the kind of cooperation, enthusiasm, and energizing effort which you have to have at all levels of an organization to make it truly effective.

Is there such a thing as negative leadership which, in time, can impair or even destroy an effective organization?

Oh, yes. I have seen this many times in my experience here in the federal government. Take the case of a poor administrator who follows one who has been a highly successful leader, and see what happens. It isn't only those who were brought in by his predecessor who leave, but many others as well. What can be even more difficult is the fact that people may continue to work but may not put their full interests, time, and effort into it. This is a much more difficult thing to get at.

I think in this connection it's important to recognize that most people in the Congress sense this point too, because this makes a difference in terms of whether an organization is able to do its job. It's not only a matter of getting enough money to carry on your program, but also of getting the kind of cooperation on legislative changes, the handling of problems affecting the constituency of a congressman or senator, or the constituency even of a committee in terms of its jurisdiction.

This is an art—a real art for an administrator—to be able to work effectively with the Congress. If he can do that, it usually also means that he's able to work at least on a viable basis with the interest groups that are concerned with his particular program. The fact is that leadership has to be visible to the staff in these matters. Ability to get along well with the press is a part of it, too.

On the strength of your administrative experience, does it make a real difference—does it make any difference at all—what we call administration? It's been tagged, as you know, an art and often a science and a combination of both as well. Does this count anymore—to a practicing administrator?

I think we have to revert again to the point of leadership and the qualities of leadership. To what extent can these qualities be ascertained and developed? To what extent can a person who is not a good administrator, say, capture these qualities if he is mindful of what you might call the do's and don'ts—what are the things you emphasize and de-emphasize?

I would say, first, that some individuals have these qualities, which I'm referring to under the loose heading of leadership, apparently without any formalized training or being aware of the rules that have been developed in the field of administration over the years.

I've been disillusioned with the how-to approach to administration, the technique emphasis. I think, as I believe you infer, there is a kind of hunch school—an it-all-depends school—which makes as much sense as an overcommitment to the methods, the organizational charts, and so on. These can easily become too rigid and an end in themselves. Of the two approaches—art or science—it's possible perhaps to say it's quite an art.

It is an art, but that is not to say—especially at the lower organizational levels—that more emphasis on managerial training is not warranted. I'm thinking here, at the moment, about our own organization, which is made up of individuals who were selected, initially, from technical fields—accounting, auditing, financial management, business management practices, and law. As the organization has grown, however, the number of problems that we deal with also has grown, and so has the number of agencies we deal with. Now we find that there hasn't been enough consideration given to selecting people at the supervisory level who have displayed qualities of leadership, and we haven't given any special emphasis to managerial training. I would not downgrade the importance of selecting individuals who have these traits of what I've called leadership—people who are able to deal with a wide variety of problems, people who have demonstrated an ability to work with people effectively, to inspire people below them, and who have the art of communication. These are things we can evaluate and make a judgment on if we do it systematically; we're moving in this direction now, in the GAO. I think the research that's been done in the field of public administration in this regard has made a contribution.

Then I think there is some value, particularly with individuals who are moving to these leadership levels, of getting what we have loosely called managerial-type training. By this I suspect that it is not so much the learning techniques, as you infer, as having time to reflect on case studies, focused on this problem of mind-stretching in the sense of looking beyond the immediate problems that you've been dealing with and looking at the context of your program in a broader setting. There should also be a greater exposure to the private, or at least the nonfederal sector, as provided by programs such as the Harvard advanced management program, those we participate in at Stanford, and the kind of thing Brookings offers. All these training opportunities play a part, particularly at the grade 14 level of the General Schedule and especially at grade 15. In GAO we systematically evaluate people moving to the grade 14 level from the standpoint of demonstrated managerial interests and capabilities. Because if they move to the grade 14 level, we would like to assume that they are capable of moving to a higher level.

I would find it difficult to rule out the need for managerial-type training—perhaps that would be called the science aspect of administration—but these two things are interrelated. You ought to select, first, those individuals who seem to have demonstrated some capability and then develop that, hopefully, by training and exposure—you might call it staff development—and by giving them broader responsibilities, including responsibilities in different settings through rotation and a variety of assignments. These play a part in it.

Now you can't live by the rule books, in a narrow use of the word science. You can't live by the organizational manual or procedures manual. There's got to be room enough here for a good deal of discretion, a good deal of initiative, a good deal of tolerance for people who want to do things a little differently, maybe, in a manner which doesn't quite fit with the rule book.

I have found, in the course of my research, that there are few who fit the stereotyped anonymous pattern of the bureaucrat, and this I find very encouraging. There are many diverse types at all levels of government. I also find a kinship between an effective official who becomes a leader and an effective teacher in terms of, as you have indicated, communication, human relations, caring enough to share, judgment, and so on.

I know students would be deeply interested in your long service under the administrations of various Chief Executives. Could you, perhaps, describe in as much detail as you consider appropriate, any personal recollections of situations that have been of some special importance?

My first presidential appointment was, of course, by President Truman in 1950, and this was some eleven years after I joined the Bureau of the Budget. One thing that might be of special interest to students in the field of administration is his ability to analyze, in very short order, and to come to a quick decision. A great deal, of course, has been said about his decisions in respect to Greece-Turkey aid and the use of the atomic bomb in World War II. What I'm thinking about here is more the day-to-day type of problems which we brought to him from the Budget Bureau, concerning which he displayed a tremendous ability in assessing issues quickly. In short, what I guess I'm saying is he had not only a very good memory, which has been publicized, but also very good mental processes. On the memory side, we could bring to him budget figures and find very frequently that he had recalled the figure that we had approved for the previous year. He is the only President, and I think I'm correct in this, who ever held his own press conferences on the budget. We found that this was a matter of his own personal interest in the budget.

. . . and perhaps courage?

I suppose courage in terms of dealing with a group of very eager, sometimes antagonistic, representatives from the press. We would provide the briefing along with the Secretary of the Treasury—sometimes there would be one session, but more likely two sessions. Mr. Truman would read the briefing book, but at the press conference itself it was only rarely that he had to turn to either the Secretary of the Treasury or the Director of the Budget for response to a question.

Were his tone and manner brisk, lively?

Yes. Quite so. He never had to generalize; he had the figures. Occasionally he would turn to the briefing book to refresh his memory. But it was quite obvious to the press and everybody concerned that this was *his* budget. This was the essential point he was trying to make. He kept saying, you know: "This is the President's budget, not the Director of the Budget's budget, nor the Secretary of the Treasury's budget."

Which was the concept the Budget and Accounting Act of 1921 tried to get across.

That's right. Of course he had served on the Appropriations Committee in the Senate and had seen the process from that side—which may have played a part in his interest in the budget.

Something else of interest occurred during the transition after the election of President Eisenhower. Mr. Lawton, who was the Director of the Budget, and I visited with President Truman the following day. We were in the middle of working up the new budget and urged President Truman to get in touch with President-elect Eisenhower to get his cooperation, hopefully to get him to designate somebody to work with us. This way, modifications could be made that President Eisenhower might want, and Congress would be able to get under way early with its consideration. It was perfectly clear that Congress would not do much with the budget of an outgoing President; they'd want to know what the budget of the new President would be.

President Truman saw the point immediately and he tried to get the President-elect on the telephone, found he was en route to Colorado for a vacation. But he sent him a telegram, and eight days later President Eisenhower had made his designation and had Joseph Dodge sitting in the office next to mine working on the new budget. It was a particularly happy circumstance that Dodge was available and a happy circumstance also that Dodge was familiar enough with the workings of government that he understood, at least in general terms, the role of the Budget Bureau and the importance of its work.

The point I'm making here is that President Truman saw the importance of an orderly transition, and his interest in the matter prompted what has since become a systematic effort to bridge one administration into another at a time of change in the Presidency.

This had been a neglected area.

Very much so. And the effort that went into smoothing this transition was great. A great deal of credit has to be given, of course, to both parties, but especially to President Truman because he could have said—probably without criticism: "Let the new administration take over when they're supposed to take over." Instead, we developed transition papers—these are essentially briefings—on a wide variety of problems and made them available through Dodge and others who were named subsequently. These arrangements made it possible to refer back to this experience at the time President Eisenhower left office. He was so grateful, he recalled so well the value of this type of arrangement, that a more formalized arrangement was established when his term ended. At that time he designated General Persons, and President-elect Kennedy designated Clark Clifford to work out the transition arrangements. What had started as briefings, or problem papers in the earlier change, became much more elaborate. President-elect Kennedy set up task forces to work with the government people. Office space was made available—in other words, the effort was much more systematic. But if it hadn't been for this earlier ground-breaking at the time of the shift from Truman to Eisenhower, then it wouldn't have been done so well, if at all. And I'm sure—as a matter of fact I know—that similar arrangements are being made right now looking toward the change of administration this coming January [1969].

Another incident which I often recall occurred in the period before President Kennedy took office. This transition, as I indicated, was highly planned and systematic. The Brookings Institution offered the neutral meeting ground and furnished some of the staff. In fact Laurin Henry of Brookings later did a book on presidential transition. But the incident that I wanted to relate was the visit that several of us made to Palm Beach to see President-elect Kennedy in December. At the time he was on vacation. We brought along a list, as I recall it, of some eighty different items that we wanted to call to his attention. In some cases these were backed up by memoranda and in others we relied simply on oral briefings on the part of Ted Sorensen, Dave Bell, myself, Dick Neustadt, and Mike Feldman. We all went down and got there fairly late in the afternoon, and we saw President Kennedy finally about nine o'clock in the evening. We didn't get out until about three in the morning and ended up in the kitchen eating sandwiches. He was tremendously interested and we disposed of a great many matters.

We came back the next morning, and this time Douglas Dillon was there also, because we were going to be talking about budget and financial matters. We ran through to lunch, had lunch with him, and then came back that evening at about eight o'clock and covered more territory. We covered a tremendous amount of ground and a great many decisions were made. A lot of guidance was given, additional staff work was planned, and a lot was accomplished in a highly relaxed atmosphere.

Perhaps this is the proper way to break in future Presidents.

Yes. Yes, indeed. It's terribly important that there be adequate advance preparation for presidential messages which come early in the new term. This need would depend, somewhat, on the background of the individual. Someone who had been familiar with government for a long time would be in an especially favorable situation. Incidentally, one thing which continually impressed me about President Kennedy was his ability to read and absorb rapidly the material we brought him. He was one of the most rapid readers I've ever seen anywhere.

Another incident that I recall particularly was the first meeting we had with President Johnson after President Kennedy's funeral. The meeting was held at ten o'clock the night of the funeral, and was attended by Walter Heller of the Council of Economic Advisors—he was the Chairman— Douglas Dillon, Joe Fowler, Kermit Gordon, and myself. And there were other staff there as well. I believe Ted Sorensen was there too. The purpose of the meeting was to plan budget strategy in relation to the tax reduction. The decision was taken that evening, about twelve o'clock, to cut more than $2 billion of expenditures off the budget, hopefully with the idea that this would be adequate to get a tax reduction from Congress. It later proved that the President's judgment was correct. As he phrased it to Walter Heller, who was at that time pushing for a higher budget figure: "You have to make up your mind whether you want to get the immediate effect of a tax reduction or a longer-term effect of an expenditure increase." It didn't take long for Walter Heller to see the point. He couldn't have it both ways—that's what President Johnson meant.

It must give you much satisfaction to have participated in many landmark decisions. Do you take equal satisfaction in the day-to-day operations of your chores?

Are you referring now to my present role?

In contrast to some of the dramatic events you have described, I wanted to know what your experience has been with the daily, nine-to-five type of work you do.

I think there's no question about the excitement and the challenge of being part of the Executive Office, as the Budget Bureau is, and working closely with the President and the White House staff, because for the most part we were dealing with important issues and problems. You don't meet just to engage in pleasantries except on social occasions. To some extent you're always on the frontier—you're dealing with issues or differences of opinion within the administration, or dealing with issues which people outside are opposed to; you're also dealing with congressional relations— in other words, you're dealing with *real problems. . . .*

. . . headliners.

. . . you're dealing with things which the press is interested in—and this adds to the excitement—there's no question about that. There's a great deal involved in the budget process which is tough, back-breaking, drudgery-type work. This never gets into the headlines, never even gets to the President, in many cases. But there are also a great many new fields to be explored and new ideas that add to what some people would call glamour. I would call it excitement.

I think that we might add here that someone has coined a phrase: the Budget Bureau has to be politically aware without being politically active.

That's drawing a fine line.

A fine line, indeed. I suppose that it's also worth noting that I hope that the Budget Bureau, as an agency, has established itself in this context. This was once by no means certain.

I don't have to emphasize that today citizens appear to be quarreling about and questioning the practices of government at various levels. At times they attack its very goals. Does this attitude affect the public official in his operations at many points or in different ways? I'm thinking more especially about the need for each person in this age to feel that it is his government. How does the official respond?

Of course, I'm not sure that there is any greater attack or greater criticism leveled at government today than there was thirty years ago when I first joined the government. If there is any difference, perhaps it is more of a feeling by most people regarding many things about the government. It's so big, so complex, so technical, that they really don't have the ability as a citizen to comprehend it. Therefore they tend to rely more on, say, the columnists who are presumably knowledgeable, the experts whom they would regard as reliable. Take, for example, the fields of Defense, Space, or the high-energy-accelerator programs of the Atomic Energy Commission. Many of the areas of scientific research and development are so foreign to his knowledge that the average citizen feels frustrated.

I think there will always be criticism of government. There are too many people! We are spending too much! Bureaucracy! I don't suppose we hear any more of general criticism today than we did thirty years ago, or ten years ago or five years ago. The concern is really the irritation that comes about from failure to get your mail on time, or maybe difficulty with the Internal Revenue Service or from some other personal contact the individual has with government.

On the central point of whether or not citizens are questioning the practices of government, I think there's some room for optimism here. Take the greater participation and involvement by private industry, including top industry people, with the affairs of government. I think this is encouraging. I'm not referring now necessarily to the National Alliance set up to deal with urban problems, or the Urban Coalition, or similar organizations. I'm referring to involvement of more and more individuals on advisory committees, commissions. . . .

Task forces?

. . . task forces and direct-responsibility assignments. The legacy here, in part, I think still derives from World War II when we had a great influx of people from the private sector to government—and many of them are still prominent in the private sector: people like Marion Folsom, for example, of Eastman Kodak, and Lucius Clay, who had been in a military capacity but has since played an important role in private industry. Then there was Clarence Randall, who died a year or so ago, who played a tremendous role as a communicator. I wouldn't use the word missionary to describe him because he didn't make this a mission, but he did do a tremendous job in industry circles through his writings and speeches. Also, he was willing to come back, repeatedly, to serve the government. Bob Lovett is another example. Also the Committee for Economic Development, as you know, has established a Committee on Improvement of Governmental Management. I had a part, by the way, in getting the committee organized. I think the chief credit for it, however, goes to Marion Folsom. Along with three or four others, we were seeking more direct involvement by private industry people in the management and organization problems of government. There had been a number of efforts, of course, by leaders in private industry to involve themselves in economic policies—or other types of government policies—but not in terms of how to manage the government. There has been little attempt to capture the experience of private industry relevant to government, to get a better understanding of the efficiency or lack of efficiency of government, and to communicate that fact back to government through publications and personnel contacts. The Business Council didn't perform this function. It has been concerned with foreign policy, military policy—very top-level policies. It had no staff to undertake studies. It had no direct involvement. John Gardner, who, at that time was head of the Carnegie Corporation, was interested, and Jim Perkins, who was his deputy and is now president of Cornell University, was interested. We had their assurance that there would be funds for a study if we could find a practical way to it—at least for a three-year period.

Our first effort was to establish the group as a completely separate organization. The problem was to get the needed leadership. We had a number of people lined up to participate, but we couldn't really find the right person to take on the leadership. Finally, Marion Folsom suggested that we attach this to the CED as a separate committee. This was arranged, and I'm glad to say it has worked out extremely well. He was the one who was able to bring this about, because of his long-time involvement and leadership within CED.

Beyond their publications, there are conferences, I believe.

Oh, yes, there are conferences. But the work has been largely in the same pattern as other CED activities: publications, research documents.

So it is not all negative. I think that most people who have served in top governmental capacities go back to private industry and become, in a sense, defenders of the quality of government personnel.

You deal almost continuously with the Congress; in fact, it may be appropriate to say that Congress is your boss. Have you, over the years, thought out ways of improving legislative and executive relations? I'm thinking of the reversal of roles in terms of initiation of legislation by the executive and, in a sense, Congress serving as an overseer or an inspector general of administration. From your testimony on the Hill, have one or two suggestions for improvements crossed your mind?

My position, up until 2½ years ago, of course, was in the Executive Office of the President. There I probably devoted more time to congressional matters than the Director of the Budget did in testifying, following up inquiries, and dealing with individual problems. I testified quite frequently, so I saw a great deal of members of Congress. But I was still basically oriented toward the executive branch, and properly so.

Now in my current role, I'm primarily oriented toward the Congress and less toward the executive branch. I had often wondered how life would be in the legislative branch. I'm not fully in the legislative branch, in the sense of being on the staff of a member of Congress or on the staff of a committee of Congress. I'm still detached to some degree. So I make these suggestions from that background and that standpoint.

The thing that appears important to me, in terms of success and failure of executive-legislative relationships, is the maintaining of a channel of communication, particularly at the top level, between an agency and the chairman and key members of the committees which have jurisdiction. It's terribly easy for this channel of communication to break down, and easy to put too much reliance upon formal, legislative liaison staff. It's especially important that committee members have full confidence in agency people, that irrespective of differences of opinion the committee is getting the honest views. There must be no attempt to hide things which properly should be brought out when they are germane and of concern to the committee, or to the Congress as a whole. In other words, if a member of Congress senses a lack of frankness, he is likely to be more sensitive than almost anybody else, because then he runs the danger of making public statements without knowing the full story.

In my experience, the most successful administrators are not necessarily those who always agree with congressional committees, but those who go to the chairman or key members and say: "Here's what's happening. You ought to know about it. You ought to know about it now, before it gets into the newspapers."

Another problem is that a member of Congress often thinks an agency head wants to get credit for things which the congressman feels should be shared, or maybe belongs to Congress alone. Or he feels that the agency head is building up fires with the newspapers to put pressures on Congress.

It becomes a kind of boxing bout.

Yes. I recall one case where a matter was in hearings with a committee of Congress, and the agency head called a press briefing. It was supposed to be off the record, completely off the record. This press briefing was in the morning, and a further hearing on the Hill was scheduled for the afternoon. In the interval one of the members of the press who had been present at the briefing broke his pledge of confidence and told the chairman of the committee all that had been said. Without revealing his source of information, the chairman asked the same questions at the afternoon hearing as the press had asked that morning and was given answers different from those supplied at the morning briefing. It was even denied that a press briefing had been held.

It's hard to repair this damage, I should think.

The damage was never repaired between the chairman of a very key committee and a very important agency head.

Future relations are destroyed to a large extent.

They could never be rebuilt.

Another factor I would suggest is the importance of adequate preparation in testifying at important committee hearings. There's a sensitivity in the Congress, a feeling that information is all on the executive side and not enough on the legislative side. Rightly or wrongly, Congress feels it's understaffed and doesn't have the tremendous resources at its command that the executive branch has, and therefore it's at a disadvantage in a hearing encounter with a witness from an executive agency. Consequently, if the subject of a hearing is of great importance, or of great public concern, then it's important for an agency head to sit down with a committee chairman, maybe with the staff, in advance of the hearing and lay the groundwork in terms of areas to be covered, any background which either side might or might not want to have put on the record, and an understanding about what is the committee's interest. It is important that when a man goes to testify before a committee, he have the answers—if at all possible.

That he do his homework, in short.

That he do his homework. There's nothing worse than a witness going before a committee who hasn't taken the trouble to do the kind of homework they've done. He has more resources and should have been able to have the information. Committees are usually very quick in sensing when a witness is trying to do a little bluffing.

Bamboozle?

Well, not bamboozle so much as appear to say he has the answer when the committee knows he doesn't.

One can always say: "I don't know."

It's much easier, much better just to say: "I don't know."

And then assemble the information.

Yes, be glad to come back or be glad to assemble the information or put it in the record. A forthright "I don't know" is far better than to appear to try to answer the question, when it's perfectly obvious to the committee members either that you don't have it or that you're giving them information they know is wrong.

Then there's a third point to be made—again, it relates to what makes a congressman react the way he does. Many times a congressman questions an administrator much more to try to bring out information than to take a position. In some instances, also, he's putting something on the record because he knows a certain constituency feels strongly about it, and he wants to make it abundantly clear that the full record has been compiled and that action—whatever it may be—is being taken. He may be as open-minded as all outdoors, and pushing a line of questioning for other purposes. Or it may be that he has a constituency rather than a personal interest in a particular matter.

He may sincerely feel that it's worth bringing into the public arena, even though less charitable people might accuse him of doing so just for home consumption in an election year. The relevant point here, in terms of congressional relations, is that before an agency head issues a blast in the press or makes a speech, he should try to understand what motivates a congressman. They may still end up disagreeing with each other, but the disagreement might be expressed in different terms.

This might reinforce respect between the two branches and confirm what Neustadt has often said regarding shared rather than separated powers.

That's right. The worst thing is to ignore a congressman who has a legitimate interest in a given problem.

May we now turn to the office you now direct. I assume you have a number of roles and wear a number of hats. If this is so, which role has the most bite—the greatest challenge?

I think I would separate the immediate from the long-term aspects of the job. I think, in the immediate sense, the area having the greatest bite is our legal responsibility as the interpreter—the final authority—with respect to authorization to spend money. That may not sound very dramatic but it takes dramatic form. A contractor, for example, may feel that he has not had an adequate opportunity to compete. In his opinion, the rules and regulations may have been violated, or there may have been departures from the law. As an independent agency he can bring his case before us for final adjudication. In effect, we have a kind of attorney general's responsibility for the final interpretation of all laws relating to government expenditures. Sometimes we get inquiries from the Congress, after they've acted on a bill, as to what our authoritative interpretation would be in the exercise of our responsibility, in regard to allowing or disallowing expenditures by a particular agency.

Do you give advisory opinions?

Oh, yes. If a committee of Congress should ask us, we would give them our opinion with the same kind of consideration as though that question had been raised by a spending agency. We can also disallow expenditures already made, if, in our opinion, the money was spent contrary to the intent of Congress. In that case, the money has to be made up somehow— by the bonding agency or the certifying officer of the agency. If they disagree, they can, of course, go to the courts for separate adjudication, but this is highly unlikely. They could more easily go to Congress and ask for relief. The idea behind GAO was to place the ultimate responsibility for interpreting all laws to spend money in an agency attached to the legislative branch.

In respect to citizen-relations, it sounds as if, to a degree, you serve as an ombudsman.

Yes, we do. It is, in fact, an ombudsman function. And while you're on that point, we have another, which is the responsibility for reviewing any claim made by an individual or an organization against the government, where he or it is unhappy with the treatment received from the agency involved in the matter which gave rise to the claim. This gives the aggrieved party an opportunity for an independent review of his case. We handle large numbers of these in our Claims Division.

I don't think the popular image of the GAO is quite fair. It may be that I'm reflecting opinions of students—as well as the average, less aware groups. Perhaps one should think of it as a stern but yet warm protector of the public interest.

The popular image, as you put it, may be a little on the narrow side— the literal side.

But in a full sense you're the friend rather than the foe of the citizen.

In this respect, certainly.

These functions, then, are the short-run purposes of the GAO.

I would characterize them as having the most bite from the standpoint of our immediate role. I think in the longer run, the area having most bite is the work we do with congressional committees. We have increased considerably, over the last two or three years, the amount of direct assistance that we provide to committees on matters of current interest and germane to current issues. We've tried to do this by improving communications with the committees in terms of our own efforts in the audit field. What we call audit, however, is what others would call management or program review. It's an audit, but not in the narrow fiscal sense.

Our work extends to the twelve executive departments and some sixty independent agencies and commissions. It takes us into over 3000 locations worldwide, including some thirty-three foreign countries. At any single point in time we may have over 1000 audits and reviews in process, involving not only government programs administered by federal departments and agencies, but also many federal programs administered by state and local governments, universities, grantees, and industrial plants, as well as by private contractors holding government contracts.

The primary purpose of these audits and reviews is to determine whether government agencies are discharging their financial responsibilities in an effective, efficient, and economic manner. Of our total staff of 4310, approximately 2400 auditors and accountants are directly involved in this work. The potential in this area, in my opinion, is great. We have a large number of assignments, of course, that we carry on for the appropriations committees and the Government Operations Committee of Congress. And more and more we are working with other committees: Foreign Affairs and Foreign Relations in the foreign aid field, for example. We also work closely with the international organizations.

I know you often work Saturdays, attend a good many meetings, testify on the Hill. It's a kind of diary of a recent week. I know students would like to hear what you have been up to; what happens; what the Comptroller General does. Is there, in short, a typical week?

It would be hard to describe a typical week, but I might give you some idea of some of the things which make the heaviest demands on my time. I find an important part of my job is to meet with groups concerned with the work of the GAO both in the Congress and outside. Most of those on the outside are the many organizations having defense contracts, and problems that arise are in connection with our audits. It's terribly important from the point of view of government relations that this work be carried out as intelligently as possible so as to minimize expense, time delays, and difficulties on government and private-interest side alike.

They don't come to you because they're in trouble necessarily. They come for information?

They come for information or I go to their meetings to discuss and debate with them and to present to them our plans, our thinking, our policies.

I've also been spending a good deal of time with state and local agencies—I think this area is going to become increasingly important. It is, in fact, terribly important right now. I'm on the Research Advisory Committee for the Council of State Governments and recently I joined the board of trustees of Public Administration Service. I have also been serving as chairman of the Ford Foundation Evaluative Committee on the Training Programs for State Budget Officers. In these connections and others, I have gone out of my way to try to spend more time dealing with problems of state and local governments. This is an area to which we shall necessarily be giving more audit attention in the future, because it's been estimated that government expenditures for these purposes will triple within the next seven or eight years merely for programs that already have been started.

In addition, in the first 2½ years here, I have devoted a great deal of attention to our own internal problems, trying to become better acquainted with our people and their capabilities. I have been especially interested in developing a staff development program.

I've read your staff development manual and it's great—speaking, let me add, as a former personnel management man.

Well, we've had many compliments on it.

It's quite readable, by the way.

We want it to be readable because we want all of our employees to read it. We felt it's important not only to have a policy but to have our people understand exactly what our policy is. We had a lot of staff participation in the development of that manual over a period of approximately a year.

Internal management problems have probably taken more of my time in the first few years than I should expect on a continuing basis. We are not a large government organization compared to other agencies, but we are highly dispersed. We not only have sixteen regional offices in the United States, but also five overseas offices. Even our Washington staff is highly decentralized because our people are located in the headquarters offices of all the major agencies. This scattering presents internal problems of communication; it means that we had to develop techniques for improving that communication. We've developed a newsletter for all our employees, a *GAO Review*, which is a professional journal issued quarterly. We hold staff meetings. We've developed methods for improving the forward planning of our work programs—a six-months program review where we systemmatically examine our work for the forward period. In these first few years, at least, a considerable amount of time has been given to these things.

Then, of course, I testify a great deal.

Is that fun?

I've always enjoyed it, if I have the time to do it right. It's best if you can go feeling that you're overprepared, ready to answer a lot of questions that you may or may not get.

I think the most challenging thing about testifying on the Hill is dealing with current problems and helping in the thinking process that goes on in a committee's deliberations. Very seldom are you going to be the key person. It would be a very rare case where you were the determining factor, but you can play an important part in shaping up the thinking, bringing in new points of view, and offering new evidence to bear on a problem.

This leads to the point that I referred to before. As guardian of the public interest, the term "watchdog for Congress" has often been applied to the GAO.

"Watchdog" is probably an unfortunate term. It was developed—and I suspect it is going to stick—because it is such a catchy phrase, but it's misleading in the sense that it sounds as if we are interested only in saving the money—the nickels and dimes—involved. Actually, even under our statute, we have a much more positive role to play: developing studies and case materials, trying to improve and strengthen management organization. Now, to be sure, we shall always be doing investigative-type work for Congress, at the request of an individual member, a committee, or the Congress as a whole through special statutory enactments. And to some degree we're always going to be ambivalent in the sense that we are performing this direct assistance role as well as the broader one. We always try to make it clear to everybody concerned in our investigations that the end product is used by the Congress or the committee as they see fit, not as we see fit. But our name gets attached to it, inevitably. In the other aspect of our work, we do determine which areas are most important to go into, and the end product is for our own use.

There is, however, a partnership between the two roles?

I think so. Much of our work in the broader category can be used in the inquiries that we make in the investigative category.

But the GAO is a watchdog, certainly, in the sense that it may disallow expenditures, which I referred to a while ago. It is a watchdog in the sense that we render interpretations of law with respect to authority to spend government money, either at the request of an agency or on our own initiative—so to that extent we are an agency of the Congress. Moreover, we report to Congress as a whole, not to a single committee, as is the practice of the countries of the British Commonwealth where the audit agency reports to a Committee on Accounts once a year. Here, we render our reports as they are completed.

In essence, the watchdog function means that we appraise the expenditure and use of federal funds and report our findings to the Congress, government officials, and the public. Our constant duty is to serve the Congress by continually searching for means of achieving greater economy and efficiency throughout the range of functions performed in government.

Could you describe some of the major, current problems now before the GAO?

One of the most significant and interesting programs stems from the Prouty Amendment to the Economic Opportunity Act of 1967, which requires us to evaluate the efficiency and effectiveness of the anti-poverty program and report to Congress early in 1969. Over 300 of our staff have been assigned to this study for periods ranging from six to ten months. We shall also be concerned with anti-poverty programs delegated to the Departments of Labor and Health, Education and Welfare. This review involves Community Action programs in a number of large cities and the Job Corps operations in selected areas throughout the country. To assist us we have contracted with several management firms as well as with experts in the fields of social, economic, health, and related sciences. This evaluation takes us in new directions, but I believe that as a result of these in-depth reviews we shall be able to provide Congress with useful data, and I hope also some workable solutions to many difficult problems facing the agencies concerned.

Another interesting program involves countrywide reviews of United States assistance to various foreign nations. This includes programs administered by AID, the Military Assistance Program, and the Peace Corps, as well as other programs financed by American funds. We have reviews in process in Tunisia, Nigeria, Peru, Guatemala, Nicaragua, Honduras, and Liberia. There is also a review under way of the Regional Assistance program for Central America, Ethiopia, Laos, Thailand, India, and Pakistan. These broad-scale reviews extend beyond individual agency responsibilities and will, I hope, provide an authoritative insight into the total United States effort in the field of foreign aid.

One final item. In the defense area we have a number of significant programs in research and development undertaken by government contractors to increase management effectiveness and efficiency in the Far East, including Vietnam, in the procurement of major weapons, the use of civilian-military manpower, the construction of military facilities, and such support activities as transportation and communication systems.

This is surely a far-flung agenda and should change the nearsighted view many still hold of your organization. In view of the term "accounting" in your title would you consider the GAO as an accounting teacher to federal agencies?

I don't think we consider ourselves in this light, but we do prescribe the principles, standards, and other requirements for accounting to be pursued by all agencies. Besides, from time to time we provide leadership and direction for improved accounting methods. Our people constantly cooperate with federal agency accountants in this process and examine their systems in operation. Occasionally we call certain items to the attention of agency officials to permit correction as well as improvement.

In addition, the Budget Bureau also has some responsibility for the promotion of better accounting in the federal agencies and, of course, the Civil Service Commission conducts many training courses that include accounting for federal programs and management.

One final point on your organization. The GAO has a reputation for saving taxpayers' money. Could you illustrate this?

In our annual report we include a fairly detailed enumeration of collections and other measurable savings attributable to our work. For example, during the fiscal 1968, total savings were almost $190 million. Many other changes are made as a result of GAO efforts that cannot be fully measured in financial terms; these are also cited in our report. One example of specific financial accomplishment is a study we made of AEC's proposed criteria and contract for uranium enrichment services. This was made at the request of the Joint Committee on Atomic Energy in Congress. Our report contained our conclusions and recommendations with respect to AEC policy concerning certain fixed costs relating to excess plant capacity; the potential for accommodating future changes in AEC policy by contract amendments; financial consequences to AEC in the event of contract cancellations by customers; and limitations on AEC for entering into contract commitments in excess of its present productive capability. As a result of this report and Joint Committee hearings, AEC made various changes to improve and strengthen its program. One was a specific change relating to the inclusion of additional charges for depreciation and interest on investment, amounting to a total of $42 million in charges for enrichment services.

May we turn now to the concept of Planning-Programming-Budgeting-Systems (PPBS), especially in view of your Budget Bureau association and your recent testimony on March 26, 1968, to the Government Operations Committee of the Senate?

I should like to comment on PPBS as an instrument for executive decision making as against its importance to the Congress. We are frequently asked, "What difference does PPBS make to Congress?" and the answer has to be, in my opinion, that PPBS doesn't make any difference to the Congress except as it may improve the quality of the justification of programs which have been proposed by the executive branch for congressional approval.

The Congress is interested in PPBS—at least it seems to me—in terms of the end product. And the end product is the justification of executive-branch proposals, the kind of justification marshalled to support a given program as against some alternative, advanced by a member of Congress, an interest group, or from some other source.

In seeking to establish certain goals, does PPBS assist the legislator in allocating priority to one rather than another of a series with an almost equal value in his judgment?

I think Congress necessarily tends to be mostly concerned with reacting to proposals made from the executive branch. Some of my friends in Congress would probably differ with me on this, but my feeling would be that if you could quantify this, you'd find that most of the work of the Congress is generated through efforts made initially by the executive agencies.

Congressmen are interested in cost effectiveness. Few would want to use that term—it might sound too academic—but there is definite interest. Title II of the Senate-passed Legislative Reorganization Act would give GAO specific responsibility for assisting Congress on cost-effectiveness studies. And as I mentioned earlier, the Congress has recently asked us to undertake essentially a cost-effectiveness study of the entire anti-poverty program.

This is a lot wider effort than in the past.

Oh, yes. We've been trying to broaden our reviews, our analyses of governmental programs, but this new proposal carries our job further than at any time in the past. Congress is now considering extending the Manpower Training and Development Act, and one amendment which has been offered would require us to undertake a study similar to the anti-poverty economic programs, in the field of manpower training.

Does all this change your total approach?

It means that we will have to develop, over a time, more specialists in this field. Also we have now established a Systems Analysis Branch in our Office of Policy and Special Studies. We have already trained five of our younger staff people at colleges and universities in a program sponsored by the Budget Bureau and Civil Service Commission under the National Institute of Public Affairs. We have three more going out next year and we've brought in a few from the outside. The head of this branch comes from the Department of Defense. We hope also, over a period of time, to develop increased capability in terms of the techniques by which cost-effectiveness studies can be made. I think the Congress can properly look to us to evaluate costs versus benefits of programs, not just the administrative costs involved.

If before a congressional committee you used the phrase "integrated management system," would it be easily understood?

No, it would not. It would be understood by a few committees which have been especially concerned with the development of accounting systems. I say a few; it would be more like a few subcommittees rather than full committees. In the minds of some people this is an area of mystery; in the minds of others it is something that Congress should be as fully equipped to deal with as the executive branch is; in the minds of still others it is something the executive branch has developed to try to obscure rather than to clarify the reasons for one program as against another.

Was PPBS perhaps oversold at the outset? I am thinking now of your statement on March twenty-sixth of this year: "Although PPBS can generate information useful to this process (you were talking in the context of national goals and determining their priorities largely through the political process), it is quite easy to oversell the PPBS contribution to the determination of national priorities."

I think it was oversold, because it was perhaps implied that this could be a "revolution" in the field of budgeting. It can't be a revolution—either as something completely new or as something that can be adopted in a fairly short period of time. To some degree it is a repackaging. As I attempted to bring out in my testimony before the Jackson subcommittee, some of its elements had been developing for some time: the five-year-projection, the development of cost-effectiveness techniques in certain programs, the development of alternatives as against a single analysis—all these things have long been in the process of evolution and development. The thing which is new and has made PPBS somewhat dramatic was that it was to be applied governmentwide, according to a highly formalized set of instructions, and accompanied by formalized documentation.

Your statement to the Jackson subcommittee is certainly the clearest on PPBS I've come across.

We've had a lot of interest in that statement, some perhaps because we tried to go back and develop the historical background of the elements of the PPBS system.

In this organization, we are certainly in favor of the basic objectives of what is being attempted. And we have revised our own principles in examining accounting systems for which we have the final responsibility of approval—that is, *all* agency accounting systems. We will not approve one unless it will supply the basic information needed to support these program categories.

Similarly, we have been pushing what you refer to as an integrated management information system as an integral part of the financial programs in the agencies. Because of the computer, all these must be related in order to produce the kind of useful data needed.

By way of a windup, would you care to add any reflections on your extended years of public administration service?

It would probably take more time than we have to do this, and I hope I could reply better, at some later date and on reflection, than I can offhand. One point would be relevant here, however: What is it that causes people to continue to bat their way in the public service when sometimes they encounter more uncertainties and get more brickbats and less pay than they might get elsewhere? I think the answer is that there are challenges in the government service that you couldn't get in most places outside of it. This would not obtain for all public administrators—I wouldn't want to be that inclusive—but certainly individuals operating at the higher grade levels of government generally have a feeling of contribution, a feeling of doing something besides earning a paycheck. I think most of them, for that reason, get a satisfaction out of their work that would be difficult to find in most organizations outside of government. Perhaps I should not include here individuals who are performing roughly the same kind of work in one place as against another. And literally hundreds of thousands of people in the government service are in this kind of work. But even in this group, many derive satisfaction from being identified with public service agencies. I think that the great problem we still have is how to attract younger people to government employment—or at least how to give them enough exposure to government to show them that there is this challenge.

Our education is still primarily geared to providing ways to supply the private sector and does not give adequate attention to governmental institutions. We have no way, for example, to bring in selected young people, say, between their senior year and the graduate program, or between years of graduate study. We do have summer programs which are useful.

Interns.

Yes; and we do have the practice, for example, right here in the GAO, if an individual performs well during his summer period, of putting him on leave without pay for the rest of his academic period, looking to permanent employment later.

I think we may swing into that—have a government agency adopt an outstanding intern and sponsor him for the concluding period of his education.

That's right. And, of course, if he's able to work two or three summers, he gets that much more additional seniority toward an increase in grade as well as toward his retirement later on, if he remains in government. But we still need to do a great deal more in colleges and universities to find ways to expose these young people to the content of governmental programs in a way that will help them to decide whether they want to throw in their lot with a government career rather than go elsewhere.

STUDY QUESTIONS

1. Do you support the views expressed on the art-versus-science aspects of public administration?
2. Reading between the lines, would you say that the Comptroller General has a philosophy of administration? What do you consider the strongest elements of his thinking?
3. Prepare a job description of his work based on information from the interview plus any data from more formal sources.
4. Can you add other proposals to the Comptroller General's on the recruitment of students into the public service?

II
LEGISLATORS
AND ADMINISTRATORS

2

STATE HIGHWAY DEPARTMENT

The financial problems of the Vermont State Highway Department had been front-page news for weeks, and the report of the legislative investigating committee that had been set up to look into its difficulties was anticipated with much interest. A comprehensive program of highway building that in 1966 had been approved by the legislature to cost $142.7 million was found a year later to have a price tag of $457 million. The voters were shocked. Was the discrepancy due to graft, and would there soon be a first-class scandal? Was it a matter of administrative inefficiency in the Highway Department, or was there some other trouble? The report of the Joint Legislative Committee assigned to investigate the highway "mess" appeared on February 19, 1968, after extensive public hearings that added drama and suspense to the plot, as apparent misunderstandings and blurred responsibilities began to appear.

BACKGROUND OF THE CASE

Vermont is a small state, with a population of only 415,000 people and an aggregate personal income of only $1 billion. Moreover, although its per capita income is below that of the national average, it bears the heaviest tax burden in relation to personal income of any state in the Union.

In 1967 the state's total revenues were approximately $90 million, of which about one-quarter, or $23 million, was highway-user taxes and fees committed to the Highway Fund. Consequently, the state was hardly in a position to stand the financial shock of an underestimate for highway purposes amounting to over $300 million! What would it do to the state's credit? And of even greater importance to the overburdened taxpayers, what would it do to them?

To add to the difficulty, the state debt of $79 million required debt service of nearly $9 million annually, which in turn was nearly 10 percent of total revenues. The pessimists—among whom were numbered the leaders of the opposing political party—saw the prospect as near-bankruptcy.

AUTHORIZATION OF THE INVESTIGATION

The Joint Legislative Committee created by the 1968 session of the General Assembly was mandated to inquire into all aspects of highway finances, with special attention to projected highway construction costs. Five years earlier, in 1963, a fairly monumental report on the highway department had been completed by an interim legislative committee after seventeen months of study. How could so much go wrong in so short a time?

The new committee found that the 1966 highway bill called for an expenditure of $142.7 million, set out specific roads to be built, and appropriated a specific sum for the purpose. Presumably, therefore, the legislature had done its job well. This same statute established a policy of planning and construction for the entire arterial improvement program to be completed by 1980. Certain designated portions, however, were to be completed by 1972. *These figures were based upon construction costs as they existed in 1966, and would have been adequate if the roads had been completed then, as of course they could not be when plans extended to 1980.*

The question arose, therefore, as to whether the $300 million discrepancy was exclusively a matter of rising highway construction costs, due to general inflationary factors. If this were so, there would be nothing further of importance to investigate. The committee soon found that this *was* a factor, but not the major one.

What, then, was the major explanation? "In complete disregard" of the figures and assurances given the legislature, said the committee's report, "the highway department had proceeded to plan 'perfect' roads instead of those authorized in 1966." Rather than the specified two-lane highways, for example, all were to have four lanes, modeled after the interstate highway system then being constructed in the state. Secondly, whereas the legislature had specifically allocated the 1966 funds to certain roads in certain parts of the state, the highway department proceeded on the assumption that *all* areas of the state should have "perfect" roads, and not merely those specifically authorized. Why? Was it the bureaucratic tendency to do everything according to a rigid standard? Or was it a matter of political pressure on the Highway Department from members of the highway industry in areas of the state not covered by the 1966 statute? The investigating committee skirted these issues gingerly, preferring to place the blame on the highway administrators themselves.

How did the situation come to the attention of the legislature at all? The committee found that the Highway Board of three members appointed by the Governor had become aware of the department's change in concept and cost as early as the summer of 1966. Secondly, it was found that facts presented in 1967 by the Highway Department to the Budget and Management Division of the Department of Administration in the Governor's office should have alerted that agency to a serious problem, but apparently did not. Thirdly, the Governor was finally made aware of the problem some time in the late spring or early summer of 1967, but the general public and the legislature did not know the situation until late in the fall of that year. When the adjourned session of the legislature met in January 1968, the Joint Investigating Committee was appointed.

So the problem was one of administration and failure of coordination, rather than inflation, and there was no evidence of graft. But if the Highway Department had continued to obligate funds at the rate it had adopted, not only would the state have been $300 million short of what was needed by 1980, but by that time *outstanding indebtedness would have been $500 million, with $14.5 million needed annually to meet the interest and principal payments on the bonds.*[1]

INTERNAL ADMINISTRATION OF THE HIGHWAY DEPARTMENT

If the Highway Department had disregarded legislative intent "completely," and if the fault was the Highway Department's own, how could this have happened? While the investigation was in course, the Governor assumed full responsibility, but pointed out that the Highway Department had for years been insulated from executive control by the Governor. This did not lessen his responsibility; he was merely stating a fact.

The investigating committee found the real difficulty in the internal

---

[1] *Report*, Joint Legislative Committee created by the General Assembly of the State of Vermont in 1968 Joint House Resolution Number 61, Montpelier, February 19, 1968, p. 3.

organization and in the lack of coordination in planning and execution in the department itself. Although the three-member Highway Board spent much time on the job and its members were honest and able, it had not established the department's *planning policy*. How then had it been established? Apparently the planning function had gone by default. Each major division of the department was a law unto itself, and coordination never really occurred.

The titular head of the Highway Department was the Commissioner, the Governor's appointee. Under him, the Chief Engineer was theoretically responsible for administration as well as for strictly engineering functions, but he was overworked and not especially interested in or qualified for overall administration. A Planning Division with an Advance Planning Section under it also was headed by an engineer and operated in a vacuum, so to speak.

To compound the problem, the investigating committee was unable to satisfy itself that decisions sent from the Planning Engineer to the Chief Engineer were thereafter submitted to the Commissioner or the Highway Board. The committee gained the impression that the Commissioner and the Board were busy on details but never got around to considering carefully problems of policy and control.

The investigating committee graphically described the lack of internal coordination:

> Few written records were maintained and apparently none were required. There was little or no communication between the finance personnel and planning personnel of the Department and the Budget and Management Division. The advance planners were in the fourth level of administration, far removed from the Board and Commissioner. The three-man board was so overworked with administrative detail and hearings that few policy decisions were ever actually made by the Board.[2]

RECOMMENDATIONS CONCERNING POLICY AND CONTROL

The investigating committee thought that since the legislature cannot exercise continual oversight, and the Highway Department spends so large a share of the state's total revenues, the key instrumentality of control should be the Highway Board, and that it should be increased in size. Its members are civilians, let it be remembered, and are paid only a per diem for their services. In the past, there had been charges that political debts were being paid by appointment to the Highway Board.

The first major recommendation of the investigating committee, therefore, was that (1) the three-man Highway Board should be expanded to

---

[2] *Report*, p. 13.

five members, geographically representative and drawn from both political parties. Greater consideration should also be given to career qualifications and individual abilities. (2) The Board should be relieved of its detailed duties and concentrate on policy, decision, and control. (3) In condemnation hearings, which previously had been the joint responsibility of all three board members, a single member *or a hearing examiner* should suffice.

IMPROVED INTERNAL ADMINISTRATION

Although the members of the investigating committee acknowledged that they were not qualified as administrative consultants, they were clear as to what was wrong and what the remedy was. The problem was too much divided responsibility, and the remedy was to make the Commissioner a real chief executive instead of a figurehead, as he had been in the past.

The committee summarized the faults as follows:

    1.   Outdated organizational structure.

    2.   Lack of the internal controls expected of a large engineering department.

    3.   Lack of communication and candor between the various divisions of the department.

    4.   Gross assumptions (arrogations) of authority and decision making by some divisions, especially the Planning Division.

    5.   Disrespect and disregard for the legislature's authority and intent.

    6.   Complete lack of concern for the state's ability to pay.

    7.   Duplication of effort, such as the preparation of a seven-year construction program and a fourteen-year planning program for the Highway Department and an eight-year program for the Budget and Management Division of the Department of Administration.

    8.   Multiplicity of fiscal programs covering such varying periods as to make it impossible to compare them with each other.

Although the investigating committee believed that improved internal coordination constituted the key to better performance and that this need could be met by vesting more authority in the Commissioner and less in the engineers—who had proved rather inept at this phase of their work— the committee also expressed concern for coordination at higher levels. Four major alternatives were set forth: [3]

    1.   Creation of a joint legislative committee to guide the state's thinking in the proper allocation of its *total* resources. (Legislation to this end had already been introduced.)

    2.   Creation of a joint administrative council in the Governor's office, to include—at the minimum—the Director of the Central Planning Office

---

[3] *Report*, p. 35.

(which had been newly created with grant-in-aid funds), the Commissioner of Highways, the Commissioner of Education (another big spender), the Commissioner of Development, and the State Treasurer. The purpose of this group would be to establish and evaluate guidelines for the future long-term capital needs of the state, to assess the economic impact of the expenditure of these capital funds, and to determine the ability of the state to finance the construction (highway and other) called for in such plans.

3.   A third possible check would be to add "independent economic and financial analysts" to the Department of Administration's Budget and Management Division, to aid in economic projections and to determine ways and means by which the state might best finance and implement its future programs. No explanation was given of "independent," but the assumption is that these analysts would be brought in from the outside, perhaps on a per diem basis.

4.   Finally, it was suggested that a new position be created within the administration to coordinate and evaluate the long-term needs of the state and to recommend the proper allocation of its resources.

Although all of these four proposals were considered alternatives, and it was suggested that "one or more" might be chosen, it seems obvious that, except for the suggested joint legislative committee, the purely administrative effects might be to dilute still further the administrative authority of the Governor and to add to the number of officials charged with overlapping responsibilities. How would the new long-term coordinator and the existing Central Planning Office divide their responsibilities, for example? Or the new coordinator and the existing Budget and Management Division?

FINANCIAL RECOMMENDATIONS

Since the Highway Department had been trying to build four-lane highways throughout the state, contrary to legislative authorization, the committee was also forced to cope with this problem. In effect, they said that although four-lane highways would be nice, the state could not afford them. In the case of the interstate highways system, which is four-lane, the federal government pays 90 percent and the state 10 percent of the cost. But for other, intrastate highways, the cost to the state is 100 percent.

It is anticipated, said the investigating committee, although in no way certain, that after completion of the interstate system in 1977, federal funds will be available on a basis of 75 percent to the state's 25 percent. Thus, if additional lanes and interchanges were built after 1977, the net cost to the state, even with rising costs, would be lower than in 1968.

The committee recommended a four-way program of legislation for coping with this situation:

1. The state should buy land for and design four-lane roads, but actually build only two-lane highways. This alone would substantially reduce the financial stringency.

2. Once funds have been allocated to construction, the Highway Board should assure itself that adequate funds are left over for bridge maintenance, secondary roads, and similar needs.

3. A study should be made with respect to the ability of cities to finance their own roads, owing to increased use by urban traffic; this might be another source of savings.

4. The legislature should move immediately to re-establish a highway construction ceiling *in the form of a statutory limitation on the amount of state funds that the legislature will allow the Highway Board to use for construction in any specified fiscal period.* In other words, quota limits should be set, and under no circumstances should the Highway Department be allowed to exceed them without securing permission from the legislature. In line with this policy, no future legislative authorization should fail to contain this statutory limit.

WHAT THE COMMITTEE DID NOT SAY

Most of the newspapers of the state seemed generally satisfied with the recommendations of the investigating committee. Being proud and thrifty, Vermont citizens were glad that the "mess" turned out to be no worse than it was. In some ways, however, the committee's report is as significant for what it did not mention as for what it did.

There was no mention, for example, of strengthened powers for the Governor or greater authority for the Budget and Management Division of the Governor's office. Indeed, these two factors were almost wholly disregarded, while emphasis was on a two-way relationship between the legislature, on the one hand, and the Highway Board and its Commissioner, on the other. It was recommended that the powers of the Commissioner be strengthened, which in some ways might be regarded as correspondingly weakening the authority of the Governor. A possible explanation is that the Governor was a Democrat, and the majority of both houses was controlled by Republicans.

There was also no reference to pressure groups in the committee's report. What part did they play in the decision to create higher standards and incur greater expense? Or was this entirely the idea of the cloistered bureaucrats?

Finally, there was only an oblique reference to sectionalism and pork barrels. The original hue and cry had occurred, for example, when the southwestern part of the state complained that it was getting relatively less than the eastern part, where the interstate system from New York and Boston to Montreal was being built. This complaint was then joined by those from the "northeast kingdom" (along the Connecticut River and south of the Canadian border), which objected that it was being left out altogether. But what was the effect of these sectional pressures on the decisions of the Highway Department in the first place? And would the matter be improved, or made worse, once the three-man board was expanded to a five-man board, with geographical distribution?

One thing that seemed beyond doubt was that the legislature felt deeply offended and abused and did not intend that this should happen again, even if it meant authorizing a new investigation every year. This zeal would be the greater, of course, if, as in the present case, the Governor was of one political persuasion and the legislature of another.

STUDY QUESTIONS

1. What are the implications of having a state board or commission develop and implement policies?
2. Basically who was primarily to blame for the development of such a situation? How might the executive have acted to forestall the problem?
3. Which of the proposed alternatives would you have endorsed?
4. Can such situations be prevented by adequate legislative watchdog methods?

3

STATE GOVERNOR

The Governor's invitation was informal, friendly: "If you would like to come up on May seventeenth, getting here in the middle of the morning, we could spend some time together."

On the appointed day I waited in the reception room adjacent to the Executive Chamber to meet Rhode Island's fiftieth chief executive. Heavy drapes bordered large windows providing a panoramic view of Providence; on the balcony, I reflected, a governor might perhaps unwind from the responsibilities of state administration and return refreshed.

Shortly after eleven Governor Chafee appeared—a man of clear-cut features, a trim yet husky build, and an encouraging smile. Above all I was aware of his voice: resonant and buoyant—a most vital person. He led me through a spacious conference room into his office, which is rather small and looks like a workshop study.

I showed him a list of questions as a tentative basis for discussion. "These are fine." I asked if there was any objection to my using a tape recorder. "It may save you taking copious notes," he replied. "Sure, use it." He removed his jacket, offered me tea or coffee; I settled for a cigar, and we began.

The Governor listens carefully and responds cheerfully. A Republican in a strongly Democratic state, he is in his third term in office. He enjoys continuing respect and popularity and is known for his strong, high standards. Forceful, well coordinated, aware of power centers, and having a strong feeling for details, he carries conviction as an administrator. He excels in compromise and persuasion but can act quickly. At ease as he is in the worlds of both thought and action, I could easily see him in many environments, but especially among students, influencing and responding to young people. In fact, he is trying to bring many young people into government service.

Governor Chafee's official biography sheet reveals his active interest in a number of related worlds:

Born in Providence, Rhode Island, in 1922, he was graduated from Deerfield Academy in Massachusetts and entered Yale in 1940. During his first year there he captained the undefeated freshman wrestling team, then left to enlist in the U.S. Marine Corps. In 1942, as a private, he landed at Guadalcanal with the First Marine Division, was subsequently commissioned an officer in the Marine Corps, saw action in Okinawa and served in China. By the end of the war, he had served four years on active duty and was released to inactive duty as a lieutenant.

Chafee then returned to Yale, completed his undergraduate studies, and went on to Harvard Law School where he graduated in 1950. Soon afterward he was recalled to active duty by the Marines and served as a captain in Korea where he commanded a rifle company. In 1952, after one and one-half years' service, he returned to civilian life to practice law in Providence.

In 1956 John Chafee began his political career in Rhode Island by winning an election as a Representative to the General Assembly. Re-elected two years later, he was chosen Minority Leader. After three terms in the General Assembly, in 1962 he ran for the office of Governor, defeating the incumbent Democrat by 398 votes. Two years later he was the first Republican governor in 34 years to be re-elected in Rhode Island; his margin of 87,000 votes was the largest attained by any governor in Rhode Island's history, and his 61 percent of the total state vote was the highest of any Republican governor in the nation. In that same election President Johnson took 81 percent of the vote in Rhode Island, his highest percentage in any state.

In 1966, Chafee was re-elected to a third term, exceeding his previous victory margin and receiving 64 percent of the total vote, again the largest percentage of any Republican governor. Moreover, for the first time in 28 years in Rhode Island a Republican lieutenant governor and attorney general also were elected in 1966. Governor Chafee lost his bid for re-election in 1968 to a former state judge, Democrat Frank Licht (who promised as a major issue that the state would not have an income tax). Mr. Chafee has since been appointed Secretary of the Navy in President Nixon's cabinet.

Chafee has served as Chairman of the Republican Governors' Association and a member of the Republican Coordinating Committee. He has also served on the steering committee of the Education Commission of the States, having served as its chairman in 1965–66. He is a member of the Visiting Committee to the Harvard University Graduate School of Public Administration, recently renamed the John F. Kennedy School of Government. In addition, he has been a visiting Chubb Fellow at Yale and has been awarded the honorary degree of doctor of laws by Brown University, Providence College, and the University of Rhode Island.

The Chafees have four sons and one daughter. Their home is in Warwick, Rhode Island.

In the course of our interview, Rhode Island's chief executive emphasized the qualities of the political and administrative leader, the extent to which the citizen's understanding of government often outdistances the politician's, and the attitude of young people toward public careers. Executive-legislative relations are another crucial area to which he devotes much thought. His use of task forces was the topic of an article by State House reporter John Hackett ("Chafee's Kitchen Cabinet," *The Rhode Islander*, May 17, 1968). Describing those who serve on task forces, the Governor is quoted as saying: "They are people who tell me exactly what they think. They are not reluctant to lay the hard facts right on the table." In a sense, this is the impression one received of the Governor himself.

From your experience in the past two terms what would you consider to be some of the most interesting challenges of the governorship?

I think that they break down into several categories. Certainly, one of the primary ones is to exert leadership in the state in a whole variety of fields. For instance, I think that the Governor has to provide leadership in the direction of excellence, try to get across to the people of the state that we've all just got to do our jobs—whether it's working on an assembly line, or teaching, or attending school, or whatever the job is—we've just got to strive toward excellence, because we live in a state that has no natural resources. We don't have any coal mines or gushing oil wells. The only thing we've really got to sell is what the people can produce.

Next, I think that one of the real challenges is to do everything possible to boost the economic life of the state. That means paying a good deal of attention to the requirements of industry, and getting ahead with the construction of roads. In our particular case here, it means spending a good deal of time and energy trying to preserve passenger and, more importantly, freight rail service. It means constantly being on the lookout for new legislation that might help attract and retain industry.

I'll give you an example of that. It came to my attention that we had no mutual funds based in Rhode Island. The reason was that we had a very, very high tax, not specifically directed toward mutual funds but which did apply to them and not to regular operating trusts. Well, with this high tax there weren't any mutual funds. So we sliced this tax down to about one fiftieth of what it was before, with the hope of having at least some mutual funds based here with all the fringe, peripheral jobs that come with them, plus the money they cast off.

Then also I think there comes the challenge of leading the legislature, which is always a difficult job, especially if the majority is of the opposite party. And, finally, there comes the challenge involved in leading the party, trying to build up your political party.

On the other side of the coin, Governor, are there equal frustrations in your responsibilities?

Yes. I think most of the frustrations come from the inability to control those that are working with you—in this instance, members of the legislature. I think that as far as I'm concerned the frustrations of this job would be reduced by easily 50 percent if the legislature were more willing to go ahead not only with some of our suggested programs but also some changes on operating budgets that would permit the state to operate more efficiently.

It's been said throughout the literature of public administration that a chief executive has to combine two qualities, those of the political leader and those of the public administrator. Are these parallel in your judgment, or just similar?

I don't think they are parallel, because I've known a lot of people who were good politicians—if that was the word—but whom I didn't think were very good administrators. It's amazing in public life how you do something that has a very dramatic appeal to the public, and will get you a lot of approval, but you do something that is good solid administration and a great step forward, and it will receive no public approval. It's quite different, I believe, from operating in an industry where the final test, after all, is at the end of the year: what's the balance sheet—what's the profit-and-loss statement? In this business, it's very hard to tell whether somebody's doing a good job or not. He might merely do something spectacular that the public can understand.

Let me just give you an illustration. I got loud approval by announcing, when I came into office, that I was having the two telephones taken out of my automobile—don't need 'em; if I need to make a telephone call, I'll stop at a telephone booth and pay a dime instead of paying thirty dollars a month for each phone. The public can easily understand that: "Gee, that's a really good save," and you get applause for it. Whereas if you undertake a real reorganization of the tenure system for state employees—which was completely out of whack—and you change it, then you come up with not only no applause but usually a good deal of criticism.

You have a question on your list dealing with public relations. I think that in political life public relations is of far more importance to a political leader than it is, say, to the chief executive officer of Textron, Collyer Insulated Wire, or some other company.

Your illustrations suggest the question, how can we enlarge citizen understanding of the governmental process and bring the citizen closer to what government is all about?

That's a tough question. I think one of the ways is for the public official constantly to use the medium that really gets across to the people more than any, and of course that's television. If you explain the problems and the way you're attempting to solve them, the people do get involved. I have found in my political life that citizens are way ahead of the politicians. The politicians always ascribe baser motives to the public than the public really has. A perfect example was all this talk about white backlash: it just wasn't there; the people aren't made that way. I think politicians also ascribe to the people a lower sense of understanding than exists. In our state I could give you many examples of that, usually in connection with the activities of the Democrats in the legislature when they will do something that is—well, here, I'll give you an example. We had a constitutional convention here which went on and on and on. They thought they'd put through measures like a complete ban on wiretapping, and allowing the legislature to license any lotteries that it chose. They thought they could just slip these things right by the people. No one seemed to protest particularly when they were brought up and so, you know, quietly they could be got by the people.

Did the proposed constitution also cover pay for the legislators?

Yes. Members of the legislature could set their own pay. That is, they could set rates for the next session, but there was no limitation whatsoever on how high they could go. But when this was all explained to the people, the proposed constitution was defeated—4 to 1—in a referendum.

. . . a healthy loss!

It's a whale of a defeat, and shows that the people can understand these things far better than the politicians ever think they can.

I find that a good many college students are disenchanted with public service. Have you, in the past several years, tried through the internship program, perhaps, to bring young college graduates into government?

Yes, we have—but I'm not sure I agree with your thesis.

I hope I'm wrong.

In my talks with some of the people—for instance, at the Harvard Law School—they've told me that no longer do the bright young men want to go down to Wall Street and make money. It's the most extraordinary thing. Not just the bright ones but all of them want to go off to some public service activity—working in the federal government or state governments, the Peace Corps or Vista. The most prestigious event when I was in law school was what they call the Ames Competition. The whole class was divided up into law clubs and everybody participated. Each club had about six members from each class and was presented cases to argue. It's an elimination contest, and to reach the finals was a very, very significant thing. Today, I am told, no one enters the Ames Competition; they're all off in Roxbury defending some indigent person in one of the lower courts, as they're permitted to do these days.

This is encouraging. Will it last?

I think it will. I'm told that down there in Wall Street they've jumped starting salaries to $15,000 in order to attract these boys. They just can't get them at $8500 or lower. Heck, when I started I went at $2400, and that wasn't so long ago.

As a Governor, you are no doubt concerned with interrelations between Rhode Island and the cities, and between Rhode Island and Washington. From your exposure to these state-city and state-federal problems, can you suggest any ways to make the states more—let's say creative—in these partnerships. I think Governor Rockefeller calls it "creative federalism."

One of the difficulties the states have been laboring under is, of course, basically a financial one, in that the federal government has appropriated to itself more and more areas that formerly were state concerns. As Professor Pat Moynihan has said: "The federal government is very efficient at collecting revenues and very poor at dispersing services." And they have a very efficient and effective fund-raising instrument—the personal income tax—that brings money in at a rate that astounds everyone, although they have a capacity to spend more than they take in.

I think the secret to making federalism better has to be a realization, by the federal government, that the federal government is poor at dispensing services, and that it must grant to the states a much greater freedom of action in the spending of these funds within the broad areas set forth by the federal government, than presently exists.

Let me give you an example. The federal government has decided it's going to help elementary and secondary education. This was decided, say three years ago, and since then, really fantastic sums have been poured into this small state of ours. It amounts to several million dollars a year. And yet I think even the most fervent advocate of federal aid to education, on these levels, agrees that the program has been a failure. As always, the federal government has tried to keep very close strings on this. It doesn't say to us: "Look, Rhode Island, you take this money and use it in the educational area where you think you need it most!" No, no. It says the money can only be used for *new* programs. And so if the state is relatively advanced and already has remedial reading programs and compulsory kindergarten and so forth, it can't use the money for that—it's got to go on to something else. Basically this attitude stems from a belief, inherited from the New Deal days, I believe, by the federal government that the states are ignorant, inefficient, and quite frequently corrupt and therefore can't be trusted.

We're on the front lines trying to do the job. If the federal government would forget the fact that Mississippi might misbehave (and therefore everything must be controlled), and realized that some states have done really magnificent jobs—every single one of them is anxious to improve its educational system—and give them a little more latitude, the whole program would be better off.

You spoke of the problem of balancing income and expenditures. Does federal aid make budget balancing in the states an impossible job?

No, I don't think so. Most of the states—ours included—must present a balanced budget. But it does mean that some fudging occurs when the state decides on a broad program. In other words, suppose you decide on bond issues for the repair and maintenance of the state's institutional buildings or its roads. Well, it is, of course, improper to bond repairs—that's something you should meet from current revenues. But it is going on to some extent, although not enough to make it that much easier to balance a budget.

The real problem all governments are running into, at the city and at the state and national levels, is this constantly increased demand for services. For example, people say they want better education. Sure they want better education. But then you find pressure groups demanding that we do more for children who are emotionally disturbed—they deserve special education. And so we've got a program here to send emotionally disturbed children off to schools at state expense—in some cases costing us $14,000 a year for one child. And then for the mentally retarded, there must be regional day-care centers. No longer is it the family's responsibility to educate these youngsters, and I can understand the difficulties involved. So now the state has new responsibilities—hard of hearing, poor eyesight, look after their teeth, care for the elderly. More and more is demanded, and more and more the people have got to expect to pay. Although I think they realize it, the situation makes it extremely difficult for anybody in an administrative position.

How does a chief executive do two things: first, keep control—tight or loose—on the way his programs are being implemented, and second, innovate and develop new programs?

Well, let's answer the questions one at a time. How does he keep control on the programs he's developed? Everybody, I suppose, has different ways of operating. My system is to find the very, very best directors I can—that is, my immediate subordinate chiefs who run the departments—and then I let them run it. I have confidence in them and I don't look over their shoulders. They also choose their subordinates. I hold them responsible, and I can see what the results are.

A couple of examples. One of the big things we want to do is get our road-building program done here. Well, it's pretty easy to tell whether your road-building program's coming along . . .

You can see it.

You can see it. And, by golly, if it's slow and if problems come up and they can't be resolved, they come to your attention pretty quickly. Then you know things aren't going right and you get on the back of the man in charge. Now we've got a man who in that particular area—the highest praise I can give somebody is to say he's a self-starter, and in our Public Works department we have a self-starter. In other words, he and I go over the general program and then he takes the ball and runs with it.

Another program we have developed here where I can follow progress, and where if things aren't getting done I can push those involved, is what we call our Green Acres program. I came to office very disturbed with the effects of this mushrooming population, and our limited amount of land space. By golly, we've got to set some of it aside or there won't be any play spaces for children in the future, or for adults. So we went into a Green Acres program, to secure open spaces. Part of it was through financial aid to the local communities to encourage them to do the job themselves, and part of it the state would do itself. This has been very successful and you can follow it. If I am curious to know how things are coming or if I don't see the results the way I want to, I call in the director.

But I don't have cabinet meetings as such. I don't get all department heads in here, because it seems to me that the problems involved in the Department of Labor just have nothing to do with the problems involved in the Department of Social Welfare, or the Department of Business Regulation. So why have them all spend their time in here? Perhaps I *should* have them in more often to just encourage more of a team spirit. We seem to have been all right on that, but I think I should have them in more frequently. In 5½ years, I don't think I've had them all together three times.

I've been discouraged in Washington with the obsession of many administrators with meetings. It's a disease that I call "meetingitis" and I'm glad to hear your views. In regard to the second aspect of the question: innovation. Rhode Island is considered a creative state. You spoke, in the beginning, of the need for excellence among your citizenry. Do you feel that in your two terms in office you have innovated in new directions?

If you mean, have we inaugurated new programs, the answer is yes. Where do we get the ideas from for the programs? Well, we can get them from a variety of places, but one difficulty is that there aren't many brand new ideas. Some of them you conceive yourself. Some of them you read about. Let me give you a little example, now.

I read somewhere in the paper that the federal government had considerable success with what, in their prisons, they call a work-release program. Prisoners who have served a certain amount of time and are going to be released, in say, two or three years, are permitted to go out and work during the day and report back to the prison at night. This way they develop good work habits and get used to the pattern that they'll have to fit into when they get out. Otherwise they stay in that cold prison, and when they are released they'll be given a new suit and ten dollars and sent on their way, which is down to the nearest bar where they meet their old friends and get in trouble again. So we adopted here a work-release program. And that idea I just got from the newspapers, seeing a clipping.

Now we do have various associations—Council of State Governments, National Governors Conference, the National Association of Republican Governors—where we pick up ideas. Sometimes also we get new ideas from task forces that I appoint, and I have found them very, very helpful.

For example: I formed a task force to look into the field of mental retardation—to see how we could do a better job here. Sure, we've got a great big institution with over a thousand mentally retarded children—but is that really the best way to handle that problem? Well, this task force came back and said "no." The better way is to set up regional day-care centers so that a youngster can be off his family's hands for every school day—180 days a year—yet stay in his family environment. That's better for everybody. It's better for the family, it's better for the youngster. When mentally retarded youngsters go into an institution, they all sink down to a lowest level, whereas if they are home—if they're with their normal brothers and sisters—then they learn how to ride a bicycle and tie their shoes and are brought up to their maximum—plus it's a heck of a lot cheaper to run a day-care center than it is to have a child being cared for as a ward of the state for 365 days a year.

Now, that's an idea we got from a task force. It's not completely original, but then I try to supplement ideas like this by getting bright people on the staff—and it's hard to get bright people on the staff. One method I have used extensively is to entice people for only a short time. "Look," I say, "I'm not asking you to spend your life working for the Department of Business Regulation. Will you come and work for me for two years and then you're free. You're not going to make a career of this. You're a lawyer or a banker but give me two years. And it's a great experience for you. You'll be making a contribution." Again, try to get them young. Our pay's as good and sometimes better than where they are in their private arrangements.

Then I also try to keep contact with a sort of a kitchen cabinet or brain trust. People who have nothing to do with government, just friends whom I respect. If I were going to make a military decision or a social welfare decision, I would rely on their judgment. I try and meet with these people to get their ideas, because they are always on the ball and alert. We developed our whole Medicare program through one of these contacts.

Many of these outsiders on task forces are critics, I suppose, but you can reject their suggestions if you wish.

A task force is a more formal arrangement than what we call a kitchen cabinet. One of the problems, I might say, with commissions or task forces is that often they are set up by the legislature. It may organize one, say, to look into the need for a department of correction in this state, rather than a division. And once the legislature creates the task force, it will then designate, quite frequently, who some of the members must be. And you always end up choosing—you're restricted in your choices to—people who really have an axe to grind in favor of a particular solution.

. . . and push hard.

And push hard, so that when the commission goes to work it's practically preordained what the result is going to be. Whereas if I can set up a task force myself, I can choose people who aren't prejudiced in favor of a particular result before they get there. This is far superior.

As you know, the President and the Presidency have been intensively examined, especially in the past decade, and many students of the subject believe that the Chief Executive may become a prisoner of institutionalization. Could we relate the problem of running a state, such as yours, with some of the administrative principles that have served as guides? For example, the literature of public administration is full of theories of decision making, human relations, delegation, communication, staff and line. Which, if any, of these have perhaps rescued you from becoming imprisoned by, let's say, formal organizational arrangements?

Well, I'm not sure I can answer that. I presume that in the federal government, the President is in a sense trapped by the bureaucracy. I remember Franklin Roosevelt saying that in the 16 years—or 14 years, or whatever it was—he was President, he never got control of the Navy Department. It was just like pushing a pillow: you push here and out it comes on the other side. There's no question that the President has great latitude and personal power, but I think he's more handicapped than a governor in that Congress is a far more equal branch of government than state legislatures are—at least here. And I think the answer is that whereas the city legislative department has restricted itself primarily to vetoing power, at the state level ultrastrong legislatures inevitably tend to get over into the administrative end of things, and at the federal level the tendency is even more pronounced. The result is to create a constrictive atmosphere in which the chief executive finds it hard to move.

There has been, in a sense, a reversal of roles: the executive initiating legislation and the legislature acting as a negative force—to some extent. Would you agree?

Yes, I think so. I don't want this to sound like an anti-legislature polemic, but there is a great difficulty here. Legislatures are caught up in this wave: "We've got to strengthen the legislature," and "We've got to have more staff," and "We've got to be full-time." It seems to me that they constantly press themselves, try to insert themselves into the administration of statutes rather than merely enacting them.

I've talked in California, where probably they've strengthened the legislature more than in any other state, and they say that interference doesn't happen. However, in Rhode Island, just the other day, they passed an act providing that a member of the Traffic Commission will be a legislator. Now he's still in the minority on the Commission—in other words, the Governor can retain control. But this is an example of the legislature constantly moving into the executive. It would be better, I think, to seek a clear-cut chain of command, or delegation or responsibility, so that you know who isn't doing the job or doing it right.

Many states are handicapped by these long-term appointive boards that are between the Governor and the administration of, say, the Department of Mental Hygiene or the Division of Corrections or the Division of Highways. If a road isn't built, the responsibility lies vaguely in the State Highway Commission of five members, each serving a five-year term; so a governor has to be in office three years before he gets control of this apparatus. Well, we don't have that problem—fortunately—in Rhode Island. Here the Governor appoints his department heads—the Chief of the Public Works Department, for example, who serves at the Governor's pleasure. If he doesn't serve right and the roads aren't built, the public can blame the Governor—and throw him out—which I think is the way it ought to be. I'm not sure that answers the question.

I think you've caught the guts of the issue. In my own classes concerned with public administration and state government, I advocate a longer term than the two years under which you serve.

I think you're right. With the short term, traditionally they say: "Well, you're hardly in before you have to start campaigning again." That's true, and the longer term would avoid that. Another point is that if you're in for a longer term, you can advocate more immediately unpopular but good programs which, if given a chance, will work themselves out in a four-year term. For instance, Governor Ribicoff, when he was Governor of Connecticut, inaugurated at the start of his four-year term a very, very severe highway safety program in which you lose your license if you speed. He was terribly unpopular in the first year and a half of that program and probably if he had run for re-election at the end of the two years he would have lost. At the end of three years, as the death rates declined, as the highways got safer, the thing was fairly in force, and people could see the validity of it—he not only came out even but came out with a great plus. The people said: "Wonderful, what he's done." That's an example of how with a longer term you can take on programs that can prove themselves in a longer time than two years.

It's been said that the test of an executive in government is the ability to manage plus the talent to build political support for all his programs. How much time do you have for problems such as race relations, crime, conservation, labor relations—and so many more? Is it not sometimes even impossible to allocate priorities?

I've often said that I spend 50 percent of my time on matters that seem to be of 5 percent importance.

It's a great phrase.

Before you were here, I must have spent 15 minutes trying to get the salary worked out for a young lawyer, whom one of the general officers wanted to promote. The matter is important, I suppose, in that if we give him too much of a raise then we've got all the other lawyers to consider. If you could just say "bing" and that's it, and forget it, you'd be better off. But you have to talk to the person involved, and to his boss to console him, and in the end you spend an inordinate amount of time on it.

I suppose that when you think you're spending time on things that are of relatively little importance, you wouldn't actually be doing so if, in the long run, you didn't think they *were* important. For instance, just this morning we had a weekly event which occurs here. We offer weekly proclamations for particular groups, so that we can declare National Realtors Week, State Women in Insurance Week, Disabled Veterans of America Week—and so it goes. We've got it well organized so that it only takes maybe five minutes a group, so with perhaps eight groups, we spend forty minutes on them in all.

And you personally do what?

I give them kind of a publicity picture and it goes out to the people throughout the state.

One of your ceremonial functions as Chief of State.

To some extent that's ceremonial. Well, these are some of the things that you just have to spend your time on. In all honesty they don't really advance the state, but they're part of the job.

True. I want to conclude with a point which no doubt you understand. Politics was once considered as entirely separate from administration in order to make the bureaucracy and civil service as neutral as possible. But today politics and administration are often invisibly merged. The phrase which describes this is the political administrator. From your vantage point as a prominent political executive in today's politics—in the Republican party—do you find at your meetings with other governors that beyond practical politics, you discuss administration?

Yes, we do. There's no question about it. Even now, that's really 80 percent of what you do at a national governors' conference. In other words, you discuss regional cooperation—that's one thing you work at. You discuss this planned program budgeting system, for long-range planning. You discuss the development of water—clean-water programs—there's no question but what you discuss government and administration. When you get together with the Republican governors—which is, of course, a more partisan group—the time is devoted much more to political things, although I'd say 50 percent of it is also devoted to administration.

When you talk administration, I think there's no question but what, in running the state, we could do a better administrative job. I suppose anybody could say this; you can always do better.

I suppose it's often hard to know "How am I doing?" because the criteria for judging the effectiveness or efficiency of a program are often fuzzy—despite academic and practical administrative experiences. There must be times when you just have to "feel" that things could be better. Perhaps this is a permanent dilemma.

I suppose so. And if you got so smug that you thought everything was going all right, there'd be something wrong.

Yes.

But I do think this. I mentioned earlier that I thought politicians were lagging behind the people in failing to ascribe to the people the intelligence and goodwill that exists in people, in the citizens. I think that one thing politicians have to learn is that people respect somebody who says "No." You don't have to give them all bread and circuses—because in the first place they know they have to pay for it. They can understand a good, firm "No," although how you say it also counts. They don't want in office somebody who's just going to be a yes-man and agree to all new things. They respect and like somebody who stands up and takes a position. I'll never forget when Bob Taft was running, you'd hear again and again the statement by people: "Well, you don't always agree with him but, by golly, you know where he stands."

And respect him.

And respect him for it. The people respect politicians who will take a position. They don't want some Pollyanna in there who gives them nothing but yesses all the time.

I sense, Governor, that you are deeply concerned with human values and troubled by the aggravation of many human problems. Do you believe that the present political and administrative process can solve twentieth-century issues?

I really am concerned with the role of the legislature. I think that's what bothers me. Maybe it's because I've spent all my terms as governor with a legislature of the opposite party. But somehow I just don't think we've got worked out yet the best system for having the legislature as effective as it might be or as cooperative as it might be. And I think the answer to that is probably a trite one: that you've just got to get in your legislatures people who have a big enough view so that they can always rise above strictly political considerations. The difficulty, as I see it, in the legislatures that I've viewed, is that too often a few strong voices raising Cain can bring the whole thing to a halt. Most legislatures are a mass of people who are not bad but not actively good either—they're just sort of ciphers. So you end up with a great mass of ciphers, plus a few strident voices raising the dickens who can grind the thing to a halt and kill much good legislation. You say to a legislator: "Why don't you pass such and such a bill?" And he says: "Well, so-and-so's against it"—and he'll name a particular individual. He may not be a person of any great consequence, but legislators seem to trim their sails to the lowest common denominator. I find that extremely discouraging. So I guess the answer is Winston Churchill's remark that democracy's the worst form of government, except for all the others.

STUDY QUESTIONS

1. What criteria would you use in measuring the administrative success of a chief executive? In what areas do you consider the Governor most effective? Least effective?
2. Did the Governor exhaust the possibilities in building better relationships with the legislature? Are his methods of checking old and introducing new programs sufficient?
3. Compare Governor Chafee's views on federalism with those of others, such as Governor Rockefeller.
4. What are the pros and cons of a longer term for state governor?

III

PERSONNEL AND
LABOR RELATIONS

4

PORT AUTHORITY

BACKGROUND

The Port of New York Authority was established by an interstate compact signed in 1921 between New York and New Jersey, and approved by Congress. Modeled in part on the Port of London Authority, it was the first self-supporting regional agency in the United States—a public corporation established outside the traditional political framework. Wallace Sayre and Herbert Kaufman, in *Governing New York City*, wrote:

> Until 1921 when one spoke of a state or local public agency in New York State . . . the reference was either to a line or overhead agency. Then a new government form appeared on the scene—new, that is, to New York State, although the government corporation device, to which public authorities are related, had been used earlier by the federal government and by some foreign governments.

The Authority's main responsibilities are to plan, develop, and operate "terminal, transportation, and other facilities" within the port district, a territory with a radius of about twenty-five miles from the Statue of Liberty, and to protect and promote port commerce. Operations are financed by revenues taken in by the Authority, which may not pledge the credit of either state. One provision of the compact stipulates that the Authority "shall have such additional powers and duties as may hereafter be delegated to or imposed upon it . . . by the actions of the legislature of either state concurred in by the legislature of the other." By additional enactments, as the needs arose, the agency's progress has been substantial, and over the past fifty years it has acquired, constructed, and operated many facilities. Today the Port Authority administers six interstate bridges and tunnels, four airports and two heliports, six marine terminal areas, two union truck terminals, a rail freight terminal, two union bus terminals, and a trans-Hudson railroad (PATH), and is constructing a World Trade Center. It also maintains some nine trade development offices to protect and promote port commerce, and its representatives often appear before government regulatory agencies.

Policies are established by a governing board of twelve unpaid members—usually leaders in business, finance, engineering, law, and civic affairs—six of whom are appointed by each governor, with the consent of the respective state senate, for overlapping six-year terms. The members elect a chairman and direct the affairs of a 7500-man organization through a chief executive officer, the executive director. In order to finance—on a self-supporting basis without cost to the general taxpayer—the land, sea and air terminals, and transportation facilities, it has been a consistent goal of the bi-state agency to create sufficient revenue potential and utilize the most modern and efficient business methods.

FORMER PERSONNEL PROGRAM

The Port Authority has its own merit system and, since it does not depend on city or state appropriations, has considerable leeway in experimenting with new and better personnel programs. The personnel director reports to the director of administration, who is in charge of three departments: organization and procedures; personnel; and purchase and administrative services.

The personnel department was originally organized on a traditional, functional basis with a director and a deputy director in charge of six separate divisions, each of which was headed by a manager: classification and salary; selection and placement; training and development; employee relations; communications; and manpower research and planning. In 1964 there were 7483 persons on the Port Authority's payroll, which amounted to $53 million a year.

In its personnel administration, the Port had earned a reputation for having a progressive program. As the director of administration told the present investigator, the Port Authority has had a history of innovation in the personnel field, and is generally regarded as being in advance of most public personnel systems. This was especially true in the areas of selection and of training and placement, and employee performance was recognized by an active promotion and transfer system.

Nevertheless, by the mid-1960s it had become apparent that, with the rapid expansion that was taking place in the programs of the Port Authority—such as the acquisition and operation of an interstate transit system, the building of the world's tallest buildings at the World Trade Center, the tremendous expansion of airports and marine terminals, and so on—it would be desirable to take a close look at the activities and the organization structure of the personnel department to see whether any significant changes ought to be made. There was a recognition by the then personnel director that his department was organized substantially as it had been in 1947, at the beginning of his tenure. He recognized that, with increasing size of the Port Authority staff, it might be necessary to find ways to decentralize some of the decision making, while retaining, insofar as possible, the essential tenet of having an Authority-wide merit system. He also recognized that there was a relatively high ratio of personnel workers in his department to the total number of Port Authority employees. Thus, with 157 employees in his department, the ratio was 1 for every 46 Port employees, higher than the norms in many jurisdictions or companies.

REORGANIZATION STUDY

In 1964 it was decided to conduct a study to see whether the personnel organization of the Port Authority was best organized to respond to new problems arising during the next decade or so, insofar as such problems could be anticipated. It was hoped that the study would enable the agency to decide how best to take advantage of new trends in personnel administration, including such matters as computer technology, employee relations, recruitment and training of minority and disadvantaged groups, and the like. It was also hoped to increase the responsiveness of the personnel organization, to reduce buck-passing, to develop better-rounded personnel, and to facilitate the implementation of a recently adopted new career plan. Otherwise, if the department were to continue unchanged, it might not be able to meet the complex problems of the future. In sum, the proposed study was to take a long, hard look ahead in order to work towards a structure capable of effective management for tomorrow. Perhaps the term "retooling" would best describe this total effort.

The personnel director selected one of his division managers as consultant to conduct the study and prepare the report, in collaboration with other key department personnel and with the assistance of a senior management analyst from the organization and procedures department. Both the personnel director and the consultant agreed on the need for a broad-gauged evaluation of the whole personnel system, including its goals and its operating methods. Topics on the consultant's agenda were: Does the personnel department fully meet the needs of its clients throughout the Port Authority? Is the present structure viable with minor improvements, or is a complete overhaul necessary? How adequate are current policies and programs? There were also questions relating to communication, field-headquarters relations, and coordination.

As the study got under way, several problems at once appeared. The first was the advisability of having an inside expert, from the personnel department itself, conduct the investigation and prepare the report. In response to a question from the present researcher, the director of administration explained this choice by saying that in his judgment it would not have been feasible to recruit an outside consultant because it would have meant a delay in breaking him in on the Port's personnel program and its history. Moreover, an outsider might not have appreciated the many subtle, interpersonal relations existing throughout the Port agency and best known to a long-time employee.

A second problem arose when, shortly after the study began, the personnel director left the Port Authority for a position in private industry. The director of the organization and procedures department was then appointed as acting personnel director, and both he and the director of administration wished to push forward rather than delay the progress of the study until a new personnel director could be found. When the present investigator asked the director of administration about this, the director replied that it might be some time before a new personnel director could be found, and that the results of the study would help the new director decide how and to what extent he wanted to change the organization. A major difficulty was the fact that no official of the personnel department was enough of a generalist to fit the specifications of the directorship, which reinforced the judgment that a reappraisal of the organization was in order, if not overdue. Moreover, from a technical standpoint and in overall administrative skills, the acting personnel director was competent to supervise the study.

Yet a third major problem was the fact that several division managers in the personnel department naturally wished to be considered for the top job. Since the study was in the hands of an inside personnel official, emotional conflicts and antagonisms were directed towards him by several aspirants in the belief that he also was interested in the appointment. This put him in an awkward position, because it made his study a topic of constant speculation within the personnel department, especially in the matter of how his proposals might affect the future of present members, and their assignments. The situation was such that no matter what he might propose, it would be opposed by all of the divisional managers except those who stood to gain by the change. It is axiomatic that few officials care to see their positions abolished or their duties reduced, especially after years of service in and contributions to an organization.

Finally, there was a problem inherent in the personnel department itself. As seasoned specialists, most of the division managers in the personnel department tended to work somewhat independently, each one able in his job and proud of his craft, but lacking the motivation to pull together with his peers in a common effort. Thus, despite the efforts of the former personnel director to secure cohesion among these specialized managers, he was relatively unsuccessful. Rarely did the managers reflect the views of the generalist, nor did they understand in a sufficiently broad way the needs of their Port clients or the Port-wide goals of the agency. As technicians in personnel administration, the managers had initially been recruited or trained for their specialist skills and they were of first-rate reputation. But because the broader view was lacking, the personnel department reflected a form of professional inbreeding based on task specialization, with the department director providing the general, overall viewpoint. In order to coordinate the efforts of the various division managers, exorbitant demands were made upon the time and energy of the personnel director. This condition could not in all cases be ascribed to unwillingness on the part of the division managers to work cooperatively; in fact, on many occasions, if and when the personnel director was personally providing leadership, they would work together superbly well.

STUDY METHODS AND FINDINGS

The reorganization report was based on information assembled from some 150 firsthand interviews conducted by the consultant and the management analyst with the principal officials at four strategic levels within the Port Authority: top management, department directors, personnel department management, and employee organizations.

Officials at the top level indicated that the personnel department had not kept them fully informed on programs and problems, that effective performance among the various personnel operations was uneven, and that services to clients (the Authority's operating divisions) was often inadequate. At the departmental level, it was felt that personnel policies were not uniformly applied, that members of the personnel department were often inaccessible for consultation, that the former personnel director sometimes made unilateral decisions without sufficient clearances among the operating departments affected, and that effective coordination among the personnel divisions was lacking. There was also the complaint that the classification process was slow and cumbersome. And although some division managers were considered to be doing a good job, overall effectiveness was less than adequate.

Another method used by the consultant was to ask Port Authority officials to rate specific personnel services as fair, favorable, good, or excellent. These designations were recognized as at least partly subjective and therefore having a somewhat different intensity of meaning in each case. Nevertheless, the attempt was made to classify the resulting evaluations and to provide an overall rating for each operation and service of the personnel department.

These evaluations were not made available to the present investigator, nor did he interview all who made them. He did, however, see the final report containing the consultant's composite evaluation of the personnel department and its divisions, and he did interview several division managers, whose comments are detailed later in this case report.

At the level of the personnel department itself, criticisms expressed to the consultant included the following: Coordination between the divisions should be more effective; responsiveness to the needs of the operating divisions of the Port Authority should be greater; participation in policy formation and application should be closer; procedures should be more flexible; top management's attitude toward the efforts of the divisions should be more appreciative; and the personnel director's management style should be improved.

Finally, criticisms were expressed by representatives of the Port Authority's organized employees and other groups, including the Employees Association, Patrolmen's Benevolent Association, Brotherhood of Railway Trainmen, Foremen's Advisory Group, and General Managers' Committee. The Port Authority's personnel policies were said to be often ambiguous, nonuniformly interpreted, and variously applied. It was also said that coordination between headquarters and field in personnel matters was inadequate.

The consultant found that the problems identified by officials at all four levels could be classified into four main categories: organization, communications, control, and a grab-bag of assorted complaints. It was also apparent that any weakness or failure in one area easily affected other areas.

As the report eventually stated, under the heading of *organization*, the faults singled out were divisional rivalries, poor coordination, fragmented functions, ambiguous responsibility, delayed action, and excessively centralized decision making in the hands of the personnel director. The *communications* category was characterized by a hit-or-miss formulation of personnel policies, insulation of divisional managers, and the fact that the personnel director was often too busy for consultation. Comments regarding the *control* factor concerned the shortage of long-range plans, inadequate performance standards, insufficient attention to a formal feedback mechanism, proliferation of ad hoc plans, and too many decisions made on a crisis basis. In the *miscellaneous* group, two examples were the need for a more effective management development program and a fair system of performance evaluation at all levels of employment.

In sum, several major and many scattered minor problems had accumulated within the personnel department, and a fault in one part of the organization often spread to others. This is not to imply that the personnel department was on the verge of collapse, but the study did reveal a consensus, both within the department and among its clients, as to the weak and faulty parts of the whole mechanism. As one former official expressed it,

> The most difficult problem was the lack of coordination between divisions. Since the managers had served for a great length of time and were unable to move upwards or laterally, they tended to become involved in over-specialization and refinement of techniques. To a great extent the personnel system had become closed and inbred. An attitude of this-is-my-division had spread to the detriment of close and effective coordination.

The conditions that the study revealed, therefore, were poor inter-divisional coordination, inadequate responsiveness between the technical personnel divisions and top management and between personnel head-quarters and field operations, excessive functional specialization and a need to develop or encourage more managerial generalists with broad-gauge views, policies scattered among too many authorizing documents, and each functional division becoming a self-contained unit working for its own special and limited objectives.

THE REPORT'S PROPOSALS

Few administrative processes compare with personnel programs in the continuous need to relate one feature of an operation to all others. It is almost axiomatic that high morale is related to effective placement pro-cedures—which, in turn, are the result of effective recruitment and sound classification arrangements. And in the Port Authority's personnel depart-ment these were sometimes being taken in opposite directions by division managers acting relatively independently of one another. According to the consultant, what the clients of the personnel department required above all was a meaningful coordination among the various personnel divisions. The director of administration also indicated to the investigator that even though client complaints were sometimes muted, they were eventually increasingly vocal as people tired of the lengthy process of going from one technical division of the personnel department to another for the solution of the problems or satisfaction of their needs.

As a remedy, the consultant considered an extensive decentralization of personnel operations, but rejected this on the ground that the department's policies were not sufficiently standardized. Decentralization would also have required more funds and personnel and might have created even more variation in policy interpretation. As an alternative, therefore, the consultant devised an integrated management system as the means of blending product, process, area, function, and client so as to secure greater responsiveness by the personnel department to the legitimate needs and demands of client departments and employees, increase technical leadership and expertise, emphasize planning and policy formation, assure reasonable labor costs, and secure effective control.

When the report appeared in 1965, it underscored the need to develop more realistic objectives and to establish subdivisions based on the type of personnel to be serviced. At one point it stressed what it called "mobilization" in order to provide an interacting and self-reviewing personnel organization involving participation, communication, decision making, and job enlargement. By these means it was hoped to encourage the quality of detached and continuing appraisal among all members at all levels of the personnel department. The overriding objective was to *coordinate all personnel operations and services into a more unified effort to meet client requirements.*

It was also emphasized that the personnel department should become much more closely tied into the decision-making processes taking place elsewhere in the Port Authority on matters affecting the agency's future activities, goals, and programs. The efforts of the separatists in the department should be redirected so as to meet head-on the challenges of the coming decade and beyond, keep the director of administration and his superiors informed as to important developments, and at the same time provide maximum opportunity for the development—in a broad sense—of the members of the personnel department themselves.

To dramatize the needed changes, the consultant urged the creation of a new department under a new name, and chose the title *personnel and employee relations* to reflect the widened scope of its responsibilities, to relate more closely to similar agencies in industry, and to carry more weight with unions and other employee organizations. The new department would consist of two main segments, one concerned with administration and the other with programs and standards, each in charge of a deputy director.

Specifically, the administration segment would include four divisions: professional and management, maintenance, operations, and administrative personnel, respectively, each one organized according to the class and type of employees to be serviced. Under this arrangement, each division manager would handle the whole range of personnel functions for the employees within his jurisdiction, from recruitment to retirement. According to the report, this plan would assure an integrated personnel function and encourage the close coordination of separate units with different goals. In time, the plan might also create needed generalists having a larger view of the personnel process, provide management with a tighter control over problem areas, and even reduce the need for special committees and task forces. It would establish real service groups capable of responding to management needs without preoccupation with long-range plans, technical improvements, or professional standards and controls except as these constituted subsidiary aspects of the primary mission.

The programs-and-standards segment of the proposed new personnel department would include the divisions of manpower planning and research, programs and benefits, audits and standards, and employee services. The main objective of this arrangement was to concentrate, at one point, all the technical services involved in developing the methods, policies, and standards applied by the administration segment of the department. Moreover, long-range plans, inspections, and controls could be integrated in a group of associated tasks. In short, this segment was to become a genuine control group for the department.

The report did, however, acknowledge the possible danger—ever present in many organizations—that staff personnel might become the department's "tyrants"; effective coordination with the administration part of the personnel program would obviously be needed. The overall plan did contain checks and balances to offset this potential hazard. Thus, manpower planning would prepare tests and seek management improvements; programs and benefits would consider social insurance and communications; audits and standards would concern itself with pay-plan maintenance and classification standards; and employee activities would have to do with public relations and recreation programs.

A final proposal contained in the report was to create a number of centers to handle decisions in personnel matters appropriate to the particular level of competence and responsibility in each case, the objective being to heighten participation among all the departments at the Port Authority and increase their understanding of the total personnel management process. These centers were called, in descending order, the personnel committee, the council, and the forum. Although the idea was not endorsed by top management, several details of the plan are of interest here.

For example, a high-level committee would advise the executive director in matters of top personnel policy. Its members would include the deputy executive director, director of administration, personnel director (to serve as coordinator), directors of finance and organization and procedures, one line director, and a staff director. This group would meet four times a year.

At the next level, as arbiter of operational issues concerning personnel, a council, meeting biweekly, would act on matters referred to it by the personnel director and would advise him on policies and procedures. In effect, this would be a procedural body concerned with daily problems. Its permanent chairman would be the deputy personnel director for administration, and its membership would include the two deputy directors in the personnel department plus its eight division heads, as well as elected delegates from the next lower level—the forum.

At the lowest level, the membership of the forum would consist of four middle managers appointed by the personnel director to advise him or the council. In addition, the assistant manager of each personnel division and two representatives from each line and staff department would serve as members.

REACTIONS TO THE REPORT

Key officials in the personnel department were kept informed of the progress of the study. At a preliminary presentation prepared for the director of administration and the acting personnel director, both considered it, according to the consultant, as imaginative and exciting in outlining a new approach to personnel administration at the Port Authority. There was some discussion as to who might fill the various spots in the proposed plan, but no decisions were reached.

Shortly thereafter, during a second presentation by the consultant, the division managers in the personnel department were informed of the tentative proposals contained in the report—and, as anticipated, reactions were mixed. They were still mixed when the final report appeared. As one official remarked to the present investigator, he took "a dim view of the entire report," finding it "pedantic and merely an effort to please the director of administration." Another manager claimed that for eighteen years there had never been a breakdown in the personnel department and he frankly saw little reason to reorganize, now or ever. He also opposed the importation of a new personnel director from outside the organization. Another official, then and later, was uncertain of the new plan and thought the same or similar objectives might have been attained by less drastic innovations.

These reactions occurred even though the report itself had sought to soften the blow by urging a cautious and deliberate approach to the proposed new plan. Thus, it was specifically stated:

> The change proposed is big with far-reaching implications and complexities . . . . This should not deter us. It should merely make us cautious and cause us to plan each step carefully, affording all who are involved an opportunity to ask questions and to discuss the change as it affects them.

Within the personnel department the groups lined up, as one official indicated, in three ways, for the most part: there were those who would swing either way, those who wanted to become the new personnel director, and those who didn't want certain others to succeed to that position. No insider had been nominated for the top assignment as personnel director, although during the tenure of the acting personnel director several had approached the director of administration to present their qualifications. In the course of the interviews conducted by the present investigator, some comments on the subject were cryptic, others were extended. One former official, for example, recorded his views in these words:

> The department was functioning at a generally professional level of competence and effectiveness. By and large, the professional quality of the staff was high and most were well motivated. While there were the usual number of intradepartmental conflicts and occasional struggles, the output was well above that which one typically finds either in government or private industry.

When asked about the strengths and weaknesses of specific segments of the department, he replied, "The output and decisions were professionally rendered and generally regarded with confidence by the departments served," even though the personnel department itself was "burdened with sometimes overly complex and time-consuming procedures, particularly in the areas of internal recruitment, salary grade classification, and decision making in the labor relations field."

In a conversation with another former official, the investigator learned that the former personnel director, although superior in his qualifications for the job, tended to keep a lot to himself and did not readily delegate; but he was able to attract and retain the services of those capable of doing a good technical job. The director was generally respected and handled labor relations mostly on his own. At the division level, most managerial positions were held by strong, experienced persons who had originally been recruited for their technical competence and had held their jobs for a long time.

On balance, said this former official, the Port Authority personnel program was "good and had accomplished a great deal." Its weak points were that each manager considered his own field as more important than the overall goals of the department, there was a strong overemphasis on functions, a lack of cooperation among division managers, and some resentment by old-timers towards some of the newcomers. In sum, "Each viewed his part of the elephant as the most important part."

There had also been some frustration with the former personnel director's leadership, and some felt they had not been sufficiently recognized for their services. Moreover, although a degree of coordination had been achieved by the director himself, the group generally tended to feel that it was obtained at intolerably high prices in terms of time and energy consumed.

Regarding the reorganization report, this former official, during the course of this interview, saw it as an attempt to move away from functional specialization to an occupational, client-oriented organization. "I agreed with the need for change, and thought the report in many ways was very sound." But this official criticized it as making "too clear a separation between planning and doing—giving all the good things to the former and the nitty-gritty to the latter." This might create a kind of two-class citizenship within the personnel department.

A real problem during the preparation of the report, and one that partly conditioned the response to it, was the fact that no one really knew where he might go if the new organization went into effect, and the effect of this uncertainty was to impair morale. Even if the report had never been written, the view was expressed that some changes would certainly have been made. The objectives of the report were not always clear, but the divisional managers tended to react less to the quality of its proposals than to "that man" who wrote it. But at a higher level, the director of administration regarded it as "a pioneer approach which would help solve the need for broad-gauged people and reduce the inbreeding of narrow specialists."

RESULTS

What happened to the report? What were its effects on the structure, work methods, and staff relations of the personnel department?

When the new personnel director was finally appointed—after an intensive search by a management consulting firm, which eventually narrowed the list to thirty-five eligibles—the director of administration and the acting personnel director (who had then served for eighteen months) handed him the report and said, "Do what you want with it."

When the present investigator queried the new personnel director about the report, the director said he agreed with many of its proposals but did not see the need for two deputy personnel directors. He preferred to train a man in each division to keep the director's office informed and to follow up on any assignments the director might make. The greatest task, he thought, was to bring all the separate pieces of the department together in a common effort. During the first few months of the new incumbent, relations at staff meetings were somewhat strained because of the report, but the director admitted the value to him, as a newcomer, of a ready-made analysis of organizational strengths and failures. He endorsed the concept of the personnel generalist and proposed to build future functions around improved services to the clients of the department.

The new personnel director adopted some of the report's recommendations and shelved others. In effect, there is now a one-stop client service, and both loud and muted complaints by client departments have been reduced. From the standpoint of organization there would be two main "line" divisions within the personnel department: one dealing with management personnel (including professionals) and one dealing with operating personnel (including clerical, maintenance, and police), along with three "staff" divisions dealing with departmental administration, classification and compensation standards, and personnel benefits and activities. For example, the management personnel division would handle all transactions involved in putting a man on the payroll, whether he be a junior executive, attorney, or engineer, and promoting, training, transferring, or dismissing him or classifying his job or counselling him for career development. Operations personnel handles similar transactions plus labor relations for clerks, maintenance and operations personnel, and police. The administrative division is concerned with testing, research, space, and budget and functions primarily as a business management office for the department. Classification is now limited to wage surveys and audit tasks. Benefits is responsible for insurance plans, health systems, and employee suggestions. According to the personnel director, the operating and management personnel divisions now maintain external relations with the department's clients and internal relations with the other supporting divisions on such subjects as training, classification, and testing. The clients in Port Authority departments such as aviation, finance, law, engineering, real estate, world trade, marine terminal, rail transportation, and tunnels and bridges appear to have reacted favorably to the changes that have been made.

No division manager was threatened with termination, said the new director, but resignations were not discouraged in certain cases where there was dissatisfaction with the reorganization. Efforts also were made to reassign some members of the department whose responsibilities had been altered. The former deputy director, for example, became manager of the personnel benefits division; the classification manager continued in his job with service to the divisions responsible for client relations but with reduced staff and functions; the communications manager was offered another assignment in administrative services; both the employee relations manager and the training manager served for a time as advisors in their specialties to the director, but the former eventually resigned. The consultant continued for a time as manager of manpower planning and research but later resigned to join a management consultant office at a senior level.

The changes finally brought about in the personnel department were substantial to the point of being considered a "shake-up." In line with a growing trend in personnel administration, the department changed from a functional to a generalist organizational structure. Former specialists are constantly being exposed to training sessions in order to develop broad-gauged viewpoints in the total personnel process. The report's innovative features concerning committees, councils, and forums, however, were discarded because neither the new personnel director nor other top executives in the Port Authority believed in personnel administration by committee.

When the present investigator asked how effective the new system had proved to be in practice, no hard evidence was presented, but those at the top management level and the personnel director himself agreed that the most significant test of the new plan's success was the fact that clients are no longer shunted from one personnel division to another, as in a health clinic for shots or treatments. Furthermore, it is apparent that broader-gauged personnel staff are being developed.

Nevertheless, some hard questions remain unanswered, or have been dealt with in only a peripheral way. Should the report have been prepared by an insider, himself eligible for the directorship of the personnel department, or for one of the two deputy director spots, rather than by an outside, unaffiliated consultant? In the best technical sense, the insider was undoubtedly the equal of any outside advisor, but this is not the point. It is rather a matter of some of the political and psychological overtones that colored the reactions to the author of the report at the expense of an appreciation of the merit of its proposals. If the report had been prepared by an outsider, would its adoption chances have been greater? It seems doubtful, assuming, of course, that its recommendations would have been similar.

Another interesting speculation is what might have happened had the consultant been appointed as the new personnel director and become responsible for putting the report's recommendations into effect. It would surely have been interesting to see how the report might have fared had it been adopted intact by the Port Authority's top management and left for implementation to the author himself.

Other questions are of enduring interest to all who are engaged in the personnel process. How, for example, can an organization avoid the troubles that concerned the Authority's top management personnel about its system—a tendency toward inbreeding, specialization, and inadequate coordination, among others? Perhaps the remedy is more frequent reorganizations, so that officials can look at themselves in the administrative mirror and see themselves as others see them.

Again, how can an organization apply the art of creating and encouraging the style of the generalist, especially when pressures toward specialization are insistent?

There remains some residual friction in the personnel department, especially among those whose administrative empires have collapsed or shrunk. Among those who resigned, however, all now occupy higher positions than formerly and all—it is encouraging to note—appear to have become generalists, as personnel directors or as management consultants.

STUDY QUESTIONS

1. What are the arguments for and against an outside consultant in situations similar to that described? What is your estimate of the consultant's recommendations?

2. Which in your opinion were the most serious complaints voiced among the four groups interviewed?
3. What stands out as innovative among the report's proposals?
4. How would you have handled your assignment as a new personnel director?

5
STRIKES BY
GOVERNMENT
WORKERS

Old-fashioned views concerning stolid bureaucrats are slowly being discarded as strikes and other forms of militant behavior continue to increase, and teachers, transit workers, sanitationmen, nurses, firemen, and policemen—among others on the public payrolls—exhibit far from timid conduct in order to attain their demands on wages, hours, and working conditions. As the *National Observer* reported on September 9, 1968:

> The signs point to even greater militancy. Unions of postal workers and firemen in recent weeks have deleted no-strike clauses from their constitutions at national conventions. And membership in the increasingly aggressive American Federation of State, County, and Municipal Employees (AFSCME) has more than tripled in the past 10 years, to 400,000.

It is increasingly evident that the condition described by the phrase, "You can't fight City Hall," is rapidly changing. The head of AFSCME, Jerome Wurf, has said that firemen and law-enforcement officers should not and cannot strike, but that unless other public employees are free to strike, many governments will not bargain seriously and in good faith. In a *New York Times* man-in-the-news close-up (September 3, 1968) titled "Public Employees' Voice," Mr. Wurf was quoted as saying: "It's not a sense of sadism that leads to a strike, it's a sense of futility."

Labor relations in large cities is almost continuous front-page news and intimately affects the lives of all citizens. In New York City, for example, strikes or other disputes can often be listed in alphabetical order, by agency, almost any month of the year. Many result in hazards to the welfare of residents and interruption of vital services, as in the case of the transit strike of 1966 and the sanitation strike of 1967. Both were full-scale emergencies and remain painful memories to many New Yorkers.

The rise of labor relations as a full-time municipal function is reflected in the agencies established in New York City to handle this problem. In 1966, the Mayor appointed Herbert Haber as city director of the Office of Labor Relations. This office represents the Mayor at the bargaining table with unions involving over 300,000 municipal workers. Under Haber's direction, city negotiators bargain with unions just as management does in private industry. In the interview that follows, Haber spells out the problems and programs as he sees them.

Closely connected to this agency is the Office of Collective Bargaining, established in January of 1968. Formerly, issues of union representation, grievances, and contract disputes were handled by the city labor department, a staff agency of the mayor. In 1965 Mayor Wagner set up a panel to "facilitate through continuing informal discussions the development of an agreement between representatives of municipal employee organizations and the City of New York on improved collective bargaining procedures." Mayor Lindsay, in a letter of January 24, 1966, requested the discussions to continue, and the panel submitted its report on March 31 of the same year. The result was a written agreement between the unions and the city to establish an impartial agency to serve as the neutral party in municipal labor relations. In 1967, the city council amended the charter to create the Office of Collective Bargaining and passed a law authorizing its powers and duties. Executive Order 52 of Mayor Lindsay implemented the law, and the Office of Collective Bargaining opened on January 2, 1968.

An OCB publication indicates some of the reasons which prompted the creation of such an office:

> Unlike most private industries, government performs many functions so vital to the health, safety, and welfare of its people that a work stoppage could be disastrous. After all, labor relations means human relations, and when human beings are involved, differences of opinion arise. As an aid to settling these inevitable differences, and in an effort to bring harmony to the relationship between the City of New York and its employees, the Office of Collective Bargaining was created.

In an August 22, 1968, editorial the *New York Times* considered OCB "the best-conceived agency for assuring equity to public employees anywhere in the country." It has also been reported that George Meany, AFL-CIO chief, considers the OCB arrangement as a "model for all public agencies."

OCB is an impartial tripartite agency with two labor members nominated by a city labor committee (membership to which is open to all certified public employee organizations), two city representatives elected by the city, and three impartial public members elected by a unanimous vote of the city and labor representatives. The present investigator spoke at length with its chairman, Arvid Anderson, who indicated that although this arrangement cannot guarantee success, it does recognize the necessity of involving the public employer, the public unions, and so-called neutrals to deal with the continuing problems of labor relations in the public sector.

OCB, in short, assists the city and the unions in resolving their differences and in securing contract agreements, often designates mediators, or arbitrators, and provides grievance procedures. All mayoral agencies and the unions representing their employees may choose to become subject to OCB jurisdiction and participate in its procedures; non-mayoral agencies, such as the Board of Education, the Housing Authority, and others also may choose to do so, subject to the mayor's approval. It cannot, however, compel unions to utilize the fact-finding or mediation process. In September 1968 both the police and firemen unions decided that mediation advice and assistance might prove helpful. Upon request, OCB recommended mediators acceptable to both the city and labor. This, it is reported, represents a gain from a year earlier when the firemen, for example, were reluctant to use OCB services. According to press and official reports the Sanitationmen's Union has opposed OCB, since it might undercut union powers. In 1968 it, too, agreed to mediation.

When questioned, Anderson affirmed that this structure must surely help to maintain labor stability, and perhaps peace, between the city and the unions. If bargaining machinery is effective, then the strike may not be necessary. It is often a question of the balance of power, since most decisions affecting conditions of work are largely political in relation to other unions. He believed that the city and most public employees have increasingly accepted fact-finding on disputes, and that in the long run the majority of these employees will have greater power through arbitration channels than by going outside of established procedures.

The New York work force of some 300,000 employees includes approximately 800 job titles combined into 200 bargaining relationships and represented by about 90 unions and employee organizations. Anderson underlined the fact that the result is often a fragmented bargaining structure, which encourages one-upmanship at negotiating sessions and quite often discourages settlement. As of September 1, 1968, twenty cases had come to OCB for mediation, twenty-two for impasse panel procedures—a form of fact-finding—and twenty-seven for arbitration. OCB, he said, encourages the parties to reach agreement by themselves and suggests the means. If, for example, contract negotiations collapse, mediation might be appropriate. If this fails, or even if mediation has not been tried, fact-finding might work. The normal procedure is to settle contract disputes by these methods, whereas arbitration is used to settle grievances. The nine-day sanitationmen's strike over a contract dispute, however, was settled by the agreement of both sides to accept an arbitration decision as binding. In short, as Anderson commented, the OCB is concerned not only with the methods of settling disputes, but also with the nature of disputes. He warned, however, that the goal of labor peace, regardless of effective machinery or skilled personnel, cannot be achieved without the support and positive cooperation of the parties involved.

In regard to strikes, he believed that many unions are going to resort to the strike as a weapon, and an absolute guarantee against its use is an illusion, since the threat and muscle are there. Stability can be established only through reason and persuasion, because the militant approach leads to disorder. Strike penalties, he added, usually make heroes of union leaders, who often proudly march into a jail cell, and the union pays the fine.

In September 1967 the Public Employees' Fair Employment Act (known as the Taylor Law) instituted a large-scale program for improved city and state labor relations. The most controversial provision states that strikes are unnecessary, in view of detailed procedures to settle grievances, and therefore prohibited. Unions *have* gone on strike, however, and OCB can merely use one sanction: decertify the striking union. The courts have on two occasions fined the teachers and sanitation unions and jailed their leaders. In both disputes, OCB was not requested to advise or assist.

In an address to the labor law section of the American Bar Association in August of 1968, Anderson summed up his labor-management philosophy:

> A definition of the public management community in collective bargaining is not as simple as it has been in the private sector. However, as the Secretary of Labor has expressed so well, if collective bargaining is to work in public employment it requires a management team with authority to say "I will" or "I won't" rather than "I can't" at the bargaining table. Obviously, the Secretary referred to the ability to recommend decisions to the ultimate authority, the legislative or the executive, over those matters which are the proper subjects for bargaining. The necessity of conferring such authority upon a management bargaining team is vital if the chief executive or the legislature wants to avoid the necessity of making countless decisions about employment conditions themselves.

In an interview, Daniel Nelson, Director of Research and Negotiations for District Council 37, AFL-CIO, SCME, said the practice used is to "tell the city labor relations representative what we've got to have." The council negotiates approximately 150 contracts each year. Nelson indicated that although Haber has paper power, the direction from the mayor should be stronger and closer. SCME dealings with the city have generally been favorable. I asked about OCB, and Nelson said that his organization is one of its "biggest supporters." One complaint, however, was that OCB often dragged its feet and held various SCME requests for arbitration for unusual lengths of time. The reasons, Nelson added, are often political.

At the time of this research, September 1968, contract negotiations were under way between the sanitation workers as well as unionized policemen and firemen. The investigator was granted an interview with the labor advisor-negotiator for the sanitationmen union's chief, and various topics were discussed. Bigel indicated that, on the basis of his consulting experience, he believes public workers will continue to use the strike weapon whenever they feel deeply the justice of their cause. This happened in the well-advertised 1967 sanitation strike when the workers were willing to risk penalties—which, however, as Bigel said, would never bust the union or put it out of business. He described bargaining not as a tug-of-war between labor and management, but rather as a ballet in which both sides take one position after another. It is vital that each side do its homework and try to anticipate all the arguments the other side will bring to bear. For example, in the sanitation arbitration proceedings, as the union presented the significance of various factors—strenuosity, walking time, potential accidents, hazards of climate—the city cited the pay scales for similar tasks in other cities. Obviously, said Bigel, the same approach would not normally be tolerated in relating city management salaries to comparable work elsewhere. The standard expression of the city boils down to the "public interest," which Bigel considered to be a tired, worn-out phrase adopted especially by the newest city commissioners.

Management is forced to align one union against another in an effort to maintain balance. Nevertheless, in the bargaining process, it is vital to bear in mind the uniqueness of the union for which one is arguing, and to take account of its special requirements. Compulsory arbitration, Bigel felt, was not the answer. To achieve better labor relations, he concluded, we have to look within ourselves and consider human relations, rather than put our faith and trust in structural gimmicks, which merely obstruct the process of communication.

A basic ingredient required in the delicate art of labor relations is integrity. Other skills may be developed: patience, judgment, and insight. To apply these composite talents in a climate of pressures, nearsighted viewpoints, and painful deadlines is difficult. And in the public arena, wage ceilings have a tax side to them; it is necessary to balance the demands of each group. All want "more," but resources must be fairly allocated. It is in such an environment that New York City's labor relations director functions.

This official, Herbert Haber, is cool and restrained. At forty-four, he has survived many battles around the bargaining table. In our discussion it was not difficult to imagine him in all-night sessions, balancing one factor against another and judging all sides of an issue. His background strongly equips him for his present role. He attended New York University and Brooklyn College, and after army service completed his education at the University of Colorado School of Law in 1948. For over twelve years he served with the Federal Mediation and Conciliation Service, first as assistant to the general counsel and later as field mediator. In this connection he served in the New York metropolitan area, where he handled over a thousand disputes, negotiations, and strikes in many industries, ranging from newspapers to the waterfront, from food warehousing to missile production. In 1961, after success in settling a newspaper dispute, he became an executive of the Publishers Association of New York City, the collective bargaining agency for all major city newspapers, and as Number 2 negotiator was involved in contract negotiations with the nine craft unions in the industry.

A *New York Times* (September 30, 1968) man-in-the-news close-up, "City's Labor Warrior," stated that ". . . Mr. Haber has won the praise of labor experts for bringing a semblance of order and organization into New York's dealings with its tangled union affairs."

I thought we might examine some of the reasons behind the establishment of the offices you gentlemen direct, and consider the legal basis under which you function.

Haber: Prior to the establishment of this office, labor relations in the city were conducted by the Director of the Budget and the Director of Personnel. The subject-matter which could be negotiated was limited to salary adjustments, exclusively.

Now perhaps I ought to step back a little and indicate that collective bargaining really began in the city about ten years ago with Mayor Wagner's Executive Order Number 49, the Magna Carta as it were of municipal labor relations. That law permitted employees to organize into unions of their own choosing to represent them in the matter of grievances. The unions organized by civil service titles on a departmental basis, were recognized by the Department of Labor, received a certificate of representation, and were permitted to have dues checked off.

Different unions organized different groups of employees in different departments—frequently the same groups in the different departments—so there was a proliferation of unions and recognition certificates throughout the city. None of these unions bargained on wages; all they could do was represent employees for grievances. The city's policy was that until a union represented a majority of a given civil service title, citywide, there could be no bargaining on wages. The city could not be put in a position of bargaining with union A for typists in the Health Department and with union B for typists in the Welfare Department, with the unions arguing and trying to outdo each other for wages for the same civil service title. These employees were doing precisely the same work under the same circumstances but in different departments.

As time went on and more organization occurred, through a sort of building-block procedure, a given union would accumulate a series of certificates in different departments that ultimately would give it the representational rights for a majority of a given title. At this point the union obtained majority status.

. . . within each department?

Haber: Within each title, across departments. Union A would pick up a certificate to be the bargaining agent for typists and clerks in Welfare; union B would pick them up in Hospitals; union A in Water and Gas, and Housing, and elsewhere. Union C might pick them up in another few places. Each time a union won an election it would, on a unit basis, get the whole group. For example, if a total of 100 people voted, and 40 voted for union B and 30 voted the other way, that union would get the 100 and become the agent for bargaining.

It sounds extremely intricate.

Haber: It was complex, but the unit rule applied—if a union won a particular election it got the whole unit. So now it might have 100 people in a given department. And then it got 100 in another department, 400 people in still another department. By actual vote it might have won each election by only a small majority, but it picked up the whole unit.

After a while a determination was made that by virtue of this collection of accumulated certificates it now represented a majority of employees in that particular occupational title. At that point it was then bargained with, on behalf of all those employees, with regard to wages.

Now, all the unions to which these employees belonged remained in existence. There might be five or six unions representing clerks and typists in different departments in the city, but one of those five or six unions represented a majority of all those employed, and it set the wage rates in bargaining with the city. Meanwhile, each of the other unions continued to represent its own members in terms of grievances and things of that sort. You had majority and minority unions, so to speak.

It seems like a hard way to do things.

Haber: It is. It was hard. It is complicated—but there's a sense and a logic to it. It was the city's feeling that bargaining and representation should be encouraged. The only way any union could get a foothold was on a unit basis—a departmental basis. While the city wanted to encourage a union to organize, it didn't, on the other hand, want to create an impossible situation for itself by having to bargain with a multiplicity of unions. So the city worked out this method. Really it's a sound one, I think—complicated, and now archaic and no longer valid, but at the time I feel it was valid. In essence, the city permitted a union to organize and represent employees, but wouldn't bargain with them until they had obtained majority status.

That seems fair enough.

Haber: Yes, I think it was. I think it was kind of silly perhaps to permit the minority unions to continue in existence after the majority unions were established, but this was done. As time went on and more and more city employees came into union organization, it got to the point where there were many unions and many bargaining units. We have something like 90 different unions with whom we deal and over 200 bargaining units. We're going all the time, negotiating contracts with majority unions in addition to dealing with all the minority unions as well.

This was *one* of the basic situations that existed. Another factor was that the city, as I say, took the position that it would not bargain with a union until it had attained majority status, and then only on wages. The city said that it would not, could not bargain on other matters because these were managerial prerogatives, or the Charter would not permit delegating this responsibility, or that certain matters were of a citywide nature and could only be bargained for with *all* city employees.

This is a logical extension of the majority concept. You can't bargain with a given title of typists on wages until the rates apply to all typists. You can't bargain with a given union on holidays, vacations, and pensions, because these are matters that apply identically to all city employees. You can't bargain with one union here and another union there; you can't have supervisors with 10 days off, clerks they supervise with 5 days off, and some related title having 8 days off. It just wouldn't work. So the city said: We can't bargain with you on that until one union attains a majority *city-wide*; then we'll bargain with you on those matters.

Well, back about 1965, there was a strike—first real strike in the city in the Welfare department. And one of the basic causes was the fact that the city had taken a position that it wouldn't bargain on anything but wages. The Welfare employees thought there were many other matters on which they wanted to bargain; but the city was adamant—and so there was a strike.

Is this an example of management prerogative?

Haber: Yes. The city insisted on a *total* management prerogative. They were going to bargain *only* on wages.

Peter Goodman (Executive Assistant): In addition, I think it bears pointing out that in the matter of bargaining on wages, at that time we were living within what we called the Career and Salary Plan—a set schedule of rates of compensation. . . .

. . . set by?

Haber: I think it was set unilaterally by the city at some earlier time.

And Peter's right. Bargaining was really a matter of adjusting wage levels. The union came in and bargained, and we'd say, "Well, we'll give you a grade and a grade adjustment—one grade this year, one grade next year. Move you up the slot." There was an eight-step frame in the system. It was a very limited kind of bargaining.

And then at some point along the way the city agreed that they would bargain on a welfare fund—setting up a welfare fund, union by union. A fixed sum of money was paid into union funds to be administered by the unions for whatever benefits they chose to make available to their employee members.

With pensions?

Haber: No. City's always had its own pension arrangements. This is supplemental welfare—incidental benefits, hospital benefits over and above what the city provided, life insurance—things of that sort. And it was completely administered by the unions. City had no part of it except that there was a rather rigid set of fiscal-responsibility rules to which the unions had to conform.

Well, we had the strike in '65 and it was settled by outside assistance. A panel was set up and its recommendations moved into very, very wide areas of operations—much too far, as a matter of fact. But one of the things that came out of it was a recognition that some kind of orderly procedure would have to be set up, *that the limited sphere of bargaining would have to be broadened*. The city agreed to set up a committee to create a new procedure. It was out of this agreement—and the early committee work—that discussion began in the Lindsay administration which led ultimately to the establishment of the Office of Collective Bargaining.

This committee was set up—a tripartite committee—with representatives from the city and from the major unions in the city, plus representatives of the public who were experienced arbitrators and educators in the field of labor relations. The whole thing was coordinated by the American Arbitration Association, which had established an office whose specific title I forget. . . .

Goodman: Labor Management Institute.

Haber: Yes. At that time it was headed by Jesse Simons, who since has become Vice-President of Labor Relations for U.S. Lines, Inc. Jesse was really the main spark plug in this thing. He was a coordinator, the driving force, kept everybody's feet to the fire and really kept it going. He did a remarkably fine job in getting the thing off the ground.

As part of that whole development, it was also agreed that labor relations, on the part of the city, had to be coordinated in one office and under one responsibility. A professional arrangement had to be set up similar to that which existed in the private sector, and this office was created. A person was sought as chief negotiator for the city with all the unions, and when I assumed that responsibility, I created this office. What has come into being is what I developed in response to a need recognized by the administration as contained in the situation that then existed. The Office of Labor Relations functions as does any office of labor relations in the private sector in any major corporation.

Under this executive-order type of authority?

Haber: I don't know that the executive order created this office, but it spells out the responsibilities and authority of this office.

I can check that out.

Haber: If it doesn't create the office, it does acknowledge its existence and indicates to the rest of the city the degree of authority and responsibility we have.

Was this development inescapable in view of the trend toward national unionism on the private level?

Haber: Oh yes. I think it fits right in with that phrase: if there wasn't one, we'd have to create it. We'd have to invent it. It was absolutely essential, although some people in the administration didn't think so because to a degree it cut away some of their authority and responsibility.

We now handle labor relations for the city. We work with Personnel and Budget, because obviously some of their functions are not only invaluable to us but are really an integral part of our operation. But it's our responsibility and our determination, and they no longer have the responsibility they once did. Nevertheless, they work closely with us, and their support is vital to us.

If you had to list one major aim of the office, what would it be?

Haber: Well, we are engaged on a long-range program of stabilizing labor relations in the City of New York with municipal employees.

How many employees do you affect?

Haber: We bargain directly with about 220,000 and we have indirect responsibility for another hundred thousand—perhaps even more than that—employed in some agencies for which the city has a fiscal responsibility but no other control—such as Board of Education, Transit Authority, Board of Higher Education, the Court systems. We pay the freight, we pay the bill, but they're independent agencies set up by the state.

We've already begun to move in the direction of creating this sort of stable relationship. For example, I indicated earlier that the minority unions had continued in existence. Now we have taken steps to knock them out of existence. By executive order the Mayor has provided for the formal recognition of the majority unions. When a union attains majority status, a new certificate is now issued, making that union the *only* union with whom the city will deal, not only on collective bargaining for wages but also in grievance representations. At the same time, the certificates formerly held by the other unions are cancelled.

But the other unions exist. . . .

Haber: The unions can exist and employees can continue their membership in them, but those unions can no longer represent those people for anything. They can no longer hold meetings on city property, they can no longer represent their members in grievances—or anything of that sort. They're just out of business with the city. *There's only one union we'll recognize for any given civil service title, when the union attains a majority. Until it has that majority, we'll deal with everybody.* Once a union attains a majority, that's it. This is the private-sector formula.

Could you list some of the major unions with which you deal, covering a big chunk of employees?

Haber: First of all, the groups we describe as our uniformed forces. By the unique way in which they are set up, they are as wide as they are tall. Their citywide title is in a department. All our sanitation men are in one department, all our police in one department, our firemen in one department.

Those are the three main groups?

Haber: Those are the main ones. There are a few additional, such as Correction—we consider those employees part of our uniformed force; also Housing Police, Transit Police, and so on. Basically, that's the uniformed force. And they are substantial in number: the police have twenty-two or twenty-four thousand. . . .

Goodman: Closer to 30,000.

Haber: Well, not in the Patrolmen's Benevolent Association. You see, there are five different unions there, but the PBA, which is the rank-and-file police, has about 22,000. The rest are in Superior Councils.

To clear it up for me, the PBA is a union with which you bargain?
Haber: Oh yes.
That's one of the biggest. . . .

Haber: Yes. In the Police Department we have five unions: we've got the PBA and then we've got a Council of Superior Officers—and in that council we've got the Detectives' Benevolent Association, Sergeants' Benevolent Association, Lieutenants' Benevolent Association, Captains-and-Above Benevolent Association. In the Fire Department we've got the Uniformed Firemen's Association and the Uniformed Officers' Association. Take Sanitation: there we've got the Sanitation Men's Union and the Sanitation Officers' Union.

There are others organized in that same way in that they fall within a particular department, such as Welfare. Of the other major unions, the largest by far is District Council 37 of the State, County, and Municipal Employees (SCME). A lot of locals are affiliated with the council. But for all intents and purposes, as far as we're concerned, it's *one* union.

Is it like a holding company of unions?

Haber: Well, yes—in the narrow sense that you're using it, I would say so. The council sends a representative in for 98 percent of the negotiations that we have with the various local unions. Some are larger than others; some are stronger—but they're all affiliated and we regard this as one union. And that is the largest union in the city. It represents a majority of people employed by the city outside of the uniformed forces, which constitutes the rest of our people. It has a membership now which I think is approaching 70,000 or 60,000—it's in that area. And it represents, by virtue of its certificates and titles, something over 100,000 of our employees.

By virtue of the fact that District Council 37 does represent a majority of our employees—a status it has only recently attained (or we've recently established)—we are now able to bargain with it citywide on issues I referred to before—that is, matters that we would not have bargained on until some union had attained a majority status.

We have just completed a three-year contract with the council in which we bargained for the first time on matters such as pensions, improvements in overtime provisions, shift differentials and holidays—matters of that sort—and we have applied these improvements across the board to all our civil service people. All the unions have derived a benefit from the negotiations with the majority union.

Now to go back for a moment to this overall tightening up: when we stopped dealing with minority unions, we also knocked out minority check-off. We said that when a union attained majority status, it got a majority certificate, and after that it was the only union officially representing employees and the only one for which the city would continue checking off dues. The minority unions could retain their membership and their dues-paying requirements. No employee *must* join the majority union—we haven't gotten to that point—and no employee is compelled to pay any dues to it. They can retain membership in their other union and pay dues if they wish, but hereafter they will have to pay dues directly. The city will no longer routinely check the dues out and pay it to the minority unions. It will do so only for majority unions.

No employee in the city, then, is required to join a union?

Haber: No, absolutely not.

What's the exact labor term for this requirement?

Haber: Union shop. Now Gotbaum, who is the Director of State, County, and Municipal Employees, has put us on notice that he is after what is called an agency shop. This means that no one has to join the union, but everyone has to pay a fee to the union—the equivalent of union dues. . . .

. . . without membership benefits?

Haber: That's up to them. If they don't want to join, they don't have to. Membership is open to everyone. You join, you're a member, you pay dues. If you don't join, you pay a fee to the union for services. Because the union is required to represent all the people in its title.

Even those who are not affiliated.

Haber: Right. That's why I said before, Gotbaum's union has some sixty thousand members but represents a hundred and twenty or a hundred and ten thousand employees. He's required to represent them. When any of those people have a grievance, he has to represent them.

Union or not.

Haber: Right. And all those people have the right to share in his welfare fund—and so on. And he has to service their claims.

So for all practical purposes, most city employees are union members.

Haber: No. I'm not sure what the statistics are, but in some categories it's not that way at all. A minority are members and the others are, as *he* terms it, "free riders"—getting all the benefits and not paying their share of the freight. And he argues, too, that if their reason for staying out is that they don't like the way the union is being run, then the best place for them is on the inside where they can vote and make their opposition felt. Whether this is so or not is a debatable point, but anyway this is his argument. And they are pressing strongly on us for some sort of representational fee arrangement, which they are calling the agency shop—which is what it is called on the outside, in the private sector.

If I were to shadow members of your staff for a day, what would I find them doing within the department? What happened today, for example?

Haber: Our people are doing a lot of things. Today, our staff has been variously occupied in negotiating contracts with unions; handling grievances at a stage immediately below arbitration; representing the city on grievances that have come to arbitration for resolution; appearing before fact-finders in contract disputes which have gone beyond negotiation and mediation and are now before a fact-finder; meeting with the representatives of the Office of Collective Bargaining on questions of representation of employees in unions: (1) as to whether a particular level of employee, because of its managerial responsibilities, is appropriately in a union, or (2) whether a particular group of employees is appropriately joined with others in a particular bargaining unit—and other questions of that nature.

This goes on all the time. In addition, there is consulting with the various departments on any problems that may come up that could result in a grievance or a work stoppage or something of that sort, and advising them on maintaining some degree of uniformity of application throughout the city. Then there are various communications between ourselves and the unions, ourselves and the departments, departments and the unions—on a whole variety of problems. These include answering all sorts of questions that come to the Mayor's office from our employees and the public as to what we are doing, and why, and how come? One of Peter's major functions is "bird-dogging" complaints that we get from city employees and taxpayers as to things we're doing—are the complaints valid and can they be resolved? We also answer the Mayor's mail in matters that are in our area of expertise.

What's the state of labor relations in New York City today for municipal employees? How would you characterize it?

Haber: I think that the state of labor relations in the city is really not too different, in certain ways, from what it is on the outside. I think that labor relations generally has been given—I don't know whether the right word is an injection or an infection. At any rate, the attitude which exists in the private sector today, in our society, our community, is also affecting the same people in their labor unions.

There's an unrest, an unhappiness, and I'm not sure just what the unrest or the unhappiness is about except that it's manifesting itself within a particular framework. This presents us with problems. There have been occasions when union leadership has negotiated settlements—fine settlements—with the city or in the private sector, and the rank and file have overturned their leadership—just ignored them.

Our sanitation strike was a manifestation of this. We had reached agreement with the leadership of the union, it had been ratified by the Executive Board and the Scale Committee; but it was turned down by the Delegate Assembly—a group of 700 representing the 10,000. They just rejected it despite the recommendations of leadership. The taxi strike, the garage strike, the theatre strike—all of these were strikes where the union leadership had reached agreement and gone back to the membership, presented the agreement, and had it overturned for a variety of announced reasons. No one's really quite sure what lies behind it, but there is this general unrest.

Coupled with that are problems arising from the fact that the unions in the city are relatively new and young. So they are trying to achieve in a relatively short span of, say, ten years, what labor unions in the private sector took, in some instances, 100 years to accomplish. The city's unions are telescoping this development in one quick push to bring themselves abreast of unions in the private sector. This makes for a great deal of difficulty in reaching peaceful solutions.

Thirdly, the nature of city employees also is a factor. For the most part they are white-collar, a breed apart which doesn't readily lend itself to organizing; so there's some discomfort on the part of city employees with this new garment that they are putting on. It doesn't really fit too well.

Interestingly enough, in the private sector the pace of organization among white-collar people has slowed, whereas in the city—the public sector of municipal, state, and county employees—it's accelerated enormously. But even so, these people are still reluctant. We've got some unions who still call themselves associations or forums or guilds. White-collar people are uncomfortable, you see, with the term "union."

Teachers were once largely averse to the union label, but now many are as militant and aggressive in some areas, as the so-called blue-collar unions.

Haber: Yes. I think teachers follow the same pattern. Actually the teachers' union has been in existence for a long time. The National Education Association doesn't call itself a union, but that's what it is.

I think perhaps its attitude is ambivalent.

Haber: Well, it's coming over. It is similar to what most of the organizations in the public sector were at their beginnings. They were in existence for many years. United Federation of Teachers has been organized for a short time—five years? They came out—boom; they're a union and they make no mistake about it. They're militant and bargain that way. District Council 37—State, County, and Municipal Employees—same attitude. They are a union and they keep pounding this union concept, whereas many of the others do not. The older unions developed more slowly and still retain some of their former identity and attitudes.

As the city unions attain this new militancy in their bargaining, they're not quite sure of what they're doing. They're uncomfortable; they're unsure of themselves; they're lacking in sophistication. So there is a tendency to overact and overreact in things that they do. I think, in time, they will mellow and become—some of them—more responsible than they are right now in their behavior.

Generally speaking, I think the labor relations picture in the city is a sound and healthy one. And I think it will become sounder and more healthy as it moves along and the unions gain a certain amount of experience and knowledge and sophistication.

May I turn briefly to the role of the press in relation to this office. It would seem—I am speculating now—that if the average citizen in this city were asked: "What do you think of the strike situation among municipal workers?" he would use some very descriptive language. Do you think the press has inflated labor relations problems—does it report accurately—does it excite?

Haber: Well, I would say that the press gives our situations about the same degree of accurate reporting that it does in the private sector—and naturally you can interpret this statement as you see fit.

There's no question that because we are in the public sector, we are under a different set of rules in press coverage than the private sector is. Everything becomes a matter of great interest and concern to the taxpayer. We're dealing with taxpayer's money; the Mayor's involved; there are political implications—so just about anything we do becomes of great public moment.

Do we see the whole picture? I think that in news accounts the total plot is sometimes lost.

Haber: Collective bargaining by its very nature has to be performed in private. You cannot carry on collective bargaining in an open forum, because all you would have then would be posturing. Each side would be defending its position and making its best case for the public.

Doesn't this go on now?

Haber: Not too much, because we bargain in private. The press aren't admitted to our sessions. They're not involved in the negotiations; they don't know what's going on there.

Goodman: In 1967 we came to 95 or 100 settlements which nobody even heard about on the outside.

I guess the good is more often lost than the bad.

Goodman: Right. The one that they heard about was our caseworker dispute because that was one in which we couldn't come to an agreement.

I think if anyone were to ask the same average citizen: "What was the roughest strike?" it would be the sanitation strike of 1967. Is that true?

Haber: Roughest for whom?

In terms of discomfort and dislocation and grumbling.

Haber: I would think so. That's been the most dramatic strike of which citizens in the city have been aware. The teachers' strike, of course, might get the vote for number one, on the part of some people—the suburban, or almost-suburban residents of the city in the middle-class neighborhoods. They may feel that the teachers' strike had a greater impact on them than the sanitation strike. They bought themselves an extra garbage can and were a little more selective in the way they packed their garbage so that during that strike they filled two garbage cans but had no real discomfort. Whereas with the teachers' strike their kids were home all the time—they felt that.

The business people in New York City, on the other hand, certainly were affected more seriously by the garbage strike than by the fact that the kids were home. Ghetto residents—they got both of them; kids and garbage, too. The ghetto people, the poor of the city, are the ones who are most seriously affected by all our strikes. They are hardest hit. They were hardest hit by teachers, by garbage, and by welfare.

Regarding the quality of leadership that you see exhibited by union officials—what do you see as the indispensable quality of a labor leader in this age?

Haber: Labor leaders are like everybody else. They have a job to perform and their own particular personalities and problems that mold them and cause them to act in a certain way under a given set of circumstances. There are a number of leaders in the City of New York whom I consider to be quite able and responsible. Their actions would seem sometimes to belie this, except that a good leader reflects frequently the sentiments and drives of his membership—that's why he remains a leader. Sometimes you have to run real fast to stay out in front of your own people.

I use the example frequently of cowboys in a stampede. When a stampede really gets going—really has a head—the cowhands will ride with it until they feel the herd tiring a little and then they'll begin to turn it. A good union leader—any leader, not necessarily in a union—frequently does the same thing. If he stood up and tried to stop his stampede, sometimes he'd be trampled. Then we'd have a new and more militant leader in his place.

Some union leaders will ride with their people until the time when they feel they can gain control and turn them. I would say, generally, that the quality of leadership among the city unions is pretty high.

One final point. Many theorists have debated the issue of whether public employees have the right to strike. How does that stack up today?

Haber: Well, it's—right now it's one of the hottest subjects of discussion in the public sector. My position, frankly, is that the debate as to whether public employees should have the right to strike is academic, because they do not. *Public employees do not have the right to strike.* There is not a jurisdiction in the country at any level which permits public employees to strike. Such strikes are uniformly forbidden, in one way or another, either by statute or constitution or what have you.

The unions argue that employees have an inalienable right to strike and that they should be permitted a statutory or constitutional right to strike. This is the thrust of their argument.

I have my own thoughts on this—I don't think they should have the right to strike, but that's as far as I want to go with respect to that aspect of it. Because from a realistic standpoint, from where I sit, irrespective of whether they have the right or don't have the right, whether they should have it or not—we have strikes. Public employees are striking. And I must conduct my business as though for all practical purposes they've got a de facto if not a de jure right to strike—because they *are* striking. Therefore, so far as I'm concerned, the concentration has to be not on whether they should or shouldn't have the right to strike, but on how we establish a climate of labor relations and a framework of labor relations, so as to obviate the need for the use of the strike as a weapon.

The nature of the employer with whom the unions are dealing makes the strike an inappropriate weapon in the public sector. We can't go out of business. We can't stockpile our product. We can't move across the river.

We're an artificial creature of the electorate—created in order to provide certain basic services that the electorate feels it needs. When unions are striking against us as management, they're not hitting us in the pocket. They're striking against themselves as part of the electorate. And the way of settling this problem doesn't lie with us. So it's not an appropriate weapon—but again, I digress.

The strike is a reality and I think that the emphasis has to be on reaching a basis of understanding with our unions, so that they feel that they are being given a fair shake, that we are dealing with them reasonably and fairly. If they feel that we are dealing with them from a position of strength based on the fact that they can't legally strike, they'll feel they've got to have a weapon to retaliate with. So we have to provide some alternate way of resolving disputes that will avoid the use of the strike.

We have now developed a fact-finding process that we think will provide a satisfactory alternative. I think it will. I think that ultimately when the unions reach a degree of confidence in their own ability and an awareness that they are here to stay and that we recognize them, then they can relax a little in what they're doing. I think then they'll come to realize that the strike is *not* necessary.

Outside of New York, most strikes in the public sector today are not over disputes or wages, but over recognition. They are still fighting the battle of having a county board recognize them and bargain with them. This is the way it used to be in the private sector. Initially, strikes were for recognition, but there are no strikes for recognition in the private sector anymore. Machinery has been established. A union files an application with a federal board or a state board for recognition. There are election procedures and so on. When that was not true, there were many strikes on grievances during a contract term. You had a problem with your boss, you walked out on the street. That's virtually out of existence except in a few select, rare instances where the parties agree that you would prefer to do it this way. But for the most part you have orderly procedures: a grievance, hearings, and arbitration resolving it.

Well, now we're trying to move away from the strike as the ultimate weapon in any kind of dispute. We set up fact-finding boards and maybe arbitration to resolve a dispute finally. And I think ultimately we may get to that point.

In many ways New York is a leading center. Has it made such strides in labor relations that you could offer them as an example for others to follow?

Haber: Oh yes. I think so. I think that we are much ahead of many parts of the country, because our unions have forced us to be. I think the procedures that we have set up for dealing with our unions and providing them with an opportunity to have their day in court, with our Office of

Collective Bargaining, is an enormous step forward. I think our procedures are better than the procedures set up in the state Taylor law. I think they are better than any I'm aware of anywhere in the country. I think we do constitute a model that a lot of jurisdictions might examine—and a number of them are.

STUDY QUESTIONS

1. Is the New York City method appropriate for most cities in handling their labor relations problems? How does your city differ, if at all?
2. Are strikes by public employees supportable under any circumstances?
3. What qualifications do you consider essential for an administrator handling government's labor relations?
4. Investigate a specific labor dispute (public) in your area and evaluate the completeness and objectivity of the press coverage.

IV
ORGANIZATION

6

NATIONAL PARK SERVICE

An act to establish a National Park Service, passed in 1916 by the 64th Congress, provided that:

> The service thus established shall promote and regulate the use of the Federal areas known as national parks, monuments, and reservations so as to conserve the scenery and the natural and historic objects and the wild life therein and to provide for the enjoyment of the same in such manner and by such means as will leave them unimpaired for the enjoyment of future generations.

In an age of ever-increasing technology, the National Park Service has now paused to examine its programs and problems. Two mandates of 1966 prompted this appraisal: one contained in the presidential conservation message to the Congress which stipulated completion of the National Park System by 1972, and the other embodied in Director Hartzog's message to all members of the Park Service. "During our 50th Anniversary year," said the director, "it is particularly appropriate that we not only publicly acknowledge our achievements, but that we also take an objective look within the Service at *how we operate* the National Park System."

A checklist of current problems, which have been gradually accumulating, contains sufficient challenges for the most astute and imaginative administrator. As samples:

1. Multiplying pressures by an expanding population for greater park use, which might, in time, impair or even destroy park resources and reduce the value of park visits.

2. The need to strike a reasonable, viable balance between preservation (or "perpetuation," as Mr. Ochsner put it in our discussion) and concentrated use by recreation-minded tourists.

3. The adjustment of the competing claims of commercial lumber and mining interests, bordering communities, conservation groups and the general public.

4. Determination of recreation facilities versus natural habitats for animals—what was described in the interview as a balanced ecological system among plants, animals, and man.

5. Determination of the extent to which parks must reflect an urban orientation, yet guard against the excesses that plague modern cities—air pollution, crime, vandalism, high-speed roads, and traffic congestion.

On its fiftieth birthday, Secretary of the Interior Udall characterized the mission of the Park Service administration in these terms: "National Parks play a part in helping to enrich the human spirit, the minds and bodies of our citizens. Consequently we are dealing with a very fragile area which is concerned as much with the conservation of human resources as with natural resources."

A few figures show something of the scope of what faces the Service in this century. Under its direction is a total of 27.5 million acres administratively divided into 263 natural, recreational, and historical areas. Whereas in 1916 some 350,000 people visited thirteen national parks, it is estimated that in 1967 some 40 million visited thirty-two parks. Noting this dramatic increase, Robert Cahn observed in the *Christian Science Monitor*, in one of a series of articles on the National Parks (July 31, 1968): "The options are: to create more national parks, provide more federal and state recreation areas to ease pressure on the national park system; expand facilities such as camp grounds and lodges at the expense of certain natural values; place restrictions on use; or a combination of these solutions."

With these mounting problems as a background, Director of the National Park Service George A. Hartzog, Jr., on July 5, 1966, established a Field Operations Study Team (FOST) indicating that ". . . a representative group of our people have been assigned to study how the Service can most effectively operate the parks to meet our growing responsibilities, while making each of our jobs more meaningful and our careers more satisfying." The seven members represented various skills and levels of the Service, and two of them—David C. Ochsner and Mati Tammaru— participated in the joint interview reported here. As a park operations research and planning program, the basic work of FOST involving studies, interviews, and conferences was accomplished during the summer of 1966. Its report suggested several concepts as new approaches to future operations and made recommendations for implementing them.

After the study team had concluded its work, a task force was appointed to prepare the concepts for Service-wide use. An action plan was developed with a tight timetable and released on March 18, 1968, by the parks director. The main goals of the study team had been to study and recommend appropriate action on functional and organizational alignments in areas administered by the Service, including the utilization of professional and technician occupation skills. For its part, the goals of the task force were primarily to develop procedures for the analysis of field functions and to write qualification and classification standards for Park Ranger and Manager and Park Technician and Aid occupations.

The task force rendered its report, *Occupation and Organization Guides for Park Operations*, on June 1, 1968. Among its recommendations was a proposal that whenever size and geography favored the arrangement, parks should be divided into management units. A unit manager would coordinate, implement and direct all approved programs, and would be the focal point for communications and directions. Such a unit would fit into one of three categories: a total small park; a segment of a large, complex park; or two or more small parks under one manager. As the task force report indicated:

> The management unit serves to: (1) give management experience to first level managers; (2) bring together all parts of the park program into a rational whole at the field operations level; and (3) open the door wider to upward communication of employees' needs, desires, and understanding of their jobs and to downward communication of what management expects from employees.

Traditionally, parks have been operated according to divisional, staff-line concepts. In operation, however, most small parks are, in fact, management units. In determining management units for larger parks, the guidelines would be based on:

1. Amount of budgeted funds.
2. Human skills required to operate the program.
3. Seasonal and permanent workers.
4. Future capital investment.
5. Geographical shape of the parks.
6. Political considerations.
7. Local supply points, transportation accesses, arteries of commerce.
8. Special interest groups.
9. Population centers served.
10. Special problems: management functions, visitor services, and area services.

The report notes that because of many variables, a standard profile applicable for all management units is unrealistic. In each case, determinations must hinge upon real, human issues, such as the challenge of the operation to first-level managers; whether size, distance, and geography will permit a manager to know his employees; and the degree to which a manager can check personally on how things are going in his unit.

Building on the management unit, the so-called clustering grouping of various small parks was proposed for use throughout the Service, wherever appropriate. This arrangement would include two or more management units, a middle manager to direct overall operations, first-level managers in charge of each management unit, and staff services specialists to serve all parks within the group. Possible advantages are high-level management representation for small parks, giving first-level managers the benefit of closer advice and assistance from top management and a more economical and efficient basis for purchase, budget, program, and reporting requirements. Each park would remain under the direction of a manager (superintendent) who, in turn, would be responsible to a group manager (general superintendent).

The report also recommended:

1. The introduction of two new occupation series: Park Aid and Technician to handle nonprofessional tasks, and Park Ranger and Management to devote more attention to professional responsibilities.

2. A broadening of the academic base of professionalists in ranger-uniform positions.

3. More flexibility in the planning of a positive career ladder within the service.

Throughout the work of both the study team and its follow-up task force, a determined effort was made to bring the Park Service into the mainstream of a modern integrated management system. As with other organizations, it examined its strengths, weaknesses, and potentials. An introductory statement and a series of questions attempted to pinpoint each of these areas. Early in the report, for example, these questions are asked:

Any organization that does not size up itself once in a while might be headed for trouble. Do we have the self-discipline for a candid look at how we are doing? Do we have the determination to adjust our way of doing our job when conditions show us a change is needed?

Reinforcing this attitude, Parks Director Hartzog said: "Our determined search for excellence in all of our management, which made our Service great during the last fifty years, remains the cornerstone for our success today. For that reason, our strength must stem from a sound park management philosophy and equally vigorous management program for people."

Park personnel have underscored the usefulness of the task force as a modern means of solving problems. In this case, a distinctive feature was the candor of the relationship between headquarters people and the field forces, their effort being to "find out what they tune in on." The total length of tape recordings with personnel ran to 26,000 feet and included interviews and conferences with superintendents, regional directors, chief park rangers, assistant regional directors, and supervisors, among others.

The task force disbanded as of June 30, 1968, and henceforth normal NPS organization will continue the implementation of its recommendations. Discussions will also continue with all former task force staff about the meaning and application of FOST concepts. All phases of the Action Plan—new occupation standards, employee placement, training, and recruitment—are tied to a specific timetable. All phases are expected to be completed as of June 30, 1969, and in the following December the FOST concepts and the success of their application will be evaluated.

The Action Plan set forth specific reorganization changes to be accomplished between February 21, 1968, and June 30, 1969. In brief, implementation will be in "feasible stages" and mainly at the hands of regional directors. Parks where organizational changes are desired will be identified and the changes installed in a "planned manner." It was anticipated that most parks personnel would fit one of three categories:

1. Staff willing and anxious to implement FOST.
2. Staff hesitant because of reluctance to change or pressures of "genuine problems."
3. Staff strongly opposed to *any* change—emotionally, for valid reasons, or both.

Stages of implementation were spelled out in precise detail. *First*, FOST will furnish guidelines to help regional directors and decide which parks can be organized into clusters and those suited for management districts on an internal staff-line reorganization. *Second*, in a maximum of about two weeks each regional director must indicate which parks are susceptible of reorganization. *Third*, action teams in regional offices will visit each park in which organizational change is proposed. At this time two factors will be considered: suitability for change and staff's attitude. *Fourth*, once individual parks are evaluated, implementation will start immediately in those where the staff is willing to accept changes and where no serious problems exist. These parks will "prepare detailed organization charts" for the regional director's review and then proceed with implementation.

In the *fifth* stage, the regional director and his action team will restudy the parks in which the staff is reluctant, but not adamant, and in which there seem to be genuine problems that interfere with reorganization. From this restudy will come plans to overcome difficulties and staff reluctance.

Finally, in the *sixth* stage, the regional office will develop plans, including timetables, for reorganizing those parks in which the staff is strongly against such change. Solutions to genuine problems will be worked out. Compromises, interim measures, staff changes, and problem-solving training will be used where necessary.

All these administrative changes are directed to the objective—once the semantics are hurdled—of park improvement in order to meet and answer new demands imposed by modern, technical changes, with their advantages and liabilities. The central issue, as the talks with park officials underscored, is the proper balance between preservation versus utilization based on the philosophy that parks belong to and are for all people.

Director Hartzog pinpoints the challenge to the Service's administrators in these terms: "A park experience means different things to different people in different places. Each area is unique. A certain historical area may give the visitor a sense of his place in the stream of humankind. A natural area can give one a new perspective on the place you have in this God-given web of life. It is recreative, refreshing."

The joint interviews reported here cover a broad range of issues. A wide variety of suggestions, gained from the task force, is being willingly accepted throughout the Service. In an organization so closely related to human demands and desires, the concept of the public interest is vividly illustrated. In fact, the closing article in the *Monitor* series on national parks (August 7, 1968) relates to this basic point, for it developed a one-page questionnaire, in the spirit of a public-opinion survey, designed to provide park officials with systematic information—beyond their own sources—for planning on a long-run basis. The responses should assist the Service to relate various elements more cohesively throughout the organization and redefine concepts by reappraisal.

Robert Cahn, the author of this interesting and objective *Monitor* series, put the issue strongly:

> The ultimate answer rests not with Congress or the National Park Service, but with all the people. Their national parks—a unique American contribution—have played a relevant role in developing the kind of nation that exists today. By the way they live, the values they cherish, and the way they treat each other as well as their great resources—in all these ways Americans will decide the kinds of parks they will have tomorrow.

It should prove valuable, in the light of these broad problems, to learn how two Park Service officials respond to a citizen's questions on this indispensable heritage. David C. Ochsner, Vice-Chairman, FOST Task Force, and Mati Tammaru, a personnel management specialist, were participants in the discussion that follows.

Gentlemen, I thought this afternoon, as an introduction to the reorganization of the National Park Service, in which you as members of a task force have been involved, I might ask how you would describe its overall mission and major contributions to this century's emphasis on leisure and recreation.

Ochsner: Originally, with our enabling legislation in 1916, we were given a dual mission of preserving land areas and providing for the public use of these areas. Bringing these two concepts together creates a lot of discussion among Park Service employees. But now we're beginning to look, I think, more toward the educational aspects of parks.

We think we still have the mission of preservation or, what I like to call, perpetuation of environment—that's the way I like to look at it. Preserve sounds as if it's locking it up but perpetuation, to me, is active management.

. . . and continued utilization.

Ochsner: Perpetuating an environment—a particular environment which is within the boundaries given to us by congressional action.

Has the act been changed in many ways?

Ochsner: Actually it's only been added to by other acts, such as the Parkway and Recreation Act of the thirties and Historical Sites Act, which I think was passed in the thirties, also. So we've gained a lot of areas through other acts. Two of the most recent have been the Wilderness Act and also the Land and Water Conservation Fund Act.

I think that many students of government recall the Timber and Grazing Act, the Homestead Act—and that's about it. So now you're blanketed under a good many legal provisions?

Ochsner: Yes, there are a great many of them. But the other side of the coin of preservation or perpetuation—however we want to look at it— is the business of education. For years and years, since the 1920s, we've had interpretative programs in which we try, through activities within the parks, to tell their meaning to visitors. But now we're looking outside the park boundaries and delving into what we call environmental education. This is, in a sense, making the knowledge about the parks as fully available as possible to *all* people. And we're working directly with grade schools and secondary schools—just beginning this program this year.

With the same personnel?

Ochsner: Basically, but it's in cooperation with local school boards and school districts—this is just starting; five camps went into operation this spring.

Tammaru: State park agencies are also involved.

Ochsner: Anyone who's interested in the material is involved—it's been tremendous! It's relating man to his environment. For a long time we've been looking at the parks independently of man. We've talked about the influences of man on parks, or the adverse effect on park lands, especially the scenic and scientific part, but we have not fully related the parks to what they mean to man.

We're doing it now not only through the school systems, but we're also beginning to change our interpretative programs in parks themselves. Instead of merely getting up with a bunch of slides and saying: "This is a such-and-such snake and here's a bear, and they all live in the parks," we're trying to relate the viewer to the scene. The two objectives are closely connected: first, to induce visitors to preserve the park environment, and second, to educate people and indicate man's relationship to his environment.

Tammaru: I would add this: one of the major contributions we're going to make, in the next decade, as far as national parks are concerned, is in the area of environmental education—making the citizenry fully aware of what is available to them, and their corresponding responsibility for it. I don't think we can separate this from, say, air pollution or pollution of rivers and streams. It is all part of the same bundle. I think we have a mission here to educate the masses and try to prevent our modern technology from running away with our political and social life in our present-day society.

Have you considered, as I have only recently, that the parks provide a safety valve, especially for people living in the cities? You've pointed out, rather dramatically, the need for an integration between parks and the people who use them. Are there certain problems which all parks share?

Tammaru: I would suggest, to start with, that one problem is the highly political climate, from a public administration standpoint, in which parks must exist. There is an awful lot of pressure placed on the superintendent of a given park, from a political standpoint. Take the elk reduction program at Yellowstone as an example. This was very much in the news last year. Senator McGee and Congress got involved to the point where not only the Park Service but the entire Interior Department, including Secretary Udall, were called in on it. The constraints of the political situation around the parks are very relevant—from the standpoint of Congress, civil groups, social forces in the states, the state legislatures, and park neighbors. They all have a great impact on the way in which we manage parks.

And yet the parks belong to all of us.

Ochsner: Sure do.

Tammaru: That, precisely, is the dilemma we are facing, talking very realistically about it. I'm sure it exists in any other agency, to a greater or lesser degree. I think this is a real fact of public administration. You have to consider it as one of *the* major problems.

Ochsner: I think another one involves an awareness, on our part, internally, of today's technology and what it means not only to the general public but to the national parks—how we fit into it and where we're heading with it.

In a sense, some of the larger western parks are "islands of time," so to speak. Point Reyes in California, which is a National Recreation Area, has been described in this way. And we spend much time in one of our training centers—week-long seminars—in an analysis of the relationship of parks to technology and mankind.

In reference to technology, do you mean increased automation, mechanization, speed. . . .

Ochsner: Right. And how we handle the tools of technology for our own purposes in managing national parks. Let me give you an example. Let's take automation, or the use of modern technological methods, at entrance stations. Should we continue doing it the old-fashioned way— serving each automobile as it comes along—despite the fact that cars stack up and motorists get madder and madder because of the delay, or should we speed up the process through some technical method which I'm certain could be developed.

Tammaru: Add to this the problem of visitors in the parks—Yosemite Valley is a good example. As a manager, how far do I go in developing that portion of the area which is to be readily available to the visitor in his mechanized and automotive state? Most camping trailers now being developed come as self-contained units—including electrical outlets and septic tanks. How many of the facilities required by this equipment do we provide the public in the parks?

In other words, how much does the visitor want to keep his home environment while he's out there invigorating himself in nature? How much do we provide for him? This creates a problem for us.

This is a clear example to me of the two competing objectives: preservation and utilization. It seems that parks have many appeals to an average tourist. Does he actually know what parks can provide, or is it up to you, from what David said earlier, to educate and influence his demands?

Ochsner: We think it's up to us. We don't think, in other words, that the public, in general, necessarily has realistic demands, and that we should bend to their demands, any more than to political demands. As I see it, this also is an internal problem: from a management standpoint, how far do we go?

Tammaru: I think the technological age and all it involves has made life very comfortable for the middle-class American. I cite the example of last summer. We had the bear incident at Glacier where a couple of girls were mauled and killed. It raised a basic question: Is it up to the Park Service, is it our responsibility to remove all of these hazards from an area where we are trying to preserve the natural scene? Should we provide people with a "wilderness" which is no different from their own backyard? Or is it the intent of Congress that we say to people: "Here is a natural environment. You come in here realizing all the risks that it entails. Natural environment is natural only because it involves risks." Personally, I lean to the latter viewpoint.

Ochsner: And I see this internally also from an employment stand-point—from the point-of-view of our employees' understanding. What types of workers do we need, to understand the National Park Service from a technological viewpoint, as well as modern society's viewpoint?

Are there any organizational and management differences among the parks that make some more difficult to manage than others? As a prospective employee, would you send me to work in one, at the start, and not the other?

Tammaru: I think a basic problem we face initially—when you take a look at a map of the United States—is that we don't select the sites. They have been selected for us. We take boundaries as given to us, and this dispersion of locations has created problems in a management sense. I think this is a prime factor. Now as far as internal differences between parks are concerned, maybe Dave can elaborate.

Ochsner: Well, our parks vary all the way from some that are almost not visited—Katmai National Monument in Alaska, for example. It's the biggest area in the system, three million acres in extent and a very, very low visitation rate. People who want to go there *really* want to go there. By contrast, Independence has a tremendous visitation rate. And then, again, Craters of the Moon National Monument in Idaho has an annual visitation rate of some 200,000.

What are the three types of operational areas under National Park Service Control?

Tammaru: We classify them as natural, historical, and recreational—the latter being the latest type to be incorporated into the Service. I think Lake Meade was the first, but a whole host have been enacted by Congress and incorporated in the past few years: Assateague Island is a good example. Then there is Cape Cod, Fire Island Seashore on Long Island—all are now under the Park Service management. Each has a different type of administrative policy and we permit the visitor to do different things in each of these areas. We'll have boating, hunting, fishing, swimming, and various kinds of activities in the recreational areas, where we might have only what we call day-use activities in a historical park. In Gettysburg National Military Park, picnicking is allowed during the day but we don't have any overnight camping. So there are various types of area manage-ment policy.

Ochsner: One other thing I want to point out about our three types of areas is that they aren't purely historical, or purely recreational, or purely natural.

Mixed?

Ochsner: Well, I mean within one area there's overlap. But one particular designation is applied to the whole area because the majority of the activities permitted there fall in one of the three categories. The Blue Ridge Parkway, for example, is certainly a scenic, scientific area. It's got a lot of scenic, scientific values. And it has a lot of historical, cultural values, too. And yet its primary designation is as a recreation area.

Does each have similar personnel, or are there specialists in certain areas? In other words, could you transfer skilled personnel readily among these areas?

Tammaru: We have had a history, especially lately, for quite a mobile organization. Our park rangers, park naturalists, historians, and archaeologists have been quite mobile from area to area. We don't preclude a man who's been a park ranger in a natural area from becoming a park ranger in a recreation area. We do send them there. The only thing we expect is that they understand the differences in management policies.

Ochsner: One of the things we ought to point out about our policies, too, is that they're permissive policies—they're stated in a permissive manner.

You, perhaps like the Forest Service, apply a policy of decentralization?

Ochsner: Actually, this is one of the things we're more specifically interested in right now for many of our activities. Some things centralize when technology affects them; other things, when human communications are involved, are often decentralized.

May we turn now to a topic which confronts most agency administrators: pressure groups—or, in your case, conservation groups. With what outside pressures are you involved, and do the pressures sometimes come in to meet you?

Ochsner: The thing that immediately pops into mind, of course, are the conservation clubs and this sort of thing. . . .

National Recreation Association?

Ochsner: Well, the National Recreation and Park Association and NRA too—I don't know if they're combined now, or not. We have right up here at 17th and Pennsylvania the National Recreation and Park Association. That's more of a professional type of thing, but the Sierra Club, the Wilderness Society, the Wildlife Federation are the ones that usually come to mind as directly connected with the activities of the Park Service.

Tammaru: There is also the Association of Park Executives.

Ochsner: Yes. In a sense, these are pressure groups on us to keep us in line, but I like to look at them as supporters, because really that's what they are. They give us a lot of flak and we get up in arms, you know, but they are our friends, too. A few weeks ago I was in a training course and we had a representative from one of these organizations. Actually, he's a free-lancer and a seminar leader: Michael Fromm. He was berating us for not *using* criticism, not being able to use it constructively. And, in a sense, I guess that's true. What we often forget about are the pressure groups that are *not* conservation organizations—construction, road-building groups— you name it.

Tammaru: Rotary Clubs, too. We are interested in these types of city organizations. We need to influence them because of their influence on the parks locally. The park becomes a part of the community. You can't divorce them, you know, and merely say, "We are a National Park—don't bother us, we won't bother you." This is where the congressional influence assumes a major role.

Do you have an overall public relations program, or does each park have its own?

Ochsner: We feel that each park *is* a public relations program. And the superintendent, especially, is *the* key public relations official within a park.

Do you criss-cross with other agencies? I am thinking of the Forest Service and other agencies in the Departments of Agriculture and Interior.

Ochsner: We cooperate closely with the Bureau of Indian Affairs in the southwest, more and more right now. We know a fellow who's a consultant—he's working on a training program to provide underprivileged, teen-age Indian children with work in parks this summer, as part of their— kind of, what do we call it?

Tammaru: Summer job-training.

Ochsner: Yes.

Internship?

Ochsner: Life-enlargement sort of thing.

Tammaru: Other agencies with which we have contact are the Bureau of Reclamation and the Corps of Engineers. We have many contiguous areas where their boundaries—that is, of the Forest Service and others— meet ours. Naturally, if we are doing our job, we know what they're doing and we're keeping up effective interrelationships so that we don't duplicate somewhere, or the public doesn't get cheated out of its due from the federal government.

Ochsner: For many years, though, we've been accused of being preservationist. Good or bad, that's the label. Some think that's a good thing to be called. . . .

It's at least an honorable term.

Ochsner: Yes, but it's this business of locking up again—locking up resources so that they can't be used by people, or by loggers or by mining companies . . . this sort of thing.

The Forest Service and the Park Service are both considered elite groups. Does this help your efforts to recruit personnel? Your seniority system must be a powerful inducement—and the fact of being involved in a meaningful program. How big is the Park Service?

Tammaru: We have approximately 7000 permanent people, and then we have a seasonal work-force that comes, during the peak of the visitation period, to ten or eleven thousand.

As an old-line agency, the Park Service must command public respect, and I should think that would make your job somewhat easier at the park level. It has permanent respect from those who use it—and yet you still run into difficulties in relating people, technology, and the concept of the park.

Ochsner: I think we run into difficulties because the usual visitor to a park doesn't really know what *his* effect on that park is. He throws away a piece of paper—does it unconsciously, as if he's on a city street. They don't do it unconsciously throughout Europe—there's a big difference there.

I know they sweep the streets in Europe more often.

Ochsner: They don't throw down as many papers, either. Let me give you an example. Occasionally, we see people throwing papers out of their cars or leaving a mess in a picnic ground, or something like that. When this happens and we speak to them, you see enlightenment all over their faces. I've done this many times—go over and pick up the trash, take it back to the visitors and say: "Would you do this in your own backyard." No, they wouldn't. One of our missions is to get visitors to realize that this *is* their backyard, or front yard, whenever they're in a national park.

Recently I read in the Monitor series on the national parks a statement by Secretary Udall: "We are going to develop our parks only to what each can bear or stand." How will this policy be implemented?

Ochsner: I think this gets into the area of "carrying capacity." And we're beginning to really face some problems here in finding out what this is, say, for Yosemite Valley.

In terms of people, cars, trailers?

Ochsner: Right. We've kind of anticipated this in some new parks. For instance, the North Cascade proposal has the whole thing roadless—just no roads at all in the wilderness portions. This may be the innovator for the National Park Service in tramways to scenic points of view.

A ski-lift type of thing?

Ochsner: Right.

This would be dramatic . . . and expensive.

Ochsner: In the long run, I don't think it's as expensive as the use of automobiles, perhaps. We're faced with the same problems cities have in many places: overcrowding with people and automobiles. Yosemite Valley, for example, is an urban problem, in this respect—we have rape, we have murder, we have burglary, we have fatal accidents—we have the whole bit. And that's just eight square miles. Except perhaps for slums, we have many urban problems to cope with.

You're as concerned and unhappy as any professional planner on this score. Will there eventually have to be some restriction of admission?

Ochsner: California State Parks have already done that—you have to reserve your place there. I don't see any reason why we won't get to that some day.

Accept a reservation limited to a certain period of time?

Tammaru: That's right.

Ochsner: We do that now with camping on most of our camp grounds.

In connection with these problems, is fire a continuing threat?

Ochsner: Fire is turning out, in some respects, to be a very interesting subject. We are now beginning to recognize the management value of wild fire. There are places, there are environments, there are ecosystems which *require* fire in order to be perpetuated. Among them are the giant sequoia groves in California. Based on the best research that we have so far, they exist *because* of fire. But now, since they've become national parks, we have excluded fire from those areas—and the other trees, which the fires wiped out, so that sequoias could grow, are beginning to exclude the new growth of sequoias to replace the old growth.

So fire has a plus side.

Ochsner: Very much a plus side. So now we're going to have a problem in overcoming the Smokey the Bear image!

Are there live, wild animals in most parks? Where, for example, would I go to see a brown bear?

Ochsner: It all depends on how hard you really want to see one—how much effort you wish to put in.

Are there species of vanishing, wild animals roaming about in the parks?

Ochsner: Grizzly bears, wolves, cougars. . . .

In most parks?

Ochsner: No, not in most parks.

You had a certain park in mind?

Ochsner: Well, Yellowstone and Glacier have the biggest population of grizzly bears left in the country. There are still wolves—I guess they're mostly in Alaska, now—we have a natural population there. In Isle Royale National Park there's a very fascinating relationship between wolves and elk which are in natural balance. It's the predator-prey relationship which is going on—naturally, for the most part.

If I had visited what might have been a typical park a hundred years ago, and one tomorrow, and then one a hundred years hence—do you think there will be more changes in the next hundred years, than, let's say, since 1865, or so? Is the future likely to be the period of your greatest administrative problems?

Ochsner: That's a real hard question because it goes back to some of this business that Mati was talking about: political pressure. For instance, in Yellowstone National Park, wolves have not been reported for many years, but there's just the barest seed of a possibility—discussion, probing —of putting wolves back in the park. But, of course, there's a tremendous neighborhood pressure against them. There are the sheep ranchers, cattle ranchers, hunting fraternities who perhaps don't quite understand the role of wolves. If we could put a fence around the park I suppose they might not care.

The Park Service seems to have every kind of administrative problem: headquarters-field relationships, centralization, delegation, human relations, coordination, authority, responsibility, public relations, pressure groups. How did the task force develop—if we could turn to that. What were the main problems? What ignited the research—dissatisfaction with the directions of the Park Service? What might have happened without the task force? What do you hope it may prove?

Tammaru: Let me take one of these questions at a time. I think one of the factors that ignited the task force could be considered an internal factor. Many of our people were hired during the thirties, during the Civilian Conservation Corps days, and, of course, many entered in the early forties. A good many have moved up in the management ranks and have achieved fairly high status in the organization. Lately, I think we've experienced an exodus from the top. And I think, just as any other agency, we are facing the need for fresh, new, talented blood to take on these management roles at the top.

From within?

Tammaru: Yes. And a lot faster than we have done it in the past, because I think we are finding a comparative vacuum in certain age levels and experience levels which we haven't had in the past.

Is this an aspect of manpower planning?

Tammaru: Manpower planning is very definitely part of our task-force consideration. Another thing which triggered our activity was the need to take a look at what our people are doing *right now*. We have been going out and recruiting college graduates as rangers, naturalists, historians, archaeologists. And yet, when they get on the job, much of their college training really isn't being used.

As Dave said: "We are at this point in time; we are a people-serving type of organization." We do have a mission of environmental education. But many of the people we've been recruiting have come because of the mystique—I guess we call it—of the Park Service: big trees, tall mountains, beautiful lakes.

Another sad fact is that the Park Service has changed. It's not a sad fact, perhaps, so much as a fact of growth and expansion. We find that over half of our Park Service total employment is east of the Mississippi. You'd never think so but that's the fact. Our parks, areas, historical monuments, recreation areas that have been growing up in the last ten years have, in many cases, been eastern areas. We need people with a particular, perhaps a different view of life from those who have been seeking the natural areas in the West—like Yellowstone, Rocky Mountain and Sequoia-King's Canyon. These are some of the factors.

Ochsner: We're also interested in some of these concepts of job enlargement such as Rensis Likert has been preaching—which to me are very exciting things. I personally think the whole Park Service should get excited about these.

> *From what Mati has said, the generalist rather than the technician might be the solution to the recruitment issue. Training on-the-job in the Park Service would be, I guess, almost three times as important as in a downtown Washington government agency. The parks man is on his own, and the qualities of foresight and independent resourcefulness are certainly to be encouraged. How do you discover the potential in those who are, as you put it, after the mystique, and does this vanish as they get on-the-job?*

Tammaru: No, I think the mystique has lasted; it's one of the strengths of the Park Service. We have a very good retention rate. But we also have the problem of moving these people through the channel of promotion to a level at which we would like to have them work—where we know their capabilities are used fully—instead of leaving them at lower-level jobs where they are not challenged to their maximum.

Ochsner: One of the points we've got to keep in mind is that it's the guy in uniform, talking to the visitor, who's the most important interface of this whole business. For want of a better term, he is the lower-grade employee doing the technician type of work. Professionals in the Park Service contact other professionals all the time—at the universities, professional societies, and so on. We carry on this sort of thing all the time, and have for years. The technician's job is to understand the visitor and relate to him, show him his place in the park.

Does the Park Service have a limited range of different types of jobs? You have mentioned rangers and superintendents.

Ochsner: We don't have a limited range—we have engineers, designers, museum curators, audiovisual specialists. Perhaps you meant depth.

Yes, that's it.

Tammaru: Our greatest depth is in what we call the uniformed service, from a professional standpoint—rangers, naturalists, and so on. We plan to consolidate this occupational growth, especially for those entering the system from the bottom. This is for professionals coming into the Park Service—meaning men with a college degree, or better. Also, there must be a better career ladder on which these people can move up as rapidly as they show progress. Naturally, there are going to be levelling-off points at various stages in the game for different people. Right now, what we have is a tight pyramid and it's quite narrow in spots. There are bottlenecks which we want to open up. This is one of the reasons we need to add another profession at the lower level; it is going to be multidisciplinary —aide and technician—where our common denominator is the Park Service.

This will be, then, the new classification?

Tammaru: Correct—the new classification we are proposing. We will take a multitude of different activities, being done in all the parks—whether in fire control, soil conservation work, public contact, collecting entrance fees and generally providing visitors' services. We will call all of it park work instead of having little segments of occupational categories throughout the entire Service. This approach unclogs career channels and lets people on the jobs see what opportunities exist for them. We are trying to get away from the assembly-line type of operation and the monotony which results.

How has the task force done, in your judgment, in terms of measured results—or is it too soon to say?

Ochsner: We're just starting to get results.

Tammaru: We're quite encouraged about our work so far. Our approach, from the very beginning, has been to secure wide participation rather than the edict approach—you *shall* do. We've used discussion to obtain an understanding between those in the field and ourselves. I think this has paid dividends.

It may be a slower approach than the alternative one, but we feel that it will provide us with a better program in the long run. People will assume this project as a personal mission. Many organizational changes, or reorganizations, often take place overnight with somebody making a big announcement. This is one program where the man on the firing line knows about the upcoming changes before they are made. We have been open, as

I said, and candid, and I would estimate a good 60 percent of the people in the Park Service are with us at this point.

What changes would you like to see in the Park Service so that certain goals will be attained?

Tammaru: For one thing, we're looking for a growth and perhaps a revitalization of our management principles, as well as for management talent. This is one real change we're looking for through this task force. We're also looking for a better orientation of our decentralized operations toward the centralized aspects of our responsibility—giving the field manager a better line of communication to both those below and above him.

From a personnel standpoint I would add that we're looking for the college graduate coming in—and, in very plain terms, getting a better shake for his money, having a career to work towards at the management level.

Did you have anything to add, Dave?

Ochsner: I would just reiterate that job enlargement, I think, is one of the main issues. On a related topic there is communication. More and more, since I've been in this work, I see organizational and communications problems as pretty much synonymous. The one we want to improve is the face-to-face kind of communication.

STUDY QUESTIONS

1. How can a balance be struck between conservation administration and the advocates of more commercial uses of our resources? To what extent does national park administration differ from other types of public administration?
2. What lessons might be taken from the methods of the study team and its follow-up task force? What is your estimate of the stages of implementation?
3. What are the strengths and weaknesses of the personnel program as practiced by the Park Service? What types of training are most appropriate for Park Service generalists?
4. How effective have the pressure groups been in support of Park Service goals?

7

TRANSFER OF THE EMPLOYMENT SERVICE

The summons from the White House came as no great surprise to the Assistant Secretary of Labor. The President's appointments secretary had merely said, "The President would like to see you and the head of the Social Security Board tomorrow at 11 o'clock. He wants to discuss the Employment Service issue." The Assistant Secretary, on the other end of the wire, had merely said, "Yes," he would be there. It really wasn't necessary to ask more.

The year was 1939. America was already "the arsenal of the democracies" in the war that Hitler had started the year before. In Washington it was a time of administrative reorganization following the Brownlow Committee report of 1937. Recommendations had been made for reorganizing the executive branch of the federal government, and most agencies in Washington were all-ajitter, wondering who was going to be next and whether their organization was on the agenda.

Since the assistant secretary was responsible for organizational matters in the Labor Department, he had naturally been doing more than his share of worrying. His was a four-way job: (1) To coordinate the bureaus in the department (the units where reorganization would be involved if the lightning should strike). (2) To head the departmental Committee on Future Legislation, which he had set up after joining the agency in 1938. (3) To act as liaison with labor unions, employees' organizations, and other governmental organizations influencing the Labor Department's work. (4) To complete the internal reorganization of the Immigration and Naturalization Service, which had proved a time-consuming job. At first, this last duty took most of his time, because he was supposed to decide "personally" every case of exclusion or deportation coming to the department on appeal, and there were literally thousands in a year's time. But that burden had been reduced when the Board of Immigration Appeals was set up, at his instigation, to decide all except the few cases that the government or the losing party chose to have decided by the assistant secretary himself.

Once reorganization became the topic of Washington gossip, the assistant secretary tried to figure out which bureaus in his department might be vulnerable. The Brownlow Committee report had merely stated that the Department of Labor should be assured of those programs that were "needed." But this was surely an ambiguous test. The Immigration Service was "needed," from one point of view, because if immigration was not controlled, labor's wages and standards would be threatened; that was why Immigration was placed in the Labor Department when that agency was created in 1913.[1] But perhaps it was not "essential," which must have been what the Brownlow Committee meant.

The other bureaus in the Labor Department *did* appear to be essential: the Children's Bureau,[2] the Bureau of Labor Statistics, the Woman's Bureau, the United States Conciliation Service, the Division of Public Contracts, the Wage and Hour Division, the Bureau of Labor Standards. But the most indisputably essential of all—or so supposed the assistant secretary as he collected his thoughts following the White House call—was the U.S. Employment Service.

The USES had been one of the first and one of the most successful of the New Deal agencies. The Wagner-Peyser Act of 1933 that, among other things, created the USES was a landmark in the history of organized labor. Labor had worked for the legislation and was proud of it. What could be more essential to a labor department than a system of free employment offices, in all the then forty-eight states, energetically trying to bring job opportunities and the unemployed together? Indeed, in the table

---

[1] Before that, from 1891, the Immigration and Naturalization Service was in the Treasury Department; in 1903 it was transferred to the Department of Commerce and Labor; when that department was separated into Commerce and Labor in 1913, it became part of the Labor Department; and by a reorganization order of 1940, it was transferred from the Labor Department to the Department of Justice, where it is today.

[2] Later, however, this bureau was transferred to the Federal Security Agency, and eventually went with the FSA to the Department of Health, Education and Welfare when that department was created.

of contents of the Department of Labor's Annual Report for 1938, roughly half of the space was devoted to the U.S. Employment Service. Surely "they" would not attempt to take "that" away from the department.

Besides, the Department of Labor was small—the smallest in Washington at that time. The total national work force in 1939 was 33 million, and a fourth of them were organized in unions, but the department's budget was only $25 million. By contrast, with only 11½ million farmers and farm workers, the Department of Agriculture's appropriation was $1.5 billion, or 60 times as much as Labor's.

Nevertheless, at a recent cocktail party the Assistant Secretary of Labor had learned from an "otherwise unimpeachable source" that the transfer of the Employment Service from the Department of Labor to the Social Security Board was being actively considered by the Bureau of the Budget, where reorganization proposals were initiated. Under the procedures, the recommendation would be presented to Congress, and if there was no objection within 90 days, would be effected by the President.

The ax had not yet fallen, but after the phone call from the White House, the assistant secretary began to think that perhaps it was about to. He had already done everything he could think of to ward off this disaster. After he first got word of what was contemplated by the Bureau of the Budget, he had made a personal call on William Green, then head of the American Federation of Labor, and on John L. Lewis, head of the Congress of Industrial Organizations, both of whom promised strong support for retaining the Employment Service in the Department of Labor. Then he had approached the railroad labor unions, and they were also sympathetic. All of these groups had legislative representatives on the Hill, and organized labor's influence in Washington just then was especially strong.

A division within the Employment Service dealt with farm labor, so the Assistant Secretary had then approached the Secretary of Agriculture, who promised to lend his support too. Next, there had been calls on the U.S. Chamber of Commerce, the National Association of Manufacturers, and the General Contractors of America (this last being one of the largest users of the Employment Service), and all had said they were well satisfied with the Employment Service and wanted it kept in the Department of Labor.

Finally, another division of the Employment Service dealt with veterans' problems, and the American Legion was known to have strong political influence in Congress. It turned out that the Legion's legislative representative, a Colonel Taylor—who always carried a cane and wore a bow tie—was strong in support of keeping the Employment Service where it was.

This seemed like a formidable enough phalanx of pressure-group support, so perhaps there was nothing to be feared. At any rate, the "homework" had been done. Of course, the Chairman of the Social Security

Board had been doing his "homework," too. The only thing now was to wait and see what the President had on his mind.

The President was affable the next day, but then he usually was, even when his cares were greatest. He sat behind his desk with its familiar mementos on it, and relaxed easily in his swivel chair. The assistant secretary and the Chairman of the Social Security Board were seated by his desk.

President: I hear tell you two have been feuding, and we try to maintain a happy ship. Both of you have been trying to gain support for your desire to have the Employment Service and it has been talked about all over Washington.

With these words, President Franklin D. Roosevelt changed his smile to a look of parental displeasure, and it was apparent that beneath his benign countenance the "old Dutch" had been aroused. The adversaries looked at each other and smiled. They were good friends, and anything they had done to gain support was merely part of their jobs, or at least so it seemed to them.

President: Now I'd like you both to tell me, in your own words, why you think the Employment Service should remain where it is or be transferred to Social Security. Which of you wants to speak first?

The Chairman of the Social Security Board signalled that the Assistant Secretary of Labor should speak first.

Assistant Secretary: This is our most important bureau because it puts people in touch with jobs. It ties in with everything else we do. We believe that the Employment Service has done a heroic job in helping relieve unemployment. We don't see how we could operate a department of labor without it.

The President had turned around in his swivel chair, looking out a window, when the assistant secretary started to speak, and remained that way, thinking. It was not discourteous; he was merely reflecting, as a judge might do.

Turning, he faced the chairman and said, "Well, brother, now it's your turn." Again he turned his back and listened.

Chairman: We want to combine the Employment Service with the Bureau of Unemployment Compensation. The latter is costing the taxpayer a great deal of money. We think the two services should occupy adjoining offices in the field, so that when a man collects his unemployment insurance, he can go across the hall and see about getting a job. But if this is going to be done, we think they should also be brought together in Washington, under the Social Security Board.

President (turning back to his desk): Well, what do you say to that?

Assistant Secretary: In the field, they are already in adjoining offices, for the most part. We agree that this is desirable. But if they were to be completely merged, we believe that the Employment Service would suffer. It's a case of the agency with the most employees and the larger budget dominating the smaller one. Besides, they have different purposes and out-looks. The Employment Service must be aggressive and sales-minded. It must go out and get the jobs. Unemployment Compensation, on the other hand, is just the reverse: It tries to get rid of the clients and to discourage them from staying on insurance when they don't need to. Its attitude is negative, sort of like a banker's when you ask him for a loan. We think that if the two agencies were merged, the banker mentality would over-shadow the entrepreneurial outlook.

President: Entrepreneurial, is it? Sounds like Schumpeter. Now let's see if I understand what you two are driving at. You both want a blend, as we call it in Dutchess County. You want cooperation, not separateness, but in one case you prefer complete merger and in the other you favor separateness in Washington but physical proximity in the field. Is that right?

Both men nodded.

President: Well, I don't know what the best solution is. I see argu-ments both ways. I don't want to injure the Employment Service, but at the same time I want Unemployment Compensation to be efficient, instead of encouraging people to stay on it.

Chairman: I guess we all agree on objectives. The only difference between us is what constitutes the best method. And as you can see, we both have strong convictions about the organizational decision.

President: All right, I'll think about it. But in the meantime, I don't want any more squabbling in the family.

The two men left and had lunch together, as good friends as ever.

The blow fell on March 25, 1939, when a headline in *The Washington Post* announced: "Employment Service to be Transferred." The Bureau of the Budget and the President had apparently made up their minds.

What to do then? Attempt to apply more pressure? The President had forbidden it. The only hope, therefore, if the Labor Department was to keep the Employment Service, would be for the pressure groups that had promised their support to speak their pieces on the Hill where the decision could still be overturned.

Meeting shortly after this, the Chairman of the Social Security Board remarked to the Assistant Secretary of Labor, "Well, they can't say you didn't give it the old college try. You lined up enough pressure-group support to win, but it wasn't the right kind."

Assistant Secretary: No. What do you mean?

Chairman: Well, in our work we have an association of unemployment insurance officials. They are close to the political scene in their states, and from time to time they have been coming to Washington and taking the occasion to call on their senators and congressmen. They are on close terms with most of them. We didn't engineer this, but in some cases [smiling] they did combine these visits with official duties in Washington.

Assistant Secretary: Well, that's one for the books. Government battles are *supposed* to be won by pressure groups having the most troops and the biggest budgets. I guess this inside-track thing introduces a new principle of pressure politics.

Compared with the hearing before the President, the one before the Ways and Means Committee of the House of Representatives was unglamorous and routine. It lasted about an hour, with both agencies represented. Prepared statements were submitted in advance, short and to the point. The chairman of the committee indicated that his personal interest was largely in costs and possible savings. "Our committee finds that mergers don't always result in savings, by any means, but generally we're in favor of trying it, in the hope that they will." That night the assistant secretary went home with the feeling that the battle had indeed been lost.

The transfer of the USES to the Social Security Board was officially consummated on July 1, 1939, as part of Reorganization Plan I. The functions of the Employment Service were consolidated with those of Unemployment Compensation Division to constitute the Bureau of Employment Security. The Employment Service thereupon was absorbed and lost its identity.

Later, meeting a congressman who had favored keeping the Employment Service in the Department of Labor, the Assistant Secretary asked him how a phalanx of the Big Three (Commerce, Labor, and Agriculture) could have been beaten by a single pressure group consisting of government employees.

"There are a number of reasons," he said. "First, the chairmen of the Ways and Means and Appropriations committees thought some money could be saved. Second, the Labor Department is not very popular with the conservatives in the House and Senate, anyway. Third—and most important—Unemployment Compensation is a state program and Employment Service is a federal one, and most members of Congress favor states' rights when they think it won't cost them anything, politically. Then, too— and this may be as important as anything—most of 'your' [meaning the assistant secretary's] pressure groups contented themselves with writing letters, whereas the state people, when they came to Washington, buttonholed their congressmen and put the screws on."

He concluded: "It isn't always the *amount* of pressure that counts; it's the *effectiveness* of it. Remember, many of those who were doing the buttonholing were put in office directly, or indirectly, by many of these key congressmen in the first place."

"But the organizational decision? Didn't they consider the merits of it?"

"Yes, perhaps. But to most congressmen a complete merger always looks like a chance to save taxpayers' money, and they aren't often inclined to delve into the question of what the administrative consequences are likely to be—they assume *that's* a matter for the executive branch."

We now leap over almost three years to mid-1942, less than two years after Pearl Harbor and three months after the creation of the War Manpower Commission. Established by Executive Order in April 1942, within the Office of Emergency Management, the War Manpower Commission was charged with assuming the most effective mobilization of the nation's manpower for war.

Every agency in Washington having important manpower interests was represented on the Commission: Defense, Selective Service, railroads and other transportation, and shipbuilding, among others—all the major industries involved in the war. The former Assistant Secretary of Labor, now in a new job as head of the Recruitment and Manning Organization of the War Shipping Administration, was an alternate member of the Commission and attended regularly.

At a meeting in August 1942, the Chairman of the War Manpower Commission was speaking:

Chairman: Our greatest problem has been that we have had to reorganize the Employment Service. This meant separating it from Unemployment Insurance and moving it from the Federal Security Agency to the Commission. The President has agreed to this.

The Employment Service is the key to everything we do. It knows all the skills that are needed; it has the registers, the offices, the know-how. In fact, all the work of the War Manpower Commission must be built around an expanded U.S. Employment Service. We could not duplicate it. It would take too long and we might lose the war in the interim.

If only it hadn't been merged with another agency in the first place, our job would be easier. I suppose the reasons were compelling at the time, but look what happened. No one in the Employment Service had any real authority. Its former head, Bill Stead, left right away and went back to teaching. The professionals soon became discouraged. Many quit and went into private employment.

A function that has become scrambled, as this has, is hard to sort out afterwards. But that is what we must do. Our number one priority, therefore, is to rebuild the Employment Service as quickly and as efficiently as we possibly can. All the work of the Commission will depend upon how speedily and efficiently we do that job.

The President's Executive Order transferring the Employment Service to the War Manpower Commission was dated September 17, 1942.

As the former Assistant Secretary of Labor walked out of the board room of the War Manpower Commission that August day, he again found himself musing:

Well, I'll be damned. The same President makes the transfer in both cases. I wonder what kind of "blend" it was in this case. Probably not known in Dutchess County.

Do you suppose the decision could have been "right" in both cases? It clearly is right during the war, as the Chairman of the War Manpower

Commission argued. And General Clay, Donald Nelson,[3] and all the others said they agreed with him.

Perhaps there's one rule for one time and a different rule for another. And with that he went home, with the feeling that the war was already as good as won.

Editor's Addendum: In 1945 at the end of World War II, the Employment Service was returned to the Department of Labor, "to be administered as an organizational entity." By act of Congress in 1948, however, it was transferred back to the Federal Security Agency, again to function as a part of the Bureau of Employment Security in the Social Security Administration. The latest chapter was written a year later, in 1949, when, by Reorganization Plan 2, the Bureau of Employment Security, which includes *both* the Employment Service and Unemployment Compensation, again became a part of the U.S. Department of Labor, where, so far, they have remained.

STUDY QUESTIONS

1. What principle or principles of organization would you say apply to this problem?
2. On whose side would you have been in the dispute, and why?
3. Can pressure-group activity be overdone in administration? Explain why.
4. How would you have decided the issue if you had been President? What has been the experience of the Employment Service since the end of World War II?

---

[3] Former head of Sears, Roebuck in Chicago and then head of the War Production Board.

8
STAFF-LINE

These four cases concern the process of staff and line collaboration in the New York City departments of Purchase, Health, Buildings, Fire, and Public Works. They illustrate how staff and line team together in the solution of a common problem.

Purchase and Health Departments

This specific case is based on efforts to simplify certain paperwork involved in purchasing supplies, materials, and equipment for the City of New York. The step-by-step process in the development of an improved system of requisitioning commodities clearly indicates the interrelationship of line and staff in two municipal departments: Purchase and Health. The principals involved in the study were the Management Analysis unit in Purchase, the warehouse of the Purchase Department that supplies city agencies with drugs, textiles, crockery, dental and laboratory items, and the Purchase Programming and Data Processing Units. The Health Department is concerned through its purchasing section and the organization and methods section.

For several years the Health Department had been coping with a difficult paperwork problem caused by the requisitioning of supplies by hundreds of clinics and custodial services under its jurisdiction. Programs of the department embrace school health clinics, dental clinics, TB clinics, and social hygiene, among others, and the primary supply problems involved these clinics. As health programs expanded through the years, the volume of paperwork correspondingly increased. The system of requisitioning supplies, prior to the investigation, had had its impact not only on the clerical work in both departments, but on the materials-handling workload of the Purchase warehouses. A typical procedure for the requisitioning of clinic supplies involved the following steps.

A Health Department employee in a clinic prepared a requisition on a form supplied by the department, listing in longhand the items and quantities requested. The three major categories were drugs and sundries, stationery, and custodial or cleaning supplies. All items requested by the clinics were stocked in one or more Purchase warehouse. For purposes of this study, description of the process will be limited to the request for items in the drug, pharmaceutical, or laboratory supplies. These are stocked in a central Purchase warehouse in the Borough of Queens. A nurse, for example, in a specific clinic (say, school health), in requesting items, listed them in no particular order, and her description of them often varied according to her knowledge or conception of them. Although each item in the Purchase warehouse carried a stock code (or commodity code number), such numbers at times were either omitted or inaccurately listed. In short, there was a lack of uniformity, standardization of nomenclature, and systematic overall method.

Next, the requisitions, prepared by the various nurses, were transmitted by groups of users to the central purchasing office of Health, according to a predetermined schedule. For example, the 1500 school health clinic requisitions were scheduled for submission on a given date, dental clinics at another time, and so on.

The central purchasing office of the Health Department checked these requisitions to insure that all clinics, in a given group, were accounted for and correct descriptions, stock code numbers, and so on were furnished. In addition, requisitions were screened by the main office to safeguard against ordering of excessive amounts by the clinics. Checking of these items as to accuracy of description and quantities was a formidable task, and inevitably errors were made. After an overall review, each item was priced on the basis of the last price charged by the Purchase Department. Next, each separate item, on each requisition, was extended to indicate the total cost per item based on quantity ordered. Each requisition, prepared by each nurse in the clinic, was copied, or typed, on a carbon-interleaved form. This showed the description of items, quantity ordered, unit price, total cost, and the overall total cost for all items combined on one requisition. Proper budget codes were inserted and each requisition was then signed and countersigned to certify the need for the items and availability of funds.

To consolidate the requisitions by borough or health district, a tally sheet was prepared for each group of clinics. For example, after the requisitions were typed and signed for each of the 180 dental clinics, a tally sheet was prepared in longhand showing how much of each item each clinic requisitioned, plus a summary. In short, a clerk would enter, next to the item, Gauze, Steri Pads 2 × 2, the quantities of that specific item requested by each clinic, and then the total amount for that district or borough.

Requisitions for a group of clinics, together with the tally sheets, were then sent to the Department of Health's Accounting Bureau for verification of availability of funds. From this latter unit, the requisitions were sent to the Purchase warehouse. At this point, the warehouse personnel encountered so many difficulties in checking the tally sheets against the individual requisitions that a mimeographed form was developed. This listed all items, in alphabetical order, according to the specific stock section wherever the items were stocked. This form was the first attempt to substitute order for chaos, and it provided the impetus for the overall survey. On this form, warehouse personnel tallied each requisition for each borough and verified amounts requested.

The Purchase Department had made, over the years, abortive efforts to work out a solution with the central purchasing agency of Health. The single employee then in charge of the coordination and review of clinic and custodial requisitions resisted all attempts to revise the system. His argument ran: "Things have always been done this way—if you wish to make changes, wait until I retire." This line man turned a deaf ear to any staff proposals or, in daily practice, negated those adopted by higher levels. Staff failed to persuade him of the dividends such change would produce.

About two years ago, owing to retirements, deaths, or other separations from service, the purchasing section of the Department of Health had to be almost completely restaffed. The new supervisor and his staff had not only to learn about the purchasing function but to cope with the staggering volume of clerical work. At the new supervisor's request and the request of the Queens storehouse, the Department of Purchase called a "problem-solving" conference. The Management Analysis Unit of the Department of Purchase, a staff unit reporting to the Commissioner of Purchase, was requested to coordinate the project. The storehouse (line) personnel became active participants, because they had encountered first-hand the problems stemming from the clinic requisitions and had made the first move toward developing a partial solution.

The Programming and Data Processing Division of the Department of Purchase, a staff unit, became a major participant, since the problem seemed to have a potential for solution by computer application. This division, together with the Management Analysis unit, had for some time been planning for automation of the stores requisitioning· process. The Health Department was a "natural" for such an activity, for two reasons: (1) multiple delivery points were involved and (2) each delivery point requisitions a fairly standard complement of Purchase stock items. The Health Department purchasing section (combination of line and staff) and the Organization and Methods units of Health (purely staff) rounded out the conference.

One of the first actions taken was to develop forms in order to simplify and standardize the requisitioning of clinic supplies. The Purchase warehouse personnel supplied copies of the forms they had developed in an attempt to simplify their materials handling problems. They also supplied the Department of Health with experience records showing which items were actively requisitioned and the quantities ordered. The Department of Health sifted through these items and, with the approval of the program heads, developed a list of standard items that a given group of clinics would be allowed to requisition. Then, a printed requisition form was developed with the item descriptions, item numbers, units of measure, and appropriate columns for listing quantities needed. In the process of developing standard requisitions, the warehouse, after discussions with the Health representatives, was able to discontinue stocking many items that had been kept solely for the clinics. Each nurse in each of the 1500 school health Clinics, for example, now simply fills in the quantities requested for each of the items listed. There is no possible room for errors in either stock code numbers or descriptions. Further, the nurse knows that she is limited to ordering these items only. Also, the new requisition form has eliminated requests for items in other than standard packaging units. Before, she did not know, for example, that gauze pads are packed 100 to a package, and so she might have requested 50.

These requisitions flow from the clinics to the central purchasing office of Health, as they did formerly, where they are reviewed as to excessive quantities but need no longer be edited as to description or unit of issue, nor do they need to be priced.

Once the clinic requisitions have been reviewed by Purchasing as to quantities ordered, they are sent to the Organization and Methods Unit, IBM section. There, IBM cards are keypunched or gangpunched—one card for each item for each clinic. The computer and IBM sections of Purchase and Health, working together, developed a location digit code for every health clinic and delivery point in the city. This location code, the item description, expense account number, and quantity requested for each item are all punched on an IBM card according to a layout used in the Department of Purchase. The Department of Health developed procedures for keypunching and gangpunching cards, which are then forwarded to the Department of Purchase, data processing division, where they are priced, totals extended, and printouts of six-part requisition forms produced by the computer. The computer also produces a consolidated requisition for each borough or health district to ease the work of the warehouse in assembling the items for shipment. The computer is so programmed that each consolidated requisition not only gathers the items for better materials handling but also shows the total cost of the items for each borough or health district. These total costs are then cleared with the Department of Health accounting section. As the requisition flows from the nurse in the clinic through to its destination point in the warehouse, *not a single item is typed, priced, or totaled. Tally sheets have been completely eliminated.* Editing of Department of Health requisitions by the Department of Purchase has been reduced to a minimum.

To date, the following clinics are requisitioning under the new system:

Type of Clinic	Number of Clinics	Number of Items Formerly Typed, Priced, Checked, and Audited
Child health	89	4,361
Tuberculosis	22	1,320
Dentistry	180	34,500
Social hygiene	14	1,176
Health centers	22	3,476
School health	1,500	27,000
Total items		71,833

The program is being extended in the Department of Health to all custodial services requests for cleaning and maintenance supplies. Tentative plans have been developed to purchase soaps and related items in commercial packaging more suitable for clinic use than the present packaging units.

RESULTS OF LINE AND STAFF COOPERATION

The Health Department reports the following results to date:

1. Reduction in costs of printing ($500 per year).
2. Reduction in clerical personnel (two clerks—$10,000).
3. Reduction in requisition processing time by at least 75 percent.
4. Uniformity of item number and description.
5. Elimination of retyping the requisitions.
6. Elimination of pricing the requisitions.
7. Elimination of two ledger entries (Audits and Accounts) for each requisition.

8. Improved storehouse procedure in filling requisitions.

9. Elimination of delays in processing requisitions that had resulted from erroneous pricing of the requested items. Often it had taken two weeks to revise the prices.

The success of the program in the Department of Health provided the impetus for extension of the project to other agencies with multiple delivery points. The Fire and Police Departments are now submitting their requisitions on punch cards for cleaning and maintenance supplies and stationery items. Since both of these agencies were already using standard printed requisition forms, however, with listings of regularly requisitioned item descriptions and commodity codes, the savings in these two departments are not comparable to those in the Department of Health.

The principal savings in these two departments are the elimination of pricing and totaling of prices for 10,000 items for Fire Department and 8500 items for Police. Requisitions need not be consolidated by divisions and commands as had been done formerly. Printing of requisition forms and consolidated tally sheets are no longer required, with a consequent annual saving of approximately $500 a year.

The departments of Welfare, Sanitation, and Public Works are scheduled for inclusion in the program as soon as possible. The Bureau of Purchase has expressed interest in the further development of the program to eliminate unnecessary routine work on the part of the buyers. This phase of the program involves a trial selection of repetitively purchased drug items, particularly those which are on annual open-market price agreements with a given vendor. This wider application of the punch-card system requires further discussion with the Bureau of Purchase and Accounts and Audits.

The Department of Defense section of the federal government issues a Federal Supply Catalog Identification List, which includes drugs, biologicals, and official reagents together with an index or commodity code number. This list is used for ordering supplies from the Walter Reed Army Medical Center and may be useful as a lead to the gradual coding of items purchased repetitively or requisitioned repetitively through the Bureau of Purchase. The compilation of an "open-market purchase catalog" has frequently been discussed as a desirable tool, particularly for the Department of Hospitals, for which coding of drug items alone represents a long-term project.

In sum, the willingness of line to permit staff to investigate operations and define certain inadequacies was the beginning of improved benefits for both units. Up to that time, line resisted and resented what it might term a staff invasion of its closed operations. Line had been allowed, to a large extent, its own way, and staff advice was either ignored or postponed until the evidence demanded a meaningful collaboration—another example of how pockets of operating people, throughout an organization, can vitiate the best plans of staff until information is shared and situations evaluated together.

Buildings Department

This case involves a change of organization and procedure within the Department of Buildings for the treatment of public complaints. These concern various aspects of housing conditions and range throughout twenty-five classes of possible violations, from rats to leaky roofs. Before February 1965 these complaints were phoned into the five borough offices of the department. Top staff suggestions towards better cooperation and less waste of effort by operating personnel were usually blockaded by traditional independence of borough offices, to whom centralization was a highly unpopular word. Politics, in short, can vitiate logic and reason. The idea to centralize was brought to a head by the deputy buildings commissioner although it had been considered by the former commissioner, mayor, and city administrator. As the deputy stated: "It was apparent from a logical point of view that to fully implement the idea of a central office for receiving complaints there would have to be a centralized number to the exclusion of other numbers throughout the city." One basic problem common to the five decentralized offices was that often a complaint was not directly related to Buildings, and the caller was required to place an additional call to the respective city department. The present arrangement eliminates this additional effort and expense, since all types of complaints are accepted. Information is then prepared and routed to the affected department. Besides, quite often there was a large duplication of calls from the same building or multiple dwelling (as about lack of heat or water) and these were individually recorded. By contrast, they are now consolidated and considered as one general complaint.

In the establishment of the new office, the deputy commissioner determined the number of telephones required for the increased load that centralization would entail, additional personnel to be recruited and transferred from the borough offices. Some borough employees were reassigned, others left, and several were transferred from departmental complaint sections. To develop these facts, contacts were made with the departmental statistician, immediate staff of the deputy, and telephone technicians. At first two options were considered:

1.   Require callers to make two separate calls, the first one to the borough, where a recording would ask each to call the central office.
2.   Transfer the borough call to a new central number.

The second alternative was chosen. All staff and line members agreed as to the goal and, according to the deputy, "consensus was considerable" among his advisors; indeed, "No real dissent was experienced." Two weeks after the idea was offered, the decision was made. A memorandum was prepared by the deputy and sent to the commissioner, who concurred.

The main problem was to coordinate the elimination of the borough offices with the installation of equipment in the new central complaint office. Details were implemented by the assistant commissioner, and within three weeks the telephone number was in use.

Organizationally there are 28 clerks, 8 senior clerks, and 4 supervisors. In the continuous, twenty-four-hour seven-day operation, part-timers bring this total to 135. Two sections are involved: incoming and outgoing. Complaints are registered by an operator and details noted on a complaint form. If the complaint concerns Buildings, it is routed to the outgoing section, which will inform and request action from the owner or landlord. The tenant also is called and informed as to what steps will be taken. Follow-ups are made until the case is closed. All noncompliance items are transmitted to the processing section so that forms may be prepared covering either housing, elevator, or boiler categories. These are finally sent to the computer section for coding.

Thirty phones are used for incoming and thirty for outgoing, and an average of ten calls per hour can be handled by each operator. The work load varies according to season. From October 1, 1965, through March 31, 1966, a total of 280,634 calls was received covering all varieties of complaints.

One of the most distinctive features of the new section is that all complaints may now be handled. The city resident phones only one central number, whereupon a Notice of Complaint is prepared and sent to the city agency having jurisdiction. Other forms are used to indicate numbers of referrals to such departments as air pollution, city rent and rehabilitation, fire, police, sanitation, and health.

This case combines various elements. It was the conviction of a new commissioner that several advantages would accrue from consolidation, despite the risk of political disturbances caused by removal of a going borough function. Sufficient time and effort spent on a comprehensive evaluation of the process clearly showed that other departments supported the move (as complaints are, at best, burdensome). Buildings is most often involved, and no firm case could be presented by the boroughs to retain this task. Explanations were fully made by staff personnel to all parties involved at frequent sessions. Line personnel were equally informed and their views invited. The amount of agreement, as the deputy commissioner expressed it, was "substantial."

In sum, the establishment of a worthwhile goal, shared viewpoints, strong top leadership, and collaboration in the problem of implementation produced a new section with both old and new tasks. It may be added that the commissioner is proud of this accomplishment and personally, as the writer witnessed, often visits the section and receives complaints himself. No function is closer to the public or a more preventive administrative medicine to forestall major eruptions of small complaints, neglected by a city department.

Fire Department

The problem of false fire alarms in New York City has been persistent and continuous, and recently it has been sharply on the increase. For a decade, staff and line officials have increasingly been aware of its tragic effects in loss of lives, economic costs, waste of manpower energies, and neighborhood disturbances.

At the request of Fire Commissioner Lowery, the Mayor on March 31, 1966, initiated a citywide campaign among various organizations to attack the problem with renewed strength and attempt workable solutions. The press release stated:

> Mayor Lindsay announced today that he has ordered the Police Department to cooperate fully with a Fire Department drive for the arrest and prosecution of persons who maliciously turn in false alarms. He also said that he would ask the courts to impose maximum sentences on violators.
>
> Mayor Lindsay said that he had been informed by Fire Commissioner Robeii O. Lowery that one out of every four alarms turned in today in the city was a false alarm. He noted that in 1965 the Fire Department responded to 32,895 such alarms, a 30 percent increase over the previous year. According to Commissioner Lowery, should the number of false alarms continue to increase at the same accelerating rate as they have over the past decade, they will by the end of 1966 exceed the number of actual structural fires anticipated in the city.

An adviser to the Mayor was assigned the task of coordinating a committee of nine city agencies, including the departments of Fire, Police, Water Supply-Gas-Electricity, Sanitation, Parks, Board of Education, Housing Authority, and Poverty Operations Board. A justice of the criminal court also was included. Other statements in the press noted the following:

> The Mayor said that fire-fighting facilities were already being taxed to the utmost in some areas of the city by the need to respond to false alarms. As a result, in as many as 15 hours out of some 24-hour periods, one or more areas of the city is without immediate neighborhood fire protection while companies are responding to false alarms and others are diverted to cover these areas.

Mayor Lindsay said that he shared Commissioner Lowery's belief that many lives were lost needlessly each year as a result of false alarms which pulled fire companies and equipment away from areas where actual fires occurred. In 1965 fires caused 196 deaths in the city and seven firemen were killed in line of duty. In addition, 986 persons and 1990 firemen suffered injuries.

The Mayor urged citizens to cooperate with the combined Fire and Police Department crackdown on persons willfully turning in a false alarm. He said such violators should be reported immediately to the nearest police or fire officer.

Mayor Lindsay noted that the penalty for turning in a false alarm, a misdemeanor under the Administrative and Penal Codes, is punishable by a year in prison and/or a $1000 fine.

He said details of the joint Fire and Police Department drive were being finalized.

The dimensions of this problem can be illustrated statistically. During 1965 the department responded to 32,869 out of 85,629 fires, constituting a 25 percent increase over 1964, and the first six months of 1966 continued to mark an increase. According to the chief of department, if fires continued to multiply at the same rate, the total would surpass the estimated number of structural fires for the remaining five months of 1966. In the judgment of departmental officials, various plausible explanations included:

1. Changing and deteriorating neighborhoods.
2. Shifting populations.
3. Increasing delinquent offenses.

At the first meeting of the Mayor's Committee for Control of False Alarms, April 21, 1966, the counsel to the Mayor presided. Departments represented were Parks, Public Education, Poverty Programs, Radio Station WNYC, Courts, Sanitation, and Fire. Fire Chief O'Hagan asked Judge Murtagh about court appearances of department members, problems of follow-up, and lack of essential information on sentencing. The judge indicated this all could be coordinated through the corporation counsel in order that a number of offenders could be sentenced at one time and information transmitted to the Fire Department. It was also suggested that wider publicity be given severe sentences, although the judge was not inclined to this approach. The Superintendent of Schools directed all school principals to visit local firehouses and speak with captains on coordination of preventive measures. Staff fire officials would be invited to address school audiences. Local poverty program officials would be directly involved in planning grass-roots campaigns. A weekly arrest report from Police Department would be sent to the Mayor's counsel and the false-alarm desk of the Fire Department. The Housing Authority alerted its protective staff to watch for offenders. In addition, the fire chief contacted the Recreation Division of the Parks Department so that staff speakers from Fire Department might cooperate on speeches and coordinating functions.

A month-to-month analysis for 1965 showed the heaviest concentration of false alarms in warmer months:

January	1800	May	3449	September	2840
February	1782	June	3416	October	3010
March	2350	July	3404	November	2821
April	2607	August	2823	December	2667

A total of 10 percent of apparatus accidents occurred in response to or in return from false alarms. In 1965 eleven injuries were recorded, whereas by July 1966 there were two injuries and one death. In a Bronx fire four children perished because the nearest assigned first-alarm companies were answering a false alarm at the same time as the fatal fire. It is estimated that each response to an alarm represents a cost of $1,200, based on total budget divided by number of alarms.

To discuss the problem, in March of 1966 the Fire Department arranged a conference of about 100 staff and line personnel. Various proposals were presented by both staff and line officials, with wide agreement among them:

1. *Education*
   (a) Fire Department speakers to schools, clubs, associations, and so on.
   (b) Literature: leaflets, posters, and cartoons.
   (c) TV, radio, and newspapers.
   (d) Use of films.
   (e) Children's visits to firehouses and training center.
   (f) Cooperation of agencies involved.
   (g) Studies of other fire-department experiences in U.S. and abroad.
2. *Engineering*
   (a) Boxes—relocation, removal, raising height of, installation of alerters, floodlights, redesign of outer doors, use of break glass.
3. *Enforcement*
   (a) Police Department stakeouts, use of cameras.
   (b) Increased penalties.
   (c) Use of dye.
   (d) Fire marshals assigned to court cases.
   (e) Special phone numbers for information on perpetrators.
   (f) Seek professional advice—doctors, and so on.

The program that eventually developed is considered by many experts in this field as the most intensive and ambitious anti-false-alarm campaign conducted by any city. As the chief of department claims, the approach is through education, engineering, and enforcement, with maximum participation by staff and line officials at all stages. In developing sound strategies on this entire problem, the following personnel were involved:

Staff Officers	Line Officers	Staff and Line
Chief of department	Deputy chiefs	Deputy assistant chief
Assistant chief of department	Battalion chiefs	Deputy chief
Deputy assistant chief of department	Company officers	Battalion chief

In addition to standard assignments and responsibilities the chief of department issued a detailed statement on the false-alarm program with an indefinite expiration date. Functions were allocated to various individual and organizational segments. The communications segment was charged with three main duties:

1. Notifies chief and duty staff officer whenever a serious fire follows transmittal of false alarms in identical area.
2. Informs police if there is evidence that a series of alarm boxes have been pulled by persons in vehicles.
3. Applies identification dyes and alerting devices on certain boxes. Identification dyes, however, have not been and are not currently in use on street boxes. Dyes were used, thus far, in one instance on boxes located within buildings.

The community-relations segment is concerned with school programs and Fire Department speakers for various civic and neighborhood organizations. Uniformed members of the Fire Department lecture on the problem of false alarms and the proper procedure to report fires. Articles and a wide variety of leaflets are prepared for the widest possible circulation to individuals and agencies. The main functions of other staff elements are as follows:

Management Planning This section makes field surveys and reviews false-alarm data to identify various aspects of the problem. Alarm boxes with high false-alarm incidence were plotted on borough maps according to date, time, location, and intensity of use. Characteristics of box locations were analyzed in respect to adequacy of lighting, proximity to parks and playgrounds, ease of escape, and related factors.

Fire Investigation This section acts in a semipolice capacity in regard to stakeouts, arrests, and disposition of court cases.

Personnel Management This section is responsible for welfare of personnel, evaluation of their false-alarm assignments, and arrangement for training and transfers in connection with this new program.

The tasks of individuals in various job classifications within the structural and hierarchical arrangements of the department were adjusted to the new arrangement. For example, firemen, as line people, are required to search areas where false alarms have been sounded and to ask questions in order to discover and develop leads on those who commit these offenses. At the next higher level, company officers participate in local meetings to promote and explain the program, maintain detailed records, and select first-grade firemen to represent the department in false-alarm arrest cases. Further up, company commanders maintain liaison with a cross section of area groups and agencies on an informal and official basis. They may arrange for speakers or work with the community-relations section of the department on this project. On the next rung of the administrative ladder, battalion chiefs are designated false-alarm control officers and confer regularly with local police precinct commanders to coordinate efforts. In addition, these control officers must supervise the action taken in connection with all false-alarm responses. Deputy chiefs are in active contact with numerous civic groups and agencies to promote the program, supervise participation in community activities, and suggest changes in the program. Both the assistant and deputy assistant chiefs are accountable for:

1. Overall departmental supervision in assigned areas.
2. Analysis of trends.
3. Determination that all available courses of action are being taken.

At the top level the chief of department is the central coordinator of all units concerned in the program.

At a discussion arranged for the writer, in the department, the following officials participated:

Chief of department: Staff and line
Assistant chief: Staff
Deputy chief: Staff
Captain: Staff
Lieutenant: Staff

Acting supervising chief: Staff and line

Where the history of the false-alarm problem was delineated and updated in its various dimensions several factors stood out:

1. The extensive degree to which all organizational levels were involved in efforts to solve a crucial problem.
2. The incorporation of this new program within the permanent context of the department.
3. The energetic contacts maintained among internal and external organizational units.

The program was meant to be a continuous one rather than a spectacular one-shot affair seeking instant results. Proposed solutions have included the following:

1. Alerters, suggested by staff and line, that sound like diesel-locomotive horns when alarms are pulled, have been attached to ten problem fireboxes in the Brownsville section of Brooklyn. As compared with 76 false alarms for June 1965, a high-incidence period, there were 28 in June 1966. This is a pilot project; if effective, it may be applied elsewhere.

2. Of the 14,000 fire boxes in New York City the locations of 300 that registered 16 or more false alarms have been listed for the chief police inspector of the Police Department.

3. Thirteen floodlights have been installed 15 or 20 feet from problem boxes.

4. Harmless dyes have been used at boxes in trouble spots.

In sum, this case has attempted to describe the systematic efforts of a city fire department to deal with an expensive and tragic problem. Under sound, shared administrative leadership, all members were involved, and the common effort was reinforced by references among all levels of staff and line members. Other departments were also notified and their views and efforts coordinated within the prime organization. Success, so far, has been modest, and individual members are aware of the critical need to continue their search for solutions.

Veteran departmental members cannot recall any time in the past when such high-level leadership and support has been given to such a program. Morale among members in the Fire Department, according to staff and line officials, has been boosted by awareness that the attack on the false-alarm problem has such aggressive backing. With the cooperation of all internal elements plus efforts by outside agencies, it is hoped that false fire alarms will begin to show a marked reduction.

Mayor Lindsay has tagged the problem "top drawer." Both the counsel to the Mayor and the fire commissioner believe the alarms are not always a form of social protest but done "for kicks." In addition, the chief of department, who is the chairman of the Municipal Committee of the International Association of Fire Chiefs, claimed that false alarms were the main problem for his department, after problems of manpower and finances. As the Mayor's counsel stated: "We have to get down to the local community. We have to show them what the Fire Department is doing for them."

Public Works Department

In January 1963 the function of sewer maintenance was transferred from the five boroughs to a central Public Works Department. In 1962 a general headquarters review was started throughout all boroughs to determine the adequacy of the entire operation. It was not realized, at the start, that one of the borough organizations was experiencing difficulties in meeting its responsibilities. As these became known to central staff, the entire survey took on a different coloration and became more intensive. Complaints of flooded basements and allied problems were received at all levels of the department, as well as in other city offices.

According to staff personnel at the department, the initial reaction was to request more line men for assignment to this critical function. On further investigation, however, and considering the situation in other geographic areas, staff came to the conclusion that a genuine personnel shortage did *not* exist and that perhaps a different solution was required. In fact, a more comprehensive analysis of the borough, by staff both in the department and higher echelons, revealed many weaknesses in the location of service units, organization echeloning and discipline, scheduling, equipment, and morale.

In respect to service units, this borough garaged its equipment in a single location, and valuable time was lost in travel to and from jobs. To alleviate this, staff recommended two other locations, which line approved, and a third was suggested, permitting a faster response to citizen complaints through reduced travel time. The result, as staff and line agree, is that organizational discipline is healthier and the number of productive hours is considerably increased. Before the change, line had to schedule about one hundred pieces of equipment from one central garage, with resulting errors and wasted time. Today, following staff's proposal and line's implementation, the scheduling of equipment from three separate groups in strategic locations makes it possible to suit facilities to local needs more effectively.

Two other items were considered. Equipment was old-fashioned and largely hand-operated. Staff suggested a major replacement program, which was endorsed, and some modern trucking equipment and power-operated sewer cleaning equipment are now in use. As one official expressed it: "Normal purchasing delays have held the acquisition below desirable levels, but considerable progress has been made in replacing obsolete and worn-out items of equipment." Staff is also developing plans for a periodic testing of new equipment in order to increase productivity as an offset to attrition of personnel in the organization. And where morale is concerned, the indications are that with better equipment and facilities, morale has improved considerably.

The deputy general manager found it difficult to pinpoint a simple, final decision on this entire problem, but staff and line collaborated in appraising it over a six-month period before the final policy pattern developed. The major decision was made at the deputy-commissioner level after various reports, meetings, and field visits. After the major policy change, many smaller decisions were made by intermediate echelons to implement the larger objective. In order to correct the series of connected problems that was involved, the appointment of additional employees was avoided, the filling of future vacancies was denied, and the total force reduced by attrition to what staff considered rational levels. An equipment replacement program was suggested by staff and adopted by line. Reorganized sewer maintenance crews were established on an area basis that allowed rotation.

9
EXECUTIVE ROUND TABLE

Firsthand investigation invigorates academic research. In the present instance the objective was to determine if certain principles of administration stood up in actual practice. Once various hurdles were cleared—telephone requests for appointments, follow-up correspondence, preliminary discussions—the investigator sent to various New York City department officials a formal agenda of topics to be covered in informal roundtable sessions with a cross section of willing executives in various municipal offices.

Specific departments for these sessions were chosen as a result of various factors, especially cooperation and interest. Several departmental commissioners discussed the feasibility of interviews with members of their staff, encountering occasional unwillingness to participate without advance evidence of the value of such a meeting to their organization. The investigator could hardly guarantee hard results but did suggest how this type of confrontation, between academician and practical administrator, could help officials busy with day-to-day details to acquire an integrated view of various wider functions, better to understand relations between staff and line, and surely to appreciate other overtones that could assist them in daily operations.

Eventually, a number of city administrators agreed to join in the proposed sessions, and the whole process started to turn. The cooperating departments were the Buildings Department, the Department of Correction, the Department of Rent and Rehabilitation, the Department of Highways, and the Department of Public Works. In addition, several commissioners granted personal interviews to discuss their views on the subject of line and staff relationships.

The following agenda served as the basis for the meetings:

> The main objective of the investigator is to discover how administrators in government administer. Many books on government administration—city, state or federal levels—continue to refer to such concepts as decision making, supervision, delegation, etc., but often leave the average reader wondering how these concepts become "real."
>
> New York City provides an excellent laboratory in which a writer on administration can develop information and explore new directions. To this end, your cooperation as administrators is appreciated.
>
> These questions might help as a starter:
> 1. What are the characteristics of a "good" organization?
> 2. How and when do you apply delegation?
> 3. What are the crucial factors in making decisions?
> 4. How can leadership be situational?
> 5. Do you believe that in administration, staff advises and line directs?
> 6. What makes a competent executive?
> 7. How do you communicate with personnel in a large-scale organization?
> 8. What are some crucial personnel problems you meet?
> 9. How do you keep informed about new developments in your own field?
> 10. What arrangements exist for interdepartmental interchange of information?

A copy of the agenda was mailed to participants several days in advance of a scheduled session, and the sessions ran about an hour, with the investigator serving as moderator. In all cases cooperation was energetic, and most topics were covered although the order of treatment occasionally varied. Thereafter, a synopsis of the discussion was prepared by the investigator and submitted to the panelists for revision and approval. These summaries were endorsed with only slight modifications.

BUILDINGS DEPARTMENT

The representatives of the Buildings Department included the deputy commissioner, director of operations, and an assistant commissioner. In the judgment of all participants, one feature of a "good" organization is that those in the field, outside of central headquarters, are fully informed on programs and policies. If this steady communication is assured, information will generally flow back to the main office to form the basis of sound and acceptable decisions. Beyond this, the group agreed that loyalty to goals, leadership that establishes the pace for initiating and completing projects, and shared purposes are all vital in making an organization "good" or above average.

Assignments were delegated as often as possible, but delegation makes it necessary to check on progress and to remain available for advice while the assignments are in course. Delegation is valuable in stimulating in those involved a higher respect for the project, a feeling of sharing in its development, and the freedom to work out appropriate solutions to new and different problems.

In making decisions, the usual problem is to secure enough relevant information so that the risk of error will be reduced. Often a decision is the result of continuous probing by individuals on their own initiative, informal discussions among staff and line people, and, naturally, the wishes and interests of the commissioner. The latter initiates many decisions on his own and sometimes confirms those developed much lower down in the organization.

Staff and line is a fairly imprecise area, and the separation between the two types of administrators is not always clear. Staff people do not step out of the picture once they render advice. They may follow up on results and even share in the responsibility for the success of the project.

In the definition of a competent executive, many elements are involved. These include a willingness to share, so that those supervised will develop their highest potentials, clarity of expression in communication, and a style that spells confidence to associates. How are executives *made*? One view was that individuals need merely to be directed in the development of inherent talent, whereas the majority believed that executives can definitely be trained, formally and informally. Such training goes beyond informal observation of how executives deal with incoming papers, however, and certain courses in simulated role-playing can be most helpful.

DEPARTMENT OF CORRECTION

At the Correction Department, the administrator, director of personnel, chief of fiscal control, a deputy warden, and the director of rehabilitation represented the commissioner. The meaning of "good" as applied to an organization was sharply questioned. The extent to which an organization fulfills its mandate is a vital consideration. Some administrators seem intuitively able to determine the rate of growth towards assigned targets, despite the delays and shifts of emphasis that easily develop. In short, a "good" organization fulfills objectives, develops strong policies and programs towards that end, and seeks generally to improve the ways in which means are appropriate to ends.

Staff and line cannot be sharply split into strict compartments. Although line does operate, direct, and make the crucial decisions, staff can and should be an energetic collaborator. Perhaps staff can best be described as an adjunct used to suggest different stresses in policy. In any case, aside from tags or labels, individuals in an organization should be put to use wherever their talents can best be employed.

Competence in executives is usually reflected in an awareness and sense of purpose that energizes the organization and inspires people to reach targets ahead of schedule.

Communication was considered a most vital factor. Regrettably, many bureaucratic arrangements frustrate maximum communication about "what are we doing" and "where are we going"—and even make it hard to know the thinking of others in the same section working on parallel problems. Communication is essential in stretching and balancing policies on the basis of shared views.

This group also stressed the need for competent staff specialists to serve as additional eyes and ears for line officials, and various aspects of executive development courses in which the department had participated.

DEPARTMENT OF RENT AND REHABILITATION

The six administrators who attended the Rent and Rehabilitation session included the special assistant to the commissioner, first deputy commissioner, special assistant to the first deputy, the deputy commissioner, chief of research and survey division, and the Manhattan district director.

In their view, staff and line officials are purposeful, coordinate partners. The former develop policies, present information and advice to top management (and for that matter, to any part of the organization), propose solutions, suggest options, and carry out various projects at the request of the top command.

For their part, line officials execute policies and direct programs, always alert to the need for changes in emphasis and direction of ongoing programs and systems. In the course of execution, however, the staff people may learn of other problems or defects and should be free to call them to line's attention. The terms, staff and line, do have meaning, but should remain somewhat pliable so that the sense of tight boundaries will not become obsessive and result in administrative and psychological frustration for either side.

Communication should be in all directions—up, down, and across. Communication is an aspect of shared goals, improved understanding, and an indispensable means to synthesize and stimulate opposing views. In communicating, administrators on all levels should always use comprehensible terms with clear meanings. An insufficient interchange of information may leave people in doubt or even apathetic, but the other extreme of overcommunication may engulf them to the point where they find it hard to identify given facts as important, less important, or of limited value except to a specific segment of the organization. Informal round-table sessions could be helpful in clarifying issues and establishing a team effort on the basis of common understandings.

The Department of Rent and Rehabilitation is chiefly concerned with the administration of the New York City Housing Rent Control Law. Maximum rents are established according to criteria contained in the law. The core of decision making, especially in the field, is in orders issued to prevent evasions and violations, and the degree to which this goal is reached is a vital standard by which the entire organization can be ticketed as "good." As one participant indicated: "Our policy has teeth in it." Other standards include the extent to which decisions of a quasi-judicial character are manifestly fair to the public, tenants, and landlords; the quality of cooperation with other departments, especially Buildings and Relocation; and the effect of rehabilitation proposals on property owners.

Decisions are a product of adversary proceedings and affect every citizen. The authority of district directors is crucial and should remain strong so that they are free to make on-the-spot choices. These, however, must always accord with the standards set by the central office.

Leadership, it was agreed, may be acquired through training, and mention was made of executive development programs conducted for municipal officials.

DEPARTMENT OF HIGHWAYS

Highway Department officials at the conference were the director of administration, the chief engineer of design division, administrator of highway maintenance, and the director of mechanical services. In their judgment the definition of "good" as applied to an organization should depend on the extent to which aims are fulfilled, information affecting personnel reaches its members, a sense of shared direction exists among employees at all levels, and cooperative relationships with other departments are adequate.

As a new department, only a few years in existence, Highways has had to readjust relationships and functions that formerly were distributed among the various boroughs. It is now highly centralized, with a mandate that impinges on those of other city departments, including Police, Fire, Traffic, Public Works, and Parks. Above all, its work affects motorists and pedestrians, both of whom, as one member of the session said, "dislike to be inconvenienced but do want the streets and roads in good condition." The department's function is to design, construct, and repair public roads, streets, and highways. It is also authorized to issue or withhold permits to builders and others to use or open streets.

Leadership was said to be the highest talent of an executive: providing a strong sense of direction, making changes compatible with the moods and often the wishes of organization members, and demonstrating a sense of awareness as to the kinds of contributions career people can make to move forward the mission of the organization.

Staff and line were considered valid concepts, since the former was often capable of taking the long-distance view of problems, bringing matters to the attention of operating people, and assisting in the solution of common problems. One difficulty, however, is that staff people sometimes adopt a wrong attitude and look primarily for flaws and faults in an operating section. This negative approach commonly frustrates cooperative working relations between the two types of officials. For their part, line officials may not always accept useful advice and assistance and are apt to become strongly impatient with the efforts of staff to develop sound solutions. Staff exists to develop information as a basis for adopting new or changed policies, but it is often difficult to split the accountability between them because line usually has an undivided responsibility for making decisions.

Competence in executives depends on personality and management style; hence it is difficult to pin down in a hard-and-fast definition. Two main elements, however, are (1) a willingness to take on more and more responsibility and meet differing challenges, and (2) not being afraid to handle small but significant tasks. Competence is closely related to delegation, which is often a matter of how tightly the reins of administrative control are exerted. For the purpose of accomplishing certain standardized procedures it is important to recognize when a balance is struck between loose and strict methods of assigning work and evaluating its performance.

Communication was considered to be a vital factor in an organization and should flow in all directions: up, down, and across. Policy proposals can originate as easily at one level as at another. This diversity also provides the top executive with new ideas that can be useful to him in reaching his program decisions.

Other topics considered were relations between careerists and top organizational people, since the former provide continuity of purpose and program, and the interchange of information at periodic staff meetings.

DEPARTMENT OF PUBLIC WORKS

The final conference in this series was held at the Public Works Department, and the four participants were the deputy general manager, director of management planning, deputy director of water pollution control, and executive departmental secretary. All agreed that the administrative climate of New York City, which has often been characterized as one of constant crisis, has a strong effect on officials attempting to build "good" organizations. Several factors can identify such an enterprise:

1. Willingness on the part of its members to fulfill responsibilities in the widest possible sense.
2. Capacity of the organization to be self-healing in the sense that it can spot weaknesses and effect cures, rather than waiting for explicit instructions.
3. Showing that it "cares" in respect to both its personnel and the paying public.
4. A personnel replacement policy so that trained successors will always be available.

Agreement at the meeting was strong on the need to recruit and retain talent that, by its willingness to contribute and move upwards to larger responsibilities, can strengthen the organization. Mediocre, nonmotivated personnel usually mean a mediocre organization. It is often as simple as that. Indeed, so important is motivation that elaborate diagrams spelling out individual tasks in neat boxes are sometimes less important than the feeling that members express towards "their" organization. Each activity can in some way be dramatized so that its importance can be sensed by those involved in it. But in addition, a sense of detachment towards an organization encourages more vital participation and creative criticism. As one member of the group described this attitude, "It should be one of missionary zeal tempered with balanced detachment."

Delegation is a matter of the administrator's style and depends on what he chooses to stake out as his own preserve, what he is willing to discuss and then either keep or divide, and what subjects he is generally willing to share. Both the amount of delegation and the method used indicate, in some measure, the degree to which an official is willing to permit growth opportunities for staff members.

In the matter of decisions these are sometimes made ahead of, or unavoidably a little behind, the deadline; therefore, a basic rule is to know when to decide. If a decision is to be delayed, it is always essential to indicate to those affected why it will be made later.

Leadership means that top management expresses policies and programs in truthful terms, considers ideas from all levels, confirms or rejects proposals for cause, holds a tight yet flexible rein on the organization, and is willing to experiment and innovate.

Staff and line is a valid concept, but often its execution is faulty. Staff, for example, may crow over line's errors, may come in as a noisy skeptic without sufficient evidence to support statements; line, for its part, may be insufficiently willing to cooperate in joint goals.

This departmental session agreed with the preceding ones that staff officials are useful to top-level decision makers. Although the boundaries that separate them from line officials are sometimes fluid, this does not necessarily inhibit their interaction and may strengthen the contributions of each. The duties and responsibilities of staff can be stretched to reflect the views, habits, and needs of the commissioners. Staff success in an organization and acceptance by line often depend upon staff's attitude in daily procedures and its willingness to exercise patience and restraint. No official among all who participated in the various sessions would abolish the staff-line concept, and regarded it as one means to better management.

Among other points stressed were the following:

1.   A need to revitalize the bureaucracy so that staff and line members of an organization would sometimes be willing to act daringly.

2.   The usefulness of executive development courses in showing that other officials in other departments encounter the same challenges and frustrations.

3.   The need for periodic internal departmental meetings to iron out communications kinks and bring those with unrelated viewpoints together.

4.   The need for departmental directors to be sufficiently close to problems so as not to be constantly shocked by conditions at headquarters or in the field.

COMMISSIONER CONFERENCES

Following these departmental round-table sessions, the deputy commissioners of the Buildings Department and the commissioners of Rent and Rehabilitation and Correction granted personal interviews to discuss their views on staff and line. In the judgment of the deputy Buildings commissioner, staff provides essential information on a wide range of subjects, develops solutions to varied problems, and investigates issues throughout the organization. The advice offered may be accepted, modified, or rejected. On the other side, line implements suggestions but is always free to change emphasis and direction. Staff may overrate its proposals and try to exert tight control, but the commissioner was aware of this problem and had adopted aggressive strategies to "push" bureaucrats, on both sides, so as to prevent possible imprisonment and reduced administrative elbowroom. Without such initiative, abuses might develop that would weaken his control over staff.

To the commissioner of the Rent and Rehabilitation Department, staff and line are helpful identifications. Since the commissioner is usually too busy to follow all processes in motion within his department, staff serves as extra eyes and ears, bringing to his attention matters that he should be aware of, now or in the future. Relationships between staff and line must be an equation of continuous trust and confidence. External and internal patterns of responsibility are established so that one staff assistant is in charge of each area. An impairment of staff-line relations sometimes appears when staff believes it is too far removed from the mainstream of crucial events and decisions. The entire arrangement requires careful observation and evaluation to insure that the potential contributions of each type of official are fully used.

In his turn the commissioner of Correction believed that staff officials kept him in more active touch, while away from his desk, with the Mayor's office, the press, politicians, and professional associations. These relations are essential for any top-level departmental director. The commissioner's practice has been to divide functions among specialists rather than call in any staff man for any assignment. A valuable contribution of staff is to act as a management critic and suggest innovations. Moreover, the commissioner can usually discuss plans with staff officials before making final decisions. Sometimes decisions are made, as in the promotion of a warden, without prior discussion among staff members. But when a decision regarding procedures, for example, is to be made, the commissioner may invite comments as to their adequacy, accuracy, and the possibility of any administrative mishaps in their implementation. Staff meetings held periodically, rather than on a fixed timetable, offer an opportunity to determine whatever may be bothering members of the organization and to discuss plans with those who must implement them.

Finally, the deputy commissioner of Police described the department as one in continuous session and requiring strict specialization among staff and line officials. Internal promotion channels are a strong stimulus to allegiance and require an intimate knowledge of assignments. No problem, underscored by staff, can be downgraded by line, although the latter's experience may suggest useful ways of reaching solutions. No problem repeats in identical form, a stubborn fact that staff must acknowledge. Each problem requires individual judgment, a sense of balance, timing, and direction. *Both* staff and line positions demand the qualities needed in decision making, leadership, and communication. Transfers and rotation are encouraged to secure breadth of experience.

Following this interview, brief visits were made to the chief inspector, chief of detectives, and chief of law enforcement, who shared the views already presented. Two traits of staff and line were especially stressed: willingness to assume maximum responsibilities, and an impulse to action.

In sum, conversations with two commissioners and two deputy commissioners confirmed that the staff-line concept is endorsed and applied. The role of each type of official involves substantial management responsibilities, and their administrative philosophies usually affect organizational processes at all levels. In planning, directing, and evaluating, the staff-line concept is a central one.

To a large extent many officials had tried to tailor the staff-line concept to suit their special organizational requirements. Not all departments put the same stress on all aspects of the concept, but all agreed that some factors are more useful than others. Moreover, few participants in these sessions discounted the long-run contribution that most administrative theories could make.

STUDY QUESTIONS

1. Which commissioner do you consider had the most effective administrative style?
2. Which department had the most innovative answers and which the least?
3. With what views were you most and least in agreement?

V
POLICY

10
AMERICAN INDIAN COMMISSIONER

The office of the Commissioner of Indian Affairs is an adventure in itself, for Indian artifacts, highly colorful photographs of the reservations, and portraits of Indians decorate the entire room and quickly put one into that world.

Commissioner Bennett soon revealed the breadth of his interests and a fine understanding of program and policy matters. His interpretations of many difficult issues show a deeply felt concern. A comfortable sort of person, even casual in his apparel, he is nonetheless stately in manner and appearance. He spoke softly and slowly, as if he enjoyed the art of arranging words properly to convey the exact meaning he had in mind. He repeatedly emphasized the human aspect of all administrative situations and the pervading stress on dignity in Indian life and administration.

He has the ability to reach out and relate problems and programs to individuals, rather than the opposite. And his views on cultural conflicts and the need to adapt administrative principles to unprecedented situations are worth underlining.

He was born in 1912 on the Oneida Indian Reservation in Wisconsin and attended public and parochial schools in the state. In 1931 he graduated from Haskell Institute (Indian school), at Lawrence, Kansas, where he had specialized in business administration. His LL.B. degree is from Southeastern University School of Law.

This is his formal resume:

> Served with the Bureau of Indian Affairs agency at the Ute Reservation in Utah. Also served in various capacities with the Ute Tribal Council and as treasurer of three Indian livestock associations in the area, 1933–1938.
>
> Assigned to Washington office, Bureau of Indian Affairs, as specialist in realty operations, 1938–1943.
>
> Transferred to the Navajo Agency, Window Rock, Arizona, 1943–1944.
>
> PFC, U.S. Marine Corps, 1944–1945.
>
> Navajo Reservation, 1945–1946.
>
> Directed training program for World War II Indian veterans, as a member of staff of Phoenix, Arizona, office, Veterans Administration, 1946–1948.
>
> Rejoined Bureau of Indian Affairs in capacity of Job Placement Office, Aberdeen Area, serving Indian groups in the Dakotas, 1949–1951.
>
> Reassigned to Washington, D.C., office, Bureau of Indian Affairs, to assist in tribal development programs, 1951–1954.
>
> Appointment Superintendent of Consolidated Ute Indian Agency, Ignacio, Colorado, 1954–1956.
>
> Reassigned to Aberdeen Area office and appointed Assistant Director, 1956–1962.
>
> Appointed Area Director of Indian Affairs for the Alaska region, with headquarters in Juneau, 1962–65.
>
> Appointed Deputy Commissioner of Indian Affairs, Washington, D.C., 1966.
>
> Appointed Commissioner of Indian Affairs, Washington, D.C., 1966.

Mr. Bennett's affiliations include the American Academy of Political and Social Science, American Society for Public Administration, National Congress of American Indians, the National Advisory Committee for Indian Youth, Board of Directors, ARROW, Inc., and Rotary International.

He is married and has six children, three of whom are service veterans.

Mr. Bennett is the first careerist in the bureau to reach the top spot and, of equal significance, the first twentieth-century commissioner to be an Indian, for he is a member of the Oneida tribe. His responsibilities include improving economic well-being and living standards for about 425,000 Indians, on or near reservations, for which Interior is Trustee; promoting the political and social integration of Indians into the mainstream of American life while restoring their pride in and respect for Indianhood and its values; and increasing responsibility of Indians and Indian tribes for the management of their own funds and resources. The balance of power between decisions at bureau level and by various tribal councils is also one of his major concerns.

In sum, as he put it, the hard-core issue is the involvement of Indians, at all stages and ages, in resolving the crisis of their own future. His method is a blend of communication, faith and trust in the Indian potential, especially its youth, and emphasis on the best of the two worlds in which Indians live.

According to the Senate Committee on Interior and Insular Affairs, to which the commissioner reports, the trusteeship policy administered by the bureau has been less than adequate in terms of economic position, housing, education, and health. The result is the traditional, forgotten Indian.

The budget estimate in fiscal 1968 for the bureau was about $241 million to be devoted mainly to these goals: work with Indian people and other agencies to develop programs that will lead to economic self-sufficiency; advise Indian landowners on how they can maximize their resources; provide educational and social services to Indians; inform Indian groups of private, state, and federal sources of assistance; assist Indians who wish to leave the reservations, mainly for economic improvement; exercise trust responsibility for Indian lands and certain Indian monies.

With these objectives, any commissioner would be hard pressed to underline priorities—generally, he is obliged to juggle the entire collection almost at the same time. A representative list of major problems would put economic conditions, housing, education, and health side by side at the top. Take the first.

Trust lands total 50 million acres, of which some are now or potentially valuable, whereas others are too mountainous or arid to be developed. Many communities are isolated from centers of commerce and industry, whereas others border on the labor market. Corporate agricultural enterprise, on a large scale, reduces the competitive edge of small farms. Unemployment runs from about 40 to 46 percent of the total work force. Comprising 0.2 percent of the population of the United States, Indians own 2.16 percent of the land. How has the bureau attacked these issues?

1. It tries to help the Indians to make better use of reservation resources, land, and minerals, manage forest and range, conserve the soil.

2. It encourages industrial enterprises on or near the reservations to provide employment opportunities and work in connection with federal, state, and tribal agencies, civic organizations, private enterprises.

3. It conducts a program of employment assistance for those who wish to relocate; this includes adult vocational training and on-the-job training programs. Since the start in 1952, by 1967 about 61,500 Indians had been provided with help towards direct employment.

4. It cooperates with other federal agencies and the departments of

Labor and Commerce in the areas of economic opportunity and industrial development.

Through seven relocation centers in major cities, 10,000 Indians have received either jobs or on-the-job training. In February 1967 a National Indian Manpower Conference was sponsored by the Labor Department. Plans were developed to provide an additional $2 million in training programs. During 1967 a total of $32 million was funded for Indian programs by the OEO, mainly for Community Action programs to help solve such problems as poor health, inadequate education, unemployment, and dilapidated housing.

To help solve the housing problem, more than 80 tribes have established housing authorities. In addition to a low-rent program, the Housing Assistance Administration of the Department of Housing and Urban Development (HUD) has developed a mutual-help program to meet the needs of very low-income Indians unable to afford the rents of even low-rent housing projects. The HAA provides funds to local tribal housing authorities for building materials and specialized labor, and participating Indian families donate their own services as a down payment on a new home. In June of 1967 about 700 houses were either completed or under construction and another 2900 units were in various stages.

Supplementing the HAA program, as the bureau explains:

> The Bureau of Indian Affairs operates a Housing Improvement Program intended to improve the housing of the most needy Indian families who do not qualify for other housing programs. Construction of new minimum basic shelter or rehabilitation of existing Indian dwellings is provided by the Bureau in cooperation with tribal governments. Since fiscal year 1964, when the program was introduced, through fiscal year 1967, nearly 400 homes have been provided or improved. As the result of increased appropriations for the program and a shift in emphasis to provide more improvements to existing housing, some 1000 homes will be provided or improved during fiscal year 1968.[1]

Moreover, in an example of interagency cooperation between the Department of Housing and Urban Development, the Public Health Service, and the BIA, a total of 375 homes is being constructed, under a demonstration program, on the Rosebud Reservation in South Dakota. Training programs funded, sponsored, and directed by the OEO, Manpower Development and Training Act, and the Department of Health, Education, and Welfare are being used to construct and improve Indian housing.

---

[1] United States Department of the Interior, Bureau of Indian Affairs, *Answers to your Questions about American Indians* (Washington, D.C.: U.S. Government Printing Office, May 1968), p. 21.

In the matter of education, in 1968 President Johnson was concerned that 10 percent of American Indians over 14 years of age had had no schooling; nearly 60 percent had less than an eighth-grade education, and half of all Indian children were dropping out before completing high school. Under an executive order of that year, the National Council on Indian Opportunity has had the problem of education on its priority agenda. In this vital area, the commissioner stated:

> A major investment which will be continued and accelerated is in education. The stress will be in two directions simultaneously: quality education and equality of opportunity for all Indians. Research and experimentation, which have hitherto been approached only timidly, will become an important element of the Bureau's educational programs for Indians, particularly in teaching English, which must often be approached as a second language. The ultimate objective is the assumption by public school districts of the responsibility for educating Indian children in local schools, with Bureau schools being turned over gradually to public school districts.
>
> Greater emphasis will be given also to programs of vocational training for adults to equip them with competitive skills and knowledge for the world of work.[2]

Indian students attend a variety of schools: public, private, mission, and federal boarding (or day) schools. A total of 56 percent of all Indian school-age children attended public schools in fiscal 1967; 34 percent attended federal schools and 10 percent were enrolled in mission and other private schools. Over 20,000 living in states (off the reservations), not included in the latest school census of the BIA, attended public schools. In sum, about two-thirds of all Indian children were in public schools during this period.

The bureau strongly encourages public school enrollment for Indian children. Its operation of federal schools is basically for two groups: students who live in areas without adequate public education programs, or those in need of boarding-home care as well as educational services.

BIA figures for fiscal 1967 show the spread of these educational efforts. The bureau operated 246 schools with a total enrollment of 51,234 Indian and Eskimo students. It also managed 19 dormitories for 4268 students attending public schools. Of those in federal schools 16,430 were in day schools and 34,804 in boarding schools. In January 1969 the Navajo Community College was scheduled to open on the Navajo reservation in Arizona. Besides the standard two-year college curriculum, required subjects will be Navajo history, culture, and language. Initial registration—

---

[2] United States Department of the Interior, Bureau of Indian Affairs, *Federal Indian Policies: A Summary of Major Developments from the Pre-Revolutionary Period to the 1960s* (Washington, D.C.: 1966), mimeo, p. 3.

Indian and non-Indian—is set at 400 students. Indian leaders selected
from the Navajo Tribal Council will serve as governing regents.

Finally, in the matter of health, the bureau spells out the problem in
detail. Among Indians, infectious and communicable diseases are more
prevalent than in the non-Indian population, mainly because of poor
nutrition, crowded housing, and lack of basic health knowledge. Influenza,
pneumonia, gastroenteritis, and streptococcal infections are the most common diseases. An Indian can expect to live to 63.8 years, whereas 70.2
years is the average life expectancy for the total population. In trying to
solve these problems, the Public Health Service works with Indian tribal
organizations, families, BIA, and local and state health agencies.

Under the present commissioner's direction, BIA conducts meetings
with tribal groups to "learn from them firsthand the conditions on the
reservations as they saw them, the major problems and their ideas, and
recommendations. . . ." It is reported that 153 tribes, or groups, had many
proposals in respect to education, health, housing, trust lands, economic
development, and sanitation—among others.

In another area—that of local self-government—in 1967 BIA Tribal
Operations Staff met with top leaders of about 40 tribes in order to make
local Indian government more effective. Indians showed a strong determination to assume heavier responsibility for running their own affairs.

The time is surely "now" for a hard reappraisal of the Indian problems. President Johnson, in his own words, issued a challenge to the new
commissioner in calling for a "sound, progressive, venturesome, and farsighted program" and an end to substandard programs. Secretary of
Interior Udall reaffirmed this approach:

> Increased sophistication of the Indian people and expanded opportunities
> now awaiting the application of normal management and financial proc-
> esses make it important that Indian people be granted a greater range of
> opportunities and options to utilize, develop, and expand their resources
> and skills.

Various members of the Congress have made their views on the
Indian problem known. Senator George McGovern (South Dakota, Chairman of Indian Affairs subcommittee of the Interior Committee) stated:
"Self-help and self-determination are the major ingredients of an Indian
policy." The news media have focused on various aspects of this problem.
On the very evening of my conference with Commissioner Bennett, CBS
broadcast a thirty-minute news special: "The Forgotten American." Although its statistics didn't always agree with the official ones, several of its
statements were deeply disturbing:

> The largest American Indian tribe is the Navaho, and most Navahos
> live on this reservation at Window Rock, Arizona, in an area larger than
> the State of West Virginia. Not even the government knows how many

Navahos live here—but it is thought that about 125,000 Indians live on these fifteen million acres of semi-arid plains and mountains that the late Indian historian, Oliver LaFarge, once said, "made the barren Gobi Desert seem like the Garden of Eden."

Not only is the Indian's land barren, but by every other material standard his life is barren. While most of the nation's attention has been drawn to the large urban ghettos and the plight of the Negro, most of the American Indians who live on reservations are at the very bottom of an economic heap that has more room at the middle and at the top than ever before in history. While the federal government says a family income of $3000 a year is the poverty level, the Indian family's income is half of that. For every two American children who die before they are one year old, three Indian children die. Three times as many Indian children die before they are four years old.

The Navaho suffers most from influenza, pneumonia, tuberculosis, and, as on many other Indian reservations, malnutrition. This Navaho child is being treated at the Public Health Service Hospital in Tuba City, on the edge of the Window Rock Reservation. At this hospital, 20 percent of the children admitted suffer severe nutritional disorders.

The average American dies at seventy; the average Indian at forty-five. Those who survive constantly live in danger of mental illness. Some form of mental disorder will strike five Indians for every two other Americans. For every young American suicide, four young Indians will die by their own hand. On some reservations—the Northern Cheyenne, for example—the suicide rate is several hundred times greater than the national average.[3]

In the *New Republic* issue of March 30, 1968, an article "Lo, the Poor Indian," by Ralph Nader, underscored similar conditions:

The Indian budget has been increasing at a rate that has doubled in the past decade. Yet the picture on the reservations is drab and grim. The present poverty tally is a 40 percent unemployment rate (with much underemployment), grossly dilapidated housing, at least 30 percent illiteracy, two-thirds the life expectancy and less than a third of the average income of other Americans, rampant disease including a tuberculosis incidence seven times the national average. Anyone who has followed Indian affairs finds these figures to be a dreary redundancy of past recitations. With the exception of some advances in Indian health, reservation conditions remain as bad or worse than 10 or 20 years ago. In the past decade a new dimension of despair has emerged in the form of 200,000 Indians in city slums such as Los Angeles, Denver, and Minneapolis. But the BIA continues to exude fads of hope—whether it is relocation away from the reservations, tourism, mineral development and the latest unfilled expectation—bringing industry to the reservations.

_____
[3] From the CBS News Special *"The Forgotten American"* as broadcast over the CBS television network, Tuesday, May 7, 1968. Copyright © 1968, Columbia Broadcasting System, Inc. All rights reserved.

In a closing article, June 5, 1968, of a twelve-part series on the American Indian, the *Christian Science Monitor* writer Kimmis Hendrick claims that the commissioner is steering the BIA halfway between the termination of federal trusteeship for Indian lands and welfare and what has been labelled the Indian nationalism view. Mr. Hendrick quoted Mr. Bennett as saying:

> I see the Bureau's role changing from paternal caretaker to coordinator of economic and social aids. The Bureau should give way to a new role by tribal governments themselves—a role in which the tribal governments will be the prime negotiators with federal-aid programs.

During my interview, I found Mr. Bennett very much aware of the width and depth of problems plaguing his Indians. He believes in going out to the reservations to see for himself. In arriving at a decision he leans strongly upon the participative approach and good communications. His working knowledge of personnel policies and programs was manifest, especially in the selection process. Highly aware of the need to build and maintain sound relations with Congress, his box score in appropriations proves the success of his efforts. Above all, he is deeply committed to a difficult objective: to change the view of government toward Indians from one of philanthropic trusteeship to one of partnership in decision making between Washington and tribal levels in the field.

Soon after his appointment, the commissioner in an address called for a spirit of partnership between Indian leadership and the bureau in these respects:

> We no longer need to "sell" Indians to the people of this country. What we need now is to draw the Indian people to the conference tables, together with the best minds in education and finance and community development and Government administration. The paternalistic approach is good no longer. It has resulted, in its worst manifestations, in a culture of poverty, and even at best it encourages a dependency approach to life.
>
> This is not the way to fulfillment of the American dream. And surely the American dream of the good life, the life of self-determination, should be the fire to rekindle in the hearts of the First Americans.

And in a more personal vein, he wrote in the *Indian Record* (May 1968) a few words upon completion of two years as bureau chief:

> I would like to say to you again that I have abiding faith and confidence in Indian people. I don't think there is anything wrong with you. As a matter of fact, the emergence and development of Indian leadership is most promising and portends a bright future for you. Like you, I was born on an Indian reservation and I am happy to have been associated with many of you as a school mate in a Government boarding school, as a member of the Armed Forces in World War II, and for 35 years in the

Bureau of Indian Affairs working with you in many situations and in many places. More than anything else I am proud to be one of you.

In terms of your own experience over a thirty-year span within the government service, dealing mainly with Indian administration, could you cite some of the more heroic major accomplishments prior to your present assignment?

I would like to mention first of all I felt it significant that the historical trustee relationship over Indian property which exists between the federal government and the Indian people is now changing—from a concern not so much about the Indian's property as about the Indian himself. I think this is a trend which is in keeping with the times. I believe it significant that we are going to be working with the Indian people to enable them to manage and control their own property rather than to be working with the property itself.

Has this, in part, originated with the Indian communities as well as with levels of government?

Oh, yes. I think a great deal of it has come about because one of the things I've always attempted to do, wherever I've been, is to create a comfortable atmosphere in which Indian leadership can flourish and function. As a result, I think they feel free to begin to assert themselves without fear of any kind of—you might say—recrimination or anything. They just feel comfortable in making suggestions. I think this is real significant.

You mentioned the key word "leadership." How, from a practical standpoint, would you define the term?

As I view it, leadership is developed in those individuals who have a background both in the Indian system—you might say—and the non-Indian system, and they are able to function either in the Indian community or in even an academic community. Some of our Indian leaders can sit in a tent with a full-blood Indian family speaking very little English, and the next day can be just as comfortable as a member of a university panel.

Surely. It's a variable.

It's a variable skill. What Indian people see—and what I have seen over a period of years—is that they do not have to be a victim between two worlds, but that they actually can have a fuller existence by being able to live comfortably in two worlds.

The phrase "victim of two worlds" indicates a certain ambivalence of loyalties as with any member of a culture which is changing. Does this represent an issue to the Indian youth today?

Oh, yes—yes it does, very much. As a matter of fact, for many years it was government policy that an Indian had to leave everything Indian behind him and that he had to go over and participate fully in the dominant culture. This, I'm happy to say, is no longer the policy. As a matter of fact, when I first went to a government school you were punished in the school for speaking your own language—you had to speak English. And so, with enlightened leadership—I mean in the Bureau of Indian Affairs—and with the Indian leaders beginning to take hold and take more of an interest, realizing that if this is going to be changed they will have to change it—a change has come about.

We see as a part of the transition that we call building a bridge—
. . . between the two systems.

Between the two, so that the young people can traverse this bridge back and forth. We have some very fine examples of it. For instance, among the Pueblos of the Southwest where the young people live in the community, they are totally immersed in the community. In the morning they leave in their cars and trucks to go to the city to work as stenographers, skilled labor, maybe unskilled labor, fully participating in every way in this non-Indian community—and then come home in the evening and immerse themselves completely into the Pueblo life.

Does the same thing happen among people in other Indian communities with other traditions and values?

Yes. For example, there is an individual, a full-blood Indian, with whom I formerly went to school. During the academic year, he now heads the guidance department in a public high school in a large metropolitan area. And in the summer time, wherever there are traditional ceremonies and dances being held, he is one of the leaders in his costume. So he enjoys, all summer long, participating with his own people in many of their ceremonies, and following their traditions. Then after the summer is over he's back in the metropolitan area, in a large public high school, giving counseling and guidance to non-Indian students.

There is no contradiction whatsoever, in my mind, in—as you put it—bridging the two cultures. And yet, tragically enough, over the years it would seem that there has been an implicit requirement that the Indian forsake his initial, original loyalties, to enter the mainstream of American culture.

This is true, and some of us have done this in varying degrees. As for myself, I have always considered myself an Indian because my mother was a full-blood Indian. And yet, since I've been gone so long from my home communities, when I do return I feel I return more or less as a stranger. I make no visits to the people related to me or whom I might know, except my sister, who always remained at home and is "in" with the people there.

Could you perhaps underscore some of the values, in this century, which a member of an Indian community retains?

Well, I think as a people they retain their dignity. They're very proud and would do without many of the material things other groups may desire and hold as something to achieve in life rather than sacrifice this dignity and pride.

You've mentioned the material possessions which have become obsessive with many today—in the cities.

This is true, and the Indian people sometimes are criticized with reference to their work habits, because they don't necessarily subscribe to this idea of working fifty weeks a year, 8 to 5, five days a week with two weeks vacation. Now. . . .

. . . the routine.

Yes. When the Indian individual has something to work for he'll work, and he'll work hard for it. It may be some necessity like a new stove in the house or something like that; once that's achieved, he has no desire to keep on working and working, to try to get hold of something else. He seems to be satisfied with less in a material sense than I believe some of the other groups are.

Beyond the quality of independence, would you list others which have almost equal force to a youngster in the Indian community?

One is the concept of *sharing.* This is still prevalent even back in my home community, which has experienced the onslaught of dominant groups for over 100 years; but this concept of sharing still prevails.

Does that also relate, administratively, to teamwork?

Yes, it does—but more than that, sharing is a built-in social security system which they've always had. Those who were not able to provide for themselves were taken care of, and those who could, had to provide for others or feel the pressure and censure of the rest of the group. It was especially significant for young children, because in the Indian community, when a young child lost his father or mother, he immediately knew who his substitute father or mother would be. In other words. . . .

. . . he was adopted?

Yes, but he knew beforehand who that person would be, so that he never had a feeling of being lost. The Indian people—many of them—consider our social system of adoptions as being very cold.

And too formalistic.

Too formalistic, you know, where children are put with strangers they don't even know.

Could we perhaps build on these values and turn the attention of the Indian youth toward government service in the next decade?

Well, we hope to do this. There is sort of an attitude that's grown up—that Indian people should always be the recipients of something or other from government. And it's partly, I guess, because some of the Indian people feel that the government treated them badly in the past. Also, I think, there is more or less of a twinge of conscience on the part of the nation generally because of what happened to the Indian people. Consequently, many people feel they have to give Indian people something in return.

But I believe the greatest loss is in the contributions which Indian people themselves can make. Right now we are setting up an internship program which will bring young Indian college graduates into the Bureau of Indian Affairs on an internship basis. They will work in our various offices in Washington and throughout the country—our area offices, our city offices, and out on the local reservations—for one year. Then they will have the option of going to other federal agencies or even into the private sector or teaching in the public schools.

Will this start soon?

Oh, yes. And we also want to make the program the means of recruiting for other government agencies. I think we are missing a real bet in not using many of these talented young Indian people in our embassies and legations throughout the world.

Does it seem to you that each student, at some point, should have a stint in the government—whether it's the military or the civil service?

I'm very much in favor of that. My three oldest boys—when they finished high school—all went into military service, and when they came out they went into college. It was very beneficial for them. They had matured, had developed some goals they could strive for—and this service experience helped in many, many ways. It is especially helpful, I think, to young Indian people, because while they may have good academic achievement, generally speaking their sophistication in competing in the modern world is not at the level it should be. I think that if we have them in an interim service in a friendly atmosphere, working with us for a year or so, we can help them. Again, it's a question of the bridge between their environment and the environment in which they may want to seek their future.

Many students today have a distaste for government service. Could you explain that from your own experiences?

Well, first of all, I might say that it's popular in these days to be against the establishment rather than use it and build upon it as I have done through thirty-five years. I think it goes without saying that I could spend a great deal of time criticizing previous commissioners of Indian Affairs.

No doubt.

But had I been in their place when they made certain decisions fifty years ago, quite likely I'd have made the same decisions they did.

Not until you're in the shoes of the administrative participants, can you make a valid choice.

It would be difficult. I like to believe that future commissioners will think of me as being well-intentioned and dedicated—and I look upon previous commissioners in the same light and try to build upon what they have done. You must always consider the changes in the world around you and respond to them. I think that everybody accepts this. So this is the way I operate. I don't want to be talking about myself but I would like to point this out. I am now at the head of one of the establishments and, as you know, we have various campaigns including the Poor People's Campaign. We will have Indian people here and we have a plan ready to receive them and to discuss matters with them, to listen to their petitions and see what government can do in response to any justifiable requests they may have.

Of course. As a practical administrator, are there certain lessons that you can apply from the writings of—if I may say so—the theorists on the other side of administration? What, for example can you take out of the various topics within the text—for example, authority, communication, delegation—that have 9-to-5 meaning? Do you feel that this is an age in which we are shaping new theories and in which the practices have outrun the old theories?

Well, in working with Indian people, because of these many special laws which have been passed by Congress on Indian Affairs, the Indian people as well as the administrators know that there is a fundamental authority for our relationship. However, through various symposia and seminars on administration, I am trying to lead the organization to develop our relationship with Indian people more on human relations than on authoritarian principles. Because everyone knows the authority is there.

I think it's the same with anything in government. Everybody knows there's the Army and the National Guard to back up the President. And as everybody in Indian Affairs knows, I have the authority to do many, many things. But we are trying to deal with people to meet them on a—you might say—man-to-man basis, to discuss our problems across the board, communicate in meaningful terms, and deal with problems on the basis of their merit rather than the fact that I have the upper hand in terms of the authority.

And so, to me this is a very interesting, a deeply interesting and challenging opportunity to encourage Indian people to take part in decision making. The Indian people like to challenge you to use your authority, while you try to find other means to convince them without using your authority.

Human relations has been, as you certainly appreciate, an old-fashioned and yet a modern term. Government, to many students, is cold, impersonal, and abrasive. What has been your experience to refute that?

Well, I don't think the Indian people feel this way. I meet with Indian groups throughout the country and, as a commissioner of Indian Affairs, I am publicly committed to the fact that I am commissioner for all of the Indians—not just for the political group that may be in power in a particular reservation. I also meet with the minority political groups when I visit reservations and listen to their side of every story. I'm trying to get all the people in the bureau to do as I've done for many years—and that is, in meetings between the Indian people and bureau officials, to discuss our mutual problems and positions. You might say we have some real donnybrooks. But when we as bureau people meet with third parties, then it's a different situation because we are identified with Indians and their problems. In other words, we're in their corner, so to speak, and they understand this.

How much travelling do you do in the course of six months or a year?

Oh, I probably travel in the nature of 100,000 miles a year.

That's all!

Could you give an example of a recent situation, in which you were faced with decisions to make, problems to settle?

Yes, we are engaged in a very challenging situation that I might allude to. This is a dispute between two tribes—the Navajo tribe and the Hopi tribe—over some territory—land. I chair these meetings and it's almost like a United Nations meeting. You have to give each side equal time, be aware of who is the host for the meeting and who starts off. You know all small details are scrutinized by both sides. Therefore, as far as I can, I'm going to be absolutely fair and impartial as between the two tribes, respecting the position of each.

At times you wear other hats than an administrative one.

Oh, yes. And then, of course, another difficulty comes about—my field man working with the Hopi is loyal to the Hopi cause and my field man working with the Navajo is loyal to the Navajo cause.

And you represent headquarters.

And I represent headquarters not only to two major tribes with different points of view, but to my own administrators with different points of view, because naturally they have to be in the corner of their tribal groups.

This brings up a crucial point. In a book which has recently come out on the subject of democracy and the public service, the author— Frederick Mosher at Berkeley—indicates the problems of developing public policy for the public interest. The term itself is subject to many interpretations. Do you feel in this situation you described that you are determining public policy for the public benefit? Is there an awareness of this?

This, I think, makes this job one of the most challenging in government. The Bureau of Indian Affairs is necessarily the advocate for a special group of people. It's a minority group, an identifiable racial group, and we are advocates for them, but it's not a political group. So some of the problems come about when a conflict arises between what advocates of this group want as against the general public interest. This is when you get into some real hot water.

And there's no book for it.

No. We have a case right in point now. The Indian Civil Rights bill was just passed by Congress.

The Ervin bill.

Yes. And this runs right smack up against the system of government of the Pueblos which had existed from time immemorial.

So we have an Act of Congress which may compete with the values of the Indian community.

Right. So here we have something which is accepted as a national policy in the public interest—this Civil Rights Act, the Ervin bill—then we have a group of people, the Pueblo people, who until this day have had their own system of government; and now there's conflict between what they have been following, through the centuries, and what is provided in the Civil Rights Act.

And as a civil servant your role is to implement. . . .

My role is to be in the middle, but it is also to implement the statute—and I'm fortunate, I believe, that I do have an understanding of what the Pueblo system is and has been. I think this is going to help me in trying to enmesh the two together. I don't think we should go out there and bludgeon these people down, you know, and put this on them. But I do think we can work the two systems together.

The Pueblos went through something similar with the Catholic Church.

Is that so?

The Catholic Church could not put down the native religion. So there was an enmeshing. . . .

And a coexistence. . . .

And a coexistence of Catholicism and the Pueblo religion. Now, you can look at this in many ways. The Pueblo government is based upon religion, it's a theocracy, and the ruling class is selected by the religious leaders. So, in effect, under the Civil Rights Act we are saying to the Pueblos: "You can have religious freedom but you can't." In other words, on the one hand, they are saying: "Religious freedom means that we can go ahead with our theocratic form of government, because it's based upon religion." And then we say: "No, you can't because if some individual member of your tribe doesn't want to follow it, he has the right to follow something else." We have some real conflicts.

And again you're square in the middle, as referee.

I am.

May I ask, Commissioner, have Indian groups generally been active as pressure groups in relation to government—including the bureau— and Congress?

They have a lobbying organization called the National Congress of American Indians, but I don't believe they quite accept some of the pressure tactics that other lobbying groups may use.

. . . the sit-down and the picket.

Again, this goes back to their question of dignity. They'll come in here and sit down—it's a wonderful experience to have them come in, because they're very dignified and firm and you know they mean business— we can have some very, very good discussions. Another thing about Indian people, as I've found all through my life, is that we may have some very heated discussions, but the minute you step out the door it's all forgotten.

I wish this human relations concept, as you've described it, were equally applicable to government and the people. We seem now to be trying to frighten public officialdom, as in student demonstrations in the universities and political conventions.

We have our militant groups, including the National Indian Youth Council which has been identified as red militants. Red power advocates. . . .

Red power has come up. . . .

Yes, but again, being the Commissioner of Indian Affairs for all Indians, I provide them with a forum. I've met with their leadership, either individually or in large groups, and we've had some very serious discussions. I'm willing to meet with them at any time and any place.

As a matter of fact, they are planning this summer to hold a seminar and we have made available our facilities at Haskell Institute, at Lawrence, Kansas—the government boarding school where they'll be housed and fed. They'll bring their own resources people in and conduct their own seminar and will probably feel perfectly free to take me and my policies over the coals.

What would the agenda be for such a seminar?

I think much of it is based on pride—they're concerned with building up their past and beginning to understand it, feeling that they have a right to be proud of it. I think they're well motivated and that if they can have pride in their past, they're in a better position to face the future. Some of our leadership, both in government and among tribes, don't quite agree with their tactics, but I think no one disagrees with their objective.

I understand you've recruited several new members into top spots at the bureau. What qualities did you seek in this process?

Well, first of all, I sought any individual with, of course, the necessary education and experience background—but more than that, how effective they have been, in the past, in working with people. We have an administrative officer called a superintendent who is in charge of bureau programs on the various field reservations throughout the country. We can take two individuals with the same background—maybe they've gone to school together, to the same colleges, and come out with the same relative experiences in some professional field. In time, we may appoint each one a superintendent, only to have one fall flat on his face and the other do a very good job. We begin to think more and more that we need better selection techniques. I firmly believe that the main thing is this human relations factor.

Communication naturally comes into this.

Oh yes. This is true.

Do you, in the course of a week, hold regular staff meetings?

Yes. We hold regular staff meetings and we have a sister agency—the Division of Indian Health, under the Department of Health, Education, and Welfare, very much concerned in the Indian field. We meet every other month to discuss mutual problems. We have sent a directive out to our field that in all staff meetings which our people hold, they invite the staff of the tribe and any other governmental or state agency that may be working on the particular reservation. So the tribal leadership is aware of what our thinking is long before action is taken so they can participate in planning it.

For many years, we have had meetings with employees throughout the bureau. We now have the practice, when we meet with staff to discuss human relations or community organization and development, of inviting the Indian leadership there also. So they get a better understanding of these matters and—more important—they also know what is expected of our people.

So it's mutual regard for the needs of each other.

That is right. I had a very interesting experience last month. We had a two-day unstructured joint tribal and Bureau of Indian Affairs meeting of all the tribal leadership in the Phoenix area. No agenda. We just sat down, and I think anyone looking at the group would have found it very difficult, when a speaker stood up, to know who was a tribal person and who was a bureau person, particularly if they're both Indians.

How did it come off?

I think it was a real excellent presentation. I enjoyed it very much. Too often we've communicated with Indian people in terms of specifics rather than concepts. We need to help each other conceptualize as to what the job is.

How does the term coordination apply?

Well, it applies adequately and is a significant issue in Indian Affairs. Right now the focus is on the charge the President has made to all federal agencies that the federal government has a commitment to Indians—not just through the Bureau of Indian Affairs but throughout the whole federal government. So for the first time, the whole federal government is getting involved in Indian affairs.

This produces a real problem of coordination. But coordination at the field level is much better than it is here in Washington.

How come?

Well, with the Tribal Council being the official governing body, everyone has to work through it on the various programs. But in Washington—here we're not compelled to do this. This problem is going to be corrected, however, through the President's creation of the National Council on Indian Opportunity under the Vice-President, to coordinate all federal programs for Indians. It is made up of six selected Indian leaders throughout the country and the members of six or seven departments of Government.

Will you report to the Vice-President on this?

Yes. We report to the Vice-President, and if there is any breakdown in coordination between agencies, that office will straighten it out. This is, I believe, something we need, and now that we have an independent agency to take the initiative, I think it'll come along faster than when one department tries to take the initiative as against another department.

In the course of an average week, do you meet with other agency officials on these common problems?

Oh yes. We have a meeting scheduled for tomorrow afternoon with Mr. Ross Davis, Assistant Secretary of Commerce, who heads up the Economic Development Administration—quite a large staff meeting between his staff and our staff. And we have had two requests within the past week for our people to be detailed over to other agencies. . . .

. . . then it is one government, after all.

Yes. And for various reasons, every time we hear that some agency is going to start a program, especially for Indians, we try to see that they recruit somebody from this office to head it up. Also I have a man at the assistant-commissioner level who is my liaison with the other bureaus of government. . . .

Full-time?

Full-time. We constantly review pending legislation to see that it can be made more effective as far as Indian people are concerned. Some of the broad general legislation that is passed has to be interpreted to see that it applies to Indians. Therefore, we try to amend this legislation before it's enacted.

How would you suggest that relations between the administrator and the legislator be improved?

I think communicating much earlier with the members of Congress than we are prone to do. To use an example, a tragedy every now and then occurs. In one of our boarding schools a boy lost his arm fooling around with a machine he wasn't supposed to be handling. Well, as in a case of that kind, after his parents were notified, I immediately called his congressman or senator and told him that we had this tragedy, how we proposed to see that it doesn't happen again, and what we were doing for the young man.

It only takes a few minutes.

It just takes a few minutes. Again, if we get wind of the possibility that there's going to be some flak in a congressman's district—maybe between an Indian and a non-Indian over some lease or some matter like that—we call him and let him know that this is liable to come up. Quite often a congressman or senator will write about a specific problem, and we use this opportunity to ask for a meeting with him to discuss a broader problem. For example, a question may come up about some student dissatisfied with some practice at school. So we take this opportunity to go up to the Hill and explain the program of the whole school, rather than one problem.

And it widens his horizon.

It widens his horizons and ours, and they're very appreciative.

Do you find yourself running back and forth quite often, to testify in committees?

Yes, I do. For instance, this week we have hearings Thursday and Friday, and more hearings scheduled for Wednesday of next week. I'm the chief legislative person on Indian Affairs for the Department of Interior.

What committees would be involved?

We have four committees, generally.

That's all?

Yes. We have the Committee on Interior and Insular Affairs of both the House and the Senate for substantive legislation. Then we have the Appropriations Committees of the House and Senate for funding, which of course get involved in quite a bit of our policy, too, in connection with justifying requests for appropriations.

Is there any advice you might offer to a new administrator on relating to congressional committee activities?

Well, I learned the lesson early in the game, fortunately, through some of the supervision I had. I remember when I was younger I got a little bit irked at so much congressional mail—you know: ·felt it was interfering with getting my job done. And I was asked, at the time, by my supervisor —who is incidentally now in Congress—"How would you like to live in a country where you couldn't write your congressman?"

So, I think that answers many, many questions. And I am a public servant. Congressmen represent a constituency which is the public for whom I work. And so I feel that I have an obligation to respond.

Over a period of a week, could you underline three continuing problems that you face, aside from those which vary? Is there a trend in your timetable?

One of the trends that's very difficult to meet is what I call program demands on the part of our operating people. Although I can say that in the Bureau of Indian Affairs we receive maybe even more than our fair share of the budget dollar, we never have enough to meet all of our program demands.

So then the problem becomes, how do you innovate and how do you get other agencies involved? We have programs sometimes where we have three and four agencies involved in developing it and getting it funded—because no one agency has the whole pie. And this is where we have complicated problems of coordination, because each agency is responsible to the government and to Congress for how it spends its money. And no agency likes another agency to tell it how it should be spending its money.

Do you just talk these things out?

Oh yes, we talk them out, and sometimes we talk them out in months and sometimes it takes six months. But we feel it's worth it when we get the job done. We have many multifunded programs. Here's a case in point. We have been talking with Indian people about the development of tourists' facilities on the reservations. We are beginning to accumulate the statistics to justify the possibility of going into this. What we didn't know was that the President was going to put a ban on foreign travel this year. Now if we'd had all these facilities programmed and could have gotten the financing for them, we'd have been in business.

Is planning a major chunk of your activity?

Oh, yes, the planning is. I think I can make this as a general statement. The better we do our job in the Indian Affairs, the more difficult it becomes. This is not an agency where the better you do a job, the easier becomes your operation.

One reason is that the more you get people involved, even to the point where you have to interpret in another language—to Indian people—the longer the process takes. But using this kind of process, I feel the results are more lasting. If the Indian people are involved and agree on the goals and participate in the planning, they get hold of the program and it's theirs.

This comes back to your original point of participating democracy in running an agency, rather than authority versus responsibility—which they know and acknowledge.

They know and acknowledge—it's there. And when the Indian people come to see me with a program, they don't come here for us to read the law and the regulations to them, because it was read to them before they ever left the reservation. They come here wanting to know, "Is there some way that we can get this done?" So then we talk to them on the merits of their proposal. If all agree that the proposal has merit, then my responsibility is to remove whatever obstacle is in the way, whether it's an exception to a regulation or a waiver to a regulation. I have no hesitancy about asking the Secretary of the Interior to make an exception, which he can do under certain circumstances. And so we can accomplish this proposal. If you sit down with the people and discuss a proposal on its merit, and it does not have merit, they recognize that, too.

Who are your bosses in government?

Well, the Bureau of Indian Affairs is traditionally under the Assistant Secretary for Public Land Management because of our trusteeship over Indian land. And then, of course, the Secretary of the Interior. And I think the Indian people are very, very fortunate to have in Secretary Udall a man as dedicated to Indian people as he is. He was born and raised near Indian people in Arizona, so he's been identified with them all his life and he has publicly stated that for his remaining months in office, he wants to do as much and get as much of the Indian business straightened out as he possibly can. And he has followed this up with action. There is more time and more interest on his part in Indian Affairs than in any other agency of government. When you consider his other responsibilities for the National Park Service, water pollution, and many others—I think the Indians are fortunate and we are trying to make the best of it.

Looking in the other direction, how big a staff do you have in the bureau?

We have in the neighborhood of about 14,000 people, but I would say about 70 to 80 percent are in education and training or related activities—school construction and maintenance, the feeding and care of children in our boarding schools, and the actual instruction.

Let me conclude with one question that must often come up in interviews. What are the most enduring satisfactions of your career in government?

Well, I think the most enduring satisfactions are seeing the way the Indian people are beginning to take hold—you might say—getting themselves involved, wanting to be involved and facing the realities of their situation. And then, of course, we have many individual kinds of things which give a lot of satisfaction, such as receiving letters, as we do, from people who have gone through our educational system and are on their way toward rewarding careers. The Civil Service Commission has a program to give people at the executive level experience in different agencies, so as to broaden them, and I think it is significant that you can't get the people in Indian Affairs to leave. They are loyal to the Indian people and to a cause and just don't want to leave. Now, the new executive director of the National Council on Indian Opportunity, under the Vice-President, was recruited from this bureau. He was asked to go, and eventually the Vice-President had to tell him and the Secretary that he *was* going.

That was an order?

That was an order because he didn't want to leave.

But I would like to say one thing in terms of the government here, and that is that I'm here as an employee of the government and to advocate and work with Indian people on programs—various government programs —trying to make them meaningful to the Indian people. At the same time, I feel a very clear responsibility to advocate to government—to speak for the hopes of Indians. I was born and raised with them, went to school with them, went into the armed services with them, worked with them for 35 years—so I think I have some appreciation of their aspirations, their hopes, and their goals. So I spend half of my time communicating upward and I'm happy that I have the environment in which I can be heard. I think the President's message to Congress indicates that government at the top level is looking to the hopes, aspirations, and goals of Indian people.

From what you have said, Commissioner, I believe that you have fulfilled the request of the President who has charged you, if I recall, to put the First Americans first on our agenda.

Thank you very much.

Thank you.

STUDY QUESTIONS

1. During its history, the Indian Service has been exposed to a number of approaches or philosophies. What do you think of this one? Is it "exportable"? If so, to what other areas?
2. Would you characterize the personnel system of the Indian Bureau as closed or open? Are there dangers in either case?
3. Would you continue, or abolish, the separate program for America's Indian population? If the former, where would you put it, organizationally?

11

JOB CORPS DIRECTOR

Arriving early for my interview with William Kelly, Job Corps Director, I reviewed my homework on Job Corps programs, personnel, and problems. Any one of its assorted goals, I concluded, represents a large challenge. Since its birth in 1964, its main tasks have been to teach reading, arithmetic, and communication skills to youth, develop skills in those who may never have worked, offer guidance to young men and women, and provide medical and dental care to all members. In formal prose, the Corps

> teaches the importance of respect and responsibility to youth who have internalized bitterness and hostility, as a result of their deprivation . . . shows young people that differences and problems are better resolved by democratic processes than by violence . . . provides the alternative of productive responsible citizenship for thousands who might otherwise have known continued poverty, illiteracy, unemployment, welfare, and delinquency.

Various centers, scattered coast to coast, are supervised by regional offices and headquarters staff. Corps members, the documents told me, have performed conservation work worth $38 million, built and maintained

4912 miles of roads, developed and improved 76 miles of fishing streams and 16,560 acres of fish and wildlife habitat, planted 15,912 acres of trees and shrubs, and improved and reforested 12,805 acres of timber stands. In addition, they have performed flood relief work, aided in salvage of crops, and assisted in fighting forest fires.

Also, I had discovered from agency papers that corpsmen had established a Boy Scout troop for disadvantaged youth at Kilmer, New Jersey; corpswomen work with retarded youngsters in Clinton, Iowa; and corpsmen volunteered 120 hours a week to work with the handicapped in San Francisco. Personnel at the centers include vocational teachers—construction, maintenance, clerical, mechanical, conservation—counsellors, and general supervisors. The total staff for the entire program in October 1967 numbered 558: 310 professionals and the balance in other skill areas. In the urban areas, subcontracts are arranged with foundations, industries, and universities who have a Corps investment to protect and an interest in results.

As with many new-frontier agencies, the Office of Economic Opportunity and the Job Corps were often headlined in controversies generated by problems with communities, internal management, or friction among Corps members—and sometimes reacted defensively to answer their critics with accumulated evidence and statistics. What were the solid achievements of the Job Corps? According to a United States Chamber of Commerce survey among 314 Corps members:

> 76 percent formerly unemployed or underemployed youths have been gainfully employed after Job Corps service; 81 percent employers rated their skills as satisfactory-to-excellent; 80 percent employers rated their training as satisfactory-to-excellent.

The *Wall Street Journal*, August 10, 1967, reported:

> National Director Kelly says many who criticize the corps don't comprehend the difficulties inherent in making useful citizens out of the "hardest core of the hard-core poor." He ticks off a stream of figures: 4 of 10 corpsmen are from families on relief; 3 of 10 cannot read or write; more than 1 in 10 has been convicted of a crime; 6 of 10 are from broken homes; and 8 of 10 haven't seen a doctor or dentist in the past ten years. Sometimes, he says, the corps must try to undertake physical rehabilitation before it can think about training an enrollee for a job.

As of February 5, 1968, a Harris Associates study made a follow-up of youth trained by the Job Corps and compared their experience one year after the Corps with their situation six months earlier. The study found that there had been a 10 percent rise both in the number holding jobs and the money they were earning; that the average hourly wage of all corpsmen working rose from $1.55 to $1.70 an hour; that the total income of the male terminees showed an increase of 20 percent over the six-month period; and that among women terminees 53 percent were working or in school.

According to a press release: "The study found that the 24 percent who are currently unemployed have not been idle. Three out of four have had at least one job in the past six months. The main reasons given for being unemployed were 'no means of transportation' (23 percent), 'hard for a minority person to get a job in his home town' (27 percent), and 'most employers demand a high school diploma' (42 percent)." According to Director Kelly, in an OEO statement: "The figures indicate that the tens of thousands of young men and women who have been helped by Job Corps are really putting their skills to use."

In a close review of materials, one gained the impression that Job Corps had friend and foe—it resembled the pillow fight most new programs endure. Perhaps it is inescapable that a new idea must submit to a tug-of-war among established agencies wanting a slice of the action; to multiple pressures both attacking and supporting it, without sufficient facts and evidence; and to bureaucratic frustration in trying to make certain its objectives are attained.

As of 1968, Job Corps started with a reduced appropriation—a reduction in anti-poverty funds cut close to the bone—and it had to close down 16 of its 124 centers, including Urban Center Rodman at New Bedford, Massachusetts, operated by Science Research Associates; Conservation Center, run by Agriculture, at Ripton in Addison County, Vermont; and Conservation Center, run by Interior, at Lewis and Clark, North Dakota Park Service in Burleigh County, North Dakota. This was done on the basis of operating costs, duration of enrollees' stay, 30-day dropout rate, gains in reading and mathematics skills, placement capability, and community relations. (Both the establishment and the dismantling of any center would provide valuable materials for future case studies.) Congress had also requested greater emphasis on rural-area candidates, stress on intensive civic-life and career-counselling programs, encouragement of new training methods, and wider sharing of information with public and private institutions or agencies.

Before the Senate Committee on Labor and Public Welfare, chaired by Senator Lister Hill, on March 6, 1967, William Kelly testified in connection with his confirmation as Job Corps Director. He spoke of his belief in the program and clarified the areas that mainly concerned the senators. From his data sheet I learned that Kelly was born in Pittsfield, Massachusetts, in 1924. I observed also that he was married, had six daughters, and made his home in Virginia. The balance of his biography I scanned but left to our discussion. Among the items pinpointed during the congressional interview, these were constantly underlined:

Question: Now how many of the ones who originally show up in camp, what percentage of those drop out or are fired before they complete their training?

Kelly: Senator, I don't have that figure in the top of my head. I *can* tell you that the attrition has been running around 30 percent in the first 30 days, and that is and has been a grave concern to me, because one of the ways that I can effect cost cuts in this program is to get that attrition cut down in the first 30 days, since I obviously have quite an investment in a kid just to get him enrolled.

I have the investment of having screened him. I have the investment of having transported him. I have got, sometimes, in that first 30 days some medical and dental investment.

Let me say that we are still in the process of doing on a rather small scale some innovative things. The whole Job Corps was innovative at the outset, and we went through much the same kind of operation, I think, that a military contractor goes through, when he is assigned the whole business of research and developing a new piece of military hardware.

Nobody had ever run a Job Corps before, and I suppose the first 18 months of Job Corps operations was just that. It was a research and development phase. We are now in the kind of situation where we have created the facility. We have trained the staff. We know a lot more about running the Job Corps than we knew even six months ago, because we have data that we did not have six months ago. . . . What we have got to do now is, one, cut our attrition, particularly in the first 30 days; two, we have got to pay much more careful attention to costs. . . .

Question: Are the training programs within those regional areas oriented to the industries which are in that regional area?

Kelly: Let me say this: not all of our Job Corps youngsters go back to where they came from. You may have a kid, for instance, who came from New Jersey, and perhaps went to a Job Corps conservation center in Pennsylvania, maybe Blue Jay, for instance, and . . . learned to become a chain saw operator. He may decide he does not want to go back to New Jersey. He may want to stay in Pennsylvania, or he may want to go to Ohio, so that in terms of structuring programs vis-à-vis the industries in the area, there is no guarantee that those kids will stay in that geographical area.

Question: Are the enrollees placed in regional camps closest to their point of origin in it?

Kelly: Yes sir; I think that you will note in any statement that one of the reasons why we have been able to cut transportation costs from $76.13 in June to $35.55 during January is because of this regional assignment.

Question: Has there been anything done to try and create a better atmosphere in the community maybe during the introductory period, or even before the selection of the location?

Kelly: I think we have come a long way in that regard. We have in the United States today about a hundred community councils . . . established by the communities themselves in the vicinity of the Job Corps camp or center. These people have gotten involved with chiefs of police, local social service clubs, the mayor in some instances, members of the city council, and the *whole purpose of this undertaking is to try and create the kind of relationships between the community and the center that are just absolutely important for the successful operation of the Job Corps centers,* in my judgment.

I was invited into the director's office. Kelly, whom I had met on the pages of various documents, was at the door: wide grin, strong handshake, lively expression. Of medium height, edging towards plumpness, he reminded me of a college coach on the sidelines of a game: crewcut, shirtsleeves, and an in-motion stance. Despite a rush-rush day, he was as wound up as if it were the start of his schedule. He sat at a small desk, uncluttered, with a few neat piles of papers and the white phone for direct White House calls.

I asked about the balance of his time for the afternoon: "It's yours, no problem." Kelly gave rapid-fire, forceful answers in a crisp, often twangy voice. A conviction at times passionate intensified many replies. As head of a crash program, he had a manner to match: energetic, cool under stress, and highly elastic in the sense that he seemed to stretch, literally, to meet the unexpected. From time to time he fingered a pencil or paperclip—later the secretary mentioned he had only recently stopped smoking. But it was not tense nerves; rather, as he dug into an answer, his hands squeezed down to give it emphasis.

As he recalled his career, rarely did he hesitate, except to repeat a question and reflect over a broad span of facts. It was easy to see how he had earned high scores in confronting congressional committees. In fact, it is known that he never sends a deputy but always appears in person with the necessary facts at his fingertips. If the man has an administrative style, it is a mix of candor, realism, and optimism. Despite hard odds, he reminds one of a fighter deaf to the count. The spirit of daring could be his trademark. Unceremonial, accessible, he is like an invigorating gust of fresh air in bureaucratic corridors.

Many of his views on the administrative process are irreverent. His legacy to many high-level programs has been strong. In an almost surgical fashion, he slices through stodgy myths surrounding such features as staff sessions to reach and communicate directly with people. And yet, despite his new-breed outlook, he has kept many galloping new-frontier programs on target and has often been the one to pull up on the reins. In an era of turbulence, Mr. Job Corps—and that's how you start to think of him—is a steady force whose contributions have already been documented. He would probably regard them as footnotes.

Perhaps he summarized the essence of his belief in his job in an address given in January 1968 at the Pennsylvania State University:

> If you can't read, you are unfree. If you are sick, you are unfree. If you are hungry, hopeless, ignorant, or frightened, you are unfree. To free those of our people who are unfree is a task for all of us, and requires that part of our character and intellect that is the best and most human in us. And this strikes me as being an ethic for our time.

Ever since the establishment of the first Job Corps centers in 1965, the organization had been pockmarked by critical attacks. Giving rise to these attacks were uncertain goals, disturbances at some centers, demoralized staff, poor press relations, problems with contractors, shortage of funds, and foes in Congress. All these issues faced Kelly when he took office.

Perhaps the closest one can come to wisdom in the development of a new enterprise is to recognize the futility of any packaged formula. Most of Kelly's success in reviving a moribund program can be laid to his almost sacred belief in what it might achieve through a warm, deep sense of concern, spreading through all levels. He cared, and everyone knew it.

During our interview Kelly gave the impression of a tough yet tender administrator with kinetic qualities. From time to time he moved quickly to grab a document, lift a report, or buzz for evidence of a specific item. And yet these merely confirmed his flypaper memory and brisk replies. A man in motion—not haste—keeping a firm hand on his program, the tough business of what he calls "human renewal."

Armed with two degrees in economics from Ohio State, recently married, and a World War II veteran, Kelly entered government service not for reasons of dedication or curiosity about administration. "I needed a job," he told me. His first civil service application resulted in an assignment as Dispatch Clerk GS-2 in a warehouse of the U.S. Army General Depot at Columbus, Ohio, February 1951. Before the end of the fifth week he took a day's leave and drove to Wright-Patterson Air Force Base where he told an interviewer ("the office was packed with hundreds of people") merely that he wanted to know what was open. The job sheet on the bulletin board, Procurement Technician, seemed to describe what might interest him. An Air Force captain spoke with him, called Columbus to secure his release, and processed him on the spot.

In March 1951 he was inducted as Procurement Technician at GS-5, which paid $3100—a leap from his initial $2400. Assigned to the Training and Professional Services Unit of the Services Branch, he was soon involved in procurement of engineering equipment for the Air Force, materials for training bases, and technical services for air support. After a six-months stint he earned a promotion to GS-7 and a new title: Contract Negotiations Specialist, at $4205. Holding the same title, he moved next to GS-9 in September of 1952, just coming under the wire of the Whitten amendment. (This was a rider to the 1951 Supplemental Appropriation Act and requiring at least one year's service in the next lower grade before promotion to the next). His new salary was $5060.

As many civil servants know, there is often a lag between actual functions and formal responsibilities. Kelly's excellent work was recognized in 1953 when Lt. Colonel Robert E. Lee, Procurement Division, wrote in a letter of appreciation:

1. The Branch would like to convey an expression of its appreciation for the excellent job done by your section in connection with several recent Management Survey contracts directed by USAF. Your efforts have prompted many favorable comments from the Branch.

2. While all persons involved are to be commended, it is felt that particular credit must be given Mr. William P. Kelly for his prompt action in connection with these procurements. In view of the probable recurrence of such projects, it is recommended that Mr. Kelly be made a Contracting Officer at the earliest possible date.

Perhaps this is a clear instance of how a job and the person shape one another. To Lee's letter of commendation, J. B. Straley, Assistant Chief, Services Section, responded in standard military endorsement style:

1. Your Section Office is also aware of the calibre of work performed by Mr. Kelly . . . probably realizing more in detail the difficulty of some of the complications and difficulties of the type procurements referred to and the quality of performance required.

2. As regards the designation of Contracting Officer, it is felt that because of the unusual circumstances surrounding many of the procurements handled by Mr. Kelly including those which must be negotiated at Headquarters USAF and in which discussions involve highly placed officials of the Air Force, it is deemed appropriate that he be designated as a Contracting Officer. It should be recognized that this is a deviation from the standard policy of the Branch with respect to designating buyers as Contracting Officers, and therefore it does not follow that all buyers who might be equally qualified to perform functions of a Contracting Officer should be so designated.

A telephone call from a deputy assistant secretary, Air Force—shocked to hear that Kelly was not authorized to sign—started a flurry of paperwork, and a few days later he became a full-bodied Contracting Officer in good standing.

From time to time Kelly was assigned to the Pentagon, which meant "playing hard ball in the Air Force Secretary's office" for special projects. Secretary Harold Talbot wanted to use consultants to evaluate several procurement programs, and for a six-months stretch ("It was a brilliant stroke of luck") Kelly worked alongside management teams from Booz, Hamilton; McKinsey; and Ford, Bacon, Davis. Next, in 1954, came the jump to GS-11, as Contract Specialist, a new assignment to negotiate with architects and engineers for the construction of the Air Force Academy at Colorado Springs. In a period from June to November Kelly's timetable looked like this:

Monday: 7 A.M. flight from Dayton
           9 A.M. Washington and the Pentagon
Tuesday: 1 P.M. flight from Washington
           5 P.M. Denver airport

This he described as "fun." Today, in his office, large-scale color photographs show the completed Academy, built at a cost of approximately $200 million.

In July 1955 Kelly joined the Big League at GS-12—"being off the clock plus a parking space." This job also involved 'supervisory responsibilities as Section Chief for the work of ten buyers and the expenditure of about one-quarter billion dollars yearly. Fourteen months later he moved into GS-13, and in July 1958 he reached the level of Branch Chief with a matching one-grade promotion and a new title: Supervising Contract Negotiator and Contracting Officer. Often long titles and high grades move side by side in government.

I asked about the art of negotiation in the procurement field. There are two main elements: "Define what it is you are going to buy, and know the jargon of the business." In the course of his career, the tag "saver" has been applied to him, and this makes him proud. And yet I was puzzled about what challenges his assignments might have offered. Dealings in vital products under strong pressures might have been exciting, yet his real gift was with people. And in fact, at this point in his career the urge to divorce his efforts from procurement responsibilities had slowly started to burn.

Asked to come to Washington ("This is where the action was"), he joined NASA in April 1959 and eight months later hit GS-15 as Chief of its Procurement and Logistics Branch. One major task was to work with McKinsey consultants in determining how the space agency should best deal with its contractors and how industrial facilities could best be utilized. During this period Kelly said he was ready to "throw in the sponge." Feeling more and more like a "faceless bureaucrat," he deeply wanted to become involved in some of the newer programs bursting around him. As he put it: "I couldn't get anyone to involve me." And then something happened that proved what he told me: "I've been lucky."

John Young, one of the McKinsey staff members, brought his name to the attention of Sargent Shriver. The ensuing phone conversation was brief: his secretary said somebody by the name of Sargent was on the phone.

Shriver: I'd like to talk to you about working for the Peace Corps.

Kelly: Whenever you say.

Shriver: How about tomorrow?

Kelly: Fine, I'll be there.

The Peace Corps was born as the result of an executive order on March 1, 1961. On March 5 (it was a Saturday) Kelly met at 3 P.M. with Shriver, who asked: "When can you come to work for me?" Kelly said: "Tomorrow." And on Sunday morning he started as Director of Contracts and Logistics for the Peace Corps—one of the first administrators in the agency—and took a crucial part in building its structure and operations. Among his first tasks were recruitment and interviewing of candidates for top spots, and advising on policy. His grade moved to GS-16 in June to hit GS-17 in October 1962.

On demand, as his reputation and aggressive leadership became better known, he was "loaned" to AID as Associate Assistant Administrator for Procurement Policies. In describing this assignment, Kelly said: "It was the first time I really felt frustrated." The agency was "structured for inaction"; ten months seemed a lot longer.

His next step was a forward plunge into general administration, more or less unhinged from procurement: to serve as a member of the Task Force on Poverty (May 1964) with Sargent Shriver. Kelly was still on the AID payroll at GS-18 as of August 1963, and the agreement between Sargent Shriver, Bill Moyers (Assistant to President), and Budget Director David Bell was that Kelly split his time 50/50 between AID business and Poverty Task Force responsibilities. This was a real staff-line combination. I remarked: "This must have been an impossible situation." Kelly: "I tried it for one day, and then found myself devoting all my time to Task Force business, despite the fact that AID was paying half of my salary and the White House the other half." Perhaps the proverb of reporting to one boss still holds!

The next step, and title to prove it, was wholly public administration: Assistant Director for Management and Administration in the Office of Economic Opportunity, created in 1964 by an Act of Congress. Kelly directed management functions under the "normal" handicaps of most new programs: limited staff and meager funds. On a volunteer and loan basis he persuaded (it might be hard to refuse him) many key people in and out of government to join the new team. Under his direction about 900 contracts, in excess of $150 million, were negotiated and administered with such firms as Philco, Federal Electric, and Litton Industries. In addition, he organized, staffed, and opened seven regional offices across the country. He also arranged to implement procedures allowing OEO to use about $30 million worth of surplus government food for the war on poverty. (This record is considered unmatched by any other government agency.) Known for tight foresight, he abolished office "frills" to save the taxpayers about $300,000: no carpets, no fancy drapes, no fancy furniture—an executive desk, including the one used by Sargent Shriver, is no different from that of a $3500-a-year clerk.

When the Director of Community Action Programs was hospitalized for four months, Kelly took over his responsibilities as Acting Director. Shortly afterwards, grant approval authority was delegated to the field— more authority than had ever before been authorized by a federal agency to field offices. Under Kelly's control, grants grew from 1388, totalling $262,379,906, to 2396, valued at $355,379,750, in 2½ months. When he wound up this assignment, the poor in 1044 of 3132 counties were being aided through 898 community agencies.

On December 2, 1966, Kelly was appointed Acting Director of Job Corps, the third in two years. Four months later he sat in President Johnson's Oval Room to hear him say: "I want you to run it." He was confirmed as Director on March 10, 1967.

To the Senate Committee that confirmed him Kelly said:

> The Job Corps is engaged in a program of reclamation of the nation's most valuable and precious resource—its youth. All of us have become greatly concerned over the pollution of rivers and streams and the air we breathe. But we have long been suffering another kind of pollution which, in my judgment, is more serious. This is the kind that results in hundreds of thousands of our young people between the ages of 16 and 21 being out of school, out of work, and out of hope.

I asked Bill Kelly what the Job Corps now means to him. He bounced up, pulled two photographs from the corner, and put one on an easel. It was a striking photograph of a youngster—grim, defeated, toothless. The second photograph showed the same youngster after Job Corps rehabilitation—smiling and confident. I said: "You're building people." His phrase "human renewal" is better. "These kids," he has said, "have got to have a better life. I don't know what the alternatives are."

He picked the Job Corps off the mat at the fourteenth round. As he put it: "It had been beaten about the head."

When the tiger was accepted as the Job Corps mascot, Kelly said: "A year ago no one would have taken bets on the future of the Job Corps." I asked what was so *new* about its character and direction. Several things, he said, and he documented each one. In a staff code—to attain a balance at youth centers between permissive administration and cement-tight discipline—he wrote:

> Many Job Corpsmembers come to Job Corps with habits of appearance and conduct that are not acceptable on a job. Job Corps must give them new habits. There are two effective means for accomplishing this goal: example and reinforcement. When a staff member sets a good example, he helps Corpsmembers learn to dress, look, and act in ways that will help them be successful on the job.
>
> The success of a center and of Job Corps in general depends to a great extent upon community acceptance and understanding of the Job Corps program. Staff members are encouraged to help this acceptance and understanding. This can be done by participating in community activities in their non-duty times, by being careful about conduct and appearance in the community, and by telling community members about Job Corps aims and accomplishments. This can also be done by taking personal responsibility for the conduct of Corpsmembers when they are in the community.

Among the features Kelly had introduced were agreements with the Civil Service Commission and the Post Office Department that would permit administration of qualifying examinations at centers to test new Civil

Service employment programs for the disadvantaged. His efforts to convince many industries to join government in fighting poverty, in his words, meant a change of focus: "Private industry has always trained workers, but not the hard-core poor. . . . This takes *not* just vocational training but human renewal of the whole man." As of October 1, 1967, the Job Corps, he said, had trained 109,610 youths, 70 percent of whom are now in jobs, and the remainder in military service or school.

With a flair for leadership, Kelly continually sets goals and identifies priorities. To him the qualities of the administrator are "courage, candor, and the ability to get people to do the things you want to do." Both students and teachers should serve a stint in government to have a sense of "participation in really important national programs." He describes the traditional bureaucracy as the "system's system," which is constructed and maintained to prevent egregious errors, while next to it is the "star system," which allows human beings to break chains and attain wider, more durable ends.

What counts in an organization? To him: "leadership, getting good people whose chemistry is compatible, coming to the 'nut' of a problem, a vital intelligence system, and loyalty." He prescribes no static formulas, perhaps because he never took a course in public administration! Though his extraordinary presence defies it, he believes in "getting people twice as good to surround him." His initial take-over ("a delicate art") was prefaced with rumors that this meant a bloodbath for Job Corps. His predecessors had left for quieter fields. Word soon circulated that Kelly was OK—and this came from "the little people," with whom he has an unusual rapport. Perhaps he's still one himself, for he doesn't seem to believe he's any bigger or better than that first grade GS-2.

Career bureaucrat? Maybe he's a new breed who knows what the system has and misses. Here are his words on Capitol Hill to some hard-headed senators:

> The Job Corps is never going to be cheap. When you deal with the poorest of the poor, there must be costs. When 80 percent of the population you serve has had no previous contact with a doctor or dentist; when 40 percent of the enrollees come to Job Corps unable to read a simple sentence; when more than half are from broken homes—there will be costs. . . . But $2 million worth of property damage as a result of a riot in the ghetto is not cheap.

He said "I stretch people." In fact, he is spending $295 million this year to this end.

I asked: "Do you hold regular staff meetings?" He doesn't—but you'll find him navigating throughout his offices with a deep concern for those who make the Job Corps breathe. Nominated for the Rockefeller Distinguished Service Award, he has been praised by many. Senator Joseph Clark has written:

Bill Kelly, in my opinion and in the opinion of other Senators, is one of the most quietly effective and skilled public servants in the Federal Government today. He rates our esteem, to begin with, for being a career government employee, a man who has not only devoted most of his adult life to government service but has worked his way up from the lowest ranks of government service to become one of the highest-level Presidential appointees.

Living through constant crises, Kelly will doubtless face many more and continue to thrive. Sargent Shriver, while still his boss, described him with admiration and affection:

Bill Kelly's competence and compassion were exactly what President Kennedy had in mind when he proposed the Peace Corps. At a time when many considered the Peace Corps a certain failure, Bill dedicated himself to its humanitarian value and eventual success. It was a courageous gamble for one who had scaled the ladder of Federal Service but was willing to risk it all on an untried venture in human development.

And he continued:

When President Johnson asked me to launch a national war against poverty, I again called on Bill Kelly for he had the administrative ability and technical talent to forge action out of ideas. . . . Thousands of young-sters will have an extra chance because of Bill Kelly.

On balance, here is a civil servant who climbed the civil service ladder, yet never surrendered to bureaucratic stodginess. He constantly renewed administrative energies by exposure to a variety of new-frontier programs. A tremendously hard worker—a self-starter and driver—with an abundance of hard common sense, willing to experiment, with a risk-taking spirit, Kelly showed a deep sense of loyalty to mission. He earned high scores with congressional committees by recognizing the need to reduce costs, by his ability to "make do" with reduced appropriations, and by his almost fingertip grasp of facts. In essence, he has a flair for building new programs and organizations, and perhaps the key to this is his respect for those working with him at all levels.

On the walls of his office hang many tributes from those whose lives he has affected—corpsmen and corpswomen, mayors and educators from communities, average citizens. A teacher in the true sense, Kelly was comfortable with a piece of chalk writing on a blackboard his view of the Corps and its meaning to this century. His is a story of ability, dogged persistence, breaks, and a dose of spunk. I asked: "Do you scare people?" And he said: "I might." If he scares them into action, the effect on the public service may never rub off.

STUDY QUESTIONS

1. Is there a specific administrative type best suited to develop a new program? What obstacles usually stand in the way of building new administrative programs?
2. Do you consider one of Kelly's greatest assets to be his personality? What were his chief strong and weak points? To what extent do luck and arriving on the scene at the right time determine executive selection?

12

CIVIL RIGHTS DIRECTOR

Ruby Martin in 1968 was one of seven government career women to receive the eighth annual Federal Women's Award. As the press release indicated: "The women are being honored for outstanding contributions to the federal government and for personal qualities of leadership, judgment, integrity, and dedication." Mrs. Martin's nomination and award were based on courageous, effective administration of the civil rights compliance program and contributions to racial justice in education. At thirty-five, she was the youngest ever to earn such a citation.

In a remarkably short span of time, she has moved rapidly to her present position as Director of the Office for Civil Rights in the Department of Health, Education, and Welfare—several hops from her birthplace of Lake Village, Arkansas. An official data sheet, civil service style, would look like this:

Confidential Assistant to the Secretary for Civil Rights, Office for Civil Rights, Office of the Secretary, Department of Health, Education and Welfare, Washington, D.C. May 1965–January 1966.

Staff Assistant to the Special Assistant to the Secretary for Civil

Rights, Office of the Secretary, HEW Department, Washington. January 1966–March 1967.

Acting Chief, Education Branch, Office for Civil Rights, Office of the Secretary, HEW Department, Washington. March 1967–October 27, 1967.

Appointed Director, Operations Division, Office for Civil Rights, Office of the Secretary, HEW Department, Washington. October 27, 1967–March 1, 1968.

Appointed Acting Deputy Director, Office for Civil Rights, Office of the Secretary, HEW Department, Washington. March 1, 1968–May 1, 1968.

May 1, 1968, appointed to her present position as Director, Office for Civil Rights, Office of the Secretary, Department of HEW, Washington.

Despite the typical stiffness of governmental occupational titles, a close-up of Mrs. Martin's present duties shows a full-bodied workload. What, for example, would a sample weekly schedule be for the director of a civil rights compliance program? Mrs. Martin furnished an in-depth catalogue of representative tasks both before, during, and after my visit, and I have arranged them here under a few basic headings:

Internal management

1. Meets with Secretary's Executive Staff to discuss HEW response to the Poor People's Campaign of June 1968.

2. Meets with staff of Civil Rights Education Branch to discuss progress in gaining terminal desegregation plans from 300 selected, formerly dual school systems. Discussion of policy on dual systems for coming year.

3. Meets with Chief of Health and Social Welfare Branch and key assistants to discuss progress in developing review techniques for state health and welfare agencies. Discussion of reports from first pilot reviews.

4. Meets with prospective OCR employee to emphasize the importance attached to the job for which he (or she) is being recruited.

Coordination

5. Meets with members of the staff of Civil Rights Division, Department of Justice, to discuss joint OCR-CRD review of performance of school districts operating under federal court orders to abolish dual systems.

Congressional contacts

6. Goes to Capitol Hill to meet with a U.S. representative concerned with the requirements that HEW is maintaining for desegregation of a formerly dual system in his district. Explains what the law requires, and how OCR proceeds to evaluate a district's compliance with these requirements.

Public relations

7. Has an interview with a correspondent from an influential Southern newspaper on progress in desegregating schools in his region. Explanation of OCR policies and procedures, desegregation statistics recently released, effect of recent rulings of United States Supreme Court.

8.   Speaks to a community citizens' association, outside the city of Washington. Explains the importance of citizen involvement in the process of guaranteeing the civil rights of Americans. Explains the state of the law, with regard to so-called de facto segregation in urban school systems.
Field trips

9.   Travels to regional civil rights office to review staff activities on a recent review of state health and welfare agencies within the region. Discusses OCR policies with HEW regional director and his top staff, to assure that all HEW executives are presenting the same information and policies to the public within that region.
Miscellaneous

10.   Reads field reports; drafts correspondence and memoranda; signs mail; has telephone conversations with various federal officials, members of Congress, state and local officials, regional civil rights directors, members of the press, and so on.

Ruby Martin, I found, is a woman of quiet charm and dignity. Attractive in manner and expression, she was deeply interested in the range of my questions and answered each one deliberately. Young in years and spirit, she generates high enthusiasm. "This program counts," is the mood her presence creates. I sensed a valuable combination of qualities in her approach to pressing problems: responsible idealism blended with a truly sympathetic understanding of difficulties involved in each step. Her responses, during the interview, were brisk and clear. Above all, one senses her eagerness to bridge the gap between noble ends and workable means to create a viable program.

In charge of 300 organizational members located at headquarters and in the field, Mrs. Martin's central goal is to ensure compliance—by schools, hospitals, welfare agencies—with nondiscrimination provisions of the 1964 Civil Rights Act. All these decisions have an impact on program officials who are action-oriented and on the front lines of administration. The penalty for failure is withdrawal of federal government monies, which thereby curbs or negates the jurisdiction of line authorities and their programs.

How does Ruby Martin view her central task? She describes it in these words:

> Among the most urgent pieces of unfinished business of our Nation is the guaranteeing of equal rights and opportunities to all her citizens. Completing this business will require change—often drastic change—in the way that government, business firms, private institutions, and individual citizens behave. The Office for Civil Rights is an important agency for such change. And it is for this reason that many of us who occupy responsible positions in the Office for Civil Rights do so, despite long hours, deep frustration, sharp—often unfair—criticism, and serious doubts as to whether we can move far enough and fast enough to really be effective. We are convinced of the absolute necessity of doing our job, and so we can only hope that it will be done in time.

For one who is subject to many cross-pressures, Ruby Martin remains calm, almost imperturbable, but always keenly aware of what is needed to convert high promises into real practices. Her willingness to accept the challenges of imaginative proposals offered by a dedicated staff is, around the office, a trademark. They respect and respond to her applied belief in underscoring their strengths and potentials. Above all, she stresses a team of balanced talents and viewpoints. Aware of normal, bureaucratic channels, she never permits them to blockade continuous lines of communication. For a new program, the emphasis is on training generalists, because flexibility is needed in meeting unprecedented situations. In relations with program people, she must often say "No further funds" unless they comply with the law. At the same time, she must have effective dealings with them: educators, school board members, and community leaders—a tall order.

Published after our discussion, an article in the *Wall Street Journal* (August 8, 1968) by its man on HEW matters, Jonathan Spivak, indicates the enlargement of a function of which Mrs. Martin had spoken to me:

> After cautiously collecting statistics and encouraging admission of more Negroes, the Health, Education, and Welfare Department has decided to begin an aggressive effort to integrate, beyond token numbers, scores of four-year public colleges. . . . Major effort, however, is to desegregate more than 30 poorly financed Negro public colleges that are part of state four-year higher education systems in border states and in Pennsylvania and Ohio. HEW's major weapon to force such integration is its power under the 1964 Civil Rights Act to cut off Federal aid wherever discrimination is detected; thus, the department could threaten to hold back funds from a state's entire four-year higher-education system unless it integrates its Negro colleges.

These developments will doubtless add to the complaints and controversies already swirling around the Civil Rights Office.

Mrs. Martin, a member of the Ohio Bar Association, is married to a Washington dentist, has a five-year-old son, and makes her home in the District of Columbia.

Mrs. Martin, you direct a vital program for the Department. Could you indicate its major goals?

The major goal of the Office for Civil Rights is to enforce Title VI of the Civil Rights Act of 1964 and to make that law a meaningful experience in the lives of the minority residents of this country. When the program was started, most of our focus was on Negro citizens, because at the time the law was passed, there was great frustration and concern on the part of Negroes. As we have developed our program we've realized that there are other minority groups on whom we should concentrate some of our resources—particularly Mexican-Americans in the Southwest and on the East Coast.

Making Title VI meaningful certainly involves school integration in the South, and, to the extent that we can do it, in the North. There are restrictions written into the Civil Rights Act itself, and elsewhere, which limit our authority to deal with school segregation problems in the North.

We're very much concerned with health care, hospitals, nursing homes, and the extent to which minority group members are afforded access to these institutions and equal treatment upon admission. Related to this, of course, is the right of Negro physicians—and other minority group physicians—to be on the staffs of hospitals and nursing homes. The problems are all very complicated, and access could mean the ability to walk in because you have enough money to pay, or it could mean you can't get in, even if you have money, if your physician is not on the staff.

Certainly the whole area of welfare is of vital concern. It means the extent to which minority group members are getting the benefit of the government's participation in welfare without regard to their race or color. I think the Poor People's Campaign (which started last week in Washington) really points up the goals of our program. If we could deal effectively with the demands of this group, we would be out of a job!

Your program—or perhaps programs—are bold ones. Do you have on weekends, when perhaps your time is more your own than in the office, some sense of satisfaction as to your accomplishments?

About once every six months, I guess I would say on weekends, I have a sense of satisfaction about my accomplishments—about the accomplishments of our office. And it usually deals with specifics: a school district that finally presents a good desegregation plan, or a hospital board that agrees to take steps to comply with the law. Of course, there are degrees of satisfaction, and I must say that if I didn't have a sense of feeling that what I was doing *was* important—and making a difference in this country—I wouldn't be in this job. So to that extent I have satisfaction every day, knowing that at least I'm here and my staff is here and we are pushing for change. If we get even a little change, that's enough to hold us for that day.

I have a very interesting staff. They're young people. They are aggressive and keep everybody on their toes. I think there aren't a whole lot of people interested in becoming involved in civil rights because of the frustrations—particularly in a big bureaucracy—but the young people here have been just wonderful. They're imaginative and challenge us—challenge me—on policy all the time. I might say that some of their recommendations are way out, some of them are good, and we've adopted a fairly substantial number—as to how to set priorities, what policies are important and which ones we have to put on the back burner, so to speak.

You have been in various other programs along similar directions. Could you indicate, in those areas, what your assignments may have been, to what extent you were involved in building a new organization and establishing objectives?

Well, the Office for Civil Rights has gone through a fairly sizeable number of reorganizations, considering that we're not very old. Let me say that as far as I'm concerned you can have all kinds of administrative reorganizations and charts and graphs but you have to build it all around people. And you have to identify the strengths of your staff rather than its weaknesses. It's essential to build around their strengths and to try to balance people. People are strong in one aspect, and you try to balance them with others who can complement their abilities. So often, in a bureaucracy, a person's weaknesses rather than his strengths determine where he goes.

For example: We have teams of investigators who go out to review the Title VI performance of school districts, hospitals, nursing homes, and so on. On our staff we have some people who are competent investigators, but they can't seem to write a straight sentence! We try to balance our writers with our investigators, and we hope that each will learn from the other—so the writer's skills as an investigator can begin to develop and grow and the investigator can learn how to write what he has investigated so very well.

I'm just convinced that the whole concept of administration has to be built around people, and the ability to deal with people, rather than some lofty notions about "channels" and "hierarchies." The staff here feels free to come to see me on anything—anyone. They know the line of command; they know to whom their memos should be sent. But, on the other hand, I don't think there's anyone that has any reluctance to come and talk to me about either a personal problem (which is a very big part of administration, I'm finding), or a policy matter as it relates to our operation. Of course, this takes time, but in order to have an effective operation, or to try to have one, I think that it's unavoidable. In addition, I might say that I rather enjoy it, because I can sort of deal with problems and people, because I can talk to a lot of people and I may know more about a particular issue than the person confronting me *knows* that I know. I can engage very much in problem solving, I think.

I sometimes think we are loaded at various levels of government with specialists. Is there still room in an organization of this character for the generalist?

Yes, very much so. As a matter of fact, on the regional level—we have nine regional offices throughout the country—90 percent of our people are generalists. Their job description and their civil service write-up characterize them as generalists. We don't have many people to put out in the regions, so we expect them to be flexible and knowledgeable about Title VI and all of its implications—whether it's a school or a hospital or a nursing home. The issues are very much the same, although digging out the facts is different. It's fairly easy to review a hospital for compliance purposes because you look at beds and you count people—things like that. On the other hand, a school district is a lot more complicated. You may have to look at school board minutes and records. You have to talk to administrators to see what went on in the community to cause a certain boundary line to be changed or to stay the way it is, despite the fact that the school may be operating at over- or undercapacity. But if our people keep the issues and the goals in mind, we think that they can learn how to go about fact-gathering fairly quickly.

I assume your contacts with those involved at the policy and administrative levels in the educational process are continuous. Do you also have contacts with college students?

We have not had any contacts—specific contacts—with college students during the three years of our program, other than as valuable summer employees. However, we have begun a program of reviewing, on a systematic basis, colleges and universities throughout the country. As you may know, last year for the first time we asked all institutions that receive federal financial assistance to submit to us racial data. On the basis of these surveys we have identified colleges which we feel have Title VI problems. They either have a low percentage of minority group enrollees or segregated housing or no Negro athletes on scholarship—those types of things. We will be making our reviews—as a matter of fact we have been to about a dozen colleges and universities already. Our primary contact, of course, will be with the school administration, because those are the people we will be gathering our information from and those are the people that we will be asking to make changes. We realize, of course, that there's been quite a bit of unrest on a fairly large number of college campuses in the last several months. To the extent that we know about organizations that are concerned about these problems, on the campuses we visit, we want to meet with them to explain what we're trying to do and to make ourselves available to hear the kind of information or complaints that they will want to give us.

Surely. Your civil rights programs cut across so many agencies in government as well as outside groups. How do you manage to deal with internal administrative problems in HEW and also keep in touch with other groups at the field and Washington level?

Well, someone once said that "Our greatest enemy in the civil rights program is not the bigot, it's the bureaucrat." I'm not sure that I would agree with that completely. I will say that we have had our problems dealing with what we call the program agencies. These are the people with the money to give, and they, of course, have a vested interest in their program. The Office for Civil Rights is a compliance agency, and we're taking money away—when necessary—from other government agencies. It's a little difficult for many of them that have been granting funds for so long to understand that the law has now attached strings to their money— constitutional strings which say: "If your behavior is such, you are not entitled to this money."

We have come a long way with the program people of these action agencies, I believe. I think they're beginning better to understand our program and, I might add, they could be—and in many areas they are—our greatest allies. They are the ones that have the continuing relationships with the hospital administrators and boards, and the college presidents and boards, rather than we. They are members of the college establishment or the hospital establishment, and many of them are now beginning to explain the Title VI program to these individuals and institutions. And as a matter of fact, they're bringing information back to us—identifying a lot of institutions that might have a Title VI problem that we would not otherwise know about.

Could you describe a sample trip that you might make outside of headquarters? Where would you go, what happens, how quickly can you make decisions and produce results?

Why don't I take you on a compliance review of a school district in state X—let's call it a Southern state. This is a district that is operating under a so-called freedom-of-choice desegregation plan. This plan very simply says that any student has the right to choose to go to any school that he wishes. Now, this sounds like a very democratic, if novel, way to run a school district. But you have to realize the history and tradition of the community—Negroes have always gone to "Negro" schools; white children have gone to "white" schools. There are circumstances and forces within that community that will prevent Negroes from choosing to attend a "white" school. We have information that there are, say, five Negro students attending a white school—no white students attending a Negro school. The faculties at these schools reflect the racial composition of the students. In other words, the "integrated" school has an all-white faculty and the Negro school an all-Negro faculty.

Prior to visiting that school we would send the superintendent a letter telling him that on the basis of information submitted to us, it appears that the district may not be in compliance with Title VI. We tell him that someone from our office will be calling to make an appointment. We ask to meet with the superintendent and the school board. Immediately upon our arrival, we will ask for permission to visit individual schools within the district. We indicate that we are going to talk with people within the community about the situation in the schools, and also that we will conclude our visit with a "wrap-up" session with the school board.

At that wrap-up meeting with the superintendent and the school board, the regional office staff has authority to agree on a desegregation plan for that district. It can work out a plan and assure the district that if it adopts the plan they've agreed upon, it will be in compliance with Title VI.

Now there's just one limitation. We're talking about abolishing the dual school system. The first thing our staff people will say is that freedom of choice has *not* worked in this district. The courts have held that where freedom of choice has not worked, its use can no longer be regarded as complying with the law. Now if the school people balk at that, if they say that they're going to use freedom of choice forever, then our people usually go back to the regional office and refer the case to Washington for Title VI enforcement action. That is done in Washington because our lawyers are here, and because we work in close consultation with the Department of Justice.

But a district may say: "All right, we're going to abandon freedom of choice; we're going to come up with a different kind of desegregation plan. For the 1968–1969 school year we'll do A, B, C, D, and E. For the 1969–1970 school year we'll do F to Z, which will result in the elimination of the dual school system."

Your record includes early involvement as a bureaucrat in government administration concerned with civil rights programs. Could you perhaps trace some of these assignments and emphasize both challenges and frustrations?

Yes. Upon graduating from Law School (Howard University), I went to Ohio to work with a civil rights agency—a local one in Cleveland, my home town. And it became pretty apparent, to me, that with a civil rights ordinance primarily concerned with conciliation, I wasn't going to get very far. I was frustrated with that job and came back to Washington and worked with the United States Commission on Civil Rights for five years. As you may know, the commission is really the source of the proposals for civil rights legislation that the Congress passed during the sixties. Many of their recorts contained recommended legislation. The Civil Rights Act of 1964 was lifted out of its findings and proposals.

Once these were enacted into law, I wanted to see whether the laws that we struggled so hard to get enacted were going to have any real impact on the country. So I moved over to HEW, which has perhaps the biggest federal role in civil rights, because HEW is the largest granting agency. Transportation spends large amounts of money to build roads, but it isn't the same as making grants to colleges and universities for research or to upgrade teachers and those kind of things.

And I will say that I've had my frustrations since I've been here— particularly in the early stages of enforcement of the act, when some of us were quite concerned that the Congress might not have meant what it said when it passed the law. This is a sensitive and explosive program. It's a target for all kinds of political pressures and political attacks. The Office for Civil Rights is often made a party to the HEW programs. If you want to get a bill passed involving public health, for example, sometimes the politicians feel that they can put a little squeeze or a little pressure on the civil rights program.

Weaken it in some ways?

Yes, that would be the objective. But the top officials, at HEW and throughout this administration have been steadfast in their refusal to permit what I call administrative repeal of the act. You wouldn't have to repeal this law in order to make it nonoperative. It could just be administratively repealed. We've lived through all of the frustrations so far, and I guess the Office for Civil Rights is considered sort of the exciting part of HEW.

The new frontier.

Yes. We touch all of the department's programs; we sort of bring them all under our umbrella—whether they like it or not—because Title VI cuts across every piece of money that goes out of here.

The one thing, I guess, that personally influenced my getting involved in government, at the bureaucratic level, was my experience in undergraduate school. I attended Fisk University in Nashville, Tennessee, and I saw the kinds of humiliating things that happened to Negro residents—and to myself. I guess I was thrown off of more buses than I was allowed to ride on. And going up the back stairs to the "colored" balcony of a movie, and paying more to go in there than to sit downstairs. These are the kinds of things that gravely influenced my desire to get involved in history-making. And I just figure what I'm doing *is* history-making. We're trying to change the course of our country.

You have to start with the premise that this whole concept of segregation was legislated in the first instance. And there are people who say: "Why do you have to legislate civil rights?" It's because you have to *unlegislate* what was legislated in the last hundred years. We're trying to undo that kind of legislation. But when you get accustomed to wearing your hat on the left side of your head for twenty years, it's hard to change it to the right side. Despite the fact that you try, it's still hard.

But I think we're going to do all right. I'm just very confident. I'm an optimist and I think that America is going to be able to come to grips with this problem for a variety of reasons.

STUDY QUESTIONS

1. How would you characterize the administrative philosophy practiced by the director?
2. What criteria might best be used to measure the overall success or failure of this program?
3. What procedures might be improved at both local and national levels?

VI
PLANNING
AND DELEGATION

13

METROPOLITAN TRANSPORTATION CHAIRMAN

Dr. William J. Ronan directs the largest mass transport program in the nation. Its origin and growth reflect careful planning and cooperation between a governor, a state legislature, and the public.

In late May of 1965 the New York legislature passed a bill to establish a Metropolitan Commuter Transportation Authority—the MCTA. The Governor signed it at Albany on June 1, and the five members he appointed to serve as the governing board were confirmed on June 22 by the state senate.

Dr. Ronan, who had headed the special committee that recommended this legislation, was the agency's first chairman. Broad powers were conferred on the MCTA to preserve and improve commuter services in New York City as well as Dutchess, Nassau, Orange, Putnam, Rockland, Suffolk, and Westchester counties. The agency was also authorized to work with similar organizations in neighboring states towards related goals.

MCTA was governed by announced guidelines reflecting the dimensions of the transportation problems of the area in and surrounding metropolitan New York. In large measure, these principles reflected the thinking of Ronan and his approach to the planning process. Crash programs, it was

197

stated, can no longer—if they ever did—meet the giant needs imposed by the transportation crisis. As Ronan said: "Immediate and long-range needs must be identified, priorities for actions assigned, and specific programs implemented to meet these needs." The entire transportation complex was to be viewed on a much more comprehensive basis than in the past; all systems of rail, rubber, air, and water must be designed and operated to support one another. Mass transit was recognized as a vital part of a balanced regional system. Neither the city nor its suburbs, as Ronan put it, "can go it alone and continue to prosper."

The first year's accomplishments for this bold new venture were encouraging: the start of modernization on the Long Island railroad, assured continuation of the New Haven railroad commuter service, testing of new means of rail propulsion, and a study of regional airport needs. The next step came on March 31, 1967, when the state legislature approved comprehensive and farsighted legislation: a law to provide the financial basis for a broad, statewide transportation system, and another creating the administrative machinery to implement the program. In November of the same year the New York State voters approved a $2.5-billion transportation capital facilities bond issue—$1.25 billion for highway construction, $1 billion for mass transportation facilities, and $250 million for airport and aviation facilities. A state Transportation Department was then created to provide centralized administration of various functions, unification of mass transportation policy direction, and control in the New York State sector of the metropolitan region under a single board. Shortly afterwards (March 1, 1968) the MCTA was expanded in membership and renamed the Metropolitan Transportation Authority.

As of 1968 several separate agencies, responsible for regional transit needs, were included: New York City Transit Authority (subways), Manhattan and Bronx Surface Transit Operating Authority (bus lines), and Triborough Bridge and Tunnel Authority. Policy direction for and control of these agencies is carried out by a single board, although each agency will maintain separate operational and legal identity. In short, MTA, with a chairman and eight members, is the unifying organization and will also serve as ex-officio board for the other three local transit authorities. The new authority, Dr. Ronan indicated, can be compared to a public holding company that "provides and promotes unified direction for related transportation operations."

MTA represents a new, integrated approach to mass transportation, and its objective is to modernize New York City's system, which since Mayor LaGuardia—thirty years earlier—had not been improved in any major way. Organizationally, MTA hopes to avoid entanglement in municipal politics and the conflicts that normally develop between cities and their surrounding suburbs. As one report indicated, the objective is "a regional approach to urban problems."

The scope of Ronan's problems can be best illustrated by a brief sketch of the overall problem. It is estimated that by 1985 the 18 million people who now live on some 13,000 square miles in the tri-state metropolitan region will have increased to 25 million. In something less than twenty years this region will have to absorb the equivalent of two Chicagos. It is also anticipated that this population growth will occur mainly in the suburbs. The population of New York City is not expected to grow very much, but it may be slightly redistributed to the outer areas, while the areas closer to the core remain fairly stable. At the same time, one MTA document stated:

> By 1985 we will add more than 2.5 million nonagricultural jobs to the regional job market. Most of the growth in blue-collar jobs will take place outside the central city area. Yet the core area will continue to house a large proportion of the region's unskilled, and the need for fast, efficient, low-cost transit becomes increasingly significant.

And a detailed analysis of future trends has meaning beyond the confines of a great Eastern city, for it concludes: "Our ability to get people to their jobs and goods to the marketplace is a fundamental challenge in a rapidly urbanizing society."

Ronan's own views are succinctly stated in his comments: "If you can't go, you can't grow," and "Unless we move to meet transportation needs on a balanced and comprehensive basis, we will continue to be confronted with such ironies as new aircraft . . . capable of flying from New York to Seattle in about the same time it takes a Manhattan taxicab to go crosstown two miles from the area of the United Nations to the transatlantic piers on the West Side of the Hudson River."

Dr. Ronan, an educator turned administrator, has long been in on many political and administrative decisions affecting New York city and state. He was chief assistant to Governor Rockefeller for a significant period of his career. As the boss now of the largest complex of rail and bus lines ever linked together in a single agency, he seems to take his job in stride.

For this interview we met in his midtown Manhattan office. Reserved and somewhat distant, he is a man of strong purpose who conveys a strong sense of confidence, but he laughs easily, and his quick sense of humor—concerning himself and his work—comes as a surprise. Tall and straight, he exercises nearly every day and appears slim. His present task requires a combination of hardnosed pragmatism and clear vision, looking ahead to the next twenty to thirty years, and he has refused to make promises that cannot be fulfilled.

For about thirty minutes we spoke of his assignments and the problems he faces. For a person with pressing deadlines, the storms he has weathered are a sound preparation. One comes to think of him as a most deliberate, highly programmed individual who knows how to account for each split second of a long day. It may be, as mentioned in the interview, that his pleasure in making decisions is his secret weapon. In any case, he faces stern, often giant tasks with an even spirit.

He was born in 1912 in Buffalo, New York. In 1934 he received a baccalaureate degree magna cum laude at Syracuse University; he pursued further studies at the Geneva School of International Studies and at Harvard and took his Ph.D. in political science and economics at New York University. He was Penfield Fellow in International Law, Diplomacy, and Belles Letters and is a member of Phi Beta Kappa.

In 1938 Ronan was appointed instructor in government at New York University and advanced through the ranks of assistant and associate professor to become professor of government in 1946. During World War II, from 1943 to 1946, he was a lieutenant in the United States Navy. From 1949 to 1952 he served as administrative head of the Graduate Division of Public Service at New York University, and in 1953 was appointed Dean of the Graduate School of Public Administration and Social Service. In addition to these duties, he served New York University as chairman of its Institute of Labor Relations and Social Security, and from 1954 to 1959 was director of the New York University Ankara (Turkey) Technical Assistance Program.

Ronan has served in the State Department and Civil Service Commission in Washington and was the first Deputy City Administrator of New York. He has also been a consultant to federal, state, and local governments, both here and abroad, as well as to private organizations.

He has served New York State in several capacities. For nearly eight years, beginning in 1959, he was secretary to Governor Rockefeller. As Director of Studies of the Coordination Commission, he conducted surveys of the state Education Department, Civil Service Department, public authorities, Bureau of Motor Vehicles and the nonjudicial positions in the state courts. In December 1956 he was appointed Executive Director of the Temporary Commission on the Constitutional Convention, and its successor, the Special Legislative Committee on Revision and Simplification of the Constitution. In 1966 he was appointed to the temporary state Commission on the Constitutional Convention.

In the transportation field, Ronan has served as chairman of the Special Committee on the Long Island Railroad and chairman of the Tri-State Transportation Commission. As chairman of the board of MTA, he now is also chairman of the Long Island Railroad, New York City Transit Authority, Manhattan and Bronx Surface Transit Operating Authority, and the Triborough Bridge and Tunnel Authority.

Among professional associations, Ronan is a member of the American Foreign Law Association, American Society for Public Administration, National Academy of Public Administration, American Transit Association, International Institute of Administrative Sciences, National Municipal League, Civil Service Reform Association, and the Railroad Club of America.

Dr. Ronan is married, has two daughters, and resides in Manhattan.

Dr. Ronan, in a rather literal sense your career combines practice and theory, politics and administration, in respect to at least three assignments you fulfilled: dean of a graduate school in public administration, executive assistant to Governor Rockefeller, and now chairman of the Metropolitan Transportation Authority. In looking back over this journey, are there certain administrative principles that you would claim have been of most profit? On the other hand, have there been some that are of less value or even useless?

Well, I'd say probably the principle that's been most useful is the simplest, but in many respects the most difficult to observe, and that is to be sure there is delegation of authority and commensurate responsibility to get anything done. It's easy to say but not so easy to put into practice. Particularly in a political situation, in government, it is always hard to really get the kind of delegation of authority that is essential to get things done.

I've been fortunate in my work with Governor Rockefeller in that he happens to be a person of some understanding of these things, and he does delegate authority—in fact, sweeping delegations of authority to people in whom he has confidence. And, of course, here is the amendment to the principle: you can't delegate authority to people in the abstract, or to positions in the abstract. No sensible person in politics does it without knowing the person to whom he's delegating.

I think that in looking at an organization chart, as the student of public administration does, one sees a box that delegates to a subordinate box that's supposed to receive it.

No people, just boxes.

That's right. It's an unreal world. Another thing that one learns is that you don't just say: I delegate. This principle of the delegation of authority and responsbiliity: you have to have a situation where people are willing to accept responsibility—to accept authority. I've lived through many a situation where I found very competent people who were really unwilling or emotionally unable to accept authority.

Just scared or fearful?

In some cases fearful. In some cases they didn't want to tie their life sufficiently to the job to accept the responsibility. They'd rather be 9-to-5:30 or have their weekends free or whatever it might be—or just not have such anxieties that they thought went with responsibility.

Are the risks, would you say, greater than the rewards of accepting delegation?

I'm afraid that in the public service we are reaching a point—if indeed we haven't already reached it—where there is a reluctance on the part of a good many people to accept the kind of responsibility and, of course, the corresponding authority largely because of the social risks involved. And this may equate to difficulties in their own status situation in the community, because they become the bogeyman of government—or their wives become concerned, rather than the man himself. His wife doesn't want to be in a situation of being the wife of a man who's doing things that her neighbors, club members, associates in the church may question or consider irritating.

And they're all geared to a going status quo.

Very much. And this therefore becomes a disturbing element, whether a person's in the welfare field and is trying to effectuate some new concepts in welfare and therefore asks someone to take on a job—or in my current operation where I try to get somebody to head a task force on developing a General Aviation Airport. And of course nobody wants an airport in his backyard. If this fellow happens to live in Westchester County, in a place roughly where we're going to put an airport, his wife may be very unhappy that her husband becomes the instrument for despoiling Westchester County, or whatever it might be.

You brought up the phrase "task force." Have you much confidence in this, and why—or why not?

I have as much confidence in a task force as I do in its members. I have great confidence, *provided*—and the provisos are two: one, you get the right people, and two, the delineation of its role is carefully set forth and there's good communication between the people who have established the task force and those in it.

By a task force I may mean something a little different from the definition others might ascribe to it. To me it's bringing together people who are knowledgeable and have great expertise in a field where the research is pretty much done—at least as of the moment. You don't have time for in-depth research, beyond what has been accomplished, so you get people who presumably are acquainted with the field. . . .

And neutral, perhaps, towards your program?

Not necessarily.

Or impartial?

They may be impartial. Or you might put on the task force people deliberately of different views but all competent and articulate—and get them together and then, again, get a leader or provide the leadership out of your own group. And hammer out, with the task force, a decision on policy or a program, representing the best distilled thinking of the group. It's a group process.

To accept or reject?

To accept or reject on our part.

Do you have now a few in process?

As of the moment we're about out of task forces. And that's largely because we've just completed the master plan for the transportation in this region. We're now moving towards an implementing phase.

I like the phrase "master planning." In a sense you in the state are Mr. Master Planner. How far ahead are you looking? According to press reports, maybe too far.

Well, our program is geared to 1985 and we really look a little beyond that to the year 2000. We recognize that when you go that far afield, the year 2000, you're dealing with a lot of imponderables. We can see '85 fairly clearly—it's a lot closer to us in time certainly than the end of World War II is. So that's a very conceivable period, so far as we can see. And while we claim no omniscience, we can pretty much calculate what the state of technology is likely to be in our field by that time. We've been, of course, in touch with the people in research and development. That also indicates there isn't as much research and development in this field as there really ought to be. So in that sense it's a field that's been moving too slowly.

In your planning, can you rest on or refer to many or some of the administrative principles that this generation was brought up on? You did mention delegation, before. Do you find yourself having more meetings, that communication is the pulse of the administrative process —beyond good people, beyond solid personnel programs?

I think that, again going back to the statement of principles of administration—going back to Luther Gulick's POSDCORB—there's been a misinterpretation to some extent. I don't think he put forth POSDCORB as the kind of sterile piece of literature that some people see it.

Surprisingly, some of it still stands.

It does stand. I would say that there's been a misinterpretation of the planning end of it by some, and the planners themselves (as we have been developing a group of people who call themselves planners, or we call them planners) are getting too far away from the pragmatism that is essential in administration.

Planning was conceived, I'm sure, by Gulick and Urwick and other pioneers in the field as a process closely related to the rest of administration: coordination and organization as examples. I've always said that planning and all the rest of the so-called functions listed together in POSDCORB are all aspects, really, of the same thing: the administrative process. It's one continuing process and these are different aspects. You can look at it from different points of view.

In an attempt to segregate planning, to isolate it and say: "We must plan"—is sometimes an attempt to move into a vacuum. Or, more important in my field, there's an attempt to stop the world while we plan. And this is absolutely impossible. It's devastating, and there's too much of it. And there's also a kind of utopianism which—I don't want to derogate too much—goes into certain kinds of planning which makes it frequently not as useful as it should be—and sometimes useless.

That's one reason why I think you have libraries full of plans that have never been implemented. And I think the planning fraternity—the planners, in attempting to establish a professional identity for themselves, run the risk of becoming isolated from the administrative process. And if that continues, they will be ignored. Because the fact of the matter is, decisions are going to be made; if planning is going to play its role, it's got to be an integral part of the process. It can't be isolated.

I've often thought that administrative theorists play games. They claim at one point that decision making is the heartbeat of the process. And then they discover that the human being counts. And then they find that human relations cares too much for the individual. Have you been so exposed to these principles that one or two or perhaps three really count—or are there certain individuals that have influenced you?

Well, I guess I've been influenced by a number of individuals in my time. I would say probably, as of this stage of the game, I've been influenced by experience, which includes individuals—working one's way out of difficult situations.

Maybe that's what administration is.

I think this is it, actually. Administration to me, anyway, is a process —it's a process in many ways by which you take ideas and put them into practice. That's about what it is.

And if they don't work?

If they don't work, you have to adjust them, modify them, drop them, or whatever the case may be. You really start with a concept or a series of concepts and then you try to take this abstract idea and make it concrete through action.

If you were looking for a good administrator—even ideal administrator—would you check off on the blackboard certain priority qualities?

Yes, I would. The first quality I would look for may surprise you. I would say the person has to have excellent health.

This is often overlooked?

Very much so.

Mental and physical?

Mental and physical. And with that I say must go stamina. Now that doesn't mean that a person who's crippled or has some kind of disease he can live with, need not be a good administrator. But let me emphasize that in administration one needs a tremendous amount of sheer physical and mental vigor to be successful.

Staying power?

A great deal of staying power. But it's more than this. The Bible says: "He that shall endure unto the end, the same shall be saved." Well that's fine, but saved for what? This is the real question. So you do need the endurance, but administration also takes tremendous vigor. It's not only to endure, but to influence others to your way of thinking.

Perhaps the pace is too rigorous.

I doubt that, because a good administrator can get—within limits, obviously—the capacity to pace himself. And some of the administrators who work themselves—quote "to death," unquote—are failures in and of themselves.

Allocating goals?

That's right—inability to delegate and winding themselves up in frustration. Now that doesn't mean that on occasion jobs don't break people who do the best they can—and that happens in life—dealing with difficult legislative committees, or bosses, or supervisors. It can be nerve-wracking, I'm sure, to people.

But I think an administrator has to have a very considerable amount of stamina—intellectual, moral, physical.

Integrity?

That's what I mean by the moral stamina. It takes sheer "guts"—to use the popular term.

Isn't an administrator a teacher? He cares enough to share, to build people, to give freely of himself.

He has to, and he's not going to be successful unless he does. In any organization of any size, no man can do it all himself. The word sounds bad, but an administrator to some extent has to be an evangelist. He's not just a teacher; he's got to be a convincer. And when he develops his staff morale, the enthusiasm for a program—in a sense, he's evangelizing a cause. Whether it's in business or government or voluntary organizations you'll find that usually your best administrators are the people who are identified with a cause.

Does this also mean that a good administrator must be a team member?

I don't like the phrase "team member," in a sense, because administration to some extent is a fight.

And a lonely one.

It can be a very lonely one, depending on the position a person has. There are times when chief adminstrators especially—and certainly this is true of Presidents, governors, and so on—have got to make decisions when all around them there may be differing points of view, representing all kinds of values. A person just has to spend the lonely hour or minutes. Often there isn't time to anguish over it; a decision's got to be made fairly rapidly. But it can be a very lonely thing.

When you say that a man's a team player, some of the more successful administrators might not fall into that definition. They are team players in the sense that they provide leadership to a team, but a team player may also be defined as being a good guy and getting along with. . . .

Even perhaps a yes-man?

A yes-man, or putting the relationship to the group ahead of the idea that has to be pushed, implemented—whatever it may be.

And his ideas may drown or suffocate.

They can, and I could give you names of people who were lifted out of positions where they were good team players and put in positions of principal administrators, and become failures. And the reason: they could not rise above being a good guy in terms of their interpersonal relationships. There comes a time—and it may be unfortunate—where a man has to put the respect of the people that are going to work for him ahead of their friendship.

Does loyalty have a strong influence?

I think loyalty is an essential in administration.

Can it be divorced from this concept of the team?

I would redefine team. I think loyalty to the organization, to the program of the organization, and to the leadership of the organization is what makes for morale and productivity, and gets things done in a very real sense of the word. And that loyalty comes only as a result of at least a two-way and maybe a multi-way street.

But the administrator who would command the respect and affection of the people has to be something other than just a shortstop on the team. When we talk about team player, remember there's always a captain to the team—and the captain calls the signals. And this has to be recognized.

And there may be too many: "I wish I were captain."

That's right. And you can overdo the committee business, in arriving at a consensus, I think, with all due deference to the committee process, brainstorming and so on. It is valuable and you can't operate without drawing on the expertise, knowledge, intelligence, and imagination of your colleagues and associates—because that's what really keeps you alive and moving.

Still, if you are the number one, as governor or mayor, you among others should never lose sight of that fact. Otherwise you're very apt to slip. I don't mean that in an arrogant sense; I'm talking in an organizational sense—in a sense of assuming responsibility, providing leadership, and explaining to your associates *why* you're doing what you're doing, so they know and understand and appreciate.

Much of the literature makes much of relations between the political executive and the nonpolitical administrator—or career man. Is this a real problem, from your vantage point in this state? Member of a cabinet and an invisible second man, as it were.

I would say that the attempt to draw a sharp line between the political executive and the nonpolitical administrator is bound to result in frustration.

For both?

For both. Now that doesn't mean that the career administrator in a government department should become a politician—in the political party sense. I think that is not necessary. I don't think it's expected anymore in a state as sophisticated as New York. On the contrary, I think it might well be resented because if there's anything that the political officeholder, who comes in as part of a political team, would resent, it would be career administrators trying to do his politics for him.

But I think there has to be an accommodation and it depends to a very considerable extent upon the rigidity of the people involved, on both sides.

You've seen, in the state, bureaucracy at first hand. . . .

Very much so.

Why, and I must ask this, is it often—if not always—scolded or spanked? Does it have a bad press? Is it the image?

Well, I think there's a lack of knowledge about bureaucracy. The fact of the matter is that any major government today, in this country, to some extent runs itself.

It often seems so.

You've got a bureaucracy, so-called, which is a group of people who have been assigned to and are carrying out jobs. There's a structure of authority and responsibility, a method of communication, established policies and procedures—and it runs. As long as nobody interferes with it too much, it'll run. And therefore you can remove, let's say, the head of a department and yet the department will go. He could take a world tour and things would still run, after a fashion.

But perhaps things would run away.

They would either run away or run down or get into a rut, which is a real danger. It becomes much more of a set course, which is not going to meet the exigencies of the time.

But within a bureaucracy, the difficulty is that when an organization settles into an established habit-pattern, the routines set up to accomplish particular policy and program objectives can lose their meaning and become rote, if you're not careful. You need to distinguish between a routine which has a purpose and what is done by rote. Just as in religion you've had practices which became routine—all once had meaning, but after a while they became rote. We have religious cults, throughout history or maybe even today, where people simply go through motions. And bureaucracy can do the same thing.

Can a bureaucracy be innovative and exciting?

It can, provided—and here's the big proviso—the bureaucracy generates—is able to generate—a great deal of imaginative, creative thinking. I would say the problem is the stultification that comes with the mechanistic kind of establishment that is too often the stereotype that the press writes about.

Actually one of the requirements when one goes into government as a political officer—I've done both—is to find out in the bureaucracy where the creative talents are—and they're there.

And squeeze, concentrate, and maximize. . . .

Or encourage and stimulate them. It's leadership again within the bureaucracy. One of the major problems that you have to contend with is to free the creative, the energetic, the doers as against the people who do just what they think will get by. Whether it's government, business, the church, philanthropy—you have different types of people, all kinds in all walks of life.

Ed Litchfield often—whenever I was in one of his informal sessions— said and wrote, as you know, about this: administration is administration, public and private. Is there enough transferability, or mobility, between the public and private worlds? Would you like to see, perhaps, more?

I think there ought to be more than there is, and I'm afraid that one of the reasons there isn't more is that there isn't enough mixing of key people in the private sector and the public sector—in a meaningful fashion.

More than just luncheon meetings.

Or just going off to the university—or wherever it may be—for a weekend and kicking it around. I think where you do involve people on meaningful projects—and this is one of the places where the task force is a very useful device—it brings together people from various parts of the business community, labor, and the professions. The cross-fertilization of ideas is, number one, very important. But number two, I think, you do develop a communication, and personal associations which tend to move across the board.

I've been interested, as a person who's spent a great deal of his life in public activity and in university activity, in the number of opportunities I've had from private business people I've been associated with, to go into private business.

Did it pull, ever?

Some of them were challenging. They didn't happen to be as challenging as what I was doing. I had no bias at all against private business and I serve on the board of a couple of private corporations, at their request, with their insistence. They were persistent, let me put it that way. And I find that the contribution a person with my background can make to those boards is rather different and unique and apparently valuable as against the contribution of those who would have come up through an accounting firm or a bank or a law firm.

Long-range view?

A very different view. It's different. I wouldn't want to say longer-range, because there are people who come into such an activity whose long-range view of the money market is better than mine. But on the other hand, being in touch—as one is in government—with social forces, with economic forces on-the-move, and having a close acquaintance with the governmental processes, the political processes—you get a basis for judgment that's very different. It's a broader base in a sense.

And you're more aware of all these nuances. . . .

Very much so.

. . . than those in the private sector—which may be an overstatement.

Well, you're aware in a broader spectrum. One thing I think political life teaches you is that you have to be sensitive to a lot of social forces, to the interests and needs of different groups of people. And you've got to have a sensitivity to public relations. A good politician has to be almost charismatic, I would say, in that sense.

And this leads you to a very different kind of an evaluation of events, than if you are a person who's been spending most of his life with figures as an accountant dealing mostly with corporate executives, and so on. And spending your social life, not going to political meetings and mixing with the crowd, but enjoying your friends and your clubs and so on. And I enjoy my friends and my clubs very much, too, and wish I had more time to spend with them—but I've been exposed, and continue to be, to a wide variety of people. Because being in politics to the extent that I've been, this happens.

Two points: What have been some of the greater satisfactions as you look back, over the years? And could you bring us into the current scene and some of your operating problems.

I think the greatest satisfactions come out of solving problems, because I have the kind of mind, I think, that likes to wrestle with problems.

The soluble problems.

Yes, and I don't really believe that there are any problems in terms of government and politics where you cannot make some approach toward a solution. Obviously, we will not solve all problems for all time, but at least we can make some progress—particularly, if we take a progressive, pragmatic point of view on them.

I would say one of the great satisfactions is seeing problems tackled and, to an extent, resolved, and new programs instituted for solving them.

One of the great things to look back on are problems that were great problems as of the time, but are not problems any more, largely because of one's efforts or those of one's associates.

That's not to say that you just wastebasket them for a while.

Not at all. These are things behind us. Let me mention some, for example, where we think we've made some progress. Let's take the field of labor relations. New York State had no minimum wage. So some of us played a major role and we now have a minimum wage. We have collective bargaining in voluntary institutions. Some of us played a role in bringing that about. And one has seen substandard wages—hospital workers getting 60 cents an hour, not even under the Wage Hour Act. Now these people are not second-class citizens but able to organize, to bargain collectively. Sure there's a special arrangement—compulsory arbitration. There is a minimum wage. These things are on the way. Well, you get a great satisfaction.

In a very different area, in terms of a different problem: the state embarked on a tremendous program to eliminate water pollution within six years in its own streams. With the leadership of the Governor, some of us worked on that program. We produced it in crash time and I won't tell you how little time it took to produce it, for others had done the research before. This is the value of a few people zeroing in. I see the press notices as they come through with the grants that are going to local communities. While nobody believes it, I'm sure, water pollution is going to go out in New York State. We're not going to have it. Now this is a great thing, and it will be taken for granted.

You have to take your pleasure, in a sense, from things that are now just taken for granted, but which you had to fight for. You have to take your own satisfaction from that.

Some things, then, are improvable.

Yes. I think we can definitely improve most things. And I think the most devastating thing that is happening in our society at the present time is that people are beginning to take the position: nothing can be done. This bothers me in the race relations field.

It's too late.

The theory is, it's too late. It is never too late. Never. It can't be, because the alternative is anarchy, cataclysm, and what not. It's never too late.

With all our administrative techniques—I don't mean to use that in a pejorative sense—it would seem reasonable to agree with you. Most things can be solved.

They can.

With just the will and the word you used before—stamina.

It takes it.

You may get tired. . . .

Yes. But this is also why I think it important that in administration, one has to know when to quit. Or if one doesn't know, others ought to be in a position to say so. Because there will come a time in a person's life when the batteries do run down, and maybe they can't be recharged. A battery that gets too old won't take a charge after a while. And I think some of the wise people get out when they have others to take on the load.

The energy people get derives, I think, from the excitement and the challenge that's in the job. I think that's true of a number of key political figures on the scene today—and always has been.

In terms of your present program, have you pioneered greatly? According to my information, you have a long-range plan for a $2.9-billion system of transport for New York City.

Well, I think we've pioneered—in this way. First, we've proposed a regional approach to transportation and have been successful in having this adopted by the state government of New York—the first state that's ever adopted a plan presented for mass transportation. I don't like that word but that happens to be the phrase: mass transportation for the entire New York State section of this metropolitan region.

This is a program that's going to total about $2.9 billion. For the first phase of it—$1.6 billion—we can see the money to build because the people passed a bond issue, which we had a large hand in helping to produce, and so we can actually build this first phase. It's going to be done by a regional agency that didn't exist before the Rockefeller administration came in. It's going to be done by putting together, for the first time under one board—which we have now—the subways of New York City, the bus operations of the City, the Triborough Bridge and Tunnel Authority—with all of its fascinating activity, including a convention hall and a zoo, and the Long Island Railroad.

And we're just now in the process of acquiring a general aviation airport at Republic. We spent the morning on it, and we're going to move on that. And we're going to build bridges across the sound—Long Island Sound. That's required of us under the law.

What we've done here is to create a structure which will ensure a regional outlook on transportation for the future. We are bringing together rail, air, water, rubber, really in a very big way.

Does this tie into Department of Transportation in Washington?

It's very materially tied in with DOT, which is fascinated with this operation. We're on very good terms with Alan Boyd [the Secretary] and John Rooks, who's just come in to head their mass transportation activity.

But let me go back to administrative principles, because in the establishment of this agency we've done something very unusual. We've created something that others had talked of and some had tried to do and failed—an agency to encompass all of this activity. And administratively it's rather interesting.

One of the things that we have learnt—and learnt the hard way in administration—is that if you have a going concern, and it's working, before you disturb it, be sure you know what you're going to do and know approximately what the results are going to be. We have also learnt that vitality lies in a degree of autonomy.

One of the main things—going back to our talk about bureaucracy—that I find wrong with bureaucracy is that we don't create enough semi-autonomous units within the bureaucracy to provide the kind of initiative, incentive, and so on, that's necessary. . . .

For each individual.

. . . for each individual and for each unit so he can feel a part of something that's comprehensible rather than something that's enormous.

Now, we took over the New York City Transit Authority, we took over the Manhattan and Bronx Surface Transportation Operating Authority, the Triborough Bridge and Tunnel Authority, the Long Island Railroad, et cetera. What we've done is to leave these as autonomous units, up to a point. First of all, we must keep out of the details of operation, because interference would be fatal.

Would it be just duplication?

Not only duplication. We wouldn't know enough to do it; we would be operating in an area where we would not have, frankly, the talents; nor could we give it the time and attention it needs.

You'd have mess and mass.

That's right. Therefore, what we've done in a sense is to create a kind of holding company structure: a single board for all of these operations with a highly intelligent, able, practical, very well-informed central staff for that board. And then we delegate to the operating agencies the authority to run them, subject to our policy direction and control. Now it's in its infancy but so far it seems to be working.

We can, by virtue of this, encompass what would be almost impossible. And I read in a couple of newspapers, from time to time, statements that we ought to take over more and ought to integrate on a total regional basis all transportation—because we've gone this far, we ought to go further.

Well, there may be a logic to that ultimately, but until we derived this formula we didn't think it would be possible to bring all these together. And under this arrangement, you see, we can add—which we will—the New Haven Railroad commuter service and we'll be able to manage it. So manageability is a very important part of this.

Are there lessons that are being applied on the West Coast, Midwest, Southern area—or in Europe and in developing countries? Is this the first as a method in regionalism that can be borrowed?

We've had the advantage, frankly, of looking at some other regional setups: Toronto, pre-eminently.

They established a really metropolitan government which is different from ours. They put their transit under this. In this area, metropolitan government is an impossibility at this point legally, and it would be almost impossible to comprehend at this juncture in terms of management.

Did you go to India and London and other places?

Some of the things we're doing here are of very great interest to people in London—and we studied London before we took our steps here. There were some things there we were very much interested in. But I think they're now turning around and looking at us, because they did not put the commuter railroads and the subways together—they went a different route. I think in both London and Paris you'll find they're beginning to come in our direction now. We were behind them before, organizationally.

I've visited the Soviet Union recently and visited with their people. We've learnt something from them—not so much in administrative terms but in terms of technology.

The San Francisco Bay Area Rapid Transit system is something we've learnt a great deal from—their successes and failures so far.

The whole area of comparative administration as well as comparative technology—we are very high on. For example, in terms of comparative management, we're about to embark on an enormous construction program. The San Francisco Bay Area program is probably the second biggest, once we get ours going. And we went out to just see how they had organized themselves to do the construction phase of it—because that's a major administrative problem we face. We're going to build railroads, subways, and all the rest of it.

There are real problems: How do you get along with organized labor—because strikes, jurisdictional disputes could kill you. There's the question of how do you get competitive bidding. How big should a project be—or how little—to get the optimum bidding.

It could be too big?

It could be too big. In other words, if you put out too big a slice of subway construction, it might mean that only one company in the country —or more likely, a joint venture by several of the biggest companies—is the only group that could do it. Well, then you don't get competitive bidding. How do you split it up? What's the optimum size?

These are all things that a comparative approach can help us with— and we pursue them.

I suggest on a weekend you write the next book on public administration. Thanks very much.

It's a pleasure.

STUDY QUESTIONS

1. How does Dr. Ronan's approach to planning and other features of the administrative process agree with views generally presented in the literature?
2. Explain the advantages and disadvantages of the structure represented by this new type of organization.
3. Can you think of a better method of solving the metropolitan transportation problems of the largest cities?

14

FOREST SERVICE

The Forest Service administers all public lands that are reserved as national forests. According to the official language:

> The Forest Service, under the direction of the Secretary of Agriculture, is responsible for applying sound conservation and utilization practices to the natural resources of the National Forests and National Grasslands. It also has the responsibility of promoting these practices among all forest landowners through example, cooperation, research, and the dissemination of information.

By law, the Service is authorized to make far-reaching decisions on a continuous, complex question: to what best use should the forest be put—wilderness, public power, dams, resources development, or recreation? These, and similar issues, require a staff highly skilled in balancing competing viewpoints, seeking hard facts in difficult situations, and weighing the impact of different choices as they affect the overall objectives of the Service.

Over the years the Forest Service has acquired a distinctive character of its own, which Professor Charles Reich describes in a paper for the

Center of Democratic Institutions entitled "Bureaucracy and the Forests" (1962): "The profession of forestry has strong elements of solidarity. A vigorous esprit de corps, a proud history, and many common experiences bind foresters together."

In order to evaluate a most-favored managerial concept of this Service—delegation—the present investigator moderated a round-table session at the Washington headquarters office, the participants being five professional foresters now serving as director and branch chiefs of the Administrative Management Division. Each of these men had started his forestry career at the junior professional entrance level and climbed the career ladder past district ranger to forest staff, regional office staff, and now headquarters staff.

Delegation has become a kind of trademark of the Forest Service. A manual, *Organization and Management Systems in the Forest Service* (December 1967) states that in order to accomplish its objectives

> ... the Forest Service pursues the following policy:
> 1. Delegates maximum authority to subordinate line officers consistent with laws and Department regulations and retention of control by the Chief.
> 2. Provides each line officer with the help and facilities he needs to carry out the responsibilities assigned to him.

This manual also defines delegation as

> ... the process whereby a line officer divides the work assigned to him so that significant portions of the whole job may be effectively assigned to subordinates. Delegation is necessary to obtain acceptable performance at minimum cost. . . . The real purpose of delegation is to give each member of the organization the freedom he needs to do the work assigned to him. For this reason *Forest Service policy requires full delegation all along the line*,[1] including necessary provision for guidance, coordination, and control functions.

The delegation process balances commitment to topside policies with respect for and encouragement of the resilience and resourcefulness of the field rangers who are concerned with program operations. As Professor Herbert Kaufman so precisely stated in *The Forest Ranger*, first published in 1960:

> The Rangers want to do the very things the Forest Service wants them to do, and are able to do them, because these are the decisions and actions that become second nature to them as a result of years of obedience. Recruits may conform to official requirements against their instincts, their desires, or even their judgment at the outset, as the techniques of over-

---

[1] Italics added.

riding their personal feelings are applied. After a while, though, they come to appreciate the reasons for the policies they execute, and they come to comply with instructions habitually, instinctively, naturally. If there were no preformed decisions and devices for discovering and correcting deviations from them, it seems likely many of the patterns of behavior that become habitual would never be established; that is, "internal" forces may well depend, at least in part, on external influences.

At the same time, the operations of the external influences may depend on successful manipulation of the personal references and perspectives "inside" the Rangers. Systematic selection and training of personnel, and procedures for building identification with the Forest Service, increase Ranger receptivity to the communications of the central office.

During the round-table discussion, theories and practices of delegation were compared by seasoned foresters as they viewed the process through their own experiences—in some instances, for a total of thirty-five years within the Service. For example, is delegation a rigid as well as a flexible instrument; how is a balance achieved between the views of those in the field organization and headquarters personnel; are there any lessons that other government agencies might adopt? Quite naturally, this appraisal of delegation led into a lively exchange around the table, on such questions as staff and line, career service, job enlargement, morale, and mobility.

The district ranger was the main focus of attention in this discussion, since, as the conferees generally agreed, he occupies a central position on the firing line of operations where the "buck usually stops." Indeed, the ranger is the key man in the Service as regards careers established, field-headquarters relations, decision making, and the translation of administrative policies into practical results.

Participants

Chester A. Shields—Director, Division of Administrative Management

W. Duncan Giffen—Chief, Directives, Forms, and Reports Branch

Lennart E. Lundberg—Chief, Management Studies and Systems Planning Branch

Russell T. Cloninger—Chief, Organization and Work Programs Branch

Donald W. Smith—Chief, Workload Analysis and Work Planning Systems Branch

Does the Forest Service encourage a combination of staff and line work in developing a career? How has it been able to generate a commitment and perseverance to its goals?

Shields: Traditionally in the Forest Service, the career-ladder pattern has been to move personnel back and forth from line to staff assignments as a requirement for advancement. A few years back, however, through analysis, it was decided to deliberately design our career-ladder pattern to provide more specific and more acceptable career ladders within specialties. An individual who aspires to be at the top of his specialty can now reach that goal through a specialty-career ladder. For example, it isn't necessarily required that a division director at the Washington level have experience as a line officer in all of the lower levels. So there has been a shift in recent years. Nevertheless, most Forest Service staff people—particularly foresters—have wanted to try their wings and gain experience in a number of different areas. This is supported by deliberate career-ladder design at the lower levels that helps to sort out interests and aptitudes at the lower levels before a more restricted, vertical career ladder is chosen.

Giffen: I think this also relates to where you are at the time you make a choice. For example, when I took my first job with the Forest Service, I wanted to be a district ranger. At first I was satisfied with being a ranger, but then after a few years I realized that I wanted to go on. This is why I think it depends upon where you are.

If you were to redesign your careers, would you do them in the same way—for purposes of training, or to train a replacement?

Giffen: Yes, I would. In fact, we had a training position in our branch and I encouraged both of the occupants of that position to go back to the field into the ranger's job. This is where all of our work is done and it gives them the background that, I feel, is essential to an understanding of all that comes later on.

Career development ties into the concept of delegation, for which the Forest Service has long been admired. This suggests a participatory democratic type of management. Are there certain features of the Service that encourage people at the lesser levels to be resourceful, even independent, knowing that they will work their way up? The ranger, I guess, is the heartbeat of the Forest Service—or not?

Shields: Yes, the ranger is the heartbeat of the national forest system. I suspect that our discussion will revolve primarily around this part of our total program. This is where the bulk of our personnel is assigned and where decentralization and delegation are most prominent. We have two other major programs—state and private forestry cooperative programs and the forest research program.

In responding to your question, there's great danger in oversimplifying. How do we get or do we have democratic, participative management? A noteworthy aspect of the Service is that field views, suggestions, and recommendations are deliberately solicited during the process of national policy formulation. The top level in the Forest Service, the Chief and his staff, insist on it.

Smith: I think Duncan made the point when he said: "This is a Forest Service attitude at the field district level, where the work is done." The work is done down at the district level and the structure above pretty much supports and helps the district get the job done. To me, this has a strong bearing on the so-called democratic, participating management.

Having come in from the field—and that goes for each one of you— it would seem that at the national level, of which you're now representative members, you can look for contributions from those with whom you've been associated. Can't you easily pick up the phone, or drop a note to a field person, on a first-name basis—someone with whom you've worked—or encourage him to come here for a conference? Communication, I should think, would be easier from Washington to the field because your careers encourage the field to contribute.

Shields: Of course you have to understand that it's a career service and that the Chief of the Forest Service—all the Chiefs—have achieved their position through the career ladder.

Do they go back into the field quite often?

Shields: In terms of inspections and field visits, they keep in close touch. They're very sensitive to the need for matching Forest Service policies with the field views and conditions on the ground, the acres of land that we manage. I can recall sitting in a staff meeting with the Chief of the Forest Service when a staff proposal was presented—a recommendation affecting the field and requiring his decision. He asked the question: "What are the field views on this?" The staff had not obtained any field views and he said—and I can just about quote: "I am not about to make a decision on this *until* I have the views of the field."

So, it's a state of mind, perhaps, throughout the organization, as well as the factor of career training.

Shields: It's built into the philosophy of the organization, but there are very specific reasons why it is needed. You have to trace the decision-making process as it relates to the resource being managed. At this level you cannot have personal, intimate knowledge of every acre of land in the 187,000,000 acres we're responsible for managing. Therefore, a man at this top level must have the facts on the local situation before he can make good decisions. He must know the needs of the local situation—not only of the resource but also the local residents who are dependent upon this resource.

You must also consider the speed within which decisions must be made. In other words, if you must make a decision to stop a forest fire in the shortest available time, you can't consult the Chief of the Forest Service. The man on the ground must have the technical knowledge, willingness, and authority to put the fire out.

I think we've got our third factor: that the nature of your program dictates that you become fully aware of field problems.

Shields: It does dictate.

Giffen: I think there's another important phase of this thing. In spite of the fact that all of us have many years of experience in the Forest Service—and at the field level, too—this old world is moving so rapidly that we must not forget this point and try to make decisions based on the way things were thirty years ago. If we do, we're in bad shape. We've got to go to the field.

Cloninger: We should not forget, though, the basic principles of running a ranger district. I don't think that we can sit in Washington and write policy and put all the stuff in the manuals without having had that basic experience in the district. We must also have some idea of the impact our policies will have from the bottom to the top.

The issue of centralization versus decentralization today is on the spot. It has many elements: bringing government closer to the people, increasing the sense of participation by the public, as well as encouraging those in a particular Service (such as yours) to contribute to the general welfare and public interest I would say we have at least three sound reasons for this decentralization in your organization: the background training of each professional, the need to delegate, and the nature of the materials with which you work.

Shields: Another is the social and political framework within which the Service operates—social needs and the direction of the administration in office. Incidentally, Forest Service officials pride themselves as professionals on their responsiveness to the administration. We greatly prize our responsiveness to whatever administrative direction is given to us.

We feel very badly when people accuse us of being so inbred that we go our own way. I could cite examples from first-hand observation of senior management in the Forest Service proving that this is not the case. Historically it may once have been so, but today we seek out and bring in laterally or at promotion—at all levels—people having special skills and experience in other organizations. In fact, we are far from inbred or restricted in our career ladders. We feel badly about this kind of criticism because we don't think it is justified.

This central core of experience, as you pointed out, started by entering professionals at the lower levels. Our career development program was deliberately designed to broaden their experience through assignments from level to level, from one geographic area to another, and from one activity to another. All of this results in a very strong identification with central purposes and goals. It also provides greater understanding of what is necessary at all levels to accomplish these goals in terms of support, training, delegation or what have you. But this is different from exclusiveness or inbreeding.

At this point let me offer a definition of delegation and see whether you agree or disagree: delegation is a systematic effort to deposit, at

the lowest practical level, sufficient responsibility and matching author-
ity so that decisions can be made with an awareness of the problems to
be met. Now that may be a bit too brief. Is it defined in this way in the
Service?

Shields: Well, this is how we commonly define it. However, you have
to consider the factor of training so that the capability to redeem this responsibility will be present. You can't separate delegation and training.
They have to go hand-in-hand.

Is delegation partly a gamble, or is it so much stressed that your people
respond well? Or, is it that you delegate heavily because you know
that they can tackle most problems?

Cloninger: Hold on a minute. I think we're missing the point. What's
the reason for delegation? We have four levels of management in the
national forest system—the Chief's office, the regional office, the forest, and
the district. Why do we have 790 districts? Why don't we combine some
of them and have only 200? Our basic mission is service to the public. Now,
if you're going to serve the public you have to move authority and responsibility down to where the public is located. These are the basic reasons
behind decentralization or delegation of authority—at least to me.

Are the terms delegation and decentralization used interchangeably by
your staff?

Shields: I don't know that we concern ourselves with semantics, except
in discussions of this type when we have to agree on definitions in order to
communicate. The Forest Service was once a centralized organization—for
various reasons, including relatively few trained people, a comparatively
low level of resource management, a small budget—a whole host of reasons.
But very quickly we found that the knowledge of on-the-ground situations,
the relation of these resources to the people who depended upon them—the
point Russ just made—and the necessary speed of decision making required
that decentralization take place. In fact, in one fell swoop the Forest Service
established regional offices and moved people in mass out of Washington.
This was in 1908.

Cloninger: One other point. Delegation per se is neither good nor bad.
In many cases, centralization and nondelegation are probably the best
approach. For instance, there's a tremendous difference in the amount of
delegation and decentralization between the state and private forestry
programs and the National Forest System programs—simply on the basis
of the mission of those two programs.

In other words, if delegation were not serving your needs, you'd
abandon it. Right?

Cloninger: Or change it.

Lundberg: There are various degrees of delegation, too. I don't think
we're heavily doctrinaire for or against decentralization. Maybe, we're

more doctrinaire about delegation, but I think it gets down to the kind of activities, the kind of things we're doing in meeting our objectives, and so on.

Giffen: I think you also have to recognize the evils in it, and a real good example is that we have three levels below the Washington office and delegations to each level. For example, a district ranger cannot make a decision or carry out a program that affects two ranger districts. This kind of decision has to be made by the supervisor. By the same token, the supervisor is not delegated the authority to make a decision which affects two forests. This has to go to the regional forester. So you've got to recognize the problems in delegation, as well as the benefits.

There are, then, minuses as well as pluses. The first minus that comes to mind is the risk that a person may be making larger decisions than he is capable of doing. But you've guarded against such a minus, it seems. He has to operate within his own boundaries.

Shields: We have organized so that we can provide specialist support to the decision maker except for emergency situations, which are well defined—fire control, someone lost in the woods, or something of this easily recognizable nature. Normally you have enough time available to acquire the advice of specialists. We're dealing with a physical resource, and generally you have lots of time to acquire the facts necessary to make the decision. This can vary anywhere from a week to a hundred years. Even though you delegate, all the specialist support at all levels—including the Washington level—can be brought in to assist this man in making a good decision. We have many mechanisms through which this specialist support operates—rather elaborate, comprehensive work-planning systems and management plans.

Does this type of consultation rub off on the field staff?

Shields: It's not a case of rubbing off. The field staff just can't do business without it. Specialists are essential working tools.

You're speaking also of the manuals?

Shields: The manuals and also the technical resource management plans that govern the management of timber, recreation, water, or whatever.

Is it possible in manuals to anticipate all the possibilities that could develop? There is something that has been called "manualitis," when headquarters people become obsessed with the need to get-it-in-writing. Quite often, this makes a prisoner of the guy out in the field.

Giffen: Our basic policies that are dictated by law and regulation must be distributed to all levels. Also, standards which apply Service-wide must be put in the manual system. But it isn't practical for us, at this level, nor is it good business, to put instructions in the manual to cover every job in the Forest Service. For example, the Washington office should not issue detailed instructions on how to mark trees. This is because the species that you mark in Florida are entirely different from the species on the West Coast. So our directive system permits supplementation at the lower levels to cover such items.

Smith: I don't think it restricts your ability; rather, it enhances it.

Giffen: Right.

Smith: Actually, I know my experience as a district ranger was that if I wanted to do a certain thing, I looked in the directive system to find the policy on the matter and determined whether I had the authority. I could then decide that I was just as capable as somebody else in interpreting the policy. And when I made the interpretation, I felt I was just as capable as anyone else of making a decision about my local situation. But when the policies weren't spelled out in the directive system, I had the feeling that I didn't know what the Forest Service policy was and therefore I had to go up through channels to find out. Here in the directive system the policies were available to me—which strengthened my hand.

It seems that you have different sizes of umbrellas—the higher policy at the top and then shrinking, so to speak, down through different levels until it reaches the man closest to the problems.

Shields: Right. A key point, though, is that our directive system is designed so that the organization, the writing, the content is all very deliberately put together for the use of the basic resource manager.

Cloninger: Decentralization—you have to work at it. In other words, you have to develop the management systems and policies that go along with decentralization. *It doesn't just happen.* In another organization perhaps it wouldn't work at all, because their whole system might not be developed in this particular way. We have an inspection system. It's geared to decentralization. Work planning, work-load analysis, long-range plans, and short-range plans are all geared to this philosophy. That's a part of the whole process. It's a working philosophy and not something that remains static.

Shields: It also requires constant renewal and adjustment. With the changing techniques and capabilities we change the level of decentralization. In some cases this is towards centralization. It's a matter of adjusting to fit the operating situation either current or that you're faced with in getting ready for the future. It must be continually updated.

Cloninger: I think that's the strength of the Forest Service—not so much whether it's decentralized or how much delegation there is. It's the ability to remain flexible and change as conditions change. That's been the case over the fifty to sixty years of Forest Service history.

You don't then have any static commitment to a rigid principle, which often might be watered down by conditions, but rather a commitment to the mission and adapt yourself to it in any direction that becomes necessary.

Cloninger: You must be flexible enough to change when the mission changes.

Shields: Let me give you a rather simple operating example to illustrate the point. For a great many years, the real backbone of our forest fire-fighting organization was at the ranger district level. The ranger had relatively complete autonomy within his own district boundaries for pre-suppression, detection, and suppression work. Within the last few years there have been lots of technical developments in terms of helicopters, aerial detection of fires, and so on. In many areas with high fire incidence, centralized detection and dispatching is now possible at the forest head-quarters level, and in some cases even higher. This, in a sense, is a real pullback of delegation from a district ranger. If you were committed to complete autonomy, you'd think: "Here's the place where the ranger *should be* the quickest man on the ground with the best knowledge of local conditions to fight the fire on these acres." Yet, technology and the ability to afford new methods have caused a shift in delegation to keep up with the times.

You still have large amounts of discretion, don't you, at the ranger level?

Shields: As far as the operations aspects of the job are concerned. It's not nearly so much when it comes to changing major resource management plans or final policies or systems designs. Discretion is more in the interpretation and use of these systems at the local level—operating discretion, in other words.

Can't we perhaps make it a universal principle: that dependent upon the competence of the subject, as proven by his record, give him as much discretion, delegate as much as you think he can carry?

Shields: Only as far as you can afford to do it. You can't afford to have every expert, every possible skill represented in every district.

Smith: Let me say something about that. I think a simplified way, for me at least, to look at this is first to recognize that our primary mission for a big segment of the Forest Service is land management. We have a number of land managers—professionals—located in the 800 ranger districts. Basically, we're giving them all of the authority and discretion they need to make all the necessary decisions about their geographic piece of land. Then we say: "Well, it isn't appropriate to give them *all* of this authority!" There are some things that should be withdrawn for several reasons. For example, it may not be efficient for the ranger to do all of his own purchasing—centralizing may make that a more efficient operation. Or to do all of his own data processing—computers may make it more efficient to centralize this, too. Then again, he may not have all the expertise necessary to do all the jobs that must be done on his land. So we withdraw, in each instance, from his total delegation, whatever is necessary to gain either efficiency or competence.

Is the ranger in on some of this planning? Does he share in making the decision on what will or will not affect his operations?

Cloninger: That is a point I wanted to make. Delegations must go along with the responsibilities of each level. In other words, the district is the doing level. The district ranger is delegated the authorities and responsibilities that are needed to accomplish his mission as a "doer." The supervisor's office is basically the planning level. Therefore, there would be no reason to delegate this function to the ranger.

Shields: Russ is not referring to operating planning, since the ranger does make his local operating plans. This is over and above that function.

So there is a balance achieved between levels. Could we turn to some of the factors that have an impact on delegation and reciprocally are affected by this process? Could you suggest a definition of staff at this point?

Shields: We have defined this term officially and yet it is a troublesome area—it always is. Any time you have an organization big enough to need and afford staff assistants and specialists, you get into a continuous operating-problem area. Not too long ago the Forest Service reviewed and redefined the entire relationship between staff and line. The delegation between them was changed officially. We attempted to remove the staff assistant positions from any direct line decision-making authority. In your own research, I'm sure, you concluded that this cannot be done in any real, true sense. You can, however, arrive at operating arrangements that revolve around a mutual, clear understanding of the roles to be played. This can be done not only between line and staff but also vertically between the various line levels. If you're really sophisticated, you can deliberately recognize the informal authority function.

Which both sides usually pick up.

Shields: Yes, and which we have tried to formally recognize within our system. Under this system we've also tried to purify the line concept to where the line official does exercise the traditional, clear line function. The staff officer, then, restricts his decision making to the interpretation of existing guidelines, policies, directives, et cetera. In addition, he has the responsibility for training personnel at the lower line and staff levels in his area of expertise and for observing, and recommending to his line superior, actions that should be taken, or changes in policy, and so on. We have specified a recognizable and accepted function between the staff officer and the lower line level that he's assisting. We call it "decision by agreement." Essentially, it is the appeal procedure.

Consensus, perhaps?

Shields: You might call it that. As long as the line officer and the upper staff office level agree on certain actions, decision by agreement takes place. Assuming, also, that the superior *line* man does not interject a disagreement.

However, if anyone disagrees, and if after negotiation and thorough review they still can't agree, then the superior officer must assume the responsibility of making a decision.

We know that staff and line can operate as partners or act against one another. As you see it, why do disputes so often occur?

Shields: Well, in my view, in order for staff officers or specialists to redeem their responsibility, they need continually to drive for a full consideration of their proposals. This is not only human nature, but I think appropriate in order to achieve a balance between specialists. The real guts of the organizational problem posed by a line-and-staff setup—or any version of it—is the coordination of specialists and the proper utilization of their skills. A balance must be maintained with all the other technical activities and other staff functions. To me it's perfectly acceptable and desirable for staff specialists continually to agitate for full attention to what they have to offer and contribute to an organization. If they're not doing this, you might want to question even their maximum efforts—whether they're really fully contributing.

And they may also ask others to accept too much of their specialty without taking the time and effort to orient them.

Shields: Our system here, you see, also poses a responsibility on the lower-level line officer to evaluate and say: "Yes, I accept," or "No, I reject your guidance here."

Then staff is advisory?

Shields: Right. If the line officer blindly accepts a specialist's advice, the first thing he knows, his activities will be biased in favor of this specialty. Consequently, responsibilities in other areas—not represented by this particular specialty—will suffer. Then he will not have a balanced program or all of the resources needed to redeem the policies and guidance of his superior line officer.

It becomes a complex, personal relationship that cannot be solved by any formal description.

Smith: I think the term "advisory" as applied to staff is much too weak. I think the real challenge of being a staff man is that you have a special program area with some responsibilities for leadership. As I see exercising this leadership, it is not by saying: "You will do this and you will do this." Instead, staff talks to line in terms of salesmanship, saying: "I have thoroughly analyzed this program area and here are the alternatives and here is the program that I especially recommend to you." The challenge to a staff man is his ability to sell line men on a course of action. This is far from being just advisory. It has a real leadership responsibility.

Sometimes when a critical staff man finds that line men are not doing what staff intended, he says: "You're not doing it the right way." A staff man sometimes seems anxious to get into the act himself.

Smith: Well, I think he may have to get a new approach to his salesmanship, or reassess his own evaluation of the program. He has to say: "Why does line reject my program? Are its reasons valid?" If its reasons are not valid, then he has to say: "How do I convince line of this and get it to adopt the program I proposed?" This, to me, is the real challenge of staff work, and it's fully equal to the challenge of line work.

Shields: I think this comes up in a case-by-case situation, where staff does insist on another hearing or re-evaluation. In my view, this is the way it should be—the door should always be open for staff to come back and point this out. We do it routinely in the Forest Service. It is an accepted practice. Staff, of course, is often disappointed when its plans are still not considered important enough to change the decision. This may be, and frequently is, appropriate, because the line officer views the situation from *all* aspects and may say: "The priorities or alternatives are such that I must make this less useful decision, or this more expensive one, for the benefit of other advantages." This is the line man's coordination of competing specialists. But he must also be available to staff for a rehearing, within reason.

Cloninger: We have a term now in government called "position management." And if you want to get along with everybody, just mention it. Here's the thing about it: position management, as such, is nothing more than the day-to-day working of a good organization plan.

An integrated management system?
Cloninger: Right.

Shields: An organizational design of management.
Cloninger: Delegation to me is the same. It is only part of the total management picture.

Is there the possibility that by insulating and concentrating on delegation, we may come to worship it for its own sake?

Cloninger: The thing I fear most is that we may get out of perspective. We spend too much time on just the word "delegation" without seeing it in the context of all the related parts of management.

Does the average forest ranger think he has enough authority and responsibility? Does he think of himself as being a proper mixture, at times, of staff and line? Is he seriously concerned about coordination?

*In short, on the basis of your own experiences as former rangers, are
these his waking, administrative concerns?*

Shields: I think, in most instances, our district rangers feel they could
take on more authority and delegation. But I also think this could well be
a natural consequence of their training and the characteristics which led
them into this kind of work to begin with. We'd be disappointed if our
district rangers didn't feel they could take on a bigger job than they have.

Smith: I think we can give you a good example of the effect of delegation on the attitude of the ranger or lower levels of the entire organization.
We have many people who resist promotion to higher levels because they
do not want to give up the meaningful authority they have for land management at their local level.

*Although promotion would have definite advantages—salary, prestige,
perhaps?*

Smith: Right. In the past few years we have actually devoted some
time to a study of the Washington-office image. This was brought about by
the reluctance of field people to transfer into the Washington office because
they would be getting too far away from the action. Now, to me, this is a
proof of effective delegation.

*I never quite thought of it in that way, but it makes sense. Does loyalty
also come into their decision, or is it mainly a matter of being comfortable?*

Smith: I think they're excited about the job where they are, and do not
see the role of the Washington office as equally exciting.

Shields: Perhaps you should explore a little our method of staffing this
office in Washington. In fact, a heavy percentage of the staff people at this
level are here for only a relatively short time before they return to the field.
The career ladders are such that it's informally understood that many senior
field positions require Washington experience. So, many people come in
here with the attitude that it's a necessary developmental step—a career-
ladder step. Generally speaking, the Washington office is not a dead-end
assignment. It does become a terminal assignment for those at so high a
senior level that there's no other place for them to go within the Forest
Service. Then there are others so interested in a particular specialty that
they want to succeed to the senior position in that specialty, and that, of
course, exists only in Washington.

*So the action is here just as fully, but it's different from the action
anywhere else in the organization.*

Shields: Right. There are a few who, due to age, remain in Washington
until retirement comes along. But this is a relatively small percent of the
cases. So, all in all, I think this is somewhat different from many other
headquarters agencies in Washington. There is continual identification with

the field both through the experience of field assignments and by making inspections, Another factor is the fairly sizeable percentage of people expecting to be reassigned in the field.

Could we perhaps turn now to some of your own experiences at the field level, and discuss some problem situations. This might support the statement that delegation, as we agreed, is not a universal but must be used flexibly and in connection with every other element in administration.

Cloninger: Here is an illustration of delegation of responsibility and the follow-up of using administrative tools to accomplish that which is delegated.

Our timber sales program at the forest level may be entirely centralized or entirely decentralized. If centralized, the authority, dollars, and people stay at supervisor's-office level. If decentralized, then all of these factors are pushed down to the district level.

When I moved into the principal staff job in charge of timber management, I inherited a centralized organization, but during the first six months, the job was entirely decentralized to the districts. This required an intensive training program for district personnel, along with more than normal supervision.

In decentralization, the mission of both the supervisor's office and the ranger was completely changed.

In the course of an average week, does a ranger make many decisions on his own, aside from those you would consider routine? Can we get down to the nub of his assignment? What would it be like to follow him around in this decision process?

Cloninger: I always like to ask this question: "How many balls can you bounce all at once?" The ranger has the timber function, the grazing function, the fire job, the maintenance job, and more. They're all connected with people. Therefore, he's spending all of his time bouncing balls and keeping them in relation to each other, and making what decisions are needed when they're needed. In addition, there is the job of overall coordination on this particular area of land.

You just used the word "coordination." How does he coordinate— what and with whom? You have been coordinators, I presume.

Shields: Well, we are coordinating every day—even today. I suppose you could talk about this for a long, long time too. But to me, I can almost oversimplify it by saying that coordination is a balanced approach to achieving specific goals and objectives.

And acknowledging priorities.

Shields: And acknowledging priorities. Now we're often accused of planning just for planning's sake. We have planning systems that are quite elaborate. Don Smith, here, is responsible for one segment of the planning system—that is, maintenance and design of planning systems for ranger district operating plans. It's a very refined system, currently undergoing review and adjustment to modernize it.

There often seems to be a gap between theory and practice, and perhaps in this instance, between theory in the planning stage and what's happening in the field.

Smith: Let's make a distinction. At the Washington-office level, we deal with a planning system, not with a plan. The ranger makes the plan. He carries it out—the action plan. We're dealing with the design of how he goes about this process. There are elements of both theory and practice. However, when you plan ahead for twelve to eighteen months, what actually occurs subsequently never exactly matches your plan. But you still have to approach planning in the long perspective.

At least it's a target and you know what you're aiming for.

Shields: Planning includes an analysis of what you have to work with in terms of manpower skills, dollars, and physical situations. It is an analytical way of getting at and facilitating the job you're delegated to do.

If I were to ask of the ranger: "What are your goals?" would he assume this to be a mere academic question? Would it be better to ask: "What are your immediate and long-run plans?"

Cloninger: To either, he'd probably say: "My goals are the same as the Forest Service's goals."

Lundberg: The greatest good for the greatest number in the long run would, no doubt, be mentioned.

Shields: Back when the Forest Service was formed, the Secretary of Agriculture delegated to the Forest Service a job to do. The delegation included the statement: "Where conflicting interests must be reconciled, the question will always be decided from the standpoint of the greatest good for the greatest number of people in the long run." The original of this letter is in a frame hanging on a wall in the Chief's office. That statement is also in all of our directives. Many people are unhappy with it because they say it's a motherhood type of affirmation. It's idealistic and doesn't really define what you will actually do. However, in my own view, it expresses a spirit of service that is useful to me—something that I'm not ashamed to cite. This is true for most of our people, too.

Smith: I think most of us can think back to a time when we were under pressure because of a decision we had made. Whenever we stop and consider: "Did we make the right decision?" we back up into this motto, saying: "Well, I made this decision in light of the greatest good of the greatest number, in the long run. I may take a beating right now but time will be on my side."

Can I lead from that into decisions made by the ranger and how he looks at these priorities?

Shields: Most of us, with the possible exception of Len, have been away from the district level long enough so that only critical incidents would stick in our mind. It would be difficult for me to reconstruct a routine day in order to give you an average picture of what the ranger does.

Does he, for example, keep a working diary of events, decisions, and so on?

Shields: For many, many years that was a requirement. The necessary management information is still recorded but not in a diary form.

Cloninger: You brought up the question about coordination, insofar as the ranger is concerned. The ranger has people, he has dollars, and he has programs. All of these are handed down to him from above. It's his job to put all of them together to accomplish work. Now at least when I was a ranger, one of the most satisfying things was to see some fat cattle coming down the road, or a load of logs, or going into town and talking to some of the people who used the forest district. That's the satisfaction of the job, and it's all achieved by the ranger coordinating all his tasks.

How does a ranger know how he's doing?

Cloninger: It is measured by all of the outputs resulting from his total effort. The outputs are what's happening on the land.

Where, right now, are some of the rangers if we could spot them on that wall map?

Lundberg: In my old district on the Ottawa National Forest I suppose there's about a 50–50 chance that the ranger is sitting at his desk in the ranger station. He might be looking at a work plan. It's right on the lake but I doubt if he has time to enjoy the view. Like a lot of administrators, a ranger has to balance pressures from all directions—all kinds, including the use of his own time. He is dealing with the forest users, people in the community, recreation facility users, grazing permitees. There are contractual relationships with a lot of lumber interests, grazing interests, mining interests. There are usually things that have to be done right away—now.

Can I come back, briefly, to the Forest Service and its mission. Is it to maintain the land as untampered with and uncommercialized as possible? I'm prompted to ask by what was just said regarding the ranger and his dealing with so many interest groups.

Shields: It's rather to protect the land and develop it, through wise use, for the public.

Smith: We make a sharp distinction between preservation and wise use.

Shields: For example, the assigned mission of the Park Service is quite different from ours. Their role is to *preserve* for the use and enjoyment of future generations. Our organic legislation provides for managed use, and our latest act—the Multiple Use Act—identifies five activities including recreation and the recognition of wilderness values.

And the ranger is at the midpoint.

Shields: He's responsible for managing the actual acres of land and resolving all of these countervailing pressures for use of the resources. You have the strict preservation recreationists who don't want any tree to be cut—and I'm exaggerating to make the point here—versus, let's say, a mining interest which feels that the minerals are more valuable than the aesthetics of the site. You have many such pressures all the time.

In this century, has the mission of the Service, as it affects the ranger, changed very much?

Shields: The main change is in degree of management, from rather extensive management to comparatively intensive management. This is because of the pressures and developing demands on the resources—whether it be for recreation, more lumber, or higher-quality water. You name it, and it has intensified.

Perhaps the ranger is best described as a resource manager.

Shields: He's the general manager in charge of the plant—the plant being a particular geographic area.

How many acres might an average ranger have under his control?

Shields: Well, let's see, 220,000 acres would be close to the average.

Giffen: I think the smallest district is somewhere around 40,000 acres and the largest is over 1,000,000.

Shields: Something like that.

Smith: You expressed some amazement at 187 million acres under Forest Service administration. If you'd pull that from all parts of the United States and put it into one package, it would just fit into the state of Texas. Then consider that we divide local management of that amount of land among 800 people. When you consider them scattered around on subdivisions of Texas and visualize the program, you begin to see the job of the rangers.

Is the Forest Service in every single state?

Shields: Forty-two states have public lands under the administration of the Forest Service.

Smith: There are relatively few land-managing agencies in government. Most government agencies are involved in some specific service to the public unrelated to specific land areas. You'd probably find the Soil Conservation Service in every state and many counties of every state. But they are not land managers—they are consultants to private land owners, whereas we are the actual managers of public land.

If a road were to cut through forest preserves, would that become a headquarters problem?

Giffen: It depends upon the class of road.

Cloninger: It becomes a problem for the ranger to coordinate, regardless of what it is.

Shields: It modifies his management of the whole area. It has both economic and biological effects.

Smith: It's an interesting point you raise here. You say, there's a decision for Washington. Actually, it would be a very exceptional case for anybody from headquarters to go out to the field to have a look. We have people out there already who are professionals, and very capable. Most of the decisions—roads, for examples—are made on the basis of their information and recommendations. In their recommendations, they must consider the effects of this road on other forest uses and the protection of the land.

Giffen: The only time the Washington office would become involved would be on an appeal from an administrative decision. In this case, the decision then comes up the line and can go all the way to the Secretary of Agriculture.

Shields: An example was a recent situation where they wanted to reroute Interstate 70 highway through a proposed wilderness area in Colorado. This went all the way to the Secretary for decision. He disapproved the proposed rerouting. That's quite an exceptional situation. Most cases never go beyond the regional office level.

How does the Forest Service, through the eyes of the ranger in a certain district, regard some of these rapid changes that technology is producing—roads, as one example?

Cloninger: Let's look at the problem from this standpoint. The ranger's major interest is in the soundest utilization of each of those 200,000 acres or so under his jurisdiction, and that includes all of its uses, such as grazing, timber, and so on. When the road comes in, it gives him a much greater opportunity to move ahead and intensify his management.

Shields: His main worries are whether resource values adjacent to the road are properly protected. If, for example, the road were improperly located, it would affect the fish in the streams, create erosion, or damage the watershed. We have and maintain road systems within the national forests. In aggregate, the total mileage is more than any single state system of roads.

How does the ranger get around his area?

Giffen: He usually drives a pickup truck and in some western areas he rides a horse.

Lundberg: Sometimes he has a sedan or station wagon. The Forest Service also has about 100,000 miles of trails—foot trails and horse trails.

Smith: We ought to tell you that a ranger spends practically no time in a fire tower. I hate to destroy what might be your image of a ranger at this point. On that other matter, we're not at all for or against roads. It's a question of putting roads where they'll do the most good and the least damage. Actually, we have an aggressive road program of our own to provide access, wherever necessary—to remove cut timber, for example.

The ranger seems to be right square in the middle of various forces, such as conservation, utilization, and other factors. How does he handle these competing viewpoints and how do they affect his work?

Shields: The main emphasis is on balanced, wise use of resources— whether the use be for wilderness enjoyment or harvesting of timber, as you would an agricultural crop. The original definition of conservation by the man who coined the term, Gifford Pinchot, was just that: "wise use." But today, especially, conservation is often used as a synonym for preservation—we would have to reject that.

So conservation and utilization can go hand-in-hand.

Giffen: Oh, absolutely. Let me give an example. The Bald Eagle is now classified as a rare species. The Chippewa National Forest is one of the principal breeding areas. It's estimated that there are 600 pairs of these eagles in the United States and 150 of them are in Northern Minnesota. Our people have located the nesting areas, put them on a map, and developed use policies for these defined areas. For example, it doesn't hurt to cut timber as long as you don't cut their nesting trees, which have to be large. But you don't cut during the breeding or nesting season. This is preservation in these areas. But naturally, we're going to continue to manage the total forest area.

Smith: It's part of the coordination we spoke of before.

I have the notion, from what's been said, that there is no stereotyped forest ranger.

Giffen: The reason is that there are no stereotyped ranger districts.

He has a core of duties, but beyond that he has to use discretion, remain flexible, ingenious at times, and highly committed to his role.

Shields: And he must have, let me add, a social conscience.

In terms of interpreting the law and an awareness of public needs, interests, and demands: It seems as if the job of the ranger never actually gets away from him. He's always in command. He coordinates, delegates, balances his pressures, and, in a real sense, blends his various tasks because he has enough authority and matching responsibility.

Shields: It doesn't just happen, either. It is the result of a whole range of considerations. We have achieved this by selecting the right kind of people with the right kind of education, and designing our organization to match the job which must be done. Then, there's internal training after selection—that's another factor.

What is the role of Washington headquarters in all this?

Shields: Headquarters offers the support of a wide range of administrative systems. These include not only organizational design but also career-ladder selection, training, the directives system, reporting system, communications system, and all the physical facilities that the ranger needs in addition to office files, clerical help, engineering assistance, and special assistance. In short, this is a total management system, interrelated and coordinated.

Smith: We keep doctoring the system, too.

Shields: It's always routinely under review. As needed, new systems are developed. Right now, for example, we're in the process of designing a whole new accounting system. This was partly generated by the requirements of the GAO and the Department of Agriculture. However, there was a lot of internal pressure, as well. Also, Don is in the process of re-evaluating the district work-planning system and there will be some adjustments there, too.

You're always in motion, so it seems; something always needs adjustments.

Shields: Always in motion, that's right. We attempt to maintain an attitude that: "What we have is never good enough." In fact, when we allocate money, we very seldom are able to allocate 100 percent of the money needed to meet the standards. Our analysis of needs always shows a bigger job than we could conceivably do. This is an incentive to always drive ahead, and search for excellence. We hope we're not so self-satisfied that we measure our achievements in comparison with other agencies. We attempt to measure our achievements against our own evaluation of what we should do. Financing less than analyzed need is one motivation for improving methods.

From what's been said I judge the Forest Service discards whatever doesn't fit its needs. In other words, if an administrative principle doesn't work—after sufficient trial—you don't continue to use it. Besides, it would seem that you're constantly attempting to improve the use of the instruments you already accept as important.

Cloninger: Situations change. You've got to stay with the situation. In other words, the work-planning system might have been fine five years ago, but the situations have changed. Now, the needs are different and therefore you must update the system to handle the present situation.

Shields: We emphasize this approach to change specifically in order to reinforce the ability of the district ranger to plan and operate better.

How independent, in the final analysis, is the ranger? As an area manager he does run programs, and yet he is evaluated by a supervisor and in turn looked after, if that's the phrase, by a regional director. These

*levels of supervision are interdependent, so he isn't fully free admin-
istratively.*

Giffen: He has only one boss, the supervisor, who operates from forest
level.

Smith: Bear in mind that there are 130 national forest administrative
units and each one has a forest supervisor. They're broken up into an
average of about six ranger districts.

Cloninger: You spoke earlier of the breadth of the ranger's supervision.
On the average he might have 40 people under him, but this can go up to
150 in large districts and down to 25 in small ones.

Shields: Or less.

Cloninger: And his budget, on an average, would be somewhere
between $100,000 and $300,000. This can go up to around half a million.
The sheer size of the operation takes a good manager. Consider just the
personnel problems which develop as well as the fiscal problems. When you
blend these into programs, he becomes a true manager at his particular
level in the organization. He is, after all, the doer.

*I can't offhand think of an area of administration that doesn't touch
him—from which he's exempt.*

Cloninger: None whatsoever—he has them all, in some degree.

Shields: In regard to this interrelationship you mentioned, the ranger's
direct relationship is with the forest supervisor or his staff. If the ranger
comes into direct contact with the regional or Washington-level people, it's
only because they are working through the supervisor. We at headquarters
have no direct authority or delegation relationship with rangers except
through the supervisor. A ranger might, on the average, see someone from
the headquarters level only every two or three years. On the other hand,
he'll probably see someone from the regional office maybe two or three
times a year. But essentially it's a layered organization on rather clear-cut
lines.

Is there much transferability among ranger districts?

Shields: Not a great deal, unless, of course, our organizational and
placement design causes this to happen, deliberately.

*The ranger, when all is added up, is a generalist in the true sense of
the word. Am I correct?*

Shields: He is, in the true sense of the word, as long as he remains a
ranger. He may transfer to another district because the organization needs
him there as an individual. He may also go to a staff position at the forest
supervisor's level or to the regional office, but very rarely will a ranger
move into the Washington office in one jump.

*Do you have many separations from the Service, by those who may
feel it was the wrong career step?*

Shields: Mainly during probation or during the initial years of the assignment, but not a significant number. Once an individual has a fairly broad range of experience and assignments, he's likely to remain with the Forest Service during his whole career. In fact, we're frequently criticized because our people refuse to accept transfers in government outside of our Service.,

Smith: The history of those who leave varies, too, according to disciplines. In the case of business managers, researchers, and engineers the tendency to stay is much less evident. In short, the specialist group may move about more in government work.

As you've been spelling out the role of a ranger, I've been trying to imagine some of the personal qualities he might have. Would it be fair to consider a typical ranger as a daring, outgoing, resourceful person?

Smith: If it helps your image, let me say that once, as a ranger, I had a white horse!

Thanks. It does help.

Smith: If you were to see a ranger at a Kiwanis meeting, I think you'd probably have trouble in separating him from the rest of the group.

Shields: I'd typify him as steady, reliable, and dependable.

Smith: Visualize him as a most active person, physically.

What do you consider to be the real challenge—or challenges—of the ranger's job? I ask this especially since all of you at one time were in this position.

Shields: I would say it is his responsibility and the relative operating autonomy. I would also include his status, both within the organization and in the community in which he is located. In many rural communities where these districts are situated, the ranger has social status on a level with the superintendent of schools, the local M.D.'s, the banker, and so on. He may, in fact, be the only representative of the federal government within the area.

Smith: He may be the biggest employer in town.

Lundberg: There's also his contribution to the local community in the course of securing benefits for the whole nation.

Cloninger: Putting it baldly, I'd like to say that the ranger is the only man who actually moves some dirt—in other words, actually accomplishes something on the ground. He actually causes something to happen; he causes this load of logs to come down the road, causes these cows to get fat, causes water to go down the creek.

Smith: Russ, couldn't we modify that to say that he manages the group that throws the dirt?

Cloninger: That's right, but he's responsible for all of these things.

Giffen: Back when you and I were rangers, Don, we threw the dirt and replaced the telephone insulators.

Smith: I've had a ranger district where I had no assistants. If a sign post was crooked, I straightened it. We've come a long way from that, because that's hardly a professional job requiring a college degree. At that time we were on what you could call a rather extensive type of management. Today, intensive management has required us to put specialists and workmen at the district level. This permits the professionals to delegate many of their jobs to their aides and technicians. We can also have specialists in districts where the work load is large enough to justify their assignment.

Can any of you cite some problems solved as rangers that provided a great deal of genuine satisfaction in making a contribution to the district? This might interest those in the process of making up their minds on a future career.

Giffen: I can tell you the greatest satisfaction I experienced in my career as a ranger. It was in southern Illinois. We established a forest there in 1935 when we acquired wornout farm land, and one of our major programs was to reforest and plant on this land. Sixteen years later, I returned to that same forest on an inspection. At the time I was in watershed management and wanted to see what some logging operations were doing to the watershed. We went over four areas where they were cutting the pine trees that I had planted sixteen years before. They were actually making the first commercial thinning of trees planted when I was the ranger. This is a real experience.

Smith: I can think of a southern Ohio district where we had a man-made lake during Civilian Conservation Corps days. This lake was subject to siltation—mud coming off the farm lands up above into the lake. You might not suppose this was part of a ranger's job, but I think it's quite typical. We actually got involved in getting cooperation from the local Chamber of Commerce, Rotary Club, and the power people in the city in which we were located, as well as from the county. These groups invited the Soil Conservation Service to establish one of their districts there. In cooperation with them, we got people to work on the headwaters of that stream to protect that lake from siltation.

So, this is part of a total land management picture which is larger than just your immediate government-owned acres. It involves the total community.

At lunch I recall Mr. Shields saying that it's a team effort that produces the Forest Service and its results. How does this team spirit affect the ranger?

Shields: We have an intimate term that we apply to ourselves—"the Forest Service family." The Chief refers to this quite often.

It must obviously be very meaningful, for otherwise it wouldn't be applied.

Shields: With our pattern of reassignment and transfer, as part of the way of doing business, an individual is soon identified with this family. When transferred, he's automatically acquainted with and knows many of the people with whom he will be associated. One feels comfortable and not as a stranger, even though it's a new assignment in a different community.

Unfortunately, because of our increase in size and specialization, this aspect of the Service is in danger of dilution or loss. For example, our engineers have some trouble identifying themselves with the family, and this affects their morale and retention rate. In fact, we've recently completed a major study of the utilization of engineer skills and identified a wide range of problems along this line. To some extent, this situation applies also to our business management people. But at least we are aware of it, and perhaps at a future date you might return and we could exchange views on our progress in solving this problem.

The basic strength of the Forest Service, I think, is this personal identification with the goals and the organization and a firm sense of accomplishment. I feel a real sense of pride in doing something that is intrinsically worthwhile, from a social point of view.

And this is a front-line problem in many organizations, public as well as private—the individual who pursues a specific technical path and tries out, as it were, many organizations until he reaches one that provides the fullest opportunity to share the experiences that the Forest Service appears to give its people.

Smith: We start out with an advantage in this regard. Consider why a young man elects to take forestry in school. Probably he is motivated somewhat by conservation interests and a desire to do something about this problem. When he gets into the Service, he finds a place to express this desire and is quite happy in being able to translate his aims into practice.

Are there some situations you encountered as rangers that would help a reader to understand more fully their responsibilities and problems?

Lundberg: I was a ranger for a pretty short period compared with the others. It was about a year and a half. The district I came to had a big job in timber sale preparation. The main problem—and challenge—was to build up the backlog of proposed sales. It was a hardwood district and it took a lot of work to build it up. By the time I left, we were really on the way. We had quite a few timber sales prepared in advance and were starting to make some headway. It was really going good. This gave me quite a bit of satisfaction. When I left, a capable, aggressive young fellow came in to replace me, and in a couple of years that district was right up near the top and has been there ever since.

Are there several ways of running a ranger district to reach the best results? I'm thinking of how much difference the personality and one's attitude have on accomplishment.

Shields: I think what we're really concerned with is the total effectiveness of the operation. As a matter of fact, we have recently completed a quite comprehensive study to determine the optimum size of a ranger district that we should work for and maintain in order to do the best total job. In size, I include all the variables: numbers of people, size of budget, numbers of acres within the boundaries, and so on. In seeking the optimum size, or the desirable range of size, we supposed the size factor to be related to the total effectiveness of the district's operation. But we were able to identify only a very, very weak correlation. As you might assume from my comment, the basic differences do seem to relate to the managerial style of the specific ranger.

Can you mention some of the styles you've encountered?

Shields: They would range all the way between two extremes. At one end is the individual who personally knows what has to be done but lacks the ability to delegate it to his staff to accomplish it as part of a team effort. The other extreme is an individual who can identify, plan, set priorities, and delegate to a staff and thereby maximize accomplishment.

What about a ranger's training before and during his assignment?

Shields: We have a wide range of on-job training assignments as well as in-house formal training sessions. Before he's given the responsibility of the job, he is exposed to all the key training experiences that should qualify him. Let me add, he also needs the training which is provided both in school and in the form of supervisory training.

Smith: In most instances, a ranger has been an assistant ranger.

Cloninger: He's been on a ranger staff from four to six years. This reduces the possibility of selecting an untrained or inexperienced man for a ranger's job.

Smith: We have only 800 rangers out of 22,000 permanent full-time personnel. So we do have quite a selection process.

How does a ranger manage to pass on his acquired experience for the benefit of those who follow him in the district?

Lundberg: My replacement came in from another district; as a matter of fact, he had been an assistant ranger on one of Don's old districts. I never saw him. I left on a Friday and I think he arrived on a Monday. He had had experience in working in ranger districts and of course my assistant was still there to pass on information. Some things were new to him technically—kinds of timber, product species, as examples. With his basic background, he could easily adjust and catch up in a short time. That's pretty much the way most rangers come in. That's the way I did; the assistant was there to help me break into the locality and meet the people. I had the background to draw on from other places. Many things were not that much different. It's still the same outfit.

Shields: There's also the supervisor's staff. They're in the district fairly often—in fact, as often as they think necessary.

What does the ranger in one district know of the problems that he may be facing and are being solved in another district?

Shields: There are periodic meetings. Some forests are compact enough to have monthly sessions. In other forests the staff meet less often, generally once or twice each year. Supervisors visit back and forth, and contact is frequent between the ranger and supervisor.

There is still this back-up of all the supporting systems, procedures, and policies, which makes it easier to exchange views on problems. After you've had qualifying experience, you could probably go to most any district and handle the work.

Giffen: In regard to the question you raised before about training, some of the forests on which I worked assigned ranger trainees to different districts and tasks. One assignment might be on a heavy timber sales district, another on recreation, and so on. The trainee would be put on all of these for different periods of time, and gain experience on all the various operations.

Smith: Len, I have the suspicion that the man who took over from you inherited an annual work plan which spelled out to him, in quite some detail, what you had visualized for the next year. I'm sure the ranger must have taken that plan and said: "I'll attempt to carry it out and I'll modify it, as needed, as I go along." Basically, he started out with a plan of work or he used the assistants to help make a new plan. This, you can see, is part of continuing training.

I'd like to turn, with the ranger still in mind, to a possible definition of an ideal administrator. How would you, as representatives of the Forest Service, define such an individual?

Shields: To me, we're talking about breadth of knowledge as to agency goals and objectives, and the technical abilities to achieve them. It is also the ability to organize and operate in a team framework.

Giffen: He's got to have commitment.

Shields: Absolutely.

Can, and does, the Service encourage this approach to building a program, sharing goals, stretching one's talents because of this commitment Duncan mentioned?

Shields: I think certain people have attitudes which can be modified, changed, or added to, and I think I've seen examples of this. Some achieve it by deliberate design and others by happenstance.

Smith: Our whole programming effort has a strong bearing on your question. We produce an annual program of work in the Washington office which outlines in rather broad terms what the Chief and staff want to see accomplished throughout the Service. In turn, each regional office—and we have nine of them—produces a similar program of work for each region, often building onto the Chief's program of work. The supervisor looks at this and prepares his own program of work—a plan of work—and the ranger does the same thing for his unit.

If a ranger tries to take off on an independent course, and his goals do not fit those of the supervisor or, in turn, the supervisor's goals don't fit those of the regional forester—what happens? The discrepancies come to light rather quickly and there's a decision or a confrontation. Decisions are made on what are we really trying to do, and what is the best way to get it done.

We've been speaking, off and on, about goals. Is it so tough to decide what they should be? Aren't most of them set for you?

Giffen: Priorities are the problem, quite often. We speak of objectives, goals, and movement toward their attainment.

Smith: You spoke earlier of the program planning and budgeting system. We've got an enormous shelf-stock of jobs that we could do. One of our basic problems is sorting out what we *should do* from what we *could do* within our available resources. To make the fit, we may have to eliminate jobs or in some cases decide that we have to lower our standards.

Then the ideal administrator must determine which of the options is to be pursued. He makes choices.

Smith: We've got a little chart in my office which we've labeled, "The Basic Choice." It says: "Must do, Should do, Like to do, and Nice to do." To me this captures the essence of the manager's dilemma. He has to continually sort through the possibilities, not only in a year's program but in his daily efforts.

Giffen: We have an example of this effort to get a lot done with a little bit, or less than you need. On the Chippewa National Forest, we had a program to increase our timber cut. The only way to increase it at that time was to advertise large sales in order to get a large volume on the market. What we completely overlooked was that for years we had been working with small operators, who had been our bread and butter. We forgot these poor little operators and right away they began to holler. We met with them and had to back off and say: "OK, we will cut only 90 percent of our planned volume, because we've got to satisfy these local people." So we made some little sales which actually cost us money. We had to do it. It was a clear-cut economic need which we had completely overlooked.

Shields: In other words, the situation made the decision once you got all the facts.

Giffen: That's right. Quite often, once you get all the facts, the situation pretty well makes the decision. It's when you have much less than perfect knowledge that you have to gamble, and either make a decision you're not quite sure of, or make no decision at all. To do nothing is often not an easy decision. In the case I speak of, after we had looked at it fully, we admitted that we had made a mistake—a gross error.

Thus far, three related issues emerge from our discussion. First, the rather close and flexible relationship between the top Washington directorship level, and those concerned with front-line, daily operations—regional directors, supervisors, rangers, and their staff. This flexibility spells itself out in a number of different ways: widespread agreement on the whole catalogue of administration practices within the organization—staff and line, delegation, matching authority and responsibility. Also, through your career ladder there seems to be an interchange whereby a man in one district can transfer to another, or may spend some time in Washington and then return to the field.

The second main point I sense is the elitism of the Forest Service, which is based on pride, commitment, and a strong affirmation of goals. It acts as a continuing igniter and also as a catalyst of one's highest efforts.

The remaining element that comes to mind is the respect the Service exhibits, from your own experiences—and they appear to be widely representative—towards the individual.

What did I omit that you yourselves have felt, over your long careers in the organization?

Cloninger: One item you might have left out is the feeling which I think all of the people in the Service share: that they do have a meaningful part in developing policy. They have a part in writing instructions and procedures, which gives them a commitment to how the policy and procedures are applied.

Smith: I think that the outfit, as I see it, has developed a real pride in the belief that they are forward-thinking in their management approach. They're constantly seeking for better management, and whether they correctly evaluate themselves or not, they keep looking for these better techniques. I think our motivation causes us to do this, but the fact that we do it, in turn, builds our morale. We feel—you notice this especially among the younger fellows—that if anyone has a real proposal for improvement, it will get a hearing. This is important.

Lundberg: The constant interchange of people between the field and the various regional offices and Washington is probably a very strong influence in supporting the sharing, contributing approach. There are a lot of organizations in which members start out at headquarters and remain there. This is their entire career experience.

Cloninger: I think something we haven't talked about is where the great number of decisions are made in the organization. The fact is that probably 95 percent of them are made either at the district or forest levels. The only decisions made above those levels tend to be ones that are too complex, or where the field staff lacks the capability or the authority to settle. Decisions then filter up to the regional or Washington levels. So the freedom to make decisions at the ranger and supervisor levels is a very strong motivation for people wanting to be at those levels.

So it comes back to the point at which we began our discussion: delegation—as the Forest Service sees and applies it—is representative, democratic, and participating management. If you give the individual ranger enough incentive and he's strongly motivated to achieve organizational goals, then delegation must almost inescapably accompany the assignment. It therefore isn't a question, as this group has emphasized, of which comes first—delegation or the action by those on the front lines—but rather that action often requires delegation as a means to an end.

Cloninger: Why couldn't you reword that and say that the management climate of the Forest Service is a democratic participating management. I think that the term "delegation" is too narrow.

In the Forest Service, delegation seems to be an instrument that must be used in conjunction with many others.

Shields: It can't be used independently.

Cloninger: I've got one more question for you. The very first sentence in Section 1230 of our manual says: "Delegation is a process a line officer uses to divide the work assigned to him so that significant portions of the whole job may be effectively assigned to subordinates, and to authorize subordinates to take specific action. Delegation is a prime management essential in successful administration of a large organization such as the Forest Service." What's your reaction to that particular statement?

It looks as if it's a catch-all and that delegation is the formula by which all the other avenues and options will be opened. It may be asking too much of delegation.

Cloninger: Well, I wonder if your definition, earlier in the discussion, isn't a little too much towards the academic, and our definition too much of the nuts and bolts. Somewhere between, there is a middle ground.

Perhaps this illustrates the gap between the actual and ideal, between the theoretician and the practitioner. I sense in the Forest Service a blend of the two elements, that you are able to lean back and take a long, hard look at what is going on, and change what may need to be changed.

Shields: One thing that appeals to me in your selection of delegation as the center of our discussion is that it provides a fine illustration of the essentiality of teamwork.

It also seems to demonstrate top management's competence in maximizing the potentials of the team at all stages and levels of the Service. Perhaps delegation could be considered a magnet around which other essential administrative elements are attracted.

Let me express a sincere thanks for this opportunity to range widely over the entire administrative arena, as it were, using delega-

tion as our focal point. Perhaps at some future time we can hold a reunion and update the dialogue in view of changing situations and developments.

Shields: We're quite anxious to participate in discussions of this kind. This is very stimulating for us and we learn something from it. I hope we're not self-satisfied with what we do. I hope you will come back, and we shall welcome you.

STUDY QUESTIONS

1. The Forest Service enjoys prestige for its administrative philosophy and performance. Others say its reputation is not fully deserved. What are the plus and minus factors, in your own assessment?
2. What have been the most effective tactics of the Forest Service in promoting its goals to the public and Congress?
3. How can centralization impair an organization in achieving its success?
4. Are there any lessons or administrative principles that might be transferred from the Forest Service to other agencies?

VII
INFORMATION SYSTEMS
AND DECISION MAKING

15

THE POST OFFICE

The following discussions center around three main elements: first, the problems associated with the establishment of a new planning and systems analysis office in an old-line, federal department having strong traditions and practices; second, the attitudes and reflections of staff participants towards organizational goals; and third, an evaluation of planning as a process and its relationship to the work of the entire department.

As the interviews with these four staff members of the U.S. Post Office Department illustrate, the problems of adding a new function to an established department are highly complicated. Members of the new section agreed that reaching their goals would require a rare combination of hardheaded common sense, persuasion, a vision of tomorrow's needs, and a strong appreciation of and belief in the contributions such a section can make to the success of a department—especially a department currently in serious administrative trouble. Rather than assemble a number of people around a conference table, the interviewer held separate discussions to compare individual views on the planning process and understandings of the section's impact on overall objectives.

Shortly after these discussions were held, the Kappel report[1] was issued. The present Post Office Department, said the report, cannot meet demands increasingly imposed on it; therefore it should be abolished and the postal function established in a nonprofit government corporation.

Following the publication of the Kappel report, Robert Cahn wrote an article in the *Christian Science Monitor* (August 15, 1968), "What a Way to Run a Post Office," which concluded with a statement of the general counsel of the Post Office Department:

> No one can stop an idea when its time has come. The idea is not necessarily the corporation but that the department must have the management authority and tools to raise capital the way any company has to operate.

Perhaps no service is taken so much for granted, by most citizens, as the postal service. Complaints usually concern exceptions to the average service: lost magazines, delayed letters, damaged parcels, higher postal rates. Few have the need or time to become well enough informed to understand former Postmaster General O'Brien's statement: "The Post Office has a race with catastrophe." Several facts that underlie this remark are the close concern of the planning staff. In 1968, for example, the department was required to provide essential service to 5 million more locations than in 1965; cost to the taxpayers of the public service subsidy on books and records was $63 million. Within ten years, total mail volume—80 billion pieces in 1968—was expected to exceed 110 billion pieces. In fiscal year 1967 the Post Office collected $4.96 billion in revenues and spent over $6.13 billion, the $1.17 billion deficit being made up by the federal treasury.

The proposals of the Kappel report are not within the scope of this introduction; however, the report spells out the width and depth of the postal problem in these terms:

> The Post Office has always been operated as if it were an ordinary government agency: its funds are appropriated by Congress, its employees are part of Civil Service, its officials are subject to a host of laws and regulations governing financial administration, labor relations, procurement, and purchase of transportation. Major managerial decisions are made through the legislative process: Congress sets postal rates and wages, governs Postmaster appointments, and approves or rejects construction of individual post offices.

Many of those interviewed confirmed the report's next statement: "The United States postal system is in serious trouble today because of

---

[1] *Towards Postal Excellence,* The Report of The President's Commission on Postal Organization, June 1968 (Frederick R. Kappel, retired chairman of the Board of Directors, American Telephone & Telegraph Company, was the commission's chairman).

decades of low priorities assigned its modernization and management needs." The discussions that follow may provide some insights on how a group of professional civil servants move forward, inch by inch, in their determined efforts to improve and modernize the postal system through PPBS.

WILLIAM J. SULLIVAN, DEPUTY DIRECTOR, OFFICE OF PLANNING AND SYSTEMS ANALYSIS

At the outset perhaps we might discuss those factors in the postal organization which, in the first instance, caused the establishment of this planning office, and second, of equal importance, have either encouraged or discouraged its growth.

Let me identify myself for the record. Up until ten days ago when I returned to the Post Office, I've been on the staff of the Kappel Commission, a Presidential commission which made a year-long study of the organization of the Post Office. Our report is completed but not yet published.[2] In June of 1964 I came to the Post Office to work on a task force set up to study the parcel post crisis. When that work ended, I came to the newly established Office of Planning.

It might be useful to begin by describing how the Post Office is organized. First of all, it includes a number of functional bureaus. The Bureau of Operations is the major operating bureau; it manages the field service, and consumes some 80 percent of the total postal dollar. The Bureau of Transportation procures the transportation, obviously an important part of moving the mail. The Bureau of Finance and Administration prepares budgets, administers information systems—a vital function—and does special cost studies and analyses. They operate the cost ascertainment system, so called, which determines costs and revenues for each class of mail. The Bureau of Personnel handles labor relations, training, and other personnel matters. The Bureau of Facilities is responsible for procuring the physical plant for the postal service. A new Bureau of Research and Engineering does the research and design work for the postal service. This is a new bureau, but it's an old office; they've been around for many years and have recently been elevated to bureau status.

Now, let me return to 1964 and the task force. The Post Office was faced with a serious problem in parcel post. Costs and rates were rising, volume was declining, service was poor, damage was high. Postmaster General Gronouski brought in an old friend, Ed Kriz, who put together a

---

[2] The President released the Kappel report five days after this interview, on July 16, 1968.

task force to study the entire parcel post problem. The task force was—if you'll forgive the immodesty—a group of bright young men who went deeply into the organization, found out how parcel post was handled, and looked as well at rate structure, and the customer relations side of it. In short, they did a *product analysis.* This contrasted with the traditional bureau administration approach, by which one bureau worries about distribution of parcels within a post office, another worries about transportation between post offices, and still another sets rates for them. The task force was, I think, successful. Parcel post service was improved and we succeeded in getting through Congress legislation which modified the rates and the size and weight of parcels the Post Office could accept. When that effort came to an end in the fall of '65, this group was given a new responsibility—that of studying the advisability of what was then called "priority mail." The question was: should the Post Office abolish air mail and provide next-day delivery for all first-class letter mail. This again was a problem that cut across bureau lines for about the same reasons as parcel post.

At that point (August 1965) the Postmaster General reconstituted the Parcel Post Task Force into an Office of Special Projects, the reason being that it had become apparent that the task-force approach was going to be needed to meet other product-line problems besides parcel post and priority mail. When I say product line, I'm contrasting the products of the Post Office with the functions which the bureaus handle on a day-to-day basis. These functions are aggregated into our planning, programming, budgeting categories and are closely tied into Post Office budget accounts. But interface with the public comes through the products we sell. The public doesn't care about mail distribution, or our other internal functions. Their interest is in our products—such as first-class mail, how much it costs, what service it gets and so on.

But because the bureaus were organized functionally, there was no product-line orientation in the Post Office. Any problem that crossed bureau lines had to be handled on an ad hoc basis, by an interbureau study group or by the Deputy Postmaster General or the Postmaster General himself—the only two people in the work force of 600,000 who had an overview of the entire postal service. The bureaus were established, I might point out, in the 1800s. Such a highly functionalized structure is considered passé in most modern organizations.

There haven't been what you might call wisdom-tooth changes, to speak of, within the department during the past 100 years. Would this be correct?

That is correct. The same kind of internal bureau structure has remained since the Post Office was made a cabinet department in 1829. From the very beginning, there was what was then called a first Assistant Postmaster General, a second, a third, and so on. From time to time they've reshuffled bureaus, but the Department has remained highly fragmented— staffed by specialists oriented around specialized functions, rather than by product.

In other words, it retained what could be called an orthodox structure common to many departments.

Exactly. In 1964 and '65 several problems were attacked by task forces drawn from different bureaus who were reporting, of necessity, to the Postmaster General. In the fall of '65 it became apparent to John Gronouski that he needed a continuing special projects staff to which he could toss problems which crossed bureau lines. On Labor Day of 1965, however, the President announced Gronouski's appointment as Ambassador to Poland, which tended to disrupt some of the plans he had in mind. Fortunately Larry O'Brien, his successor, was very much oriented toward the need for strong executive control.

It is probably obvious that the existence of a Special Projects Task Force, working directly for the Postmaster General, tended to diminish the authority of the line people in the postal system, as well as that of the staff bureaus. Traditionally, the Postmaster General—and let me overstate this for brevity—was the captive of the bureaus, which he nominally directed. And the existence of a continuing group to study interbureau or cross-bureau problems would give him leverage in the sense that it would provide him with information and would raise questions which otherwise might not get asked. I think, generally, the heads of organizations succeed insofar as they have accurate and meaningful information on the organizations they manage. The McNamara story at Defense is my reference here.

When Gronouski left, the plans to convert this small group of about twelve or so (essentially outsiders, but with a few very capable old-timers who worked with us) into a standing office of Special Projects—those plans were frustrated. But concurrently on October 12, 1965, the Bureau of the Budget issued its Directive 66-3, which created PPBS in the civil agencies and directed that each one set up a small group of analysts reporting directly to the Secretary, or head of agency, to analyze proposed programs.

This was a little different shift. The Special Projects Task Force in the Post Office was oriented to problem solving. The Budget Bureau directive said: "Don't wait till they're problems; while they're still proposed programs, have some group of dispassionate—I mean, not associated with operating people—analysts review and analyze the program. As part of your annual budget submission (which is the Budget Bureau's leverage on the world) give us a detailed program memorandum explaining and analyzing, on the basis of economic standards, the proposals that you're making." The result was that with almost no loss of time, the little group that had been planned was, in fact, set up. And it was set up, to some extent, with the same individuals.

The Special Projects people, I would think, would be a natural to inherit this new assignment.

Yes, and in fact they did, despite the change at the Postmaster General level. The new group was created and called the Office of Planning.

Wasn't it an outgrowth of Special Projects?

Special Projects had never been really legitimized. It was always an ad hoc group.

The plan of the Postmaster General was to make it into a standing special projects group.

Give it a permanent home?

Yes. Let me run through the chronology to make certain the picture is clear. The parcel post task force was an ad hoc, one-shot type group. That work finished, they got another ad hoc problem—priority mail— which they were asked to report on to the powers that be. That program has not yet moved into action; it's a bigger thing than parcel post; it's moved along, but it wasn't neatly tied up the way the first project was.

OK. So, seeing the value of a group reporting directly to him—and not committed to any of the bureau chiefs—the Postmaster General exchanged memos to establish a permanent Office of Special Projects on his staff, to handle whatever problems the Postmaster General wished. But before that could happen, Gronouski left.

When O'Brien arrived, he picked up the idea, reinforced by 66-3, which said: "Set up a special group of analysts," et cetera, as I indicated. O'Brien was a strong Postmaster General and had a strong management orientation. He set up the Office of Planning, using for the purpose a man he borrowed from the Budget Bureau, named John Haldi. O'Brien had talked to quite a few in government who had this curious mix of economic background, public service orientation, and analytical ability but didn't find anyone willing to take over the job. So as I get the story, he said to Charlie Schultze—who was then Budget Director—"Look, if you want me to follow through on 66-3, you've got to give me someone who can run the thing." So Schultze loaned him Haldi, who was Harry Rowan's assistant. Haldi worked here for a four- to five-month period as Acting Director of the Planning Office. When Ron Lee's assignment as a White House Fellow was completed, he became the first director of this office.

So, you're an infant organization but your roots go far back.

Yes, the roots do go back to a few ad hoc attempts. The office was established on February 6, 1966. I might be off a few days. It was formally established while John Haldi was acting director with a very small group of four or five. I was one of them.

We went around to the bureaus and said: "Well, what do you think an Office of Planning in the Post Office Department should do?" We were welcomed with a great deal of enthusiasm: "Oh, we've needed this for years. You guys are really going to get this place organized. Nobody knows which way we're going. We can't make plans because those people over in the other bureaus won't tell us which way they're going," and remarks of that type. It seemed quite clear that there was wide recognition that the bureau structure was not the right way to run a railroad, but everybody, so it seemed, was willing to live with it.

Did they admit a need for coordination?

Everyone complained of a lack of coordination.

Usual disease.

Yes. The disease is widely recognized, clearly diagnosed, and perpetually tolerated.

That really covers it.

Gene Walton and I, who made some of these rounds, observed some interesting reactions. The bureaus were willing to give us a charter on the future: "Gee, if you guys can think about where we ought to be five years from now, we would really like to know about it. You'd be a great help, but we've got control over next year's budget—and the year after that we know exactly what we want to do. So, you get a good fix on 1984 and let us know what you think. This gives us time to decide whether or not we're going to adopt it."

Someone has said—and this is parenthetical but appropriate—that planning is intelligent cooperation with the inevitable. And to the extent that forces in the environment and within the department are moving of their own impetus in a certain direction, it behooves the department to identify them, even if we can't change them. At least someone should be watching them.

Isn't the initial purpose of the Planning Office to identify and pre-scribe? Perhaps if it doesn't go beyond that, it's a futile experiment; however, if it starts with this, can it fully justify its existence?

I think so.

But, and I'm speculating here, you wouldn't settle for less than identification, prescription, and the cure—the surgery for the diseased situation. There are, I'm sure, a lot of impotent planning offices.

You're absolutely right. Top management of an organization clearly must not only anticipate what's going to happen but adjust the organization to it. The first role, chronologically at least, of the Planning Office is finding out what's ahead. If you're going to cooperate with the inevitable, you have at least to identify it. To a large extent, however, what's ahead is what we put there. Naturally, in our operation the economy-at-large will, for the most part, determine what the demands will be on the postal service.

Population growth, urban centers. . . .

Exactly. These are the planning activities of the Post Office, and our office should, if not do all of them, at least see that forecasts are made.

Now, having estimated, or ascertained on a best-guess basis, what the future holds for the department, the next step is getting the bureaus to cooperate intelligently with what is coming. This is the job of top management. The Planning Office, I feel, is not the agency to force bureaus to change their behavior. Our function is an informational one in two senses: it provides the environmental data I've just described, and it anticipates some of the technical changes in the way mail will be handled so that we can compare the future demand for mail service with our projected capability to supply it.

To push the bureaus in certain directions today is one thing; but won't you eventually push them tomorrow and the day after?

Through top management only. Through the Postmaster General.

They do the hard shoving.

Yes. When the day comes that the Office of Planning loses the support of the Postmaster General and tries to shove on its own, it's shoving with an empty boot.

As I see the Office of Planning—and again this is editorializing—as long as we can be useful to the Postmaster General in drawing his attention to the important issues, our function is legitimate and significant. And in many cases there is an attempt—an institutional attempt—to obfuscate the important issues. This is not, I think, unique to the Post Office at all. Since the median tenure of Postmaster Generals in this century is 2.6 years, the Post Office tends to feel that the top man is its captive. The bureaus tend to resist innovation, although they themselves may develop many changes. I don't want to characterize postal management as stick-in-the-mud or static or old-fashioned or negative. It's not; there are really good people here.

What about scaring top management into action by showing the appetite that Planning may have for innovation?

I think it's a widely used technique, and frequently proposals for change are accompanied by predictions of dire consequences if they are not adopted. Earlier I alluded to the Kappel Commission. It was established because Larry O'Brien recommended that the Post Office Department should become a government corporation, asserting that the department was in a "race with catastrophe." So, this is a recent illustration of the point you make.

I'm not characterizing the O'Brien statement as scare tactics, because he had a valid point: the Post Office is headed for trouble unless some major changes are made. Internally the Office has been able to raise, with the Postmaster General and his principal advisors, a lot of the key issues that the department should be worrying about. Now in the past these issues normally are raised by an agency outside the Post Office—the Budget Bureau, for example.

Have some Postmaster Generals been management-oriented or, at least, do they manage, even in their short tenure of office, to acquire a sense of what is sound management practice?

The most noticeable characteristic about Postmaster Generals, as a rule, is that they are political figures, and I don't use that in a pejorative sense—Jim Farley, Arthur Summerfield, Larry O'Brien. I stressed the latter's management skills because one wouldn't have expected that. And there's a long list of Postmaster Generals who were rewarded with the job rather than challenged by it.

With one exception in modern times the Postmaster General has been an outsider. Harry Truman appointed a letter carrier who had worked his way up, and by all accounts that I've heard and seen written, he was a total failure. There's a different kind of skill required to deliver a letter than to manage this big organization. I don't have to belabor that point.

Postmaster Generals, for the most part, have had the same problems as Secretaries of Defense. That is, they were people who came to an organization that was clearly and widely recognized to be unmanageable, and unmanaged it for four to eight years, or a median of 31 months in our case. All that changed when Secretary McNamara arrived. He used his "planning office," the Alain Enthoven systems analysis shop, to ask the important questions and advise him when certain proposals, made for institutional reasons by the various services, were not in the best interests of the Defense Department as a whole. Let me add that, as you can appreciate, the acquisition of information is more often than not the secret of influence in a big organization—public as well as private. McNamara, in short, was able to do what no man had ever done in the department before him: namely, manage the Defense Department. We have not yet seen a Postmaster General who has been able to manage the Post Office.

Is it ungovernable, or does it seem, as many government agencies and departments do, to run itself almost?

It runs itself.

With a peculiar momentum, or even a negative momentum—and perhaps this ends up as none at all.

If by peculiar you mean extremely small. I think the term to be applied is inertia, if I may say, rather than momentum. The productivity of the Post Office demonstrates the point rather dramatically. Over the past ten years in the Post Office the increase in productivity has been 2.3 percent; that is for the entire decade. The comparable figure for the economy-at-large is 3.2 percent per year, or 32 percent for the decade. Salaries in the total economy have increased some 44 percent since 1956. The difference between salary growth and productivity growth represents a rise in unit labor costs, which is normally reflected in higher prices. In the Post Office, productivity has risen 2.5 percent since 1956 and salaries have risen about 56 percent. You can see what has happened to unit labor costs. These figures show rate of growth, of course. In dollar terms, postal salaries are still far behind most industries.

Who does, or should, this bother, besides the taxpayer?

The Post Office is not efficiency-oriented; in fact, people here resist the term because it suggests efficiency experts and speedups and all that, and I don't really mean it in that spirit.

Many people within the department—and I include many congressmen who help run it—believe that the Post Office is merely one more government agency. And they point out that every government agency runs at a deficit. If there is no cry of alarm about the Department of Defense deficit or the Treasury deficit, why should there be one about the postal deficit? Let me say that this line of reasoning in our view—and I mean the Kappel Commission, and I think our Planning Office—misconceives the nature of the postal service.

The Post Office is a public utility. Postal services are no different, no more essential than telephone services. The nation's telephone system is no less important than the nation's postal system. They're obviously different technologies. Indeed, if I had to lose either one for a week, I'd have no trouble in making a choice. But the Post Office is surrounded with much tradition, as you've already said. At one point in our history the Post Office was the only means of communication, linking the frontier to the centers of power and government.

Rather a glorious history.

A glorious history which we often relive. I guess I could say the Post Office was once a *policy* arm of government. Transportation subsidies were extended to fledgling industries, through postal mail rates—that is, to steamship, canal, railroad, stage coach, and most recently, airlines. The government, it often seems, is in business to give subsidies. The postal service has been the channel for many subsidies and I think the country has profited by it. Today, people worry about building roads, but for many years, in the 1800's, the Congress exercised its influence on highway construction through the building of post roads—they were part of the postal subsidy in eighteenth-century America. For many years the Post Office was organized, as it were, in partnership with the Congress as a policy arm of government. I say "partnership" advisedly, because the alternative form of organization is corporation, and that may be what lies ahead for us.

The world has changed; the Post Office today is not in the business of moving your mail to your relatives. Only 14 percent, a recent study showed, of all mail is from one household to another. The rest of it is mostly from household to business or mostly from business to household, business to business, business to government—government looming larger in all our lives. Our Post Office is a major advertising medium. It is, I believe, the fourth largest advertising medium in the nation: only news-papers, magazines, and television exceed direct mail advertising. It's a unique and highly specialized form of advertising, whatever a householder may think about "junk mail"—a phrase that we don't use. It's a form of broadcast communication: one sender and millions of receivers of the same message. In fact, the Post Office is moving into the "broadcast" business in a really big way because of the computer revolution. I don't have statistics for you, but the point is beyond debate. More and more mail is addressed by computers at high speeds and it goes into the mail stream untouched, in the words of the poet, by human hands. But it's touched by human hands when it gets into the mail, because the Post Office is so highly labor-intensive. In fact, 80.2 percent of the postal dollar pays salaries, wages, and fringe benefits. The processes haven't changed much, but the products of the Post Office and the users of it certainly are chang-ing. The Post Office organization is the same one—with some title changes and some allowances for buzz words that have come into being—it's the same as it was one hundred years ago.

It may be that it's remarkably—in quotes—"efficient," and yet doesn't know it, or doesn't admit it.

Well, you may be right. I've heard it characterized as one of the less important subsystems of the American economy. It just goes on and on and it isn't really that important to the nation, as a whole, whether it operates at peak performance or not. Indeed, we wouldn't want it to operate at this level, if it meant sacrificing other things that are good—the sanctity of the mails, for example, which, in this country, is a real comparative advantage. The casual confidence (and I'm quoting from something here) with which the citizen drops even the most personal letter in his corner mailbox speaks volumes not merely about the mails but about his form of government. That's a quote from a report you'll be reading soon by the Kappel Commission. So the mail system, by and large, jogs along.

Hardly a reflection of the jet age.

It's not and won't be, because mail is not in the jet age. The jet busi-ness means moving by electronics and the telephone; broadcasting com-panies will develop that market, when it's technologically feasible to do so, with a readout device in every home, for example.

In the long run, how do you regard planning's future, say, during the next five years within the Post Office? Will you remain in business and be able to influence the operating bureaus to an increasing degree?

I think we'll be in business.

Regardless of the turnover at the top?

Yes, because we're in business not because we're the favorite of a particular individual or indeed a political party, but because we have filled a void that existed and would exist if this office were abolished. We would soon be replaced by another office that did the same thing. Forgetting about titles and names, the Postmaster General, whoever he is—or the "Head of the Post Office," should the title change—will always find it necessary to have, a la McNamara, a small group of specialists whose job is to analyze whatever the organization should be doing and is doing, and give him the questions he should be asking, so that he will have at his fingertips the facts, the answers that Congress needs, that the bureaus need, the information that he needs to do a 9-to-5 or, further, a 9-to-9 job.

You are, then, basically . . .

. . . an extension of the Postmaster General's hours.

A lengthened shadow, as it were, sitting beside him—prodding and nudging.

You put it very graphically, and I think we have done this. There is no possibility that any one man can run a business this big in an 8-hour or 10-hour or 32-hour day. The president of General Electric has given up trying—he has five people sharing the presidency. The trend is toward not merely a good strong staff for the top man but several top men.

Staff people function as technicians more, sometimes, than salesmen for their ideas. The two elements don't often go hand-in-hand. What's your view on the best way staff can make its influence felt right here?

I think planners have to be promoters. Earlier I said that Post Office planners themselves could not implement the changes. They must do it through the Postmaster General. It sounds Machiavellian, but I don't mean it that way. The fact is that in any organization, promotion and selling are an important part of "implementation."

If a staff remains purely advisory, it may not push hard enough for its own convictions. On the other hand, what if the Postmaster General allowed your proposals to suffocate or be mothballed in storage? Can you sometimes anticipate the degree of support you may get from him for a proposal in the embryo stage? I assume he may also ask you to work on a certain project.

Yes, those are the easy ones. Our real contribution comes in telling him those things he should be worrying about which, in fact, he's not. The Postmaster General who knows what to assign us really doesn't need us.

I see our role as a little more than merely doing things he doesn't have time for. It's telling him what he should be doing with his time. The scarcest resource in this building—in this department—is the time and attention of top management. We're short of funds, but we can get money. We're short of buildings, but we can build them. But there are only 24 hours in a day and the things the top management spends its time on become the most important things it does.

So you identify possible options.

Yes. I don't want to make it sound too systematic and smooth and well oiled, because it isn't. On many occasions this office has made proposals which have been rejected. Those are the ups and downs.

Does the present Postmaster General encourage, let's call it "creativity" on the part of this office?

Yes. The phrase he uses is "controlled conflict." He is fully aware—even though he's a short-timer himself—of the organizational anomalies built into the Post Office. No more than the President of the United States, can he press a button and say: "I want this done," and have it done. I refer you to Scheslinger's book on *The Kennedy Years. . . .*

And Neustadt's Presidential Power. *At this stage, what would you be willing to put down as major accomplishments by Planning for the department?*

I'd like to be able to list many accomplishments—I don't think I can. We have been the prime movers in getting the PPB system installed—that doesn't require a definition. We're by no means the only ones involved in this—the Bureau of Finance and Administration has also run with it—in fact, run in a slightly different direction than we had hoped at first. But that's all right.

Perhaps up there in Planning, in a broad sense, you're teachers in a partial role.

That analogy has come up often.

Sometimes, from my observation, "teacher" is not as dangerous as some of the tar-and-feather terms often applied to management analysts, systems experts, or just plain planning officers. If I limited you to one main problem, or disease, in the department you don't think you have yet managed to cure, what might it be?

"Cure" is, I think, a little too final.

Perhaps "disease" is too strong.

No, I don't think it is. To restrict myself to one single problem is not unfair, but it is difficult because many compete for attention, and different interpretations and definitions could be given to the very word "problem." Perhaps when you have a chance to read the report of the Kappel Commission, you might gain more by identifying, in your judgment, the so-called biggest or worst problem.

Insofar, again, as accomplishment is concerned, it would be the adoption of the PPB system, which was formulated in this office. After the breaking-in period, this took on a life of its own. It became changed in some ways, diverged from what we had in mind, but basically it's a sound system and has been, with much reluctance, adopted by the rest of the department. This, I believe, is our most meaningful accomplishment. Now that it's launched it's no longer a planning problem and we are properly backing out of it, because it's clearly tied into the budget and there is a pretty well-established budgeting system that is now accomplished much more rationally than formerly, through the planning and programming system. Our principal concern has become *product planning*, through which we try to see the services the Post Office offers through the eyes of the customer and raise some basic questions about the kind of business we should be in.

We have also, let me say, introduced the concept and practice of the formal study—and that, by itself, may be an important contribution.

DR. JONATHAN A. CUNITZ, ASSISTANT TO THE DIRECTOR, OFFICE OF PLANNING AND SYSTEMS ANALYSIS

I thought we might move by stages toward a consideration of the Office of Planning and Systems Analysis, in which you serve as the Assistant to the Director. We might discuss the reasons for establishment of the office, then have your views regarding the purposes of the program, and finally take up the measuring of results.

Why don't I take it from the beginning chronologically and trace through what we've done.

When PPBS came into being in August 1965, the federal agencies were, in effect, notified by the President that a new planning and budget system was coming into being. Then in October 1965 the Bureau of the Budget issued Bulletin 66-3, which, in detail, prescribed what PPBS would be like, what it encompassed, and the deadlines for different stages in its development in the agencies. During fall 1965 the Post Office Department was undergoing a change in head: Postmaster General Gronouski had resigned and Postmaster General O'Brien had been appointed by the President. Whenever this happens in any agency, as you may have noticed, decisions come to a halt. It's a lame-duck agency; people are afraid to make decisions for fear that they will be reversed, and afraid to bother with groundwork for fear that it just won't be used. They want to see how things stand and what the new Postmaster General wants.

But the problems continue.

Right. There were some specific requirements placed on the Post Office Department by the Bureau of the Budget. The department asked for a moratorium in applying PPBS because of the switchover. When the new Postmaster General arrived, he decided to support PPBS completely. This decision was actually reached before he came here, but once this was confirmed and acknowledged within the ranks, work commenced very quickly on meeting the Budget Bureau's requirements.

Was PPBS a mandate from the White House?

Right. It was a definite requirement for 21 civilian agencies. We were told we had to do it. Now it's a matter of how well you're going to do it—you can pay lip service to it, and some agencies have, or you can try and apply it properly. I think the extremely strong support from the top is the basic reason for its success—not complete success, but adequate success.

Did Mr. O'Brien call for immediate implementation, or for its application by stages? In other words, how did he give his support so that members of the department could understand needs and goals?

In a staff meeting during the week following Mr. O'Brien's arrival in the department, he made it specifically known that he was supporting PPBS. He asked his White House Fellow, the present director of this office, to develop within three days specific recommendations on implementing PPBS in the department, as well as the organizational changes required to establish the system.

The White House Fellow responded within the deadline with a whole list of required actions and specified the organizations that should be introduced for the successful implementation of PPBS. If you read Bulletin 66-3, PPB has some specific requirements for planning and systems analysis. The bulletin stated the need for a centralized planning and analytical group. It was felt that if the system was to be given proper emphasis in the Post Office Department, a special office would have to be created within the Office of the Postmaster General.

Prior to PPBS, an Office of Special Projects within the Office of the Postmaster General had been involved with parcel post legislation and had started working on PPB. But it had a small staff and was associated too closely with other matters to be able to handle major PPBS responsibilities. So the recommendations to the Postmaster General included the creation of an Office of Planning and Systems Analysis, an Executive Planning Board, to operate as a top-level decision-making forum, and three new divisions within the Bureau of Finance and Administration—Budget, Review and Analysis, and Programming. Of these three divisions, Programming has done the greatest amount of the PPBS work.

PPBS requires, as I understand it, that all cooperate at the systems level, the program level, and the budget level for—I'd guess you'd call it—an integrated system in the long run.

Right.

You worked with what you had plus a new arrangement. Is this correct?

This office, the Executive Planning Board, the Programming Division, and the Review and Analysis Division were all new organizations. The Budget Division was reorganized. Thus, new staffs, new organizations, and new responsibilities were introduced in response to PPBS.

After these recommendations were approved by the Postmaster General, a Headquarters Circular was prepared which implemented the organizational changes. [A Headquarters Circular is a document within the department used to introduce official changes and regulations.] In February 1966 a Headquarters Circular 66-9 created the Office of Planning, the Executive Planning Board, and the three new divisions, and delineated their responsibilities.

Even before this, however, the Postmaster General, his White House Fellow, the Director of the Civil Service Commission, and the Director of the Bureau of the Budget had begun an intensive search for someone with enough sophisticated management skill to head up the Office of Planning. They considered quite a few candidates from the Defense Department, private industry, educational institutions, and other governmental agencies for the position. These men had salaries ranging from $25,000 to $75,000 and were generally high-calibre people. Several were interviewed by the Postmaster General, but none was actually hired for the position. A few were acceptable to the Postmaster General but their circumstances would not permit them to join us at the time. The applications of others were merely screened.

Did this position require a special breed in terms of talent?

It required not so much a specific background or an experience in government as it did an attitude, a personality, and an education in terms of the skills that were required here. The department needed someone with a very high level of professional education and who was also dynamic and progressive, because in any bureaucracy you need someone like this if you want to get anything done. The Postmaster General did not want a professional bureaucrat.

Rather, a creative innovator.

Exactly. Finally, a high official of the Bureau of the Budget was offered to the department on loan to establish this office. He had been associated with PPBS from the Bureau of the Budget side. Now to be quite frank, there were two reasons the department thought he would be good for the position. First of all, because PPBS was being introduced by the Budget Bureau and he had come from there. We thought he would make an excellent liaison with them, understand their requirements, and meet them satisfactorily. If anything went wrong with the department's PPBS work, it would be much harder for the Bureau of the Budget to criticize, because their man was on loan to us. Secondly, he could be used as a catalyst to get certain changes introduced quickly and then leave. Here was a high-powered man coming from the Bureau of the Budget, here for a short time to get something done.

In February of 1966, when the office was created, this man became acting director. To staff the new unit, two men with graduate degrees—one an MBA from Harvard and the other a Ph.D.—were selected from the Office of Special Projects, which had been another office in the Office of the Postmaster General. In addition, five men were assigned on "detail" from other bureaus within the department—one each from Facilities, Transportation, Finance. These were 90-day loans and supposedly the cream of the bureaus, even though it was hard for the bureaus to do without them. Gradewise, they were GS-14's and 15's, primarily.

Program people? Take the Transportation representative.

The Transportation representative was a woman, who had her Ph.D., was the head of a line division within Transportation. The man from Facilities was a staff member within the Procurement Division. They weren't picked so much for their positions within the bureaus as for their expertise.

By means of these "details" we got some staff within the office fairly quickly. They served several purposes. First of all, they provided quick manpower. Second, they hoped to relieve any apprehensions within the bureaus that the Office of Planning would be unreachable by the bureaus. And finally, they gave the Office of Planning a chance to scrutinize potential future staff members for permanent positions.

Was there a selling aspect to the PPBS program?

Of course. This is to be expected with any new program—a tremendous selling and educational process.

In March 1966—a month after the office was created—the screening of applicants for permanent positions within the office began. During the next year and a half, over 300 applications were received and over 100 people interviewed for the 25 positions within this office. Generally speaking, those selected for the professional positions had had extensive education and came from outside the department.

The initial work of the office centered around special studies for the department. This was also suggested by the Bureau of the Budget's Bulletin 66-3. The acting director of the office felt that staff could get started on special studies without much resistance from the bureaus because studies are hard to fight; no one is against them. They may not do anything with them once they're done, but they're not against their being done.

They can usually be filed, if nothing else.

Well, even if the bureaus don't agree with the results of the studies, they still can't effectively oppose the basic idea.

Would you say that you moved cautiously?

Well, not cautiously. There was a calculated strategy. There wasn't anything haphazard. You want to get established; you want to get staffed up; and you want to get something done that will give you a firm basis and won't kill you off right in the beginning when you're still in the embryonic stage.

That puts it very accurately.

The director—I remember a discussion we had soon after I came here—hoped that after we became established, and our footing became a little more sure, the staff could get into research for rate changes (although this never came about), organizational changes within the department, and some basic changes in the way we do business.

In other words, the office was not solely for the development of the broad concepts in PPBS. It also had related ambitions. Was this true?

Well, it was created as a professional, analytical staff at the Postmaster General's level that would survive with or without PPBS, but at the moment was geared to implementing PPBS to bring about its success.

When you assemble a highly professional staff within an agency, at the top level, it doesn't get killed off that easily. You've invested too much in it and it's too badly needed within any agency. It was our intention that the office be identified, in a professional sense, and respected, no matter which Postmaster General it worked under—though there were some very close ties between this office and Mr. O'Brien. Mr. Watson has now come in as Postmaster General, but our status has not changed enough to hamper any of our efforts.

What are the problems associated with the Post Office which (a) are peculiar to it, and (b) which, in priority order, this office started to attack?

Priorities within the Post Office Department are very difficult to ascertain. Everyone has a different version of what gets top priority; after a point, everything's top priority. Even in our post offices, postmasters say: "We have 150 different studies, projects, or programs from headquarters going on. Which ones do we give priority to?" Our office decided to take a look at some basic problems. We put together a shopping list of problems, of potential matters for study, and we attacked them. Our initial approach was to develop study proposals on a number of these topics. I can read these off to you. Some of the initial proposals were on methods of selling postage, evaluation of railway post offices, improved collection service, lobby services (transactions that occur with the public in the lobby of a post office), air transportation containerization, intercity mail transportation, the Vertical Improved Mail program (a delivery method in high-rise office buildings), mail service levels (standards of service), plant acquisition criteria, intracity mail transportation, and space and mechanization problems within post offices. Studies followed on a number of these, although some others didn't get very far at all.

Who proposed such a list?

The shopping list was prepared by the staff members of the office, and the study proposals were prepared by members of the office—either permanent members or "details" assigned to us.

Did any proposals get on the list from others in the department?

Not immediately. Those I mentioned probably covered about the first year or so. We also left ourselves open to suggestions from other bureaus and offices. Some of the ideas we developed arose from other bureaus working through their details to our office. We also asked our regional offices for study proposals or ideas. There were a small number that actually came in from the regions. The study proposals, themselves, as I said, were prepared by our staff members. Some have worked out fine, developed into studies and resulting action, and some haven't.

The other early activities of the office centered on developing an official format, or guide, for preparing study proposals, and was put out in the form of a headquarters circular. Another activity was the development of a long-range planning system composed of plans up to twenty years in the future for the department. These were based upon bureau submissions and were formulated in terms of the PPBS program category structure.

This is where the Post Office should be, or might be, over that period of time?

These are the activities that should be undertaken to bring the Post Office Department to where it should be at that time.

I take it that the Post Office never looked too far into the future. Is this a fair statement?

This is a very fair statement. There is one key constraint within the department in that the environment forces us to become involved in day-to-day problems and the annual budget cycle. Anything further than the budget cycle is irrelevant to most managers.

Was the Planning Office considered an upheaval? Was it regarded with some skepticism by Capitol Hill?

Congress couldn't care less about the work of our office; they don't get involved in it. They usually don't get involved with individual organizational changes within a department. They have too much else to do. They're involved with our annual appropriations, postal rates, constructing federal buildings, and so on.

It seems that no government activity affects each individual citizen so such as your service. And if it is to be improved on a long-range planning basis, certainly it comes ahead of many other departments. I am surprised it's been so neglected.

Well, there is certainly a need for long-range planning, but you can't blame anyone for neglecting it because they weren't under any pressure to consider it.

But the service is far from excellent. . . .

Present service is not generally affected by long-range planning. The service is mostly affected by immediate problems. If you want to improve service ten years in the future, you plan. Long-range planning is not going to help you two years, or three years, from now.

I see—it's not a plan, it's planning.

Right. Our intention for a long time back was to develop an integrated planning system for the department, composed of long-range plans and two other elements: a forecasting system covering the same time period and relating to the category structure, plus the setting of department goals or objectives.

As of now, we have headquarters circulars establishing department goals and another describing the forecasting system. Individual forecasts are now being put together. The goals are still confidential. The office has been involved in a number of other areas, too. You can tell from our list of responsibilities what we've worked on, and I could talk for hours on what we've accomplished. What we've discussed here covers only a small part of what we've done up to now.

The three prongs of this integrated planning system—plans, forecasts, and goals—all are interdependent, and they're also dependent on the special studies performed either by our office or by other groups in the department.

Do you feel at this point that the results have been solid?

I have my own viewpoint on the successes of the department in different areas. I would say the Office of Planning has had a definite impact on the department, has succeeded in introducing a considerable degree of change, has served as a catalyst in many other areas, and has easily justified the expense and the effort spent to develop it.

One other point: Are there some lessons from the experience of this office that could be shared by others in attempting to set up an office of planning and systems analysis?

There are a number of good things done by this office and there are a number of lessons to be learned from our experience. I would rather you tried to ascertain them yourself at this point. And also, we had better get on to Dr. Armstrong.

Surely.

DR. JAMES C. ARMSTRONG, ASSISTANT DIRECTOR OF PLANNING DEVELOPMENT, OFFICE OF PLANNING AND SYSTEMS ANALYSIS

I thought we might begin by discussing the problems encountered by this office during your assignment, and later consider the success with which you and others believe some of these issues have been solved.

I assume you're familiar with the standard problems that any new—spanking new—office has when it's born, and placed in a position of high leverage. There is the initial resistance of—if I may use the word—the bureaucracy. The bureaucracy is bound to resent the establishment of any office, particularly when not only the office function but those involved are new to the service. Most of the analysts here are young compared to old-timers with twenty and thirty years in the Post Office Department. A large number of these old-timers feel that systems analysis has no part to play in helping them accomplish their day-to-day operations.

To establish systems analysis in a fairly new organization might be somewhat less frustrating, I would guess.

Much less frustrating.

Perhaps it's too obvious but I'll risk the question: Are you still on trial—which is not always a bad condition—or merely regarded with some doubt in the department?

"Regarded with some doubt" describes our position quite well. As to whether we are on trial, I would say, yes. By its very nature—that is, by its objectives—this office will continue to be on trial. To a certain extent it's a healthy condition. The question is: "Can the antagonism generated become lethal?" We're usually identified as the office which spots problems and finds things which should be changed.

Won't you, in time, benefit the entire department?

Absolutely. But there is some question in the minds of those in the old-line operating bureaus as to whether or not the benefits to the department—assuming that they accept the notion there is some benefit—are worth the price one has to pay. The price, you know, can be in the form of fewer jobs, bad politics, or any of a number of other unpleasant or inconvenient consequences. The situation will doubtless improve, as it did in Defense, for instance. There—the analogy isn't quite perfect, but you could associate the old-time bureaucrat, say, with the military people—there, you can see a straightforward response to systems analysis. The military simply discovered that the way you fight systems analysis—and systems analysts—is with systems analysts.

If you could ever get to that stage here, in all senses, it becomes a very healthy way to work. The antagonism is an academic one. And once you academically prove a point, everyone shakes hands and goes off and prepares for the next battle. Currently here, you open up a wound and you leave a scar.

And it's a continuing uphill climb, if not a knock-down and drag-out bout.

That's right. The nature of the office as an antagonist is not understood in an academic sense, but rather as antagonism in a very real sense. They—the departmental personnel—think they are actually being attacked, and they respond in the manner in which I would guess, from my limited experience, most bureaucrats would respond—namely, politically.

As well as: "It's not the way we've done it in the past." You're surely accused of upsetting settled ways of doing business. So you have a selling job. And second, a human relations task. Perhaps, third, your techniques are easily misunderstood. All this must be a drawback. But, on the other hand, you're working from a posture of strength from the very level you occupy in the organization.

I would be the first to admit there have been a great many mistakes made here, and I think elsewhere too, in the introduction of systems analysis in government. In general, we try to move too fast. Here, in the Post Office Department, I think this office was too sophisticated. The PPBS structure, for example, was frequently viewed by old-timers as an elaborate presentation of something which originally was a very simple notion.

What about the position of systems people—the in-group—in any organization?

To a certain extent, they're the in-group. That is true, in a very real sense, here, for instance. Of the 700-odd thousand employees within the whole Postal Service, almost none of them—a small fraction, at best—know anything at all about PPBS and what it is. The people here in the Washington headquarters building know about it, of course, but the vast mass of Post Office employees have no feeling for it, because it's never been part of their lives. Those people—the vast majority—do not contact the department through this office, but rather through the Bureau of Operations—one of our chief antagonists. Again, I use that word in the sense of saying: "We could do things better, why don't you?" This is the payoff. Actually, the idea of systems analysts as members of a small in-group has its disadvantages. If you look at it in that light, you realize that the whole PPBS could suddenly disappear without a trace. It would only have created a ripple.

As I've been listening here, I have gained some impressions of the Post Office. Every organization has its own special administrative personality. In my judgment, the Post Office is kind of overweight, beyond middle age, and overtired, and has been performing its services in about the same old way for about as long as the Republic has stood. "Leave it alone" has perhaps been the attitude by some insiders and outsiders, as well. And yet, despite a crisis, now and then, it has offered good and even superior service. Is this a fair estimate, bearing in mind that it is inevitably superficial?

There are, let me say, some unfortunate misconceptions about the department. It's certainly true that it's an overlay of one step after another —200 years of layers up to the present time and its present structure. It's big and it's cumbersome. But perhaps most important is the fact that tangled in the layers are a number of legislative dictums which confine the department to a particular mode of operation. Within those confines you can change things, but not much. The real changes, such as Mr. O'Brien's suggestion of going from a cabinet position to a public corporation, require breaking out of these confines.

Changes have been made—perhaps not enough, but some have been significant. Mr. O'Brien's announcement of priority mail, in the first part of this year, is an example. I think we should have done it before. The Zip Code is another case where in retrospect one more or less dreams about what you *could* have done. The concept, from inception to implementation, took a number of years. In the scheme of things—the Post Office scheme— it went very fast.

Perhaps the Post Office hasn't quite understood the quality of introducing change. I'm speculating here, and doubtless this is merely the tip-of-the-iceberg sort of thing with many deeper reasons below the surface.

I would suspect that change in any large, old-line organization is difficult for the old-timers to understand. The Post Office Department is probably not an exception in that regard. Going back to your previous question, I might mention again that the changes one would like to make are frequently not within the power of postal officials to make—so that criticism of postal officials is often misdirected.

Some critics suggest that they could do our job better. A frequently cited example is United Parcel Service (UPS). The fact that they stay in business must mean, so it goes, that their customers are getting a better deal than the Post Office can provide. But it should be noted that UPS doesn't take on the job of delivering parcels to nonprofitable areas. If you just look at the geography of the country, you discover that most of it is nonprofitable for delivery service. But we are by law required to give the same quality service to large cities, small towns, and rural areas.

What, among the various problems you face, now stands out as the most difficult to shake down?

The single, biggest problem in making PPBS work was the lack of solid cooperation by the operating bureaus. This varies in degree, and from person to person; in some cases we did receive good cooperation. But the resistance of the bureaucracy to taking part in the new system essentially means its death, if the resistance continues.

And yet, weren't you, as I suggested earlier, after improvement of the total operation?

Absolutely. I came a year ago and was not here when the PPBS structure was originally drawn up. I can look at the program structure without feeling any sense of authorship. From my position, I feel that the initial system was overly sophisticated. There were attempts to place requirements on the bureaus which they could not meet—without really some very uncomfortable stretching.

Could this office have done a better job of breaking in the non-systems people?

This office, of course, does not represent the total effort to install PPBS. There is a group in the Bureau of Finance and Administration concerned with programming. I would say, to your question, that more thought should have been given to breaking in the non-systems people. It's really the same problem that people in operations research have known for a good many years—namely, that solving the problem is 10 percent; the other 90 percent is selling the answers. And PPBS, to a certain extent, had that aspect. It's also true that if you have the leverage, the quickest way to obtain results is not to placate and compromise and struggle on, but to take the direct approach.

Short of being ruthless, it is a clinical handling of organizational innovation: the wisdom-tooth approach means that the tooth has to go.

That's right. I think if you try to describe the approach used here, it amounted simply to a decision to go in and say: "This is it." But you can't do that sort of thing by unpopular edict, because the system must be fed with information, and getting it requires cooperation. The people down at the Post Office level have to tell you how many hours they are working at a special-purpose window, or a general-purpose window, and so on. If they don't tell you what you need to know, then you can't tell if they're making money or losing money.

I guess you're bound to poke a good many nerve centers of the organization. Are there, for example, departmentwide problems so serious that without the establishment of this office the Post Office might be headed for real trouble?

There are two frequently recited points of view about the troubles of the Post Office Department. One is that it is heading for a catastrophe. The other is that it is struggling along and will continue to struggle along, albeit inefficiently.

Like a fat lady waddling slowly to cross the street, perhaps.

Nothing will happen to her. She may be inefficient and slow and taxpayers may have to pay a bit more than they would if this were subcontracted. For a systems analyst looking at these two views, the second is just as horrifying as the first. You don't have to have a catastrophe to know that you ought to change things.

It should certainly be a challenge for any systems man looking for better ways to perform these vital tasks.

Exactly. It's a chance to examine the entire anatomy of the organization. The Kappel report is the most intensive recent study of the overall Post Office operation. I'd be very interested to see whether they claim the Post Office is simply an inefficient old lady—in a sense—or whether the place is heading for a catastrophe. I mean by a catastrophe the sudden breakdown of the whole system. I have the feeling that if you exclude from the definition an isolated breakdown of a part of the system, the Post Office Department is not headed for a catastrophe. The Post Office Department is an inefficient, tired old lady, and if you pull out systems analysis altogether the Post Office will continue to roll along. It's not going to die or run into a disaster.

The challenge of effective systems analysis is dulled by the traditions of the department. The idea, for example, of "Get the mail out today—and don't worry about five years from now," can seriously cripple planning and thorough analysis. This office has, on occasion, been tied down with short projects, a situation which we refer to as "fighting brush fires." The fact that the topics are considered urgent and are assigned by higher authority means that you have to do them now. But they're frequently time-consuming, and many other opportunities must be foregone or delayed. Looking at the other side, on the other hand, in many decisions for the future, today's decisions bear directly on five-year plans. For that reason we have been involved in some specific analyses which have immediate impact. In fact, some people within the department have criticized this office because: "You people are supposed to be involved with long-range planning."

That's surely a clue to much more than merely a current attitude. How do you think systems analysis influence has actually rubbed off? Has it, to any degree, infected the operating branches and in some measure aroused their energetic cooperation in new directions?

It is not, let me say, of epidemic proportions. That's for sure. Trying to promote the infection and get this thing rolling is a big job. If, as I said earlier with reference to the Defense Department, you can ever reach the point where you were fighting systems analysis with systems analysis, then it would all be downhill. There has never been any study within the department which shocked me with its profound elegance and analytical approach, but there have been some which appear to be honest attempts. These are few and far between, and I think until you reach the point that you have solid studies, it is difficult to claim real success.

One final item. Aside from the frustrations, have you had some satisfactions in the kinds of challenges which cross your desk?

I have, in general, been disappointed in the fact that the challenges are there but one can't get to them. In that sense, it has been frustrating—perhaps not in capital letters—because there have been some steps taken and we have made some progress. Take the recent restructuring of the program system. It was done with the cooperation of the operating bureaus —a new approach. There have been arguments and a continuing dialogue between the bureaus and this office. Not all of that discussion has been what I would consider rational, but at least it's discussion. The structure that evolved does have the approval of the operating bureaus and us. Maybe the last 2½ years were a necessary prelude to this.

I hope, as an observer, that the next several years will prove somewhat better but we will let you do the praying. It might be fair to state that at least they couldn't be much worse.

I wouldn't think so.

MRS. WILLIAM P. McLAUCHLAN, MANAGEMENT ANALYST, OFFICE OF PLANNING AND SYSTEMS ANALYSIS

I should like to start with the question: How do you look at the overall role of the Planning Office—as an information collector, synthesizer of scattered facts, as a catalyst to energize the operating bureaus—or a bit of each, perhaps?

I'd say the latter is probably the case: as a catalyst. We don't have the staff to go out and dig up very many facts on our own. Most of the digging is done by other bureaus and offices. We'll find out information from one bureau that another bureau really ought to have, and would not discover except through our office. Our responsibility extends across bureau lines and is concerned with a particular area of activity. So we tend to know the people who are related to that area in every bureau, whereas members of the various bureaus may not necessarily know each other.

In other words you're not assigned, through a particular series of projects, to a particular bureau for most of your postal career?

Oh, no. It happens that in our category we mainly work with the Bureau of Operations because it does the things in our area. It's a big bureau and, as I say, we do whatever coordination there is between it and the other people involved.

Your work, I understand, goes all the way to the top of the department.

As far as we know, it does. We raise these issues for the consideration of the Postmaster General or the Departmental Planning Committee or other fairly high-level decision makers. We don't just have them resolved by the head of our office. He forwards them to others—that's the whole reason for our existence.

And yet, it's not an inert role. You are staff, in the best sense of the word—advisory, rather than operational—a group of suggesters.

That's right.

As I remarked in another discussion just this morning: nudgers of the operating people.

I would say that's true. We have been working on pushing a particular policy point of view with one of the operating bureaus, for example, for some time. We ourselves have no line responsibility whatsoever in this area. So we can't go out and tell the people in the field: "You shall do such and such." Whatever effectiveness we have is through our ability to persuade the other bureaus or the appropriate decision maker to tell the bureau in question: "You must do such and such," even if they don't agree.

I've heard the term "persuade" in other talks today in the Planning Office. How do you make it work? What implications does it have?

It means that you must secure the agreement of the other party. It doesn't matter what your opinion is; you have to work with the other person and come to a mutually agreeable solution of a problem. You can't say: "You shall do such and such"; rather, you say, "The best thing to do is this," and they say, "No, it's not that," and then you both discuss it.

Does it ever put the Office of Planning on the defensive? You don't have less information, certainly, than the operating people; presumably you have more. But you're in a position only to persuade, and you can't insist that a certain course of action be taken.

That's right.

Nor if it is taken, can you supervise it. You can't walk out and say: "We want it done our way and we're going to look over your shoulder." Let me put it even stronger—doesn't this situation prevent you from being assertive, or aggressive, in your efforts to persuade?

It depends on the level of political interests and your particular problem. If the Postmaster General has expressed particular concern, and the

Budget Bureau has raised the issue, then it's important enough to worry about. You're in less of a defensive position when the information you're presenting is, in fact, considered relevant—otherwise it may never come to the surface.

How innovative in such a department as the Post Office can you get?

I would say very innovative. That's the whole function of the Planning Office.

For its own sake?

Well, no, there's no sense in producing a completely far-out idea if you have to persuade another person. But if you think of a good idea, that's fine—provided it will work.

Does sponsorship by top leadership in the department greatly help, or make the crucial difference, in promoting a new idea?

I'd say yes, that definitely helps.

What about orientation toward the management process by the bureaus? Wouldn't they have to understand your views before you started to persuade or promote a new idea?

Their view is influenced by high-level decision makers. That is, when O'Brien says, "You shall be interested in planning," we tend to have very good acceptance in the bureaus. But it's because the Postmaster General said it's a good idea, not because they're very interested in long-range plans. That is my impression, anyway.

Generally, how would you characterize relations between the Planning Office and the bureaus, formal as well as informal?

I'd say our relations are very good informally, and some of the bureaus are developing more interest in planning as we work with them. One thing in our favor is simply the fact that it's obvious that the department cannot go on functioning the way it has for the past 100 years. The word "catastrophe" may be a bit overdone, but I think that it is becoming more and more apparent, not only to the public but even within the department. Before, people were concerned mainly with their own particular area of interest, and now there's more of the sense: "We've got to work together to do something to solve these issues." High-level people in the department are interested in these ideas. Before, when this crisis-type situation was lacking, the mood was, "Why should a bureau develop any new ideas in the first place?" Because there was no place for these ideas to go.

Besides top support and the attitude of the bureaus, you've added pressure from the public, which is beginning to insist on some type of change.

I think that's definitely true.

What about the impact your office has already had in applying some of these new ideas to improve departmental operations? Can you think of positive results of which you, and others, can say: look, this is something new and better?

I think the most important overall result is this general change in atmosphere toward planning and coordinating, being concerned with the issues, and making sure, in fact, that issues are checked with everybody involved. In the category of my own work, I can think of specific accomplishments—some are still open issues. We are still pursuing them and I think we'll come up with some concrete results.

Would the actual specifics of what you're developing be too narrow to recite—that is, in respect to the overall planning functions?

I think pretty much. Our victories tend to be small ones. That is, we raise an issue that you've got too many of this kind of a machine, and they say: "Yes, indeed; we never realized this before." What we did in planning was to bring the information together, not that anybody wouldn't ultimately have found this situation in need of repair or correction. We found it first. Not all of our discoveries are dramatic breakthroughs. They're the little sort of things that keep you going because you *think* you're accomplishing some good. I think you just don't solve the major issues that we're working on, overnight; just raising those issues in the first place and keeping them alive is a victory of sorts. I personally wouldn't really be happy until we'd made our point on the issues—that is, until we'd won.

It's been said that to identify and prescribe cures might be a sufficient justification for your office. What would you say?

I don't think we can come up with cures for these illnesses all by ourselves. We don't have that many ideas or that much staff. But the department coming up with its own cure, because we have acted as a catalyst in bringing everybody together and everybody's experience to bear on a given problem—I think that is very important. That's what our office can do. For example, we can't come up with *the* ideal postal system—on the seventh floor with a staff of about twenty-five. It's extremely small. But when we develop a new idea, we check it out with someone in a bureau who has some background in the matter, with someone else who may have a different approach to it, then we bring it to somebody who can make the decision—that's how the process works, the process of change.

You've described some of the elements of the process of creating a new idea. Have you found in your postal experience, many, I won't say, dreary bureaucrats—let's say those who just don't respond to different ideas that might lead to better ways of doing old things?

I'd say there are a great many dreary bureaucrats—people who do not respond—who would rather not respond. They will, however, respond if they are forced to do so. That's in fact one of our functions: to make the issues so hot, and by nature many are, that the bureaucrats have to do something about them. On the other hand, there are pockets of very creative people in the bureaus, and our office tends to find them. I know that in a certain bureau, the guy to contact is so-and-so because his answer is never "No." His answer is: "Well, how can we work this out?" In fact, there's more of that approach than I thought existed when I came.

Do you feel the job is often frustrating?

Actually, I don't really feel that way. In a sense we keep ourselves going. The office has a great deal of esprit de corps. We feel we're out to save the Post Office Department, and this also extends to the various pockets I mentioned in other bureaus and offices. If any one of us were alone, we would be stifled overnight, practically. We sort of reinforce each other: don't give up; this is just one issue that you've lost; there'll be another battle tomorrow.

In the matter of disappointments, don't some—or even many—planning ideas as presented get lost, shelved, or buried?

That is a very big disappointment, especially when the issue is shelved simply because there's no one to make a decision on it, or because it's been considered and they've decided it's a bad idea. Sometimes it's shelved simply because you don't have the energy to keep bringing it to people's attention. I think I've mentioned the problem of the change in top-level people, of the change in the decision-making body—you know, the problems of a lame-duck administration. You do get very frustrated because, in fact, there is nobody to decide the issue. It's not that you get an adverse decision; there's just nobody to listen to your side of the story. Of course, as you appreciate, we're fighting on several fronts at the same time. So during these periods of frustration, we tend to focus our attention on other areas which have festering sores, so to speak, in them.

The Planning Office is rather young in terms of age of staff compared with standard government groups, I believe.

I think part of the reason that it's young—and this is pure speculation—is that not many young people would think of coming to work for the Post Office Department in most of its bureaus. But they come to work here in the Planning Office because it's a great opportunity for those just starting out. Those with established reputations in some other department of government wouldn't be interested.

I would assume that a good many people consider the Post Office loaded with clerks and mail bags.

I would never have considered working for the Post Office. It was purely accidental that I came over here.

Perhaps you can become the sales representative to recruit others.

We're trying.

What are some elements you think essential in an ideal administrator? I'm asking this mainly since you must deal with many postal administrators, and therefore I'd be interested to know if you have found some of these elements right here in the department.

I think it's very important that an administrator have an open mind to new ideas. I also think he must be aware of what's going on in his own organization. There's a great tendency for administrators to get very involved with particular, high-level, very hot political projects, and the daily operation absolutely goes right by them. That's a very bad thing to happen, because over a period of time the day-to-day operation will just fall apart. They're interested in one top-level issue after another.

Isn't the Planning Office supposed to relieve the minds of these administrators of concern for the next ten years, or so? If this is true, shouldn't they become more involved in these daily operations?

They have to have an overall awareness of both. Some of them, however, do the exact opposite and run the organization on a day-to-day basis and forget completely about tomorrow. The ones I have in mind are concerned with pressing political issues today and the day after, and so on. You should, I admit, have the long-range view of where your organization is going, but also some awareness of what, in fact, it is doing right now. You surely have to know what issues are being considered and solved by your subordinates. Some are solved and never surface.

You planning people, as I said in another interview with one of the staff, are teachers and can alert operating heads to priorities. This, it seems, is the art of balance: what comes first and what counts the heaviest.

You just picked my favorite word, because in so many of the programs it's: "Do we do this whole program or this whole program?" rather than: "Should we consider these aspects of these proposals first, and these aspects of another item next?" and so on.

Are you optimistic about the next year or so in the Planning Office? What success do you think you might have in putting your ideas across?

We might have some success if we can ever get to the point where the political situation settles down. It's difficult, as you can understand, in a lame-duck type of administration.

I understand the average term of a Postmaster General runs about three years, or even less.

It is very short, and I've been here that long!

One feature I've noticed in my study of the Planning Office and talks with some of its staff is a certain rhythm of enthusiasm. Many of those with whom I've talked care for the Post Office in an affectionate and yet demanding way. They get angry enough to put their best efforts out in working for desired and essential change.

That's true, I guess. I never really thought of it in those exact terms. I know I put in any number of hours for the sake of the organization and hope, in the long run, it does some good.

Anything you want to add as a footnote to our discussion?

I think that timing is very important in introducing change. It's difficult to say that you should go very slow, or very fast either. If you suddenly push too much on people, they can't accept it. They feel like they're shuffling papers because they have to produce this document to satisfy this person, and they get involved in your planning operation as merely another bureaucratic operation. So you don't want to demand too much all at once.

And, as I've discovered, too much pressure becomes coercion and has thin results.

That's right. You can't successfully persuade someone in this kind of relationship. On the other hand, if you move too slowly and take account of all the objections, you're never going to get it done.

I guess again it comes back to a sense of balance as well as an intuitive sense of feel.

We depend on human relations a great deal in this entire process.

STUDY QUESTIONS

1. Which of the four discussions provides the most understanding of the Post Office's problems?
2. Do you favor a government corporation for the Post Office? Provide the pros and cons.
3. Can PPBS be successfully applied in Post Office operations? Better than in some others? Why?

16

AMBULANCE SERVICE

This case analyzes the efforts of two New York City departments—Police and Hospitals—to develop a new solution of a serious situation affecting the welfare of city residents: an improved ambulance service. Prior to this study, proposals had centered on (1) improvements of the service entirely within a single department—Hospitals; or, (2) attempts to prove that another department—Police—was perhaps able to provide the service at a more efficient level of operation.

In this report's analysis, operations and efforts of both these departments have been merged—for the first time—in order to maximize the potential benefit for all people in need of this service. It represents the first time, also, that New York City has used the new method of computer simulation to aid the decision-making process. Evidence is strong that additional steps will be taken to use computers in the improvement of other situations within city administration.

The proposals were imaginative and responded to the urgent needs of a faulty service. Many historic practices were questioned and new concepts developed. Short-run innovations were installed, and at the same time further proposals are on the agenda for implementation, once results of the initial effort are available.

These factors are described in detail in the body of the report that follows.

From a March 8, 1968, letter to Mayor John V. Lindsay of New York, signed Timothy W. Costello, Deputy Mayor-City Administrator:

> In the course of our study, which utilized computer simulation and cost-benefit analysis techniques, we developed some proposals for a greatly improved emergency ambulance system which are being evaluated in detail and will be reported in the future. These proposals including separating the emergency ambulance service from its historical, but perhaps obsolete, link to hospitals; placing the emergency ambulance service under direct, centralized control; dispatching ambulances directly from the Police Communications Bureau, without intermediaries at garages; abandoning the entire concept of hospital districts as far as ambulance service is concerned; distributing ambulances in a widely dispersed geographic pattern, rather than grouping them in garages; and locating ambulances at on-the-street ambulance stations rather than in garages.
>
> You will note that the last two proposals, besides being cost-effective, serve to bring visible government close to the people being serviced.

New York City ambulances serve a potential ten million persons around-the-clock—the service never stops. It is a system with plain purposes: to save human lives, reduce suffering, and provide some comfort for those who, often on an instant's notice, must use these facilities. Since 1870 the city has supplied emergency ambulance service for residents and transients. During the decade from 1957 to 1967, as population increased, so did demands for service. For example:

1957	1967
349,457 calls	501,466 calls
46,160 transfers	64,658 transfers
395,617 total trips	566,124 total trips

Two departments—Hospitals and Police—cooperate to provide these services. Effective, split-second merger of efforts is vital. In this respect, the city administrator believed that improvements were imperative. As a result of three related factors—traffic problems, abuse of the service as a substitute for the family physician, and awkward communications—by the 1950s a "critical situation" had developed.

Since 1950 reports on the situation had been prepared by the Hospital Council, the Hospital Review and Planning Council, and the New York Academy of Medicine. Early in 1967 Mayor Lindsay requested the city administrator "to organize a task force for the purpose of evaluating the recommendations made in the past and to develop methods for the adoption of new proposals."

The task force began its work during the summer of 1967 and submitted its report—*Emergency Ambulance Service*—to the city administrator in March 1968. Mathias L. Spiegel, a first deputy city administrator, had overall responsibility, and the work on computer simulation and cost-effectiveness analysis was directed by Dr. E. S. Savas, a deputy city administrator, assisted by members of his former staff at the New York Scientific Center of IBM. Daily operations were supervised by Thomas F. Loughlin and Leonora L. Burkholz of the city administrator's management staff. Four Urban Corps interns were assigned to specific tasks at the central headquarters and in the field. In the preparation of the report, the following provided information and suggestions: New York City Department of Hospitals and Police, Budget Bureau, and such professional organizations as the Greater New York Hospital Association and American College of Surgeons.

HOSPITALS DEPARTMENT

The task force found that the Hospitals Department had a fleet of 114 ambulances, 10 hearses, 50 station wagons, 2 premature ambulances, and 4 disaster units. *All were supervised by its transportation division but located at hospitals scattered throughout the city.* The bulk of this equipment, 60 municipal ambulances, remained on emergency call between 4 P.M. and midnight, when requests are heaviest. From midnight to 8 A.M. 43 were available, and from 8 A.M. to 4 P.M. 56 were on duty. Assignments to the five city areas were as follows:

	Midnight–8 a.m.	8 a.m.–4 p.m.	4 p.m.–Midnight
Brooklyn	14	19	23
Manhattan	12	15	15
Bronx	9	14	14
Queens	6	6	6
Richmond	2	2	2
	43	56	60

The Hospitals Department contracts yearly with voluntary hospitals to meet their emergency service requirements. Payments are made according to total of calls answered and processed. At the time of the study, 31 hospitals were contracting for 49 ambulances costing about $1,900,000. In short, a voluntary hospital purchases the ambulance and is reimbursed each year, on a sliding scale, by the department—up to 3500 calls runs to $35,000; 3501–5000 calls is fixed at $37,500; and beyond 5000 calls the price is $40,000. As illustrations:

Knickerbocker Hospital, New York City	$120,000 contract
Long Island College Hospital, Brooklyn	100,000 contract

Brooklyn Jewish Hospital, Brooklyn	40,000 contract
Booth Memorial, Queens	37,500 contract

These voluntary-hospital ambulances operate on the following schedule:

	Midnight–8 a.m.	8 a.m.–4 p.m.	4 p.m.–Midnight
Brooklyn	13	15	15
Manhattan	17	18	18
Bronx	1	1	1
Queens	10	11	11
Richmond	4	4	4
	45	49	49

Total combinations of *municipal* and *voluntary ambulances* on the three-shift basis are as follows:

	Midnight–8 a.m.	8 a.m.–4 p.m.	4 p.m.–Midnight
Brooklyn	27	34	38
Manhattan	29	33	33
Bronx	10	15	15
Queens	16	17	17
Richmond	6	6	6
	88	105	109

A total of 566,124 calls for both types of hospitals was completed in 1967, divided this way:

	Total Calls	Transfers	Total Trips
Municipal	285,816	38,444	324,260
Voluntary	215,650	26,214	241,864
	501,466	64,658	566,124

For municipal hospital service, the average cost for each call was running slightly over $15.00. Although specific data were not available on voluntary hospitals, they claimed to operate at a loss during the year. New York City pays a $40,000 maximum rate to reimburse voluntary hospital ambulance operations, and quite often the cost to the voluntary hospital runs about $60,000 per ambulance.

Since 1942, trained attendants have been regularly assigned on trips, whereas formerly interns filled these tasks. Under certain critical conditions—train wrecks, plane crashes, maternity cases, or when a patient requires medical treatment without removal—a physician is sent. Generally, these attendants are nurses' aides with training in first-aid practices.

POLICE ROLE

As a rule, an ambulance service request is processed through the communications bureau of the Police Department. (An exception would be if an ambulance crew spotted a need for service on return from a call that did *not* require service.) Emergency ambulances have two-way radios that permit communications to and from the Police Department, but they are not normally in contact with the hospitals at which they are based.

The internal procedure includes a series of steps: communications bureau receives request; duty patrolman determines type of call, screens sick and accident calls or other types (disaster situations), and determines need for ambulance; makes assignment to nearest hospital equipped to perform emergency ambulance service; usually a radio car is sent to the scene.

As the task-force report indicated:

A policeman usually remains with the patient to obtain full information. However, he may respond to a more urgent police call if an adult is present at the scene. . . . As a rule, the police are able to obtain most of the information at the scene, but on occasion they must accompany the patients to the hospital to obtain further data, following which they return to their active police duty.

The requirement of police personnel at the scene of all ambulance calls has been considered *questionable* for two reasons: current shortage of manpower, and diversion of trained personnel for this assignment. Other people are usually available in sick-call situations, at home or business, to remain with patient pending ambulance arrival. On the basis of Police Department spot checks, 45 minutes is involved on these calls. During August 1966, evidence was obtained to estimate total potential police manpower involvement, during an average year, in the sick-call category on ambulance cases. It is the belief of Hospitals Department officials that this percentage remains constant for the year.

August 1966
Department of Hospitals
Sick Calls

Type	Percent of Total Calls
Cardiac	5.8
Asthmatic	1.9
Overdose	1.3
Unconscious	2.9
Colds	1.0
Body aches	6.3
Fever	2.4
Abdominal pains	5.4
Other sick	13.8
	40.8

As the report stated: "In these instances policemen were dispatched to the scene and *there is a real question about the value of their assignment to approximately one-half of these calls."* In addition, evidence was obtained which proved that more than one-half were classified as non-emergency, and did not demand the presence of a police officer.

| | Sick Calls | | |
	Rush	Nonrush	Totals
Cardiac	1,807	537	2,344
Asthmatic	398	325	723
Overdose	342	193	535
Unconscious	822	328	1,150
Colds	116	282	398
Body aches	843	1,641	2,484
Fever	294	652	946
Abdominal pains	795	1,377	2,172
Other sick	2,101	3,136	5,237
	7,518	8,471	15,989

Besides, over 70 percent of sick calls were in homes or at businesses, where attendance of a policeman was least required.

The report concluded: ". . . it is estimated that *in at least 14 to 20 percent of the cases there is no need for a police officer to be present* at the scene of an ambulance call for patients classified as 'sick.' " On the assumption that the 40 percent sick call (August 1966) is applied to the yearly total, then an estimated 216,000 calls would belong in this category. In all these situations, the need for a police officer can be seriously questioned. Based on a 45-minute average for each call, the *loss of hours from regular police work will range from 2835 to 4050 tours of duty in an average year.* In the report's words:

> If all the sick calls (40 percent of annual calls) were considered in this, the estimated amount of police tours of duty lost in this activity would amount to over 20,000 tours. Indeed a substantial drain on police manpower at a time when this city needs all the police force it can muster.

Time estimates were assembled in a single police precinct and the figures considered as more suggestive than conclusive. The elimination of this function for police would make considerable time available for strict police work, perhaps releasing about 100 police. The report suggests that: ". . . further data should be developed in cooperation with the Police Department." Along the lines of additional investigation, it was proposed that the Police Department gather data to determine the nature of the services rendered and time involved in responding to ambulance calls, especially "sick" calls. On the basis of additional facts, procedures should be constructed to provide safeguards for patients, utilize police time effectively, and obtain public acceptance.

If police cars (as emergency service vehicles) were used only in limited instances, the results would be to provide additional tours by reduction of police time away from normal tours of duty, improve police communication and the public image of the police, and reduce the number of calls with extensive response time. Average response and round-trip times should drop. In short, the issue remains: in what situations should police vehicles be used to transport emergency cases to hospitals?

The task force studied a number of component factors within the overall problem, including creation of satellite ambulance stations, direct radio communications, improved supervision, restoration of siren use, supply of ambulances, and revision of dispatching forms.

SATELLITE AMBULANCE STATIONS

In early 1967 the city administration was under constant pressure for additional ambulance service in certain districts scattered throughout the city. The Hospitals Department, therefore, decided to try to reduce ambulance response time by creating a *satellite ambulance station unattached to hospitals*.

Funds for several satellite stations were requested and made available; the Hospitals Department pushed for a decision, by the city administrator, to initiate the program. Noting this plan, the task force stated:

> This office was aware of the fact that the available data by itself was insufficient to justify such a decision in terms of improved service. However, it advised the Department of Hospitals that it was receptive to such a decision while it simultaneously would seek to refine and analyze the available data.

In a sense, this was a cautious yet encouraging reaction. The city administrator then decided to develop available information based on resources at hand and to obtain outside technical assistance in respect to a simulation and computer program. The project then moved forward on an experimental basis; it proved useful to the task force in showing what might be done in this area.

Based on Hospitals Department information, three ambulance districts were judged suitable for establishment of a "prototype satellite ambulance station." A total of five factors were applied in the selection of the district for station location: size, number of calls, dispersion of these calls, base hospital characteristics, and hospital ambulance service.

For this innovation, the Kings County Ambulance District was selected, the reasons being that it was one of the larger districts, contained areas of very high and low density of calls, and had a large, well-administered municipal base hospital and efficient ambulance service. Besides, its community groups had expressed, consistently and energetically, criticisms about "alleged delays in ambulance response time."

To reinforce this choice four medical students as Urban Corps interns conducted a district field study, observing at first hand the ambulance operation of municipal and voluntary hospitals; members of the Kings County hospital administration—garage foremen, drivers, attendants, dispatchers—were interviewed; and students rode on all types of ambulance calls and in 24 hours covered three tours of duty. This study "supported the conclusion that this was a logical district in which to establish a satellite station prototype."

Housing the new facility raised a number of questions. One option was to use police precinct houses. After a review of precincts within the area it was decided that space for vehicles and staff facilities was insufficient. A call-density map showed that both the 73rd and 75th precincts in Kings County Hospital District contained the highest concentration of all borough calls. Each, however, was some distance from the hospital.

Further analysis was made of true emergencies and of non-emergency as well as unnecessary calls. A recanvass of police station houses in these precincts confirmed that there was limited space for cars and staff. The next step was to seek private facilities, and a suitable private garage was finally located. The new service opened on December 27, 1967, as a branch of the Kings County Ambulance Service. A total of 35 staff members included drivers, clerks, and attendants. Five ambulances were available for service. As the report put it:

> This pilot installation will make it possible to test many new methods, cost-effectiveness procedures, and will produce data for evaluation of the need for such satellites in other parts of the City.

DIRECT RADIO COMMUNICATIONS

A second area for possible betterment concerned emergency ambulance and Police Department communication. Existing procedures involved the following elements: Police Department receives original request to provide service and transmits assignment, by telephone, to appropriate hospital. Direct police radio communication with the ambulances is used to cancel calls or reassign vehicles. In fact, an ambulance crew must radio-advise police as soon as available for reassignment. (This happens when no patient is located or patient is not to be removed to a hospital.) As stressed in the report:

> ... in order for the hospital where the ambulance is based to be informed of its activities either at the scene of a call or when returning from a call it is necessary for the police to advise the hospital or for the crew to telephone their home base.

A hospital dispatcher can contact an ambulance only through police radio. As a result, each ambulance is under police control immediately upon leaving the hospital garage.

In January 1968 the Hospitals Department installed a transmitter at Kings County Hospital to control its emergency ambulance activities. During each 24-hour period it has been used about thirty times, operating in cooperation with the Police communications bureau. Two results were indicated: ambulances could be rerouted to more serious calls; rerouting could also accommodate response from cancelled calls to new requests. Undue delays in response time might also be prevented. It was believed that this "new link could form an essential part of the total communications system and would increase efficiency in the service. . . ."

Naturally, if such a system were applied to all hospitals, additional manpower and radio equipment would be required. Estimated cost for 69 dispatchers would run about $552,000 and for 13 radio transmitters ($700 per unit) about $9100.

Under a new Police Department electronic system, the exact location of all squad cars will be known at all times. Besides, radio call assignments will be more rapid. A change in the improved ambulance communications, the report underlined, should be geared to this new system (coded as SPRINT).

IMPROVED SUPERVISION

Until this survey, supervision for emergency ambulance service—5 P.M. to 9 A.M. weekdays, and 5 P.M. Friday to 9 A.M. Monday—was not provided. If an emergency arose, the director of service was contacted on supervisory problems, usually involving personnel matters. Such lack of control impaired ambulance service efficiency and often delayed the making of proper decisions. However, the Hospitals Department had requested budget authorization to employ supervisors for this period. Backed by the task force, this request was approved in August 1967, and seven new positions were created. Two changes were made in the emergency ambulance service:

1. Four supervisors were assigned to evening tours involving hospital garage visits, inspections, and submission of written reports to director of service.
2. Three supervisors handled daytime boroughwide responsibilities, with one each assigned to Manhattan, Bronx and Queens, Brooklyn and Richmond.

In the main, this group has charge of field operations of the total emergency ambulance service, including staff and vehicle assignments, inspection of city and voluntary ambulances, and cooperation with the Police communications bureau—all under the direction of the Ambulance Service director.

SIRENS

The issue of sirens also came up in the survey. For many years they had been used on police radio squad cars, fire apparatus, ambulances, and other emergency vehicles. Although the usage is obvious, abuses have sometimes resulted in accidents.

The Hospitals Department discontinued ambulance sirens in 1955 on the ground that the high accident rate was connected with siren use. Because of today's heavy traffic, however, it is difficult for ambulances to reach emergency scenes promptly and to return to hospitals with patients. Naturally, any delay is crucial, and the task force believed that the Hospitals Department should reconsider the use of sirens.

A decision was made to use them on ambulances during the summer of 1967 at Kings County Hospital and later at Bellevue Hospital. Test results indicated that less than 5 percent of emergency calls required sirens under controlled conditions and that continuous motion of an ambulance was more essential than great speed. In short, proper use of the siren assisted in unblocking traffic congestions.

The Hospitals Commissioner on December 1, 1967, authorized the use of sirens on a citywide controlled basis for voluntary and city ambulances. Various procedures must be fulfilled: en route to an emergency, sirens will be used when the Police communications bureau grants permission at the time an ambulance is requested; on the return to the hospital, either the ambulance attendant or a physician on the scene determines whether the siren should be used; for each use a siren report is required. It is the Hospitals Department's plan to monitor the entire procedure to ensure that siren use is not unwarranted or excessive.

SUPPLY OF AMBULANCES

What low-cost means exist to increase the effective number of ambulances? To answer this question, several areas were evaluated. First, attention was paid to tighter screening of calls; about 15 percent of all calls were found to be unnecessary. In this area, the police play a prominent part. The report indicated the pros and cons:

> The argument will be made that a policeman should not have to make a decision to deny service to anyone. A rebuttal is that the policeman decides now whether or not to send a doctor along, he decides priorities, and he

can detour an assigned ambulance to a call he deems more urgent. To give him the additional authority to deny service is not a major extension, in practice. Furthermore, the present system really means that the most irresponsible person . . . the one who calls unnecessarily for an ambulance, in effect assigns the priorities and deprives a legitimate patient of the prompt service to which the latter is entitled.

At present there is no authority to refuse ambulance service, and to punish those who call for ambulances for trivial reasons does not appear workable. On each ambulance call, a police car is sent. The report emphasized that ". . . the role of the police at the scene of an ambulance call must be thought through carefully, and a closely reasoned, objective set of guidelines must be formulated for the dispatcher." Perhaps only a minority of calls justify police presence.

There is also the matter of overtime pay, which does not now apply to ambulance drivers and attendants. Consequently they are often reluctant to work beyond normal tours of duty. If overtime pay were extended to this group, more ambulances might become available. An employee, winding up his work shift, might thereby be prompted to continue on a second shift in the event his replacement was absent. According to the report, high rates of absenteeism put ambulances out of service.

Supervision of ambulance staff operates at two levels: attendants report to the nursing service at hospitals, and drivers are responsible to a garage foreman. Time schedules also differ. The report points out a practical problem:

> . . . if only a driver reports to work at one hospital, and only an attendant at another, pairing the two men to provide one ambulance, instead of keeping two ambulances idle, is administratively awkward.

Among ambulance attendants, 60 percent are male, 40 percent female. When women are on duty, the Police Department must often provide assistance in removal of patients. Efforts to limit attendants to males have been unsuccessful, one reason being that ambulance duty provides nurse aides with an extra $240. Both positions are in the noncompetitive class, and incumbents may be assigned without examinations.

On balance, three major problems face the Hospitals Department: lack of interchangeability among ambulance crews, method of recruiting attendants, and divided responsibility for the ambulance crew—nursing service versus transportation unit. A fairly simple solution would be to provide identical training for drivers and attendants. A new designation could be ambulance driver-attendant, under a single supervisor. Since drivers are now in the competitive class, the personnel department and the union would have to collaborate. As the report states: "It is recommended that the Department of Hospitals develop the plan to establish a new title and employ males in this category."

Still another aspect of the entire operation was listed and a change suggested. Certain cases, mainly psychiatric, require the crew to remain at the hospital for an extended period before release of the ambulance. Admission-acceptance procedures should be revised to increase ambulance availability.

FORMS

Various forms are used in connection with ambulance service. The basic one is a dispatching ambulance form, which is given the attendant assigned to the call. Time stamps are recorded as follows: receipt of call from Police Department, notification to garage for vehicle dispatch, attendant leaves with ambulance, and return of attendant from call. Additional information is recorded as to action on the scene, type of treatment, and case disposition. An attendant must also record secondary information such as patient's occupation, nearest relative, address, and phone number, all of which belongs elsewhere. This form clearly needs to be simplified and the data on it so arranged that it could be used in electronic data processing. The report asserted:

> The design of this form should lend itself to fact-gathering, and form the basis for meaningful statistical data. Suggestions for the modifications to be incorporated have been obtained from field investigations, data-processing experts and others. . . . A draft of a new form has been developed and transmitted to the Department of Hospitals for its review.

Basic Systems Factors

The Emergency Ambulance Service, in the final analysis, fits into an overall Emergency Medical Care System with three major elements: communications, transportation, and medical treatment. Preventive health care is also involved, since this reduces needs and demands for emergency care. Each element, cited above, was evaluated in the following terms:

> I. *Communication subsystem* involves the means by which aid is summoned for a patient, including the procedure for screening, assessing, and establishing priorities for calls. It also includes requirements and facilities for communication among dispatchers, ambulances, and hospitals.
> II. *Transportation subsystem* involves means for conveying a patient to a medical facility, transporting medical facilities to a patient (doctor, attendant, resuscitation equipment, antidotes), boundaries of ambulance districts, location of ambulances and hospitals, and finally the total number of ambulances.

III. *Medical treatment subsystem* includes nature, speed, and adequacy of emergency medical treatment according to personnel qualifications and availability, organization, procedures and equipment of emergency rooms, and ambulance equipment.

The report underscores the interdependence of all subsystems: "Improvements in the transportation subsystem could be vitiated . . . if no doctor were available immediately after the patient is carried into the hospital."

TRANSPORTATION SUBSYSTEM

The central emphasis of the analysis concerned features of the transportation subsystem, including geographic distribution of emergency calls in most severe city problem areas and number and placement of ambulances required for effective service. The essence of the total scheme was in the merits of a *"proposed satellite ambulance station"* according to objective, criteria, options, and selection of the best alternative. Each of these factors was appraised by the report.

Objective

What, after all, is improved ambulance service? Two factors must be judged:

1. *Response time*   period from receipt of call at ambulance station and arrival of ambulance at scene.
2. *Round-trip time*   period from receipt of call at ambulance station and ambulance arrival, with patient, at hospital.

In the report's view:

Prompt arrival of an ambulance and trained attendant on the scene is satisfying to the public and produces confidence in the service on the part of the general citizenry. Round-trip time is more important from the clinical (and the individual patient's) vantage point, because it measures the time needed to get the patient to the hospital for professional medical treatment.

The target adopted was the decrease of response time in a specific area—Kings County Hospital District of Brooklyn.

Criteria

Cost plus effectiveness of any new method was obviously considered. In short: what would be the capital and operating costs of more ambulances and satellite garages? Effectiveness meant minutes of average response, or round-trip time, as well as percentage of calls whose response time *went beyond a certain level.*

The crux of the problem could best be spelled out by tackling a typical district served by a hospital. All ambulances are stationed at the hospital. Calls, according to a density map, are not uniformly scattered; certain areas "exhibit rather dense clustering of dots; i.e., there is a high demand for ambulance service from those areas."

A superficial suggestion could be to station ambulances at a satellite garage in the center of one of the clusters. It was reasoned that an ambulance could collect and deliver a patient to the hospital in one-half the time. However, three factors should be considered: various delays that contribute to total round-trip time would *not* be reduced by relocation of ambulances; ambulances will continue to be called to service requests from *all* points in the district; round-trip time must be connected with number of calls. Specifically:

> . . . infrequent calls from the area around the satellite can be assigned to waiting ambulances and in this case a substantial improvement would be realized. However, as the frequency rises, the ambulances would be spending more and more time shuttling back and forth between the hospital and the high-demand area around the satellite, calls would queue up to await an available ambulance. . . .

Therefore, it might not make any difference whether a busy ambulance were at the satellite, the hospital, or an intermediate point. In fact, the establishment of satellite stations, owing to their high visibility, *might encourage more needless calls.*

Five key factors must be considered, therefore, in an effort to improve level of service: geographic spread of calls in a district, frequency of calls, number of district ambulances, hospital location, and location of ambulance garages.

The report claimed that "the basic idea of a satellite station . . . to put the ambulances where they are needed is a sound one that warrants a detailed, quantitative analysis in order to provide valid estimates of the improvements to be expected."

As an instrument of analysis, computer simulation was used to forecast results of proposed decisions "where there are many interrelated factors, where the expected effects are complex, and where trial-and-error experimentation is costly or impractical." In brief, about 160,000 calls were simulated, corresponding to more than three years of Kings County Hospital ambulance service, and attention was centered on the 4 P.M.-midnight shift (peak load). The simulation suggested three options: (1) satellite with *no* additional ambulances; (2) additional ambulances *without* satellite; (3) satellite and additional ambulances.

OPTION 1   If seven ambulances were kept but redistributed between hospital and satellite, what would be the avearge round-trip and response time? As ambulances were removed from the hospital to satellite garage, times continuously decreased. In terms of ambulance service, the *satellite is at a better location for the hospital than is the hospital itself.* Why not, then, move the hospital? The solution is to redraw hospital district lines and redeploy ambulances.

How much was average round-trip time cut? It slid from 33 to 31.5 minutes, or 5 percent. This decrease of 1.5 minutes applies, as welL, to average response time, constituting an 11 percent improvement over the present 13.5 minutes.

OPTION 2   What would be the result of basing *more ambulances at the hospital*? Average response time dropped by 0.3 minute as the number of ambulances went up from seven to ten; after that no improvement resulted, *regardless of how many ambulances were added.* As the report underlined: "Once one reaches the 'elbow' of the curve, one is operating on a plateau and *additional ambulances are wasted."*

Two elements must be measured. First: *waiting time*—the period between receipt of a call at an ambulance station and assignment of an available vehicle. Literally, this factor is a segment of overall *response time.* As more ambulances are added, what effect does this have on *waiting time?* It drops to zero, and, in turn, *response time* levels off so that it depends almost wholly on the next factor—*travel time.* This, however, is a fixed characteristic of a specific district and depends on its size and shape, location of ambulances, traffic routes, and conditions.

Finally, ambulance utilization—fraction of time spent on a call—decreases as more vehicles are added. In the report's words: "The increase in idle time (decreased utilization) is the price paid for reducing the average waiting time, that is, for assuring that an ambulance will be available for prompt assignment when a call comes in."

Specifically, minimum response time achieved, when waiting time is zero, corresponds to a utilization of 42 percent. This compares to a current utilization of about 60 percent. In short, the *utilization factor is an index of service; it can be used to manage the ambulance system.* Within the present boundaries for Kings County Hospital, if utilization is greater than 42 percent, *improved service can be achieved if ambulances are added.* If it is less, however, ambulances can be released and service level will not decline. The report spells this out in great detail.

Next is a consideration of work load (month-to-month calls) and ideal utilization (which corresponds to negligible waiting time). This latter factor is not constant; *it increases as load increases.* In short, if the load is doubled, less than twice as many ambulances will provide ideal service.

What are the policy implications? A group of small districts—each with a small load and one to two ambulances—needs more ambulances to provide a given level of service than would be required if districts were consolidated into one large unit with ambulances pooled under a unified command. Or, for that matter, district lines could be ignored and the nearest available ambulance assigned.

OPTION 3   This option would increase ambulances that service the district to ten and establish a satellite station. We notice two points: (1) with six vehicles at the satellite and four at the hospital, response time drops to minimum of 10.9 minutes, a reduction of 19 percent from 13.5-minute average; (2) if more than six vehicles are at the satellite, service worsens. Why? Because the satellite area is then "oversaturated with ambulances," which means a waste of resources. Under normal conditions, therefore, service to this area is better than the district average. In response time, for example, a satellite subarea has a 10.1-minute average—21 percent better than the previous 12.8 minutes. A more distant area has a 15.1-minute average, a 6 percent improvement from 16.1 minutes.

In short, there would be a decrease in average response time from 13.5 to 13.2 under option 2, to 12.0 under option 1, and to 10.9 under option 3. In average round-trip time, the reduction would be from 33 minutes to 32.7 under option 2, to 31.5 under option 1, and to 30.4 under option 3. On this latter aspect the report commented:

> Even if fifty ambulances were servicing the district . . . there is a finite probability that fifty-one calls will some day come in within a half-hour period and someone will then have to wait an unconscionably long time for an ambulance.

There is, from the evidence, an expectation that a satellite-station operation would result in "substantial" improvement.

After intensive analysis, some conclusions appeared:

1. Option 3 would reduce average response time (19 percent) as well as greatly delayed calls (50 percent).
2. Option 1 would also reduce response time, since ambulances would—it was agreed—be near the greatest demand point.

Why not endorse option 1, since (as the report spelled out), it

> . . . has the lowest ratio of cost to effectiveness, $0.43 per minute, lowest monthly cost, and lowest cost per call. . . . It must be observed [however] that alternative 3 produces a greater absolute improvement.

Does the evidence permit other evaluations? None of these suggestions is a cure-all. Improvements are only moderate when all factors of emergency medical care are considered. The report admits: ". . . this does not hold promise as a general policy to implement throughout the entire city."

Additional Factors

Beyond the analysis of these three options, other factors studied by the task force were *ambulances location* and *patients delivery*. It has often been suggested that improved service might depend on redistricting New York City to make district boundaries more rational in respect to hospitals location and calls distribution. On the other hand, perhaps hospitals are of secondary importance. Why not, instead, concentrate on the ambulances and *station them close to the patients*? In fact, patients should be taken to the nearest center for treatment rather than headlong to the same hospital.

In the matter of *ambulances location*, if treatment is considered independently from transportation, then two factors become important: (1) distribution should be citywide in relation to demands, and (2) as the demand pattern changes geographically, ambulance distribution should adapt—and also change. In view of this approach, one may easily wonder why the transportation service remained so long cemented to permanent hospital installations. The report provides a partial answer:

> . . . having ambulances stationed at hospitals is no doubt a leftover from the time (before 1942) when medical interns rode in attendance on each call. What began as a logical necessity survives as a custom, although the need disappeared 26 years ago.

Should no ambulances be anchored at hospitals? Not unless the distribution of calls justifies a hospital's serving as an ambulance station. Assign, therefore, the nearest ambulance available, when calls come in, irrespective of district boundaries.

Other questions arise:

Should there be two or more ambulances at one location? To shrink response time, dispersal of vehicles is essential to bring them closer to high-demand points. In fact, maximum decentralization—even a single ambulance at a single station—will perhaps mean better results than a congregation of ambulances.

When would more than one ambulance at a station be appropriate? When the area is small and demand is heavy and uniformly distributed.

Would all vehicles have to be garaged at such stations? Not if on-street ambulance stations were adopted.

How would this work? Just as taxis and buses maintain, in some instances, certain stops, ambulances could navigate and then pull up to a particular stop or even wait there.

Are there advantages to this concept? Costs would drop. Service could be seen. Delay in dispatch might be reduced.

Any handicaps? People might be putting through needless calls, and psychologically it might be disturbing to see ambulances constantly exposed. During cold periods, mechanical difficulties might develop.

What about dispatching of ambulances? The communications bureau of the Police Department would be the central point. The garage dispatcher would *not* be involved.

Can this now be done? Yes. Each ambulance now has a two-way radio and is in touch with the police dispatcher.

How will the new police communications strengthen the system? According to the report:

> The forthcoming computer-based command-control system (SPRINT[1]) at the Communications Bureau will enable the ambulance dispatcher to provide even closer, minute-by-minute control over the status and activity of each ambulance in the city system. Furthermore, SPRINT can automate the process of selecting and assigning the nearest available ambulance to each call, despite the wide dispersion of ambulances . . . .

What choices will a dispatcher have under this new system? The computer can advise whether to assign a call to an available ambulance at some distance or to wait for an ambulance now assigned that will soon be available closer to the demand point.

What about supervision? The Hospitals Department would have three sources of control and information about each call: the police dispatcher, the crew on the ambulance, and the hospital emergency room. In addition, complaints regarding delays may also come in: "The ambulance never got here!"

Are there still some criticisms of the plan to divorce the two systems: transportation and treatment? Two remain, of uneven significance. First, hospitals often use ambulances as "general-purpose" vehicles when they are not involved in their major mission. Second, a physician is sometimes required on calls. This, however, can be solved when the ambulance goes to the hospital to pick up a doctor.

Finally, in the matter of patients delivery, to reduce round-trip time where should a patient be taken? The report puts it this way: "The ideal answer is to deliver him to the nearest appropriate treatment center." This answer, although not immediately applicable, is similar to the provision of medical attention at either first-aid points or health clinics in various neighborhoods.

A number of questions arise here. For example:

Why not continue to use hospitals? Two factors are involved: is its emergency room adequate and is a bed available? If it is not a city hospital, then other problems arise.

What, if anything, can be done about emergency rooms? Surely, if upgraded facilities would allow patients to be brought to a hospital— especially if its location reduces round-trip time—this should be considered.

---

[1] Special Police Radio Inquiry Network

How does the non-city hospital fit into the systems analysis picture? On this, the report commented that:

> . . . a non-municipal hospital's policy of selectivity is outside the realm of practical systems analysis. Existing hospital district lines in some cases result from such selection criteria. Analysis can serve to identify those hospitals whose participation, or fuller participation, in the system would substantially improve the emergency ambulance service, thereby providing some direction for policy-making officials to negotiate and otherwise bargain with the private institution to secure its participation on mutually acceptable grounds.

Why is bed availability the heaviest problem? Mainly because hospital capacity can rarely hit the anticipated need in a specific district. Two results are apparent: transfer of patients and overcrowding.

Is there an ideal way to solve this problem? In its concluding pages the report notes: "The ideal situation would be for the control dispatcher to have up-to-the-minute information on the actual number of beds available in each hospital in the system." A computer-based inventory to tackle this problem for city hospitals has been initiated by the Hospitals Department. In the interim, perhaps monthly quotas of emergency cases could be allocated to all hospitals.

Summarized Suggestions

The report, in its final pages, spelled out various proposals derived from "insights and results obtained from the simulation study of one district." Although they have not, as yet, been subjected to "rigorous examination and cost-effectiveness analysis," the proposals to improve New York's emergency ambulance service "appears to offer very promising, low-cost, innovative methods." These proposals include:

1. Place direct, centralized control of all emergency ambulance operations under the Hospitals Department.
2. Place ambulances where needed—in a widely dispersed pattern—to reduce average response time; hospital garages are not necessarily the answer.
3. Attain optimum distribution of ambulances—without consideration of hospital locations and present district boundaries—by using on-street ambulance stations and satellite garages.
4. Place dispatch and control of ambulances under the police communications bureau. This can be accomplished without the resources of SPRINT; however, steps to utilize its maximum capacity should be taken with all deliberate speed.
5. Minimize average round-trip times by identifying hospitals able to accept emergency patients.
6. Improve emergency-room facilities of these hospitals and arrange, through negotiation, to secure their active participation; try to secure an

agreement that such hospitals accept a certain number of emergency patients per month.

7. Keep a current inventory of available beds in all participating hospitals in order that an emergency patient can be delivered to the right hospital.

8. Tie in the bed-inventory system to SPRINT so that the dispatcher can assign the right ambulance and hospital for each call.

Short-range suggestions were applied experimentally as the study was being conducted. A list of these accomplishments—still in the process of improvement—includes:

(a) A satellite ambulance station opened in order to improve ambulance service in a most serious problem area.
(b) Strengthened supervision of field operations.
(c) An experimental, direct communication linkage established between a specific hospital and its ambulance.
(d) More rapid response achieved through controlled application of sirens.

Other short-run improvements are also being studied but as yet have not been applied. Some approaches in different areas are as follows:

Police   (a) Dispatch of police cars *if* no ambulance is available. (b) Reduction of time spent by police "responding unnecessarily" to ambulance calls.

Calls   More careful screening of calls to reduce wasted trips.

Procedures   Revised hospital admitting procedures so that ambulances can start out more rapidly to their next call.

Personnel   Revised personnel practices to increase the effective number of available ambulances.

Data process   Provide better information with which to manage the service.

The report claimed that prior ambulance service studies generally had emphasized two factors independently of each other: improving the service exclusively within the Hospitals Department, or, on the other hand, attempting to prove that another city department, usually Police, might provide a better service. This report, therefore, pioneered in the sense that the city recognized its problem as a joint one concerning two city departments, each in a major way. Also, computer simulation was used as a means to decision making. In its closing remarks the report stated: ". . . this represents a first step in a move to use computers more creatively in municipal management."

The report has been favorably received by the Mayor, the Department of Hospitals, the Police Department, and the Greater New York Hospital Association (with minor reservations). Efforts currently are being made to implement its proposals as promptly as possible. A grant of $130,000 has been received for this purpose.

STUDY QUESTIONS

1. What factors usually militate against cooperation in municipal administration?
2. Can you think of any options not pursued by the city administrator?
3. How does one go about measuring the overall effectiveness of such a program? Will PPBS do it?

VIII
THE PUBLIC

17
SCHOOL SUPERINTENDENT

The *Providence Evening Bulletin*'s front-page headline, April 15, 1968, announced: *O'Connor Leaves in August.* The school superintendent was quoted as saying: "It's time for a change, a time for me to change."

A few days later I had lunch with Charles O'Connor at the Turks Head Club in downtown Providence to discuss arrangements for an interview, which I had requested some weeks earlier. At a corner table near the entrance, a constant stream of "good lucks" from friends in the business and professional world punctuated our discussion.

O'Connor admitted that his new job with HEW's Denver regional office as director of adult vocational education and library services would be a welcome change from a four-year fight for bigger budgets and better schools. The news story announcing his resignation had commented:

> Mr. O'Connor also is leaving the post at a time that many observers feel is a turning point in the city's public education because of a citywide call for a model school system, more school funds, and vast improvements. He is known to have favored the movement and viewed it as a way to put public pressure on city hall to get a larger school budget.

It appeared that O'Connor had thrown in the sponge as a result of battle fatigue, and he confirmed this in our later interview. The previous superintendent had served twenty-seven years and his predecessor eight years. Among considerations important to a school superintendent, Providence has a population of about 180,000, of which blacks comprise about 16 percent and the black school population 20 percent. As of September 1967 the entire elementary school system was integrated on a 70–30 basis, accomplished by busing some 2600 children, both black and white, to various schools within the city. As in many other cities, the Providence school system needs more money, negotiates with teachers' unions, and faces pressures from parents and community groups.

What constitutes the average superintendent's world? In O'Connor's case, the continuing feature was finance to match his strong ambitions to improve the schools. In a period of four years, there were three surveys on this problem and related issues. The Bosland report of 1963 stated:

> If Providence wishes to have a school system that presents to its children a well-balanced program . . . and if it is to keep its salary schedule attractive to better teachers, and provide school rooms that are reasonably conducive to education, somewhat larger expenditures are desirable and necessary.

O'Connor had to administer a program with certain limitations that sometimes dampened his persistent enthusiasm. In 1925 the Rhode Island legislature had passed the Strayer Act with two main aims: (1) to free the Providence schools from politics by electing the school committee on a nonpartisan basis, and (2) remove the school budget from city council control. The statute also provided that the school department automatically receive 35 percent annually of the city's general tax revenues.

By 1954 the allotment had become inadequate and the city departed from this method. An amendment to the Strayer Act provided a guaranteed tax revenue for the schools equal to 1.1 percent of the assessed city property valuation, the aim being to provide more funds than the 35 percent formula and also to make the schools more independent of political budgetary controls. Unfortunately, the new formula produced less revenue than the original one. Therefore, the Bosland report suggested: "A return to the apportionment provided under the Strayer Act appears again to be the way to fiscal adequacy and fiscal independence for the Providence school system." Supplemental, annual appropriations by the city council had become a standard practice and it was expected that these would continue. If the people want good public schools, said the report, the absolute limit of property taxation has not been reached.

This restoration of an earlier arrangement would require an increase in city taxes to a 3 percent maximum, which was believed to be within the city's fiscal capacity. The report ended on a strong note: "The major recommendations of the Committee can be realized only with the whole-hearted cooperation of the people of Providence, who must support their School Committee and City Council in their efforts to provide good public schools."

The Bosland report's proposal, however, was rejected. The next major study during O'Connor's administration was the Cooperative Planning for Excellence (COPE) report under a federal grant of $100,000. This comprehensive evaluation of the Providence school system was initiated by the superintendent's efforts and conducted by five local colleges and universities. The report indicted the School Department for operating in obsolete buildings, for its outmoded curriculum in most areas, failure to maintain fiscal stability, and failure to maintain adequate books and supplies. As O'Connor said: "I knew all of these things, but I needed somebody else to say it before I could move." And he continued to implement many of the report's suggestions until his resignation.

The Mayor of Providence had frequently argued that the separation of financial responsibility for the school system, between his office, the city council, and the school committee was neither practical nor workable. Even though in principle the committee is politically independent, its financial needs weaken this independence. To find some solution for a vexing problem—City Hall had to raise the funds to keep the school system going—the Mayor in May 1965 appointed a special committee of leading citizens to study this problem. It stated:

> . . . the Strayer Act formula has failed to provide for the basic fiscal support of our schools. . . . The responsibility for raising the necessary funds for education falls upon the politically elected official who has no authority or responsibility with regard to the making of policy for the schools.

The main proposals were for a school committee appointed by the Mayor, subject to city council confirmation, and rather than a guaranteed minimum income for the school system, a budget formulated by City Hall. This would, perhaps, alleviate two problems—a "school committee which prepared its own budget but lacked authority to assess taxes; a city council which appropriated school funds but lacked the powers to revise the school budget." For fiscal 1967–68, the supplemental appropriation was $2.5 million.

In a special referendum, August 1968, the voters of Providence rejected a plan for an elected school committee with independent taxing powers and empowered the Mayor to appoint the committee, with city council approval. According to news accounts: "Mayor Joseph A. Doorley, Jr., elated over the referendum outcome, said he plans to name the members of the new school board as soon as possible."

O'Connor ran a system with thirty-nine elementary schools, six junior high schools, two middle schools, four senior high schools, and a student population of 27,000. The teaching faculty consisted of some 1300. For 1967, the budget was about $16,500,000. His salary was $30,000.

For the interview we met in O'Connor's office, located in a forty-year-old high school building. The desk was covered with papers, neatly stacked according to various types of action. On both sides of the room were storage files with sliding panels, and his secretary remarked, "He knows, among hundreds of papers, exactly where every one is and can always find it, fast."

O'Connor is just over medium height, borders on stoutness, and is a youthful fifty-eight years—his grey hair merely seems premature. Immaculately groomed, he prefers solemn colors. In our discussion he never once referred to a note but poured out information at horserace speed. His diction is of stage quality, and one has a sense of the dramatic, almost rehearsed. He expands easily on any topic concerning schools, education, or teaching. Although his pace has been compared to that of a tornado, it never seemed frenzied.

As a local school superintendent, his early experience included work in many school systems throughout the state, and even his critics have admitted that often the results were solid, if not spectacular. The longest time span in one community was sixteen years as teacher and principal, interrupted by a four-year stint as first lieutenant in the army. He has also been an educational consultant to AID in Washington, visiting lecturer at various Rhode Island colleges and the U.S. Naval War College at Newport, and a speaker at adult education programs throughout the state. Constantly involved with various professional groups in the field of education, he participated in various White House conferences on education and in meetings of various regional and national organizations.

O'Connor holds an A.B. degree from Manhattan College and a Master of Education degree from Rhode Island College of Education; he is a candidate for an Ed.D. at Boston University. In 1964 he was awarded an honorary Ph.D. at the Salve Regina College in Newport. He is married, has seven children, and, until his Denver assignment, had made his home in Newport.

As school superintendent, O'Connor was often in the "hurricane's eye" of serious controversies—integration, funds, union demands. Some attacked him for undue haste in changing the structure of the school system; others considered him too slow in meeting the demands of those who wanted better schools. His day often stretched to sixteen hours and included negotiating with unions, appearing at one PTA session after another, and meeting deadlines for federal funds. On the day of my visit, a sit-in of parents on a school issue was in progress outside his office.

And yet he continued to strive, sometimes seeming even to enjoy the drama of his job and the splashing headlines. When his routine included demonstrations, boycotts, and pickets, he was sometimes said to be easily accessible, and at other times he was criticized for avoiding those with complaints. He believed that a full commitment to quality education inevitably costs a great deal of money: "We need quality education," he said. "We've been shortchanged. I mean shortchanged for a good many years. I'm surprised there hasn't been an uprising before this."

With the aid of formal studies to reinforce his convictions and federal funds to implement their proposals, what of his scorecard? By 1964, elementary school libraries had increased from none to 18, and two were pending when he resigned; the number of teachers of reading had climbed from one to 28; a total of 29 reading centers with special materials had been opened; three curriculum revision projects for all grades had been initiated in mathematics, science, and social science. And he had been largely responsible for Project Discovery, by which all high school students were provided with free repertory theatre.

Views on his success differed. The school committee chairman refused to say whether O'Connor had resigned under pressure, either from protesting parent groups or the work load. He contended that with a competent administrative staff at headquarters, the heavy work load was largely a matter of the superintendent's refusing to delegate authority. The chairman added that it would be "very difficult to find a replacement with his ability and energy." His resignation was a "tremendous loss." Other members of the committee shared these views, defended the headquarters staff, and praised O'Connor, but, contrary to custom, there was no testimonial on the record from the committee as a whole.

On the heels of O'Connor's resignation, a Committee to Eliminate Racism in the Public Schools called for a black superintendent to replace him. The chairman of this group said:

> The political pressure and years of inbreeding have been two of the most obvious causes of the present critical state of the Providence system. The school committee should begin at once to undertake a nationwide search for a black superintendent, a completely new administrative staff. The school system must be taken out of the area of politics and put upon a new basis of imaginative leadership.

Two days after the announcement of O'Connor's resignation, the lead editorial of the *Providence Evening Bulletin* claimed:

> The four years the superintendent spent in Providence were difficult for him and the city. He was obliged to work with a school committee having disastrously low horizons on public education. He carried most of the administrative burden because of a dearth of quality in the second tier of school administration. He had to do business with city hall, which was reluctant to provide enough money to run the department well.

O'Connor is a sound educator, continued the editorial, but unwilling to fight openly for his principles. Controversial situations, in the paper's judgment, snowballed into crises. It concluded with criticism and praise:

A more aggressive superintendent would have appealed directly to the people for their help after giving them the facts about their school system. Only a few weeks before announcing his resignation on August 1st, did he state unequivocally that public pressure on school committee and city hall is essential to get better schools. After some delay and drift, he laid the foundation for a program to integrate city schools, and that will stand as a high mark in his work here. The Providence Plan . . . has been described as among the most complete of programs in major cities of the United States.

It may have been a serious weakness that he never devised the means of reorganizing the bureaucratic cage within which he was forced to operate. Instead he huffed and puffed along. It would be unfair to assert, as one account did, that he deliberately stirred up crises; these were bound to develop in any case because of his strenuous efforts to make good on his determination to integrate the schools. He once threatened to resign unless the committee and the city agreed to let him see this program through.

O'Connor is a most complex individual, and he may have tried to do many right things at the wrong speeds. Intensely involved in his own sense of mission, he promoted his goals with every ounce of his strength. Despite editorial criticism to the contrary, he fought a long and hard battle for a principle. If he had administrative weaknesses, they were to be a spell-binder, to leap from one arena to another, and sometimes to fail in following up certain proposals.

O'Connor surely thought of himself as an innovating fighter in a world of tax ceilings, deficits, and school board and city hall pressures. During our discussion he appeared harassed and worn out, yet buoyed by the unwrapped challenge of a new appointment. One would have to ask if it were true courage that propelled him to support a real integration system, or a grandstand play. By allocating most of his efforts to this, as top priority, perhaps he neglected to try to widen the structure of the system and solve the fiscal problem. The limitations of the one-man band are real ones.

Dr. O'Connor, you have held a variety of appointments as school superintendent in a number of Rhode Island communities—Warren, Newport, and now Providence. Could you indicate some common administrative problems that you've faced in all these systems? Is this kind of mobility helpful or harmful, and to what extent are the problems you face in one situation matched by those in another?

My candid opinion is that as far as any administrator at the top level of a school system is concerned, he should stay on the job no more than five years. If he's going to do anything in the job, he is going to create certain enmities that eventually will limit his usefulness in the system. A doer seems inevitably to cause some dissatisfaction with the people that he's doing it with. I think that this is true, first, from the point of view of the student body. If the student body is excellent, why there's no need for a superintendent. But we take it for granted that everything's not perfect and that some changes must be made to improve the status quo.

These changes, as I have seen them in virtually every system that I've been a part of, concern the basics everybody has been talking about in education for the past twenty years. One of them, number one I suppose, is in the field of reading—Johnny can't read! And I think the paramount reason is that teachers have not been taught to teach Johnny *how* to read.

As far as the city of Providence is concerned, I was extremely grateful that under Title I of the Elementary and Secondary Education Act we were able to pick up some half a million dollars to train 76 teachers who had some inclination to teach reading. We helped them to get a master's degree in their specialty, and they became expert in the field of teaching reading.

This job developed another perspective, however, and now we've got to teach *all* teachers to teach children how to read in the same way the experts do. If this doesn't have a follow-through, we don't know anything.

When I was in Warren, some ten or twelve years ago, Sputnik was launched by the Russians, and it indicated that in the United States we were deficient in the areas of math and science, because we had bought the Dewey system. Not that I'm totally opposed to John Dewey, because I think there's a great deal of merit to what he had to say. But I do think that the implementation of Dewey's philosophy, in the Providence school system or any other school system, caused us to neglect the formal disciplines. I think that as far as Warren is concerned, if the Sputnik situation hadn't developed exactly when it did, I would have been run out of town. Because I had been saying that the children in our high schools were going to have to have five periods of English and five of math and five of science and five periods of social studies—come hell or high water! This was a complete change from allowing anybody to choose any subject they wanted and to take it at any time. For instance, some students were taking business arithmetic in their senior year when maybe they had taken algebra in their first year and geometry in the second one. They simply completed their math requirement by taking this far-out subject that was an easy, coasting course, so as to get that extra A in the senior year and make them eligible for college. And *when they got to college they'd fall flat on their faces*—because the discipline hadn't been carried to the point of developing an adequate knowledge of a subject area.

So I say that in *any* school system, no matter what has been going on, you've got to do something to develop a change and it has to be in the improvement of the disciplines that we all believe in.

In the Providence school system I have been fortunate, with the help of federal monies, in being able to establish what I think are truly viable programs. We now have a director for a reading program for the entire system. We have the same for a math program and a science program. From kindergarten through grade 12, we have a social studies program for the entire system. We picked up some $240,000 for this purpose and involved the vice-president of Rhode Island College in the development of a suitable curriculum.

These systemwide programs are a revolution as far as Providence is concerned. It means that 1300 teachers must be brought into an in-service training program to develop these new curricula and then to implement them in the schools.

Now you know that when you have 1300 teachers, one-fourth of them are going to be teaching mathematics at one time or another. But modern math is a brand new field, a brand new area. Some 50 percent of our teachers have been with us for twenty years. They don't know what modern math is—they've got to go to school again to learn to teach it. And when you have a system as large as this, you naturally have problems in developing in-service training programs. It's not enough to send teachers to the universities and say: "Get this, helter-skelter."

. . . for a mere summer session.

Right. Instead, you have to bring the college into the school system and say to the college teacher of math: "Now you teach these people how to teach modern math at the first, second, or third grade level." If you develop it along these lines, there is a normal productivity as a result of a normal continuity.

It would seem that you have two roles when you go into a new community. First, you are a critic, and second, on the strength of what you find, you are an innovator.

You're a catalyst. This is the way I see the role. You've got to be a catalyst. And as I say. . . .

. . . shake things up?

Right. What you do in this—let's talk about students for a minute. Students who have been resting rather happily on their laurels for the last several years, and who find something new that's going to make them work a little bit harder, aren't going to like it. And so as far as the student body is concerned, immediately they become upset. And what about the faculty that have to go back to school—to restudy, to retool, to be able to accept the new modern curricula? They're going to be upset, too.

And what do the students do? They go to their parents and tell them that things are getting too tough for them. So then the parents become a problem.

I think it is absolutely necessary that a rapport be established between the superintendent and the students, between the superintendent and the faculty. It isn't enough for a superintendent of schools to say that something is wrong. In Warren, what I did was bring down Brown University and have the faculty told what changes had been taking place in the disciplines and how they had to react to them. Then it was no longer the superintendent of schools who was saying: "You've got to do so-and-so." In Providence we had the COPE Report—a $100,000 expenditure of the federal government—in which the entire curriculum of the Providence school system was analyzed by Providence College, Brown University, Rhode Island College, Bryant College, and Rhode Island School of Design. Each participated to the extent of their own ability, in the area of their own expertise, and told us what was wrong with our system and how to change it.

It's through these changes that we are bringing the faculty of the colleges into the school system to tell the system how it can develop its line. What I'm saying is that faculty, student body, parents, school committee, politicians are all going to react to this. The politicians are going to react because this program costs money, and whatever costs money is harmful to the normal tax base. If this is the case, then is education worth it? You've got to prove that it is.

I think that every one of the other agencies concerned with education has also got to be convinced that what you're selling is worth buying.

Do you consider yourself an innovator? And if so, what are your most satisfying accomplishments in all these systems?

Well, I think that we all have a commitment to education. I don't believe that any one educator has all the answers. As far as my commitment is concerned and my expertise—if you want to call it such—I think that the success that I have had in certain lines has made the job, at least to my point of view, worth doing.

In the Warren school system, as I have suggested, it was a question of merely beefing up the curricula. In the Newport system, I established a gifted-child program. I tried to bring all of the higher-quality children, from grade 4, into a separate school, and according to their abilities I moved them into a greater educational experience than they had ever had before. As far as Providence is concerned, if I could point with pride to one single thing it would be to dramatizing the English curricula—and this through a federal grant of $1,000,000. This brought the Trinity Players into the school system. Forty thousand youngsters in the state of Rhode Island are now participating, four times a year, in live drama, as a result of a federal program: Project Discovery. It has not only allowed the children to go to the theatre to see—before their very eyes—Shakespeare on the stage, and many other dramatic representations, but has taken the theatre to the school and allowed the students to participate in this art form, as well as this literature form, with results that they'd never get in any other way. These were paid professionals who went into the schools and developed a rapport that was the most healthy thing I'd ever seen.

I can believe it.

In the beginning, children were taking advantage of this school "outing" to stay out of school—until the second performance. And then they felt as though they had been cheated if they hadn't gone—and they all went. I think that in one more year—and I'm truly hoping that this will be the case—the demand of the community and the state-at-large will be such that this program will be sustained by local monies rather than by federal monies. And if this comes off, as I anticipate that it will, I think that this will be the greatest achievement of my life—to bring live drama into the school curricula.

You know what we have been fostering in the line of "pap" in teaching literature in our schools—and the lack of direction as far as this is concerned. Now here's an opportunity for us to do something that's truly viable and in a different way.

Providence has been spotlighted throughout much of the country for many of your own substantive achievements. Have you had reactions from other communities? Are there some lessons that you think could be nationally applied?

Perhaps the greatest single thing we have achieved in the city of Providence, because of the racial composition of our community—17 percent black versus 83 percent white—is that we have integrated the school system. And in a sense, we have integrated the largest school system in America.

New York City, as you know, is having many painful experiences on this. I'd like to hear what has happened locally.

It's my considered opinion that there is no such thing as quality education in a segregated school. It's my considered opinion, as a result of positive observation of the situation, that little or no learning occurs in spite of the pumping of thousands of dollars into ghetto schools. The only thing that's going to achieve any degree of excellence, as far as the black student is concerned, is his association with a white middle-class or upper-class community that will bring about a change in his own personal aspirations.

Let me just give you one example of this. Last summer, through the Neighborhood Youth Corps, we had approximately a thousand children employed, whose economic and social deprivation made them eligible for this program. We had one hundred girls participating in a tutorial capacity. They were seniors, over sixteen years of age, who had been living in the ghettos for the most part and now were eligible as tutors. In a sense, it was an opportunity for them to be reacting with their peers in trying to improve their educational status. Of these hundred girls, sixty have now decided that they want to go into education. Now the mere fact of their decision is revolutionary, but even more important is their recognizing that they *can* go into education, and that scholarships, and the like, would be available to allow them to participate in the educational community.

Not only this, but virtually all of the colleges have opened their doors to these people and said to them, "We want you to come." I think a new dimension has been established in the education of the youth of Rhode Island.

This, in my opinion, is a throw-off of the program we established; we had no reason to suppose that this would happen. It's a spin-off that we couldn't have anticipated, and yet I think it's great.

There have been a number of "gimmicks" to integrate the schools, such as busing, and there are many violent arguments on that score. Am I wrong in calling some of these "tricks" rather than techniques?

Busing, per se, I think is not an extremely valuable attribute of education. I have tried to minimize it. Now, for instance, on the east side of Providence we had four elementary schools, one of which was 95 percent black. The only way to integrate them was to siphon off the children of the largely black school into normally white schools. But instead of taking that one school and busing everybody out of it, we made two schools prekindergarten through third grade, and two schools fourth grade through sixth. Then we redistributed blacks and whites in such a way that only half of the population was being moved. We bused from the black Lippitt Hill School to the white John Howland School, and bused the whites from John Howland to the black school. Both groups, it seems to me, profited by this operation. In addition, we adopted a nongraded program which allowed each child to achieve at his own level—not on a track system, but in each area of the school curricula.

In the elementary school we have children from the first through the sixth grade level, though for reading they are actually in the fourth grade. All were encouraged to progress because everybody with them was proceeding at virtually the same level—and they had an opportunity to go to the top in their level.

. . . and develop their potential.

And develop their potential. They don't stay with this same group all day. In math they may find themselves at a higher grade level than for reading. And in each case, the result is a greater development.

Then we have put a guidance person in virtually every building, and social workers in each building. Moreover, as you know, we have developed a model school in the heart of the ghetto. We did this with purely voluntary busing. We had to bus three-quarters of the children out of the school but we left 150 blacks there. Then we developed a class system so that there were no more than 25 students in a class. The whites have volunteered to come into the school to such a degree that we now have a waiting list of students who want to come.

We did this by making the school attractive. First, no class can be larger than 25. We arranged that teachers and students should have an opportunity to participate in reading laboratories, in math laboratories, in science laboratories. We brought in the Rhode Island School of Design—which, in my opinion, is one of the greatest schools, in its area, in the United States. We got from it a full-time professor and four student assistants to give children from kindergarten through grade six an opportunity to participate in an art program that you couldn't find in any other school in America.

In other words, there was everything for them: charcoals, water colors, oil paintings, sculpture, ceramics—and all taught by experts. And I think if nothing else comes out of it but art appreciation, it will be wonderful. But if something even more tangible doesn't come out of it, like a development of skills in these areas—why I will be extremely surprised and greatly disappointed.

I think a superintendent's jobs—and I make that plural—are often misunderstood. It would seem that you have, crossing your desk, more problems, and that you wear many more hats than seem humanly feasible. You are concerned not only with integration but also with the maintenance of schools, recruitment of teachers, balancing of a budget, meetings with the school committee, and currently, according to today's newspaper headline, the possible involvement of the state education board in an investigation of the city school system. Is the job almost unmanageable?

The point you make is a good one.

I'm sure that I'm speaking for virtually every large-city superintendent in America when I say that we sometimes wonder whether we are involved in education at all, because of the demands made on us in other areas. I think that very quickly in America we are going to have to set up city departments to handle labor relations. With 1300 teachers who belong to a union, and are represented by a union, it's absolutely necessary that a union contract be developed and that the city administration and the union participate in the development of this contract. The superintendent does not have either the time or the necessary expertise in this area.

It cuts into your whole schedule.

Right. We've spent almost six months in the development of a contract here. If the school superintendent is to be involved in this, he must give up perhaps two days out of every week to the job. We are just going to have to have experts in this field who will do this kind of work for us. I think that the larger city systems have had something like this for a long time, but with a system even as large, or as small, as Providence, with its 1300 teachers, it too needs expertise in this field.

If I could break down one of your average weeks, would it include a staff meeting? I'm interested in how you communicate with administrators and teachers and, for that matter, with pupils. Do you sometimes appear in a classroom?

Communication is one of the most difficult things a superintendent does. It's a fairly easy operation when one has a school system, as I once did, of 6000 students. You *can* know every teacher by his first name and you *can* know many of the student body. And your rapport with the community will depend upon whether you stay one year or five. When you go into a system that's double in size, you reduce by half your communication. And in a system four times as large, communication is limited to such a degree that you don't even know your teachers. This becomes a real problem.

In my first year in the city of Providence, I spoke 97 times to 97 different groups, which means 97 different nights in the course of a ten-month school year. This constitutes a fairly long working day. Perhaps not all of those 97 meetings were necessary, but I felt that they *were* necessary for the sake of exposure, education, articulation, and communication. I have never felt that I was anything less than a salesman for education wherever I have gone.

Are you concerned with building an image according to what public relations people advise? Or is this a secondary feature? Does it just happen?

I think that one thing a system as large as this needs is a public relations office.

Oh, you have none?

We have none. The public relations office in the Providence school system *is* the superintendent of schools—and this is a pusillanimous pair of legs that's walking around because of the limitations naturally imposed by other obligations of the job.

What is your relationship with the press? Do you give periodic conferences on "hot" issues?

As you know, we have one city newspaper, and it assigns one reporter to our schools. In the course of the last four years, we have had four different reporters, each of whom has gone on to higher echelons in his own specific field. But I think as a result of his participation in the Providence school program . . . .

You've educated him.

Right. Very quickly this reporter becomes an expert in the field of education. And his participation, his enthusiasm, and his compassion for the system are revealed in the newspaper stories. As far as I am concerned, I can say nothing but good of the people who have represented me specifically in this area. I think that most of our sharpest critics have been outside the milieu of our own system. By this I mean editorial writers or those who have been assigned for a single night who didn't know the background of a specific situation.

Who, basically, owns the schools? In many American communities with increasing militancy on the part of students, as well as teachers and parents, it would seem that many of these professional amateurs can veto many of your programs and indeed your policies.

I do think that the professional amateur can be a thorn in the side of a superintendent, if he can't take advantage of them to achieve his own goals. Generally speaking, in a system as large as this, there is a kind of negative attitude towards education. So when anybody *is* interested in making some improvement, one should encourage them and try to run with them.

In spite of the problems we've had in this school system, if we've done nothing else we have at least awakened in the citizenry of the community an appreciation of the importance of education. Dissident groups *have* caused innumerable problems, but it is also true that as a result of their participation in the school situation, we have improved it.

As an administrator, in much of your work you are developing public policy. In such a case, do you have any formula as a guide to securing the public interest?

I think this goes back to how individual parents feel about a specific school. What do they want for their children? Are they going to be satisfied with anything less than the best? We have established a model school in Providence—the Flynn School. The parents in this community reacted favorably, and now others are saying: "Why can't we have this?" And the answer is they *should* have it! But this is going to require the expenditure of thousands and thousands of dollars.

One example: in virtually every other elementary school in the city of Providence we spend approximately $400 per pupil. But in the model school we're spending $650. If these children in the model school are not being given more than anybody else, why then we certainly have failed. And if the parents in the other schools are not insisting that their children are entitled to the same expenditure, then those parents are *not interested* in their children.

One result of this model school experiment is that the school committee has created a subcommittee that's presently meeting with 150 people, half of whom are members of the community at large, plus the presidents of the PTA's, the League of Women Voters, the East Side Committees, et cetera, et cetera. And all of these groups are interested in developing a program.

What are they going to do? They're going eventually to come to the school committee and say, "We want this." What is *this* going to cost in the city of Providence? It's going to cost $3½ million to give every elementary child what we are giving to those in the Flynn School.

You appreciate that the Bundy report recently issued in New York has advocated—according to its critics, at least—an excessive degree of decentralization. On the basis of your own professional evidence, do you trust a community to maintain its schools and seek excellence? Or do you feel that decentralization might result in antagonisms among communities, and perhaps emphasize the racial character of neighborhoods? There are no quick answers, I realize.

I really don't pretend to be any expert in the large system, such as New York City or Philadelphia. I am inclined to believe that in a huge monolithic system—as in these two cities—it's rather difficult to develop, in each area of the city, a public consciousness or awareness of the needs of their children. And then to take that awareness to somebody who will listen to them . . . .

And translate it into practice.

Right. I understand that in Philadelphia, these smaller areas are in the charge of assistant superintendents and separate school committees. This arrangement might be highly desirable for an extremely large system, but for Providence, I believe that one school system is sufficient.

On the other hand, I think that in systems even as small as ours we are giving responsibility to too few people to manage segments of the city. Here I have tried to set up head principals, each one responsible for eight to ten schools. Actually, if you recognize Rhode Island for what it is—39 communities—each one of my head principals in Providence is virtually superintendent of a larger school system than many of the other systems outside of Providence. When you consider Jamestown with its one school system, with one superintendent . . . .

You could tuck it in a corner.

Truly.

You spoke earlier of the school committee. Is the concept a mixed blessing, or is it out of date for the needs of this century? What, may I add, are your relations to it?

I consider it my role as superintendent of schools not only to relate to but also to communicate, and on a day-to-day basis, with the members of my school committee, because it is another link of communication with the areas of the city. As you know, in Providence the school committee is elected from districts, and the members try to represent their districts. If in some cases they represent them to a greater degree than I would like, I nevertheless feel that their representation, or participation, in the educational community is a viable one—and one that we have got to respect.

Each of these districts has its own built-in problems and needs that can be met only if each community has a degree of representation.

Is the school committee a coordinating instrument, sharing with you in policy construction, or is it more an inspector general of the system?

Generally speaking, I would like to consider the school committee as responsible for policy and the superintendent responsible for the implementation of that policy. The policies have got to be broad; the implementation becomes specific. For instance, the school committee has stated that the community at large should have the use of the schools—not on just a five-hour basis, but on a 24-hour basis. The superintendent, then, should see to it that the schools *are* open 24 hours.

We have developed nine so-called community schools, which are open from nine in the morning until nine or ten o'clock at night. We have a tutorial program that starts when the regular school day stops. And we have professionals and tutors from the colleges—as many as 600 volunteering to participate in a tutorial role in these programs. In another instance, in Rhode Island very little was done with school libraries below the secondary level. Today, virtually every elementary school has its library. In the beginning these libraries were tended by volunteers. Eventually we are going to put a professional librarian in each area. It would be hard to say it wasn't desirable to bring these people in to help establish a program that was vitally necessary.

The record shows that you have pioneered in many areas and new directions. You still have problems: overcrowded schools, buildings in need of repairs, shortage of teachers. What does a superintendent, in a community of this size, do in the face of these odds?

Well, I think that expediency becomes a rule in many instances, and in this situation allows for the development of a curriculum that is highly desirable. I alluded previously to the COPE report, in which Brown University recommended that the Providence school system change from a 6-3-3 graded program to a 4-4-4 graded program. We have underpopulated high schools and junior high schools, and overcrowded elementary schools. So by bringing four grades rather than three into the junior high school, we can eliminate many small, obsolete, four-room elementary schools presently in our system.

The problem, here, of course, is one of parental rebellion against the children moving out of their neighborhood. If we can keep the children in their neighborhood from kindergarten through grade 4, and insist upon their travelling from grades 5 through 8, rather than 7 through 9, then we have solved the problems of housing and education. I happen to believe in the middle school philosophy. No longer can we prepare children for college if we start them on a college curriculum in the eleventh grade, or the tenth grade.

Too late.

We've got to start as early as the fourth grade, in my opinion. And I think that no longer is the elementary teacher, in a self-contained classroom, going to be the solution to the problems of education of our youth in even the fourth grade. I believe that departmentalization is necessary, at least to some degree, even from the fourth grade on.

I should like to see the math teacher as a separate unit, even in the fourth grade. I think we have also demonstrated the need for a reading teacher in every elementary school. And if science is to be taught by teachers who have been in our system for twenty years, then we must have in-service training programs for certain teachers who have expertise and an interest in science, to give them *more* information to give to the children. Even at this level we must develop higher, more sophisticated curricula in math, in science, in anything that you might mention.

You have, I judge, a wide knowledge of the system. What do you think of today's student and today's teacher?

Well, in spite of all the criticism that has been levelled in both areas, I don't believe there has ever been a time in the history of education when children were better prepared than they are today. Nor has there ever been a time when teachers were better prepared. One of the criticisms of the city of Providence is that we have over 200 teachers on emergency certificates. Now, bad as this sounds, it's not really so, because one of the things that has gone further than many of us were prepared to admit is certification requirements.

Let me give you an example. The average student who graduates from a liberal arts college is likely to come out with perhaps 18 hours in the area of English—but perhaps not. If she has had only 12 hours, she comes to our system on an emergency certificate. Is it desirable that she should have had the 18 hours? Yes. Are they available to us with 18 hours? No. And so we have to bring in people who have emergency certificates, or less than the full certification requirement.

It seems reasonable.

Right. Library teachers are as scarce as it's possible to imagine, because the certification requirements are so broad. I've had a library teacher in one of my schools who worked in the Harvard University library and in the Vassar library—but she can't be certified, because she doesn't have a master's degree in library science.

This doesn't say she's an inferior teacher; it merely says that she's got to do more, in the line of preparation, to meet the certification requirements. In the meantime, I do not feel that the children are being cheated or that she is an inferior teacher.

In Rhode Island our certification requirements are that every teacher should have a master's degree within five years. States contiguous to Rhode Island are not demanding this. So teachers who have less than our certification requirements can certainly step into a classroom in Massachusetts, and there is no criticism levelled at them.

Do your salaries, generally speaking, match those of neighboring states?

In the last four years that I have been a part of the Providence school system, salaries have gone up each year on an average of $400. This year the school committee has just agreed to a contract containing a salary schedule from $6200 to $10,000. This will be the highest in Rhode Island. We are the largest city in the state; we should have the highest salary schedule in the state of Rhode Island. It's a more difficult job for a teacher to teach in Providence than in any other community in the state. The teacher in the ghetto has to face different problems than the teacher elsewhere. Now if we could eliminate the ghettos, we might make every teacher's load about the same.

But you know the teaching load in a classical high school, for instance, might be entirely different from one in a central high school with commercial courses. If we consider that one child may be eager for an education, while another has a potential that has to be developed through a higher degree of motivation—then the teacher in one case is not fighting the same battle as the teacher in the other. So compensation is vital to the continuation of a viable system.

One last question. In a review of an exciting and extensive career, what would you say were your major success and disappointments?

I think that, to answer the last question first, it's always disappointing to find that there isn't a universal appreciation of the need of better education. And there are also the frustrations that come from not getting complete support from the administration—I mean the city administration—for the development of sophisticated educational programs.

In terms of what I'd consider the achievements in the period of the past four years, I think that the whole face of education has changed in America, and we are doing our best to keep pace. What we have achieved in the areas in which change has occurred has been very heartwarming, as far as I'm concerned.

STUDY QUESTIONS

1. What are the usual problems that arise between a school superintendent and a school board? How do they differ from problems of city management?
2. What are the arguments pro and con for decentralizing school administration? What do you think of O'Connor's public relations?
3. Would you consider the superintendent a success or a failure in resigning?

18
BOARD OF ETHICS

This case illustrates the evaluation of accumulated practices regarding expenses for city entertainment of important visitors, usually chiefs of state, and a proposed solution. The Mayor's request of the Board of Ethics extended the appraisal to an exploration of a city's proper relationship to present and future benefactors.

The analysis describes the elements that entered into the board's decision, the desire of the city council to gain spotlight attention, the background of the Board of Ethics, and its contribution in a vital situation.

Emphasized here are the opportunities presented to the public for contributing either their talents or gifts and thereby becoming better citizens of a city.

The report was stamped OPINION 100. Other cities could use it as a guide. The central issue: Should a city accept donations from private individuals and corporations for official entertainment purposes? In the final analysis, the decision in response to an inquiry by Mayor Lindsay touched upon the entire field of gifts to the city. To answer this ticklish question was a task of New York City's Board of Ethics—a nine-year-old agency, legis-

323

latively assigned to provide "advisory opinions" to municipal officials and employees.

HISTORY OF THE BOARD

On December 18, 1956, the City Council of New York, stung by public criticism in the press concerning actions of some councilmen, commenced an investigation. Public hearings were held, and two prominent members of the council resigned. Its counsel in those proceedings, Stanley Kreutzer, recommended a code of ethics for the city. The City Council appointed a Special Committee on Ethics and Standards to study the charter provisions concerning duties and obligations of councilmen, city officers, and employees on matters in which they might have financial interests. Five council members, including the majority and minority leaders, constituted the committee. Shortly thereafter (February 5, 1957) an advisory board was appointed by the council to advise the special committee on the subject-matter involved.

> The advisory board membership had impressive credentials: it included Hon. Charles C. Lockwood, former Justice of the New York State Supreme Court, Hon. Joseph M. Callahan, former member of the Appellate Division, New York State Supreme Court, Cloyd Laporte, former President of the New York State Bar Association, Edwin L. Weisl, member of the Character Committee of the Appellate Division.

From the outset, two connected problems were on the committee's agenda: (1) clarification of charter provisions dealing with conflicts of interest, and (2) their implementation through a permanent code of ethics governing all city officials and employees. On February 11, 1957, the council adopted an interim code for its members, based on the New York State Code of Ethics, and expressed a desire for a permanent code containing general standards of conduct for city personnel.

The work of the special committee extended over a two-year period. Information was gathered from writings of experts, textbooks, law review articles, court decisions, statutes of cities and states, opinions of corporation counsels, statutes of the federal government, regulations of federal agencies, and evaluations of studies produced by federal, state, and municipal legislative committees. A large share of this intensive effort was personally stimulated and contributed by Stanley Kreutzer. Contacts were also made with officials of 96 American cities, with 45 state governors, and with the mayors of 29 foreign cities to obtain comprehensive information on present or proposed codes of ethics.

The report of the special committee was released February 3, 1959, and contained two major proposals:

   1.   Adoption by local law of a code of ethics as part of the administrative code.
   2.   Creation by local law of a board of ethics for officers and employees.

The report also contained a ringing passage on the scope and true meaning of the problem:

> Ethics in government is a matter of serious concern not only to our City but throughout the entire fabric of government—municipal, state, and federal. Government has grown enormously in size and complexity, and problems of conflicts of interest and ethics cannot always be easily resolved in the present-day structure of modern society. This Committee is deeply concerned with its responsibilities to the people of the City of New York and to its more than 200,000 officers and employees, the vast majority of whom serve with integrity, loyalty, and devotion to the public welfare.

As a controlling guide the report underscored the role of all public officials. "The paramount obligation of a public servant," it declared, "is to avoid basis for the suspicion that any special or private interests may affect his official action." He should "be guided by the highest public interest in all official acts." This is imperative in order that "his decisions, views, or opinions shall be free from any influence that would interfere with the objectivity, impartiality, and integrity so basic in the consideration of municipal legislation." The admission of the special committee that ". . . it is not possible to anticipate every conceivable situation" serves, in part, as a cogent preface to the present case.

Public hearings were conducted after the report's release, and final recommendations for legislative action were submitted to the New York State Legislature and the City Council. On April 20, 1959, a new section was added to the city charter and became law after enactment by the state legislature and approval by the Governor. Later, on September 3, 1959, local laws on this subject became effective after City Council enactment and approval by the Board of Estimate and the Mayor.

The Board of Ethics consists of five members—three selected from the public and appointed by the Mayor, and two city officials: corporation counsel and the personnel director. Each member has one vote. All serve without compensation. Public members have a four-year term. The board's main purpose is to render advisory opinions, on request, to officers and employees of the city based on a given set of facts.

GIFTS TO THE CITY

Over the years, city officials who entertained foreign dignitaries did so without any unnecessary expense to the city treasury. Large corporations were usually pleased to cement relations with overseas clients by signing the tab for expenses as co-host. Much of this entertaining was done at the request of the United States Department of State, since most visitors made it a practice to "stop off," after White House receptions, in New York City.

Grover Whalen, the city's first "greeter," initiated the custom of contacting former business associates to aid. Former Commissioner of Public Events Richard C. Patterson established a list of corporations who purchased tables for these events. (He always refused to publicize names of donors.) In the same spirit, the present commissioner, John S. (Bud) Palmer, said: "Donors insist on anonymity. They are afraid of crank letters. We have a carefully drawn list of noncontroversial persons. We are only trying to save the city money." On another occasion Palmer flatly refused to admit who, or even how many, paid the expenses for the Metropolitan Opera party (at its opening) attended by Mrs. Lyndon B. Johnson and other notables. Later on, in response to public newspaper pressure, he did release names of sponsors. According to the record, former Mayor Robert F. Wagner, Jr., recalled that "a lot of companies contributed in the past to such affairs and I thought it was all right, because no one, to my knowledge, benefitted by the practice. I don't recall just what companies did. Perhaps there might have been as many as forty. But they were usually small affairs. If the expense was large, I insisted that the city pay."

On October 3, 1966, a supper party was given by the city to honor delegates to the United Nations, and the fact that it was paid for by Pan American Airways aroused immediate criticism. The next day Mayor Lindsay wrote the chairman of the Board of Ethics for an opinion, underlining the scope of the problem on which it was requested:

> Since I have been in office as Mayor, we have encouraged the private sector to involve itself in many aspects of the life of the City. As you know, the parks of the City . . . were alive with music and other performances during the summer, especially at night. Almost all of it was a result of private donations from corporations and individuals.
>
> Then, of course, there is the continuing involvement of the private sector in other aspects of the City, most especially museums and libraries.
>
> Much of this is a continuation of past practices and policies. During this administration, we have expanded it substantially. We have also continued the practice of allowing the private sector to help the City in giving recognition to foreign dignitaries who visit. . . . Many of these functions are at the specific request of the Federal government. . . . In order to provide a dignified environment we have changed it a good deal in style and approach. Rather than having a dinner for Mrs. Ghandi or President Marcos at a midtown Manhattan hotel, we used our great cultural institutions, which is a means of showing them off at the same time that we honor our visitors.
>
> We have continued the practice of having members of the private

sector, individual and corporate, co-host and assist in the cost of such functions, which is a matter of public knowledge, and indeed, during the course of each occasion I have introduced and publicly thanked those who had made possible the event.

Is recent days, questions have been asked concerning these efforts to help show off our City. This may have an impact on the private sector and discourage individuals and institutions from helping. The questions have included the recognition that our City is giving to the United Nations —a recognition which, in my opinion, is long overdue. Since then, someone has even raised the question about the new wing in the Mansion, because it has been funded privately, with a long list of major corporations included.

Regardless of the question of jurisdiction, I want to submit the question to the Board of Ethics and hope that you and your colleagues would be willing to examine the whole problem, discuss it with the Commissioner of Public Events, the Commissioner of Parks, and ultimately advise me on the matter. I think this would be very helpful, not simply because questions have been raised, but because I am deeply concerned that the forward motion that we have begun in New York to make this a better looking and more exciting place for residents and visitors, may be discouraged.

Chairman Laporte replied: "Pursuant to the request . . . we shall consider the questions presented to us and submit our report to you as expeditiously as possible."

Councilman Robert A. Low, a rival of the Mayor, indicated the views and plans of the City Council regarding the same issue. In a letter to the board dated October 10 he cited a resolution sponsored by 13 council members (there are a total of 35) calling for an inquiry into the practice of financing official and semiofficial functions through funds from private individuals and corporations. It was to be introduced the following day. In brief, his letter stressed these central points:

1.   The present Code respecting gifts and favors applies to individuals while the present question . . . involves the receipt of gifts by the City itself. But I have confined any question about this practice to those cases where the donor has business dealings with the City.

2.   Certainly, an unhealthy relationship may develop where a request for funds is made from the Mayor's office, or the office of an agency responsible to the Mayor, to a corporation or private individual having business dealings with the City. I am particularly concerned about those cases where a private individual or corporation may be seeking a special permit, privilege, or consideration from the City.

3.   The heart of the problem . . . is that there may be a suspicion . . . that the gift may influence an official action. That possibility degrades public servants in the minds of our citizens and unnecessarily casts shadows about important public decisions.

Councilman Low concluded with a request that the board submit "such legislative recommendations as it may deem fitting to extend the provisions of the Code to cover receipt of gifts by the City under such circumstances."

On October 20 the board received a letter from Robert Sweet, an executive assistant to the Mayor, asking for comments on the council's proposals. Counsel Kreutzer replied: "It is our view that Resolution 547 should await the Opinion of the Board of Ethics in the pending matter before us. We believe this to be in the best public interest." These exchanges were widely reported in the press, which continued to maintain a lively interest in the proceedings.

HEARINGS OF THE BOARD

Upon request of the Board of Ethics, Commissioner Palmer prepared an itemized list of functions and sponsors connected with various events for a ten-year period. Major items included:

Sponsored prior to Mayor Lindsay's administration

> October 21, 1957: Waldorf-Astoria luncheon for Queen Elizabeth and Prince Philip. (American Tobacco, Joseph E. Seagram and Sons, J. P. Morgan, Colgate-Palmolive, Standard Oil, Thomas J. Lipton, Inc., General Motors, U.S. Steel, IBM, Pepsi-Cola, and Continental Can were the major subscribers.)
>
> April 10, 1958: Stag luncheon for the Secretary General of the United Nations, Dag Hammarskjold.
>
> April 28, 1959: Reception and buffet for the Society of Foreign Consuls in New York.

Sponsored during Mayor Lindsay's administration

> July 5, 1966: Dinner for the Right Honorable Harold Holt, Prime Minister of Australia, and Mrs. Holt at the Metropolitan Museum of Art. (Alcoa Aluminum)
>
> July 29, 1966: Luncheon for the President of Israel and Mrs. Shazar at the New York State Theatre in Lincoln Center. (Trade Bank and Trust, West Side Federal Savings and Loan Association as major contributors)
>
> September 19, 1966: Official dinner for President Marcos of the Philippines and Mrs. Marcos at the Cloisters. (Standard Oil)
>
> September 16, 1966: Official opening of the Metropolitan Opera and reception. (Various individual patrons)
>
> October 3, 1966: United Nations supper dance for the opening of the 21st Session, General Assembly, at the New York State Theatre of Lincoln Center. (Pan American)

City paid

> March 30, 1966: Luncheon for Prime Minister Ghandi of India at Philharmonic Hall of Lincoln Center.
>
> September 8, 1966: Official Reception on the lawn of Gracie Mansion for the Consular Corps and their wives.

A similar list was prepared at the Mayor's request for Councilman Low.

On October 19 the board conducted its hearings. In his testimony Commissioner Palmer indicated that his department has an allotment of $100,000 for entertainment purposes. To aid the Mayor's economy drive, he has tried to save city funds by extending invitations to have the private sector act as hosts. Since he took office, there has been a change in the number of invited guests, the manner, and the location of each event. Instead of the Waldorf-Astoria's Grand Ballroom (with a guest list of 2000), Palmer has complied with the Mayor's wish to hold such affairs at various city cultural institutions with a reduced guest list of about 200. According to the record, the commissioner claimed that participating sponsors are never concealed; in fact, as the Mayor's communication underlined, the sponsors are always introduced and publicly thanked. Once former Commissioner Patterson had attempted to initiate a "general fund," which did not succeed. Corporations, it was explained in the hearings, prefer the publicity and would not achieve the same effect through such a fund plan. Palmer ended by raising no objection to Kreutzer's suggestion that there be a public filing of all contributions.

On the same day Councilman Low testified, expressing a fear of gifts to the city by private corporations, especially when they might stand to benefit at the expense of other corporations. One example he cited was the invitation of the Parks Department to several architectural firms to compete in designing a refreshment stand. At the same time, Parks was offering a prize to the winner of a contest it had arranged, and accepted the donation of a prize from one of the competing firms. Low advanced two suggestions: (1) that corporations disclose all pending matters with the city through a formal questionnaire; (2) that a community chest be established to which all corporations could contribute.

Counsel Kreutzer asked: "If disclosure were made by a corporation making a gift to the City, would the gift then be considered all right?" Low: "No, for the simple reason that once it is established that there is a pending matter with the City, there arises a suspicion in the public's mind of a quid pro quo." Further, Low suggested that the Board of Ethics be empowered to receive corporation questionnaires and decide on the appropriateness of proposed gifts. It was also suggested that the Mayor's representative in Washington try harder to secure financial contributions from the federal government for official entertaining by the city.

OPINION OF THE BOARD

The board considered many alternative solutions, among them: creation of a citizens' committee to receive gifts for a community fund; distinguishing between a gift of money and something concrete, such as a gift of services on a particular project; stress on the vast contributions of the past so as to minimize Pan Am's gift, which was currently being criticized; public discussion of the problem of whether a whole city may be corrupted by a gift for the benefit of the whole community; the making of future guest lists "representative" to include labor, Negro leaders, Puerto Rican leaders, and minority groups generally; and the creation of a public filing system in the city clerk's office for disclosures of gifts, earmarked or otherwise.

Current issues concerned contributions to the wing of Gracie Mansion (where $500,000 was yet to be raised); the possibility of "arm-twisting" (for example, by those under indictment or by arms manufacturers); the appearance that private sponsorship might give of commercialism and the exploitation of visitors; and the possible political credit or discredit to the Mayor. The Board of Ethics wished to avoid impugning anyone's motives and to make it clear that gifts to the city had often been made in the past as an established course of conduct, much like a habit. It was necessary now to discuss the general problem of future gifts to the city; there should be a filing for gifts of money or property, and such contributions—as in the case of "vest-pocket" parks—should be commended and publicly acknowledged.

The board then proceeded to examine the "whole problem" of private contributions of which the Pan American case was an illustration. A first step was to ascertain "so far as possible the nature and extent of gifts and contributions to the City from private sources." From its earliest days, New York City has been considered a "natural object of the bounty of its citizens." Private contributions, in a true sense, have been a well-recognized "manifestation of citizenship."

The board then classified various types of contributions:

1.   Personal services from professional leaders rendered without cost in the fields of art, science, industry, education, business, and finance. These public benefits have been "incalculable" and strengthen the vitality of the city. For the most part, even if the city could pay for them, these services would not have been available for hire.
2.   Volunteer services by individuals, who number in the thousands. Many citizens give freely of their time and money "without asking for or receiving formal recognition." As a result, New York City has established a Volunteer Council to encourage and coordinate this type of assistance.
3.   Gifts of real property and tangible personal property, such as works of art, parks, and public improvements. There have also been gifts of money, for either general purposes or specific causes and objects.

Among the business concerns that have contributed funds, equipment, and services to the Parks Department, Schlitz Beer Company supported the New York Philharmonic concerts in the parks of each of the five boroughs; Consolidated Edison participated as a donor for dance concerts; Pepsi-Cola sponsored an Amateur Youth Festival; American Machine and Foundry paid for bicycle races and provided bicycles as prizes in cooperation with the Bicycle League of America; *Cue* magazine served as host for fashion shows in association with four leading department stores. All these events, said the board, "combine the use of City facilities with contributions of money and services from the private sector."

Additional public benefits made possible by such methods included vest-pocket parks, Park Avenue Christmas lights, construction of a new wing at the Mayor's residence (Gracie Mansion), a children's zoo in Central Park, corporate scholarships to needy students, medical equipment to city hospitals, gifts of money, television, and radio sets to schools and libraries, funds and staff for government research, studies and task-force assignments, and services to assist the city in providing job opportunities and training programs for disadvantaged youths.

Millions of dollars have come to the city from the estates of prominent benefactors. "In many, if not most cases," said the board, "we have no doubt that the donors or contributors had, have, or will have business dealings or other relationships with the City."

Various statutes, the board indicated, already apply to federal, state, and city governments in regard to gifts, and "The general tenor of those statutes is to approve the acceptance of gifts for the public benefit." These examples were cited:

> 1.   Under the statute creating the United States Information Agency, a section provides that "The Secretary [of State] shall, when he finds it in the public interest, request and accept reimbursement from any cooperating governmental or private source in a foreign country, or from State or local governmental institutions or private sources in the United States, for all or part of the expense of any portion of the [USIA] program undertaken hereunder. . . ." Under another section, ". . . it shall be the duty of the Secretary to utilize, to the maximum extent practicable, the services and facilities of private agencies . . . through contractual arrangements or otherwise."
>
> 2.   Under at least nine separate applicable statutes in New York State, governmental agencies are permitted to accept gifts. For example: Section 20 of the General City Law of New York State provides that subject to the constitution and general laws of this State, every city is empowered: "To take by gift grant, bequest or devise and hold and administer real and personal property within and without the limits of the city, absolutely or in trust for any public or municipal purpose, upon such terms and conditions as may be prescribed by the grantor or donor and accepted by the city."

The board concluded that "many pages of the indices to the compilation of federal and state statutes are required merely to list the laws enacted by the Congress or the New York State Legislature for the acceptance of gifts." It underscored the point that these laws are in contrast to those which "specifically prohibit public employees from accepting gifts for themselves or which confer a direct or indirect personal benefit upon them including, in certain cases, prohibitions against solicitation of gifts for private purposes, such as charitable organizations."

The board carefully considered whether the gift statutes should not be qualified by an express or implied ethical prohibition against acceptance of gifts where the "donor has interests which may be affected by action of a City official." Its opinion deserves full quotation:

> . . . contributions of money, property, or services by the private sector for a municipal purpose are not only proper and ethical but a mark of good citizenship. We are aware, of course, of instances where public officers have subverted or corrupted their office. To hold, however, that contributions for public purposes pose a "possible" conflict of interest or have the "appearance" of impropriety is to conclude that a substantial part of our public service is diseased to the core. This is a conclusion that can be reached only if we accepted the view, which we reject, that corruption or impropriety have so substantially infested the public service that officials neither individually or collectively can be trusted to honorably, properly, or objectively perform their sworn duties as public servants even in situations where their personal interests are not involved.

PAN AMERICAN AIRWAYS AND THE UNITED NATIONS SUPPER PARTY

The facts concerning the specific matter before the board were not in dispute. At the New York State Theatre (Lincoln Center) a supper dance on October 3, 1966, was given by the City of New York to honor United Nations delegates. Expenses were paid directly by Pan American Airways "at the suggestion" of the Public Events Commissioner. The Board of Ethics report underlined the fact that this action was in "accordance with the existing accepted practice of long standing." Numerous individuals and corporations for many years "have contributed to similar functions in like manner."

At the time, New York Airways had already applied to the city for a continuance of its permit to use the Pan Am Building heliport for its helicopter service to and from airports. When the United Nations affair took place, this application was pending. Pan American owned a "substantial interest" in New York Airways and a 10 percent interest in Grand Central Building, Inc., an independent New York corporation, which owned the Pan Am Building.

Does the Commissioner of Public Events have any official responsibilities or duties in connection with the renewal of the permit or with any phase thereof? None, whatsoever. In fact, the report made it quite clear in these words:

Neither he nor his Department has any power or authority to exercise any official function directly or indirectly with respect to such application, permit, franchise, or privilege and he was not aware of the pendency of the application. The Commissioner of Public Events does not have any official or unofficial responsibility, directly or indirectly, with respect to any other Pan American activity which is supervised, restricted, or otherwise affected by our municipality.

The only officer legally designated to decide renewal or continuance of the New York Airways permit was the Commissioner of Marine and Aviation. In fact, he conducted a public hearing at which "all parties favoring or opposing the renewal or continuance of the application were heard." About one year earlier, both the City Planning Commission and the Board of Estimate held public hearings prior to the granting of the original application for the permit. Besides, the Mayor, the City Council, and the Comptroller had the right to inquire into any aspect of the entire matter. In conclusion, insofar as this item goes, the board stated: "No personal benefit, profit, or favor was directly or indirectly received by or conferred upon any City official. We are of the opinion that there was no impropriety in regard to this entire matter."

In view of the Mayor's request to explore the entire matter of gifts, in its maximum sense, the board went on to reflect its views and establish its official posture. One paragraph has a stirring ring to it and puts the whole matter of gifts—whether the governmental level be city, state or national—in proper focus:

Contributions for public purposes should be encouraged. They reflect citizen responsibility. For citizens to give of themselves, their money or their property to advance the public good is a manifestation of a high concept of democracy. Such acts strengthen our community, result in greater participation by our people, and provide more effective citizenship. The character of a city depends not on an abundance of wealth, or on large revenues or imposing buildings; its strength consists in the quality and courage of the men and women who make up its population. Its character is determined by the public spirit of its citizens, by its leaders in and out of government; and by the degree to which its citizens are willing to be involved in advancing the public purposes of a city. It is not merely a question of whether or not the City could pay for certain of its activities itself but more importantly it is the fact that the ready acceptance by the City of gifts from its citizens enlarges the scope of the active participation of those citizens in the ever-expanding area of public service to all the inhabitants of the City.

In respect to the point of whether a corporation or individual has occasional or continuous business dealings with any city agency, the report claimed that owing to the complex structure of city government, "it is impractical to require the head of a particular agency" to make this determination. In fact, it is more difficult to require him to decide whether such a person or corporation not now having a matter with the city "may well have one in the future." Since every individual and existing corporation has the prospect of future dealings with the city, a blanket prohibition, it concluded, "would be a disservice to the City and its people."

POSITION AND POWER OF THE MAYOR

Section 8 of the City Charter provides that the Mayor shall exercise all the powers vested in the city except as otherwise provided by law. Section 70 of the 1938 charter vested these reserved powers in the Board of Estimate. The present charter vests them in the Mayor. The practice concerning acceptance of gifts to the city was well established under former charters. Under a simple procedure, (1) offers to make valuable gifts to the city for the public welfare were referred by the city official or department concerned to the corporation counsel, who (2) issued an opinion as to their legality; thereafter (3) the matter was referred to the Board of Estimate, which, after consideration, voted to accept or reject the gift. Under the present charter, the Mayor makes the final decision as to the acceptance or rejection of any gift. In its report, the board stated: "We consider it desirable that this procedure be continued," the reason being that the Mayor is in the best position to (1) order an investigation, if he considers the area a sensitive one by reason of the relationship existing between the donor and the city; (2) make an informed decision as to whether the gift in question should be accepted or declined.

"For all the reasons stated above," the board concluded, "and in view of the safeguards existing and suggested herein, which we realize are not perfect, we believe that no further restrictions should be imposed."

PROPOSALS ON ENTERTAINMENT OF CITY GUESTS

The board proposed the establishment of a nonprofit corporation "for the purpose of receiving and making available to the City, funds from private individuals and corporations for entertainment of guests . . . and official and semi-official functions honoring them." It added that this specific area is a small segment in the total area of private donations for public purposes, but nevertheless it is important to New York City and the nation. Often the federal government requests these functions, and any great city would consider them its responsibility. The board believed the federal government "should bear or contribute to the cost of many such occasions but there seems to be little hope that it will." In fact it is fortunate that there are private individuals and corporations who, for business or personal reasons, plus a "sense of civic responsibility," would have these visitors properly received. For such purposes they are often willing to offer substantial gifts of money.

The board suggested that the Commissioner of Public Events be designated chairman of the proposed nonprofit corporation and that the Mayor name ten additional directors from the public at large, from lists submitted by the Commissioner, City Council, Citizens Union, Board of Trade, Commerce and Industry Association, Foreign Trade Association, and so on. Of the ten directors, four should be selected from the commissioner's list, three from the City Council's list, and three from the list submitted by the various community organizations such as those mentioned. In short, such a corporation "would provide a vehicle for wider participation and support for such functions."

In summary, the board's main proposals were the following:

1. Gifts to the city should be encouraged, since they foster citizen interest and participation in municipal activities.
2. Prohibitions by law should be avoided.
3. A distinction can properly be made—and should be made—between gifts for entertainment of city guests and gifts for other purposes.
4. Concerning all gifts, the existing procedure, whereby valuable gifts are referred to the corporation counsel for review and to the Mayor for decision, should continue.
5. A nonprofit corporation should be created to receive gifts from the private sector for the entertainment of guests of the city.

On January 23, 1967, the board's chairman addressed the following letter to Mayor Lindsay:

Enclosed is a copy of the opinion of the Board with reference to the matter of gifts to the City which you referred to us. In the event that you should wish to discuss any phases of this opinion with me or any other member of the Board, we shall, of course, be available.

The Mayor's reply was to the board's counsel:

Thank you for the excellent and constructive report which the Board of Ethics has prepared on the matter of contributions by the private sector to the City of New York.

I regard this as a very important recommendation to the City government and be assured that I shall be guided by it.

Thank you for the very professional and careful way with which you went about the preparation of this excellent report.

STUDY QUESTIONS

1. Do you agree with the methods used in developing a decision in this situation? What is your estimate of the final decision of the board?
2. Do you favor a separate agency of this kind? In all governments? What has been the experience with similar experiments?

Key to Using the Cases

It is our judgment that many of the cases can be used to illustrate more than one topic, though they have been organized in this casebook under a single topic. In real life—from which these cases have been drawn—it is rare that administrative situations involve a single theoretical problem. Therefore, as a guide to an expanded use of the cases, we offer the following table:

TOPICS	CASE NUMBERS
Administrative abilities	1, 3, 10
Administrative values	10, 18
Agency rivalries	7
Arbitration	5
Boards and Commissions	2
Bureaucracy	11, 12, 13